Mine (and Yours)

Objective Analysis of God

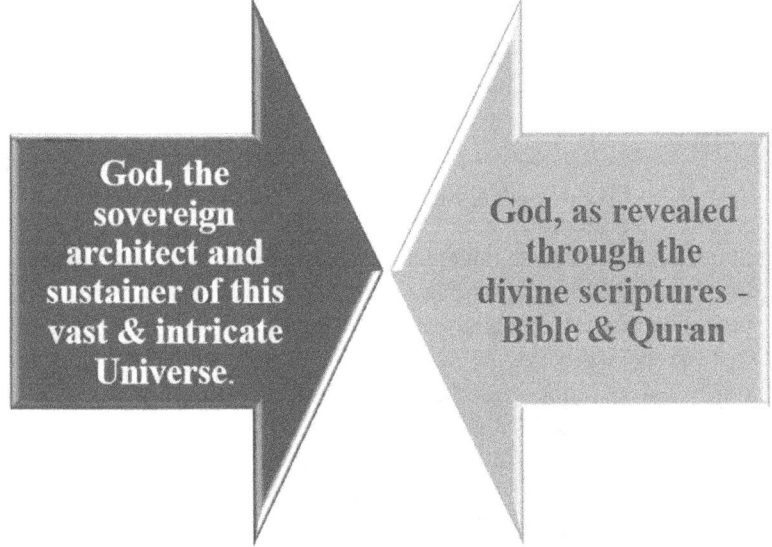

A Simple, Common-sense Approach,

to Explore *Yourself, Your Faith,*

and Your Cage.

Objective Analysis of God

Copyright © 2025   "M A"

All rights reserved. No part of this publication may be reproduced, stored in a retrieval system, or transmitted in any form or by any means—electronic, mechanical, photocopying, recording, or otherwise—without the prior written permission of the author, except for brief quotations used in reviews, academic discussion, or scholarly critique.

This book presents personal reflections, opinions, historical analysis, personal inquiry, and critical perspectives on theology, belief systems, and the deconstruction of faith. The views expressed are those of the author and are intended to provoke thought, not prescribe doctrine. Readers are encouraged to engage with the material critically and respectfully.
Published by "Independently published"
ISBN: 978-1-0695809-1-7
First Edition: August 2025
Written under the pen name M A
Contact: Approach me through:
- ✓ website https://www.my-oag.com/
- ✓ email as "one@my-oag.com"

Here we will try NOT to look at the question of:
God or no God

But will try to understand:
Which God is the GOD

This book offers over 500 pages of clear, logical thinking—no heavy philosophy, and only light calculations (which you can skip if you prefer). We will explore various historical, linguistic, capabilities, and possibilities to conclude a big question:
Can the Creator of this vast and intricately designed universe be the same as the God described in the sacred texts of the Abrahamic religions—the Hebrew Bible, the Christian Bible, and the Quran?

We have two key sources to explore the nature of God:
1. The Holy Scriptures (Hebrew Bible, Bible, and Quran) – Divine revelations claimed to be from God Himself.
2. The Observable Facts of the Universe – The laws of nature, cosmic complexity, and scientific discoveries that define reality.

In this book, we will compare the descriptions of God in the Abrahamic scriptures (primarily the Bible and the Quran) with the empirical truths of the universe. Does the God portrayed in these holy books align with the Creator of such an awe-inspiring cosmos?

We will use simple commonsense logic and a mathematical approach, without going into philosophical, lengthy arguments.

This is not just a theoretical study—it is an interactive exercise. As you engage with the questions presented, you will evaluate the evidence and determine where you stand on the spectrum of belief.

Objective Analysis of God

Me ....

I, the author, am a Muslim by Birth but have chosen not to reveal my name, considering the general trend in the Muslim world about Negating Islam and its consequences, even extending to my extended family.

I lead a routine life, completed my Engineering and Business Administration degrees,
Worked in a big Multinational for many years, achieving a reasonable multigeographical growth, and finally retiring. Like most of us, I spent mindlessly following the religion I was born into and practicing its rituals, but I was never comfortable with what was told and what I was doing. I never received a satisfactory response to my questions from Amy, the religious scholars I met, or those I encountered on social media. I also continue to drift away from religion, and after retirement, like many others, I organized my thoughts and shaped this book.

Living and spending life in the corporate world instilled in me several key traits: being objective, Data-Driven, and comfortable making decisions with 80% confidence. I have translated that into this book.

Objective Analysis of God

Factual compilation of known Knowledge - covering all the Theological, Scientific, and Historical aspects (it will be a roller coaster ride), along with a complete analysis of most of the critical Information you need to know to understand Abrahamic GOD vs scientific facts of God who created this universe.

- It is not written for religious clergy to prove it wrong, but it is for Common People who want to understand their religion.
- It is not a philosophical, a hypothesis, or a psychological debate, but an analysis of objective facts.
- You will tabulate your results and opinion about different facts to reach your answer about GOD.
  Ideas discussed are:
- What is the main flaw in "GOD vs No God" debates
- What is the biggest hurdle to understanding the Universe
- Numerous calculations proving "GOD" is wrong
- Why the Bible does not exist as the words of God
- What benefits did the Romans get when they supported Christianity 300 years after Jesus's "Crucifixion"
- What is the main flaw in the Divine principles of Islam?
- What are the sources of the Quran's "scientific" knowledge and "validation" of the Quran's statement
- The caste system introduced by Islam
- What are the fundamental issues with Darwin's Theory
- What could have happened to make life possible on Earth

Objective Analysis of God

I dedicate this book to my Father.

AB

Who nurtured my curiosity and gave me the courage to challenge the status quo.

Objective Analysis of God

Table of Contents

Table of Contents 9

SECTION 1 - MUST READ 1
- BOOK'S APPROACH 1
- BOOK'S STRUCTURE 8
- MY JOURNEY 11
- SELF-ASSESSMENT 14
- PREMISE 21

SECTION 2 - UNDERSTANDING THE UNIVERSE 24
- FROM UNIVERSE TO GOD 24
- UNDERSTANDING ENORMOUS NUMBERS: 26
- CONCEPT OF "LIGHT YEAR" 28
- UNDERSTANDING THE SCALE OF THE UNIVERSE 29
  - *Universe and Its Space* 33
  - *Universe and Its Time* 42
  - *Universe and Its Complexity* 44
- PROBABILITY & STATISTICS - THE LAW OF LARGE NUMBERS 51
- PUTTING IT TOGETHER - THE UNIVERSE AS A CASE STUDY ... 55

SECTION 3 – RELIGIONS 58
- FAITH OVER FACTS: WHY BELIEF PERSISTS 58
- PREMISES OF ANALYSIS 65
- RELIGION 67
- RELIGION'S HISTORY: 71
- ABRAHAMIC RELIGIONS: 79
- INTRODUCTION TO RELIGIONS' SCRIPTURES 81
- GENERAL ANALYSIS OF ABRAHAMIC RELIGIONS 84
- MAIN POINTS FROM PREVIOUS DISCUSSION: 84
- DEVELOPMENT OF MORAL VALUES - RELIGION OR SOCIETY 86
  - *Religion – not the reason for Moral/Ethical Values* 86
  - *Moral values are tied to social values:* 89
  - *Contribution of religions to building Moral values:* 90
  - *Moral fallacies of the Bible / New Testament* 92
  - *Moral fallacies of the Quran* 93
  - *Outside religion -Historical Moral development:* 98
  - *Why Religious Morality has failed* 102
- GENERAL QUESTION FROM BELIEVERS 104
- ABRAHAMIC RELIGIONS 136

Judaism *137*

SECTION 4 – CHRISTIANITY 141

CHRISTIANITY 141
    My Argument: *141*
    Christianity - Main concepts: *141*
    History before Christianity *144*
    Christianity - History *146*
CHRISTIANITY AS USED BY THE ROMAN EMPIRE 149
HOLY BOOKS - TANAKH & BIBLE 156
    Tanakh - Old Testament or Hebrew bible *156*
    The Hebrew bible and the Hammurabi codes *165*
    "Development" of the Bible: *176*
    Old Testament (Tanakh in the Bible) *176*
    Analysis of the New Testament *178*
    Bible - Content *180*
    Analysis of the Bible's content *190*
QUESTIONS FROM CHRISTIANS 192
    Bible - Order of Universe Creation *258*
    Christian God's Moral Values *263*

SECTION 5 – ISLAM 267

ISLAM: 267
    Islam – Main Concepts: *267*
    History: *272*
CENTRAL CLAIM OF ISLAM: 278
    Islam is Deen-e-Fitrat (Natural Religion)? ... *278*
FREE WILL VS FATE 287
ANALYSIS OF THE QURAN: 292
    Quran - History: *292*
    Quran – Content *294*
    Quran in the Arabic Language *298*
    Leading to Sectarianism: *318*
    The basis of Prophet Mohammed's knowledge *321*
    The Pre-Islamic era was not that backward. *328*
QUESTIONS FROM MUSLIMS 334
    Scientific facts revelation – Debunk *388*
CONCLUDING RELIGION TOPIC: 465
RELIGION'S SOCIAL BENEFIT: A PLATFORM FOR HUMAN CONNECTION 466

SECTION- 6 – DIFFERENT ROADS 469

ATHEISM - WHERE EVOLUTION FAILED ME..........................469
SEVEN (7) LIMITATIONS OF EVOLUTION............................471
   1. *Evolution is Reactive, Not Proactive*....................471
   2. *Evolution Lacks Contingency Planning*................472
   3. *The "Good Enough" Problem*...............................472
   4. *The Mystery of Selfless Acts*................................473
   5. *Irreducible Complexity*..473
   6. *Non-Adaptive Traits*..473
   7. *Universals' Moral*...474
EXAMPLES: WHERE NATURE DEFIES THE EVOLUTION PROCESS
....475
   Incredible Creatures That Defy Evolution:...................483
THE IDEA OF "INTELLIGENT DESIGN":...............................487
BOTH SIDES FAILED..491

SECTION 7 - POSSIBILITIES 493

WHAT MIGHT HAVE HAPPENED?..493
EARTH'S PROCESS FOR EVOLVING LIVING CELLS 493
   Starting from hydrogen in the universe:.......................494
   From Elements to elementary compounds – gases........495
   From elementary gases to complex living compounds....497
   Overall summary of the process...................................500
   Other contributing factors:..502

SECTION 8 – ENDING 507

INTERPRETING YOUR NUMBERS:...507
MY CONCLUSION..510
CLOSING THE LOOP…...514

Objective Analysis of God

Section 1

Must Read

Section 1 - Must Read
Book's approach

God or No God?

– that is **NOT** the question we are trying to answer in this book. The primary focus of this effort is to analyze the possibility that the Abrahamic God—Yahweh, Jesus, or Allah—could be the God, as described by the respective religion. So the question we are trying to address is :

Which God is The God?

We will limit our discussion to the three foundational books (Tanakh, Bible, and Quran), along with some basic logic and established historical facts, as I consider all the remaining books to be equivalent to Today's social media.

Like many others, I have embarked upon this journey. This book compiles my findings and the related questions I encountered, presenting them primarily after providing foundational background knowledge and supporting evidence. I believe that proof of the unknown lies within you, and everyone cultivates it as per their experience and thought process. Before proceeding, I would like to present the approach I have adopted in this book and outline the target audience.

Various ways to experience it
You can start reading this book from any section and still enjoy it. For instance, non-mathematical minds can skip all calculations, and Muslims can skip portions of Christianity. But to gain maximum, please:
- Follow the "flow"
- Take pauses to rewind what you have read previously
- Record your reply after reading all previous sections of text.

Objective Analysis of God

- Please do approach me through the website https://www.my-oag.com/ and email as – one@my-oag.com

Audiences:

- My audiences are religious scholars, and I am not looking for them to attempt to analyze it and provide their arguments. Yes, criticism from people like them is more than welcome.
- Audiences are Normal/laypeople (from religious aspects) who spend most of their time and effort earning or performing their daily jobs or spending time with family/friends/hobbies. They are intelligent and possess excellent knowledge to analyze things around them, but lack the time or commitment to perform this analysis. They are simply following the religion of their parents because that is what they were taught, but they have reached a maturity level where they want to understand what they were taught and what they are practicing – does it make sense, or perhaps they wish to explore their faith in God? With the following mindset:
  - Persons who do not understand the philosophical, psychological or sociological arguments given about the existence and non-existence of God.
  - Persons who want to understand God using common logic and a simple, objective argument.
  - Persons who think they give "priority" to their belief system, but it is only in their minds, not in action. In reality, their knowledge about their belief system comes last. When I say 'last,' I am not talking about the time they spend on prayers or in churches or mosques, but rather last — in terms of whether they understand why they are doing these rituals.

I am not primarily addressing religious leaders (e.g., Rabbis, Priests, and Mullahs) or scholars, nor do I seek their debates on the content of this book. My focus is on ordinary working individuals, encouraging them to explore their lifestyle and beliefs. I believe that religious scholars benefit from the very concept of religion while misleading the public.

- Having said that, anyone trying to prove me wrong will help me understand the truth, which is why this book comes with an associated social media two-way communication system on

Section 1 - Must Read
Book's approach

each question and topic. I have researched and have a reasonably good understanding of the arguments presented by religious scholars, but those have not convinced me.
- I have used harsh language against religion, mainly to prompt the public to have the motivation to counter me, triggering their thought process.
- As mentioned at the end, I am just a student or non-biased analyst looking for truth, perhaps by the process of elimination, an approach in which I have tried to remove things that do not make sense, straighten the clutter, and remove the haze so that I can see and analyze better.

Approach:
I have adopted different approaches in different sections of this book, while remaining:
a) As objective as possible.
b) Getting help from numbers, calculations, and simple common-sense logic.
c) Using only established historical facts and only three main holy books – "dictated word-for-word by God himself"

The language and approach I have tried to use mainly involve asking you aggressive questions and poking your mind to help you make objective decisions.

English is not my mother language, and this book is not written as any literary piece, so please bear with my style.

So, the main points about this book are:
1) This book may not provide a definitive answer to all questions, but it will intrigue your mind and let you decide the direction.
2) This book will provide analysis and questions to help YOU decide. I will give my argument based on simple logic and "intrigue" your mind.
3) This book appears to have been written by an atheist, but I do not consider myself a complete atheist. On the last pages, you will see the reasons and objections I have with the pure Evolution theory. My quest has brought me very close to this result, but I also have many questions that science and evolution cannot answer. With this book and related communications, I am reaching out to get those answers.
4) My objective is not to prove that God exists or not, I aim to let you decide whether GOD (Yahweh / Jesus / Allah) as presented by present religions can exist --- or be the God

Objective Analysis of God

- I will analyze each faith separately.
- The God mentioned in this book is the God described by the respective Abrahamic religions.
- The Christian concept of God is different, but in the Trinity, the Father God is the main God (as I will discuss), and I will mainly be referring to Father God.
- The Islamic interpretation of God in different sects is not discussed

5) Please note that I am not objecting to religions -- but addressing followers of that religion and their "objective" approach and thought process, while following that religion.
6) This book is primarily composed of bullet points. Rather than giving you big, convincing paragraphs, it gives you small, bite-sized information and lets you explore further.
7) My approach is to ask questions and let you draw your own conclusion and direction.
8) I am merely planting seeds for your thoughts. To get the most out of this book, take frequent pauses, reflect on what you've read, and allow yourself to explore your ideas deeply.
9) It adopts a different approach, shifting away from lengthy philosophical arguments and toward objective and logical analysis. My arguments primarily involve proving things by presenting calculations and straightforward common sense.
10) None of what is written requires any detailed knowledge about religion, considering that most of us do not know about other religions. I have only captured some basic concepts of each religion.
11) I started this book to address all major religions (Christianity, Islam, Hinduism, Buddhism, Daoism, Sikhism, and Shinto), but halfway through, I realized that, based on concepts and interdependencies, there are mainly two branches of religions.
12) The growth of two distinct sets of religions in two separate geographical areas also indicates how religion influences adjacent beliefs and the evolution of religions over time in the neighboring regions.
13) Addressing all religions in one book is challenging, so I have opted to focus on the three Abrahamic religions. This book is for religious believers in Jews, Christianity, and Islam, who make up about 55% of the world's population.
14) Abrahamic offshoots of religions share many commonalities and can be considered branches of the same tree. They endorse their predecessors' beliefs and concepts, but also

Section 1 - Must Read
Book's approach

claim that their own religion is the correct one, as the old one has been compromised. For example, Islam endorses Christianity and Judaism but says that followers have made alterations in the basic principles of faith.

15) So, negating one religion sometimes comes close to negating the rest or the previous one. Like if I am highlighting issues with the Quran about Christianity, I am addressing all three religions, Islam, Christianity, and Judaism

16) Many aspects of Judaism, Christianity, and Islam are similar at the grassroots level and can be addressed in common questions.

17) I have combined all related or common questions/objections (common to all three religions) in the "General question section."

18) The General Section is followed by religion-specific issues, mainly for Christians and Muslims.

19) As there are numerous sects in each religion, my discussion will remain within the approved scripture (like the Bible and the Quran) only, endorsed by almost all sects of that religion.

20) While addressing the Old Testament part of the Bible, I will also address Judaism.

21) *Now I come to my main approach: while all religions present a concept of God, none provides a direct method to interact with Him. Therefore, I will examine God indirectly—through His characteristics and attributes—as described in the primary religious scriptures (the Tanakh, the Bible, and the Quran)*

22) **There are two main premises of my approach,**
   - The most prominent manifestation of God is this universe, so I will strive to understand God and His Attributes through an understanding of the universe.
   - Then compare those Attributes with the image of God provided by religion -- as mentioned in their scriptures and established belief system, while taking help from *their history*

23) We will explore the Bible and the Quran in depth, how they were developed, and what is written in them.

24) As in this book, we will also ask you questions about your thought process, so we will ask you many questions at the end of each main section, which you may record to have a better understanding of where you stand, objectively.

Objective Analysis of God

25) I will present my case with a discussion point (mostly one-pager), stating facts and analysis, then follow that with a simple logical question, which you need to mark or give a number, considering the following spectrum.

Strongly Disagree								Strongly Agree	
1	2	3	4	5	6	7	8	9	10

26) In the end, we will try to analyze your thoughts based on our initial evaluation and present our opinion about you.
27) While answering and putting numbers against the above, some bias will kick into your mind. Controlling your thoughts and restricting them to analysis and questions will be essential to obtain realistic results.
28) Please pause and reflect frequently, especially before putting your number
29) **Again, the objective of this book is not to prove or disprove "A GOD" but ONLY to address" The GOD" as explained by the Abrahamic religions.**

> *Here, I will not explore whether God exists or not. My focus is to challenge the idea that a God capable of creating the universe is necessarily the same God portrayed in religion—specifically the Abrahamic traditions of Judaism, Christianity, and Islam. The question is not about existence, but about identity: can the architect of cosmic laws truly be the deity described in sacred texts?*

30) As mentioned, I am planting seeds for thought, so even if you do not follow the above guidelines (filling your responses), but continue to take pauses and think about each question, it will serve both of us well
31) At the end, I will provide my conclusion
32) There are some lengthy calculations that you can skip, but please read the conclusion to understand what is proven with those calculations.
33) There are a few novel Ideas (at least in my mind) as I have not come across those thoughts in my research
34) The Topics covered in this book are not all completely novel, so you can consider it a compilation of ideas. I insert my

thoughts here and there, which may help you analyze your idea about God.

35) I restricted myself to the following numbers of questions
    - 30 for the followers of Abrahamic religions
    - 60 for the followers of Judaism and Christianity
    - 90 for the followers of Islam

> *As an acknowledgment of Nikola Tesla, as he famously stated that understanding the numbers 3, 6, and 9 would unlock the secrets of the universe, and his stand against J.P. Morgan.*

36) I have also listed some issues, contradictions, and incorrect statements mentioned in the Holy books; religious leaders have always presented counterarguments. I have considered their general responses, but I will not delve into analyzing their argument. Instead, I will present both points to you and let you decide by providing answers to the questions.

37) While evaluating my argument, remember that these texts (Bible & Quran) are said to be coming from THE GOD, all-knowing, all-intelligent, all-powerful, etc., so our criteria are also strict. My argument is how can we expect even a little issue/mistake/discrepancy from Him, considering that those three books are the only communication (as per each religion) He has to guide us to the way he wants, which in turn is the reason for creating this whole universe and heaven and hell, etc.

38) Main areas of comparison will be:
    - Logical comparison of the religious God and the Universe God – explained later on
    - Holy scriptures' internal conflicts
    - Historical facts
    - Scientifically incorrect/incohesive
    - Moral values as given by God

Objective Analysis of God

Book's Structure

This book presents facts and an objective analysis of the possibility of a God. Here, we will make God very simple, having basic characteristics and attributes. The religious God entity analyzed in this book has the following main characteristics:
1. Creator of this universe and sustainer of its order
2. Creator of Humans, to judge their deeds in this world and reward them / punish them in the afterlife
3. Creator of Heaven & Hell and creator of the rules of who will spend eternal life in heaven or hell.
4. God exists in every time frame and every place
5. God is all good, merciful, loving, just, omnipotent, knowledgeable (past / future), etc.

Different sections of this book deal with the following topics:
1) I will start by discussing general concepts about the Universe, its vastness, and its complexity. Then, I will create analogies to help my readers understand large numbers. I have also discussed how such huge numbers contribute to increasing the possibilities for slight anomalies or unprecedented events from a statistical perspective.
2) Then I moved on to analyzing the concept of God in religions and have tried to see if there is any possibility that the God of religion can be the God who designed and built this universe and is maintaining it.
3) After that, we will analyze God and the three holy scriptures, which are supposed to come from God Himself.
4) My approach is to present facts related to God's Characteristics and then present a question on those facts and analysis, asking you to rate the possibility of a God with that characteristic on a scale of 1-10, as explained earlier and below:

Strongly Disagree								Strongly Agree	
1	2	3	4	5	6	7	8	9	10

5) Ultimately, I have shared my perspective on religions and what our approach should be. I have also listed a possibility about what could have happened, resulting in the present Earth and humans.

I have included my journey in this book, which will provide a background and may give you a better understanding of where I am coming from and how to approach this book.
I have used internet resources and AI platforms to research and validate calculations and information. I have also used AI extensively to rephrase my text for two main reasons:
- To compensate for my English language barrier
- To adjust my text so that it can fit in most of the boxes and tables I have.

I encourage readers to utilize these AI platforms to ask their religious questions rather than consulting their spiritual leaders, who, in my opinion, are biased as they have a vested interest in people continuing to follow their beliefs – I have provided evidence to support this.
Please always validate the AI answers, as they often provide incorrect responses. Consider that AI may provide a good path to follow, but not necessarily the correct destination.

Towards the end, I have included my Conclusion and have provided an analysis of your answers and numbers to help you explore yourself and take action if you truly want to find the truth.

Objective Analysis of God

Self-Assessment Section

This short self-assessment helps you reflect on your thoughts and actions. It's designed to show the difference between what you think you believe and what you may do, because actions speak louder than words.
Before reading the book, take this quick check to:
- Understand your current mindset on this topic.
- See the real picture of your thoughts and behaviors—not just what you say, but what you do.

This will provide a clear starting point and illustrate how your perspective may shift after reading it.

This book is structured so that readers can start from any second-level heading. For instance, Muslims may be interested in the Islam section and may not want to explore the Christianity section.
However, for a complete understanding, please start at the beginning and follow the flow. It is challenging to relate to a religious God without comprehending the vastness and complexity of the universe.

If you are a believer, please do not miss

"Faith Over Facts: Why Belief Persists"

My journey

I was born in a Muslim Family, and my childhood exposure was practicing the Muslim way of life. I always had questions about different concepts of Islam, for which I never got substantial and convincing answers from Muslims Scholars or the Quran.

I am a Mechanical Engineer with a Master's in Business Administration. I have spent my life analyzing numbers and facts, so Philosophical arguments and lengthy explanatory paragraphs are not easily digestible for me. I have also adopted the same approach in this book: be objective and logical, rely on facts and numbers, and present these in bullet points.
My journey started with the following verse of the Quran:
2:170 - *"And when it is said to them, 'Follow what Allah has revealed,' they say, 'Rather, we will follow that upon which we found our forefathers.' Even though their forefathers did not understand anything, nor were they guided?"*

What I got from this verse was that Allah wants us all not to follow a belief or religion just because we are born or raised in that family/environment. He wants everyone to explore and validate their own beliefs. This objective is further strengthened by Allah mentioning a similar approach at least 14 times in the Quran -- that is, all individuals are responsible for their deed and their actions alone, meaning that Muslims will not get a benefit if they are born in the correct religion.

> *If you are a believer and have confirmed faith that you need to work in this life for reward after death (in eternal life) and you do not spend time to find out that what you are following is the correct path or not – then IMO you are not a true believer – so you should stop calling yourself Christian or Muslims – because you are not.*

Therefore, everyone must embark on their journey of exploration and reach their conclusions about faith and belief. Suppose someone dedicates their life to sincerely seeking the truth—the right faith or religion—but does not find it by the end. In that case, Allah may view them more favorably (considering the above verse) than

Objective Analysis of God

someone who unquestioningly follows their parents' beliefs without reflection, inquiry, or effort to seek the truth.

A person engaged in the sincere pursuit of truth can stand before Allah and submit that they were fulfilling the Quran's guidance by actively searching, even if they could not reach a definitive conclusion. In contrast, what justification does a blind follower give someone who adheres to a faith simply because they were born into it? Even if they happen to follow the true religion, such as Islam, what answer would they give if, on the Day of Judgment, Allah were to say:

> *"You followed Islam because you were born into an Islamic environment. Had you been born into a Hindu culture, you would have followed Hinduism. For that reason, you do not deserve Heaven."?*

My target was to know and understand my beliefs enough that I can argue or perhaps convince a non-Muslim, and that will be my way of telling my God "Allah" that I am Muslim, not because I was born in a Muslim Family, but because I know that is the proper way of life and purpose of my existence.

With an Islamic background, I read the Quran and found many issues and questions regarding how Tafaseers (explanations of the Quran by different scholars) present the words of the Quran. I discovered that these scholars, in their "Tafaseers," completely changed the meaning, totally misrepresented the words, and twisted them to arrive at their interpretation.

So, I tried to find a translation that was as accurate as possible, and read only that, with the aim that if I got the answer from it, that would be fine; if not, I was satisfied as a searcher.

> ***After becoming frustrated with religious doctrines, I began exploring God on my own. I realized that perhaps a better way to understand God was to examine His most evident and confirmed manifestation—the universe.***

As I attempt to grasp the vastness of the universe in terms of time, space, and complexity - both at microscopic and telescopic levels - I realize that a significant hurdle in understanding God through His universe is that our minds cannot fully comprehend the Universe in its true sense. The human mind is not capable of understanding & comprehending such big numbers. I also realize that the Universe is so huge and complex in every sense that its maker, if any, must be an extremely intelligent and capable entity.

In the following pages, one of my main areas of argument is how a creator of such a magnificent, complex, massive, and vast universe can make blunders while writing his holy texts or instructing his followers on how to conduct their lives.

So, I have transformed my frustration into a question in the following pages. I have tried to make these questions as simple as possible; almost all of them do not require extensive knowledge of religion or history. You mainly need your logic and common sense to answer these questions.

Hopefully, this will help you understand God's overall concept and provide you with the direction or steps you need.

Again, the main object is to "use questioning as our way to truth".

> *During my journey, whenever I raised these questions in gatherings, people accused me of making their Eman (faith) shaky. My response to them is this: if someone like me—a lifelong ordinary office and family man who only began researching less than two years ago—can shake your Eman simply by asking basic questions, then, with all humility, you never truly had Eman. What you had was the illusion of faith—ritualistic practice without genuine belief.*

Self-Assessment

The main reasons for this self-assessment are to provide three essential facets to your journey through this book:
a) Take a pause and reflect momentarily upon your life and your beliefs, your strength of belief, your attitude towards your religion, and your approach towards other belief systems.
b) It provides a starting point for comparing your journey of self-exploration before going through this text.
c) Provides an objective lookback opportunity to see if there were some changes in your mindset before and after reading this text.

This book is also accompanied by a website that allows you to monitor your progress and evaluate the results of your answers using a simple online tool. This tool automates your response recording systems and provides feedback based on your responses.

https://www.my-oag.com/

AT the start, please ask the following question:

> *List the top 3 reasons that have convinced you that your religion and beliefs provide the correct and accurate path.*

Section 1 - Must Read
Self-Assessment

Question:
I am following my "Birth" religion and belief system

S1

Analysis and background:
What we mean here is that, up to this point, you have adhered to the belief system instilled in you since childhood—what you heard, observed, or were taught by elders and those around you. You embraced it with heart, mind, and soul, convinced, at least to some extent, that this belief system represents the proper, correct, and accurate path.

Conclusion:
I am convinced that the belief system introduced to me in my early childhood is the correct one, and I am comfortably following it.

Please rate this Conclusion:

Objective Analysis of God

Question: I am a practicing believer	**S2**

Analysis and background:
Here, we mean that you are practicing or participating in religious rituals, much like your parents or the people around you did. This aspect relates more to actions than to inner belief—it is about what you do, not necessarily what you think. You might rank yourself lower if you feel uncomfortable with these rituals, but still follow them out of tradition or to conform to family or friends.
Example: You might give yourself an eight if you attend church or a mosque at least once a week for prayer.

Conclusion: I am, for the most part, still performing the same rituals that I was introduced to during my early childhood, even though those rituals have evolved over time or with changes in geography.	Please rate this Conclusion:

Section 1 - Must Read
Self-Assessment

Question:
I have a reasonable understanding of my beliefs

S3

Analysis and background:
When was the last time you were confronted with a different religious belief, and you were able to argue and take part in defending your belief system?

We do not mean that you were able to convince others, but rather that we are limited to evaluating whether you participated well in the argument.

Example: Give eight even if you do not recall any such incident, but have read at least five books related to your religion during the past two years.

Conclusion:
Based on the above description, I have a reasonable understanding of my beliefs.

Please rate this Conclusion:

Objective Analysis of God

Question: I am familiar with other sects within my religion and their perspectives.	**S4**

Analysis and background:
Here, we mean if you have done any of the following:
a) Reading 2-4 books of other sects, which go slightly against your beliefs
b) Listen to lectures 5+ lectures of other sects, and reflect upon those later on, during the past 6 months

Conclusion: I have explored other sects within my religious beliefs and analyzed their validity in comparison to mine.	Please rate this Conclusion:

Question:
I know about other major religions

S5

Analysis and background:
Here, the question pertains to religions (such as Christianity, Hinduism, Buddhism, and Islam) rather than sects (Catholic, Orthodox, Sunni, Wahhabi, Shia).

If you belong to any of the three major religions, have you explored the belief systems of the other two religions (like if you are Christian, do you know what Islam and Hinduism teach)? You can consider and count social media content promoting their belief system.

Example: Give eight if you have read their holy books, even 15%, or if you have attended 5+ lectures (min 1 + hour each) delivered by their religious leaders (Priests and Mullahs) promoting their religion.

Conclusion:
I have some understanding of at least one or two religions.

Please rate this Conclusion:

Objective Analysis of God

Question: I never had any agreement or thought about what was being said by my religious leaders.	S6

Analysis and background:
Here, we mean the moments when you critically reflect on your beliefs while attending rituals or listening to a religious leader's lecture. Do you ever find yourself thinking, 'What are they saying? This doesn't make sense.

Example: Give 9-10 if you have always found those lectures or books completely logical and aligned with what you have learned and know about this universe.

Conclusion: I am entirely comfortable with my beliefs and consider those to be the truth. These findings align entirely with scientific knowledge and other facts about our world and the universe.	Please rate this Conclusion:

Premise

We will discuss it again; my approach is as follows:

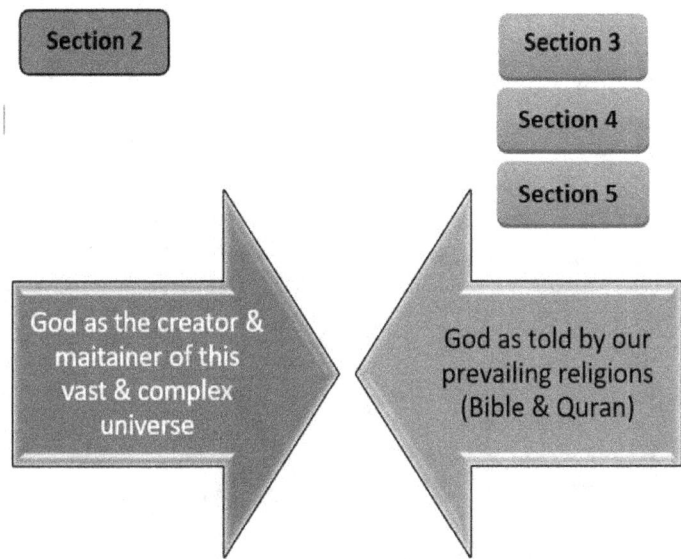

Before proceeding, I invite you to take a moment to pause and engage fully with the diagram before you. Consider not just what it presents, but what it implies—its assumptions, its logic, considering present human knowledge, and its potential consequences. Ask yourself: Does it hold up under scrutiny? What perspectives might be missing? By reflecting deeply and exploring its validity, you may uncover valuable insights and appreciate the pages you are about to read, and hopefully, embrace the changes that will follow.

Objective Analysis of God

Please see the following few examples to support the model shown on the previous page:

The entity that could have created the universe	Entity (God) informed by Religion
Having almost infinite special access – the whole universe of trillions of trillions of trillions... km	Only communicated with humans within a radius of less than 5,000 km.
Has been active for billions of years	Only communicated for 3000 years maximum
Extremely far-sighted in developing planning for billions of years	Cannot even foresee what will happen in the next few minutes
Extremely detail-oriented.	Extremely superficial, instructing humans to pray without explaining the steps
Highly organized and method-oriented – laws of the universe	Could not even develop simple ethical laws in which He plans to judge humans
Extremely capable and powerful, as He created the universe	Extremely whiny and weak - Cannot handle his minute creation – Satan - Cursing an old lady (Quran)
Incredibly imaginative and creative, consider the diversity of creations	Cannot even come up with an idea on how to communicate religion – keep trying the same failing method repeatedly

Section 1 - Must Read
Premise

Section 2

Understanding the Universe

Section 2 - Understanding the Universe

Now we will start by analyzing section 2, covering the topic of understanding the universe:

From Universe to God

This is the main thought that we will first try to understand the universe, before embarking upon understanding its creator.

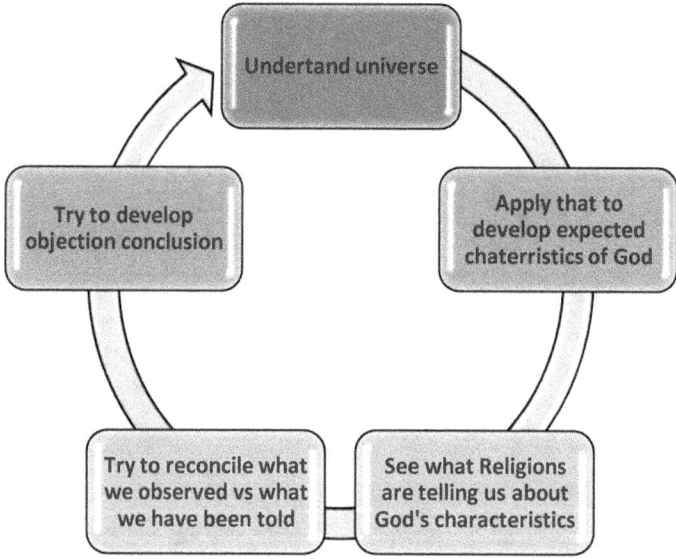

Please note that I have presented the above in a circle, as I consider this process to be iterative in nature. Humans are only trying to scratch the tip of the iceberg we call the universe. As you will see, we do not know how much we do not know. However, while scratching humans have done on the tip has revealed so much to us, since the time we started understanding the universe, no new prominent belief system has taken root. The more we know about the universe, the more we understand about religion and /or its realities.

Section 2 - Understanding the Universe
From Universe to God

This iterative sequence has been proven again and again in our history. The universe's incomprehensible enormity has fascinated and puzzled humanity since the dawn of civilization. From ancient philosophers to modern astrophysicists probing the depths of space with advanced telescopes, the question of how big the universe is and what lies beyond our reach has remained central to our quest for knowledge. Despite significant advancements in science and technology, the sheer scale of the universe continues to elude human comprehension.

We have not even explored our world—the Earth. Approximately 80% of the ocean remains unexplored, and more than 15% of the Earth's land surface remains unexplored. In effect, we have only reached about 60% of Earth's surface (80% of 71 and 15% of 29 ~ 60%). Additionally, exploring the depths of the oceans will only exacerbate our limited understanding of the planet we call home, which we have inhabited for thousands of years.

This is only the outer surface. If we add depth to this equation, we might conclude that we perhaps know less than 5% of our Earth. To give you an idea of the depth, if the Earth were reduced to the size of a Billiard Ball, a cricket ball, or a baseball, its surface would be as smooth as glass. All these big mountains, trenches, and valleys will be gone, transformed into a smooth surface. This may give you an idea of how deep we can theoretically explore.

On the other hand, although it seems that we have made great strides in understanding the laws of nature, the realities of the Quantum world have opened our eyes and struck human scientists with the statement that "you know nothing." What to talk about in the universe?

Many religious scholars and Pro-believers use this lack of understanding to give us analogies on God, with statements like:

- Look how stable this universe is
- If evolution is true, why are humans not evolving now
- How can living things come out suddenly

They do not realize that what they see is just one second of a 50-year period. If you spend one hour in Switzerland in summer, without any news, and try to judge the condition of the world we live in, you will say that everything is peaceful, organized, and stable. This is far from the facts of the world we live in nowadays, and the condition of the Earth and humanity.

Objective Analysis of God

You need to understand 50 years, take many steps back, and consider the big picture. Then, you will realize how dynamic and unstable the universe and the Earth are, and how things take millions of years to happen and changes evolve over a long period. And our life and historical record are too small to capture that.

The following lines explore the vastness of the universe, the challenges humans face in understanding its scale, and why this understanding remains inherently limited.

Understanding enormous numbers:

Now, we are changing gears and laying down some foundations to help us understand our next topic—the universe. To understand the universe, we must grasp the vast numbers that comprise it.

I will continue to explore this topic with various approaches and analogies, emphasizing that large numbers often fail to convey their enormity, and most of the time, they fail to convey the intended idea. The primary reason is that our minds struggle to comprehend these enormous numbers.

The following table illustrates the relationship as we progress from one million to one billion, attempting to understand the change by adding only three zeros. So, here is our first attempt:

Number	Figures	Scientific notation	Equivalent time in Seconds
One Thousand	1,000	1×10^3	~ 16 minutes
One Million	1,000,000	1×10^6	11.5 Days
One Billion	1,000,000,000	1×10^9	31.7 years
One Trillion	1,000,000,000,000	1×10^{12}	31,688 years
One Quadrillion	1,000,000,000,000,000	1×10^{15}	31,7000,000 years

Observe the propagation or increase in numbers from millions to billions. In everyday conversation, we transition from millions to billions, but our minds do not usually grasp the magnitude of the increase in numbers it represents.

One trillion is 1,000 times one billion. While "billion" and "trillion" may sound like they're just a few steps apart, in reality, it's a

Section 2 - Understanding the Universe
Understanding enormous numbers:

massive leap, just like the difference between walking a mile and walking around the Earth 40 times.

From one million seconds, equal to about 12 days, to a billion seconds is less than half of our lifetime, but one trillion seconds would take us to over 31,688 years. That would have been around 29,679 B.C., roughly 24,000 years before the earliest known civilizations began to take shape. Adding three more zeros, the amount jumps to 31.7 million years. The Main reason for showing it is to illustrate how quickly these numbers increase (exponentially), as our brain tends to draw an increased concept based on a previous value. It is challenging for our brains to comprehend the magnitude of the difference.

This is a fundamental concept to grasp as we move on to discuss huge numbers. You may appreciate that if we are talking about 1×10^{22}, how enormous that number will be.

One billion seconds back (mid-1990s), we saw the rise of the Internet and the Dot-Com boom. Back in one trillion seconds (approximately 30,000 BCE), we were in the Ice Age, Neanderthals were fading out, and present-day Humans (Homo sapiens) were in the Stone Age, perhaps drawing animals on cave walls while living alongside mammoths and saber-toothed cats.

If you stacked 1 billion 1-mm-thick staple pins, the pile would stretch 1,000 kilometers, which is equivalent to the distance from Cairo to Mecca or New York City to Chicago, Paris, Barcelona, Beijing, and Shanghai, which is about just a small fraction (0.025 times) of the Earth's circumference. Whereas, if you stacked 1 trillion staple pins, the pile would go around the Earth 25 times.

Now I will try to introduce the same concept in a different form. If you understand the graphs, please explain how big a step is, considering the previous numbers:
Let's discuss jumping from one billion to one trillion:

Objective Analysis of God

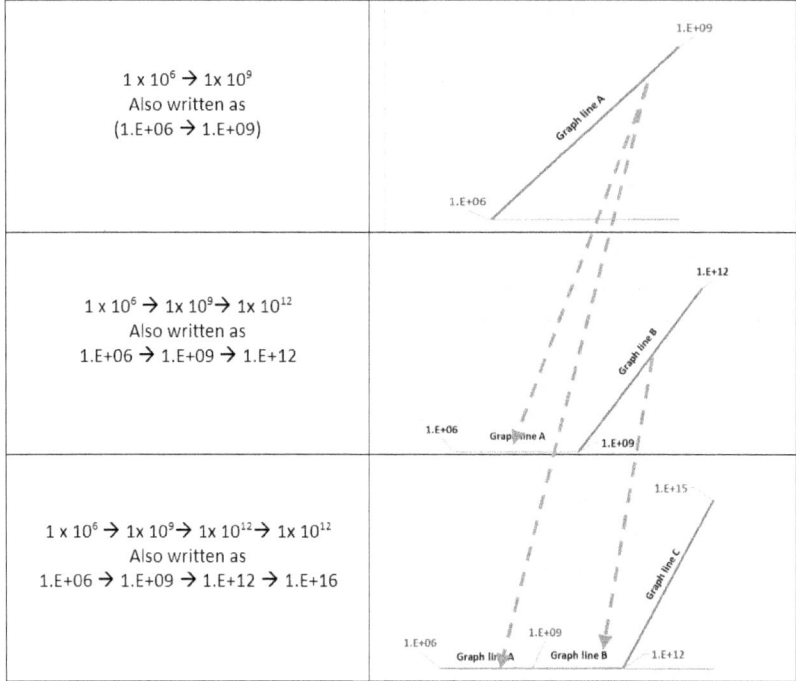

The main reason for showing these graphs is to give you an idea of how graph line A becomes almost flat compared to graph line B and how graph line B becomes practically flat compared to graph line C. We will revisit this topic, as we will need multiple cycles to begin understanding these enormous numbers.

Concept of "Light year"

We will discuss the concept of the "Light Year," what it represents, and why it is needed.
Firstly, a light year measures distance, not time. The universe is so vast that our distance-measuring unit cannot adequately describe it, so humans have devised the concept of "light-years." It helps us grasp how unbelievably big space is!

What is a Light-Year?
A light-year is the distance that light travels in one year. Since light moves incredibly fast (about 300,000 kilometers per second or 186,000 miles per second), a light-year is a considerable distance—about 9.46 trillion kilometers (5.88 trillion miles)—equivalent to

taking 236,000,000 circles around the Earth – 236 million circles around the Earth.

Why Use Light-Years?
Space is so vast, and customary units like kilometers or miles are too small to represent it accurately. Saying a star is "4 light-years away" is easier than saying "37.8 trillion kilometers away."
The following are a few examples and analogies to help us grasp this unit, "Light Year."

a) The distance from Earth to the Moon is about 1.28 seconds of one light year.
b) The Sun is eight light-minutes away. Light takes 8 minutes to travel from the Sun to Earth. So, if the Sun suddenly disappeared, we'd only know 8 minutes later!
c) Proxima Centauri (the closest star after the Sun) is 4.24 light-years away. This means its light takes 4.24 years to reach us. If you look at it tonight, you'll see how it looked over 4 years ago!
d) The Milky Way Galaxy is 100,000 light-years wide. If a spaceship could travel at light speed (impossible for now), it would take 100,000 years to cross our galaxy!
e) If a light-year were a football field, our entire solar system would only cover about 1 millimeter! – less than the thickness of a grass blade.
f) If the Sun is reduced to the size of a grape (2 cm wide), the next star (Proxima Centauri) would be 560 km (350 miles) away!

Understanding the Scale of the Universe

Our premise is that if God has created this enormous universe, evolving it, maintaining it, and making changes in it, then what could be a better way to understand His capabilities than to observe this universe that He has created?

The universe is unimaginably vast, stretching far beyond the limits of human perception. To grasp its scale, we must begin with our solar system, a speck in the grand cosmic expanse. The Earth orbits the Sun, a star that is one of billions in the Milky Way galaxy. The Milky Way spans approximately 100,000 light-years in diameter and contains an estimated 100 to 400 billion stars. Yet, the Milky

Objective Analysis of God

Way is just one of an estimated two trillion galaxies in the observable universe.

The observable universe, the portion of the universe that can be seen from Earth, has a radius of approximately 46.5 billion light-years. This means that light from the farthest reaches of the observable universe has travelled for 13.8 billion years to reach us, nearly the universe's age. However, the observable universe is not the entirety of the cosmos. The universe may be infinitely larger, extending far beyond what we can observe.

To put this into perspective, consider the following analogy. If the entire universe were scaled down to the size of the Earth, our solar system would be smaller than a grain of sand, and the Milky Way galaxy would be about the size of a football field.

The Challenges of Understanding the Universe's Vastness
Despite our best efforts, humans struggle to comprehend the scale of the universe due to several inherent limitations:

1. Limitations of Human Perception
Our historical development, sensory organs, and cognitive abilities inherently limit human perception. We are biologically adapted to perceive and interact with objects and phenomena on a human scale, ranging from the microscopic to the macroscopic, but not on the scale of galaxies or the universe. Our brain cannot intuitively grasp distances measured in light-years or the concept of billions of years. For example, the idea that light from distant stars takes thousands or millions of years to reach us is difficult to internalize because it lies far outside our everyday experiences.

2. The Limitations of Language and Analogies
Language and analogies, while helpful, often fall short when attempting to describe the universe's scale. Words like "vast," "infinite," or "enormous" are attempts to convey the enormity of the cosmos, but they are ultimately inadequate. Analogies, such as comparing the universe to a grain of sand or a football field, provide a sense of scale but cannot fully capture the universe's true magnitude. The failure lies in our inability to comprehend the vastness of our Earth. These tools are limited because they rely on human-scale references, which are inherently insufficient for describing something as immense as the universe.

3. **The Limitations of Human Imagination**
Human imagination is constrained by our experiences and the physical world in which we live. While we may use large numbers and distances, we cannot truly conceptualize, visualize, or internalize them. For instance, the number of stars in the observable universe is estimated at around 10^{24} (1 followed by 24 zeros). This number is so large that the human mind can't fully grasp its significance. As we tried earlier, and I believe we started losing track of how big the jumps were from 6 to 9 zeros, now imagine the leap of 24 zeros. Our imagination struggles to bridge the gap between the familiar and the cosmic numbers.

4. **The Limitations of Scientific Tools**
While telescopes and other scientific instruments have allowed us to explore the universe in unprecedented detail, they too have limitations. The observable universe is bound by the speed of light and the universe's age. We cannot see beyond the cosmic horizon, the farthest distance from which light has had time to reach us since the Big Bang. Additionally, much of the universe is composed of dark matter and dark energy, which are invisible and poorly understood. These limitations mean that our understanding of the universe is highly incomplete. Also, note that we can attribute all these learning and developments in the last 1,000 years, which is nothing when discussing the universe's times.

5. **The Logical and Existential Challenge**
The massiveness of the universe also poses a logical and existential challenge. It forces us to confront our insignificance in the grand scheme of things. The Earth, and by extension humanity, is an infinitesimally small part of the cosmos. This realization can be both humbling and unsettling. It raises profound questions about our place in the universe, the nature of existence, and the possibility of life beyond Earth. These questions are challenging to answer and often lie beyond the realm of empirical science. We will use this thought in our questions.

Now, we will try to understand the same topic from another angle: Why is the Universe's Vastness Difficult to Understand?

The difficulty in understanding the universe's vastness stems from its vastness, comprising scales and timeframes that are entirely alien

Objective Analysis of God

and outside our realm of human understanding. The universe is governed by physical laws and phenomena that are often counterintuitive and beyond our everyday experience. For example:
- The Scale of Time: The universe is approximately 13.8 billion years old, a timespan that is difficult to comprehend. Human history, by comparison, spans only a few thousand years. The idea that the universe has existed for billions of years and will continue to exist for billions more is challenging to internalize.
- The Scale of Distance: Distances in the universe are measured in light-years, the distance light travels in one year. Light travels at approximately 300,000 kilometers per second, meaning that:
- The distance between Earth and the Moon can be covered in 1.3 seconds
- One light-year is about 9.46 trillion kilometers.
- The nearest star to Earth, Proxima Centauri, is 4.24 light-years away, while the farthest galaxies are billions of light-years away.

These distances are so vast that they defy human comprehension.
- The Scale of Complexity: The universe is vast and incredibly complex. It contains phenomena such as black holes, neutron stars, quasars, and dark matter, which challenge our understanding of physics. The interplay of these phenomena on a cosmic scale adds another layer of complexity to our understanding of the universe.
- On the other hand, it is contemplated and "designed" at a highly minute level how atoms and molecules of different elements can form compounds and continue transforming and providing value to all beings on earth.

The universe's vastness is a testament to the grandeur and mystery of existence and its creator, if there is one. It stretches far beyond the limits of human perception, imagination, and scientific tools, making it inherently difficult to comprehend. While we have made remarkable progress in understanding the cosmos, much remains a mystery. The universe challenges us to expand our minds, question our assumptions, and embrace the unknown. Doing so reminds us of our place in the cosmos—a small but curious species striving to understand the infinite. The journey to comprehend the universe is not just a scientific endeavor but also a philosophical and existential one, inviting us to ponder the profound questions of existence and our place within it.

Humans have come a long way, but we are still in a very early stage of development. We'll all be back to living in caves if we take away the following five developments from our entire history:
1. **Agriculture**
2. **Language and writing**
3. **Electromagnetism**
4. **Converting energies**
5. **Digital development**

Just think how much more is out there – unexplored.

I will continue to try to explain the universe, as this is one of the key messages of this book. The primary purpose of following analogies is to flex your brain so that you can start (maybe) putting your head around the vastness of the universe.

Universe and Its Space

The vastness of the universe, in terms of Time, Space, and complexity, is very difficult to understand, considering the limitations of our minds, which have developed based on the exposure they receive. We have already touched on this lightly, but now we will delve deeper.

We are still in the very early stages of understanding the universe, or rather, the observable universe. Therefore, we will first explore the observable universe and then discuss what remains unexplored.

So, to understand the universe, first we need to put our brains to some extensive exercises of understanding big numbers, some of the examples are below:

"Below is a comparison between the number of planetary bodies in the universe and the number of tablespoons of water in all of Earth's water resources" (oceans, rivers, and lakes). This will flex your muscles and give us a sense of how the vastness of the universe compares to the total volume of water on Earth measured in tablespoons.

As it is impossible to count all the numbers of planetary bodies or the number of spoons in any oceans, we will take estimates and try to calculate these by making a few assumptions, as explained below:

Objective Analysis of God

Estimating the Number of Planetary Bodies in the Universe

As an engineer, I have been crunching numbers and financial figures, so the following examples are more comprehensible. If you are not interested, please skip the calculations and proceed to the text immediately before the Lake Ontario map to understand the concept.

Again, attention, the following is a long example, but like any other example that goes into this depth, it will be that long and may not be suited for many people with a mathematical background, so that they might skip this portion (with a colored background)

Secondly, I need to consider an earthly and relatable analogy, which is very difficult, as I couldn't think of anything with such big numbers that a general audience is exposed to.

The universe is incomprehensibly vast, containing billions of galaxies, each with billions of stars, many of which have planetary systems. To estimate the number of planetary bodies, we'll need to consider:

Number of Galaxies: Current estimates suggest that about 100 to 200 billion galaxies are in the observable universe.

Stars per Galaxy: On average, a galaxy like the Milky Way contains about 100 to 400 billion stars. Our Sun is one example.

Planets per Star: Observations indicate that many stars have planetary systems. Estimates suggest an average of at least one planet per star. Our sun has 8 Planets, one of which is our home, Earth

Total Stars in the Universe:

- Lower estimate: 100 billion galaxies × 100 billion stars/galaxy = 10^{22} stars (1 followed by 22 zeros)
- Upper estimate: 200 billion galaxies × 400 billion stars/galaxy = 8×10^{22} stars (8 followed by 22 zeros)

Now moving on to Total Planetary Bodies:

Recent studies suggest that many stars have multiple planets. If we assume an average of 1.6 planets per star (a conservative estimate based on exoplanet discoveries), it is a very conservative estimate, as we already know that our solar system has eight planets

So, the estimated number of total planetary bodies will be somewhere in between

- Lower estimate: 100 billion galaxies × 100 billion stars/galaxy x 1.6 planets per start = 1.6 x 10^{22} stars (1 followed by 22 zeros)
- Upper estimate: 200 billion galaxies × 400 billion stars/galaxy x 1.6 planets per start = 8 × 10^{22} stars (8 followed by 22 zeros)
- Total planets = 1.6 × 10^{22} to 1.6 × 8 × 10^{22}
- = 1.6 × 10^{22} to 1.28 × 10^{23} planets, or we can say that

In between:
16,000,000,000,000,000,000,000
---- to -----
128,000,000,000,000,000,000,000

For estimation purposes, we can say that the number of planetary bodies in the universe is approximately in the order of 10^{22} to 10^{23}, or can be considered an average number of 72 x 10^{22}

Now, to calculate the Number of Tablespoons of Water in Earth's Water Resources, we will first attempt to determine the total water in all oceans, rivers, and lakes. We will use a combination of satellite measurements, geological surveys, and mathematical modelling. Here's a step-by-step explanation of how scientists estimate the total water in these bodies of water:

Analogy 1:
1. Measuring the Volume of Oceans
The oceans contain about 96.5% of Earth's total water. To calculate their volume:
- Surface Area: Satellites like NASA's Jason series measure the ocean's surface area, approximately 361 million square kilometres.
- Average Depth: Based on sonar and satellite altimetry data, the average depth of the oceans is about 3,688 meters.
- Volume Calculation: Volume = Surface Area × Average Depth
  For oceans:
  - 361×10^6 km² × 3,688 km = 361×10^6 × 3.688 x 10^3
  - ≈ $1,331,368 \times 10^6$ km³
  - ≈ 1.332×10^9 km³ of water.

2. Measuring the Volume of Lakes
Lakes hold a much smaller fraction of Earth's water. To estimate their volume:
- Surface Area: Satellites and topographic maps are used to determine the surface area of lakes.

Objective Analysis of God

- Depth Measurements: Depth is measured using sonar or bathymetric surveys.
- Volume Calculation: Volume is calculated as Surface Area × Average Depth for each lake.
The total volume of all lakes is estimated to be about 176,400 cubic kilometres.

3. Measuring the Volume of Rivers
Rivers contain an even smaller amount of water compared to oceans and lakes. To estimate their volume:
- Flow Rate: Scientists measure rivers' flow rate (discharge) using stream gauges.
- Volume Calculation: The total volume of water in rivers is estimated by multiplying the average flow rate by the time water spends in the river system.
The total volume of water in rivers is approximately 2,120 cubic kilometres.

4. Adding It All Up
The total volume of water in oceans, lakes, and rivers is the sum of their volumes:
- Oceans: 1.332×10^9 km^3
- Lakes: 176,400 km^3
- Rivers: 2,120 km^3

Total Water Volume:
$1.332 \times 10^9 + 176,400 + 2,120$
$\approx 1.332 \times 10^9$ km^3 = $1.332 \times 10^9 + 176,400 + 2,120$
$\approx 1.332 \times 10^9$ km^3

The total volume of water in Earth's oceans, rivers, and lakes is approximately **1.332 billion cubic kilometres**, with the vast majority (96.5%) in the oceans. While lakes and rivers contribute a much smaller fraction, they are critical for freshwater resources and ecosystems.

Which has the following assumptions and restrictions
- Dynamic Nature of Water: Water constantly moves through the hydrological cycle (evaporation, precipitation, runoff), making it difficult to measure precisely.
- Inaccessible Areas: Some remote lakes and rivers are difficult to measure accurately.

- Groundwater: This calculation excludes groundwater, a significant reservoir of freshwater.

Now converting KM³ of water into tablespoons of water
Volume of 1 tablespoon: 1 tablespoon = 15 milliliters (mL).
And 1 km³ = 1 × 10^15 ml.
Convert total water volume to milliliters (ml):
- 1.338×10^9 km³ of water = $(1.338 \times 10^9) \times (1 \times 10^{15})$ mL
- 1.338×10^{24} ml.

Now, as for calculating the number of tablespoons in the above volumes of water:
- Number of tablespoons = Total volume in mL / Volume per tablespoon.
- Number of tablespoons = $\dfrac{1.338 \times 10^{24} \text{ ml}}{15}$
- $= 8.92 \times 10^{22}$ tablespoons.

So, there are approximately 8.92×10^{22} tablespoons of water in Earth's oceans, rivers, and lakes.

Comparing the Two Quantities
- Number of planetary bodies in the universe: 72×10^{22}
- Number of tablespoons of water in Earth's water resources: 8.92×10^{22}

Still, the number of planetary bodies (all stars and planets) is about 8 times more than the total number of tablespoons in all the water in this world (contained in oceans, rivers, and lakes)

Again, attention, the following is a long example, but like any other example that goes into this depth, it will be that long and may not be suited for many people with a mathematical background, so that they might skip this

---

Analytical Remarks

If you could count every tablespoon of water across Earth's oceans, rivers, lakes, etc., then completely drain and refill them, only to repeat the process—counting each time—you would need to do this eight times to approach the staggering number of planetary bodies in the universe.

Objective Analysis of God

It is an enormous number, and Earth is just one of those.
So, next time you visit a lake or ocean, take out a tablespoon of water and look at that body of water. Imagine the world's water, and then see your spoon representing the earth.

Taking this example further, I live in the Toronto Area, so for reference, look at Lake Ontario, which goes from Niagara Falls to the Thousand Islands. It is about 250 km long, with a width of about 85 km and an average depth of 86 meters—about the height of a 25-story building.

Now, examine the following map of Lake Ontario (using a Google Maps image). While standing on the beach, you (the 🚹 red person) can hardly see the surface of the water marked with the yellow ◯ circle, less than 5 km into Lake Ontario.

Now close your eyes and imagine a big pool of water—how many tablespoons of water will there be?

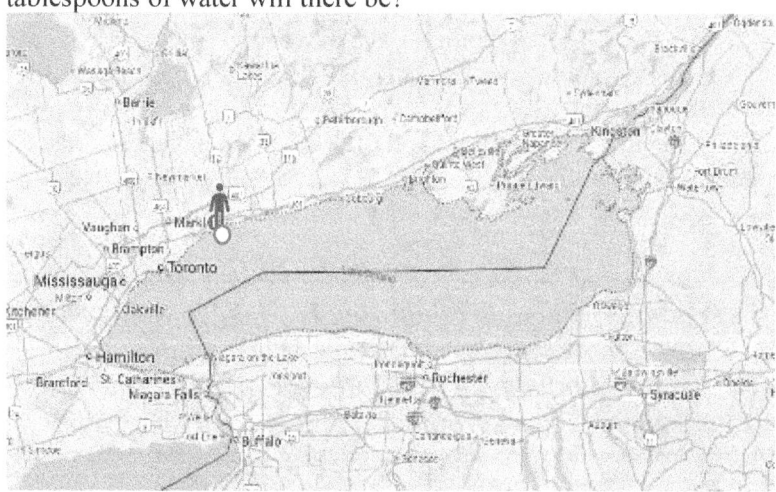

Please note that the total water in Lake Ontario accounts for only 0.00012% of the total water being considered.

Above is only to flex your brain muscle to comprehend the universe's vastness.

One tablespoon of water represents our Earth (one planetary object). How many planetary bodies will there be out of all the water in all oceans, rivers, and lakes? Then imagine that this will only cover bodies in the universe, where 99.9999% of the universe is empty space. You might need to go through the above multiple times while trying to understand the vastness of the universe—at least I did, eight to ten times, and still cannot wrap my head around it.

Now try to empty Lake Ontario with a tablespoon

We will continue to explore this concept to help us understand big numbers and the vastness of the universe. Let's examine it further with other analogies and look at it from another angle.

Universe distances are so massive, and scientists need to develop a new way to measure these distances – LIGHT YEAR – A light-year is a unit of distance, not time! It represents the distance light travels in one year, moving at about 299,792,458 meters per second. This equals roughly 9.46 trillion kilometers (5.88 trillion miles).

Even if you are familiar with this concept, please pause here and re-read the definition of light-years above. Then, consider the following analogy comparing the distance between Earth and the Moon with the total distance between the two corners of the universe – the observable universe.
The distance is calculated in light-years -- so if the distance from Earth to the moon is equal to the blink of an eye, then the following lines calculate the total observable distance of the universe (This comparison highlights how "infinitesimal" the Earth-Moon distance is compared to the vast scale of the universe).

To understand this time and space analogy, we need to establish a relationship between the time it takes to blink an eye and the distance from Earth to the Moon, and then scale this up to the size of the universe. Here's how we can approach it, and again, if you want to skip the calculation, skip the following shaded section:

We are establishing a relationship between the time it takes to blink our eye and the distance from Earth to the Moon, and then scaling this up to the size of the universe. Here's how we can approach it, considering the journey of a hypothetical rocket going from one edge of the universe to the other edge of the known universe, while travelling at the speed equivalent to the speed with which it can go from Earth to the Moon in the blink of an eye (0.3 sec).

Objective Analysis of God

Analogy 2:
We already know that
- Blink of an eye takes about **0.3 seconds**.
- The average distance from Earth to the Moon is **384,400 km** ($\approx$ **3.844 × 10⁸ m**).

Step 1: Calculate the Rocket's Speed
First, we find the speed (v) of the rocket:
$$v = \frac{\text{Distance to Moon}}{\text{Time}}$$
$$= \frac{3.844 \times 10^8 \text{ m}}{0.3}$$

$v \approx 1.28 \times 10^9$ m/s

It should be noted that, in developing this analogy, we are not considering many proven scientific theories and concepts. Like s ~**4.27 times the speed of light** ($c \approx 3 \times 10^8$ m/s), which is impossible according to Einstein's theory of relativity (nothing with mass can reach or exceed c). But for the sake of this hypothetical scenario, let's proceed.

Step 2: Define the "End of the Universe"
The observable universe has a radius of about **93 billion light-years** ($\approx$ **8.8 × 10²⁶ m**) due to cosmic expansion. If we assume the "end of the universe" refers to this distance:
Distance = 8.8×10^{26} m

Step 3: Calculate Time to Reach the Edge
Using the rocket's speed:
Time = $\frac{\text{Distance}}{v}$ = $\frac{8.8 \times 10^{26} \text{ m}}{1.28 \times 10^9 \text{ m/s}}$ $\approx 6.875 \times 10^{17}$ seconds

Convert this to more familiar units:
- **Years:** $\frac{6.875 \times 10^{17} \text{ s}}{3.154 \times 10^7 \text{ s/year}}$ $\approx 2.18 \times 10^{10}$ years
  - That's ~ **21.8 billion years**.

Key Observations/assumptions:
- **Relativity Violation**: The rocket's speed exceeds the speed of light, which is impossible under known physics.

- **Universe Expansion**: The universe is expanding faster than light beyond a certain distance (Hubble volume), so the "end" is unreachable even at light speed.
- **Time Dilation**: If the rocket could approach cc, relativistic effects (time dilation) would make the subjective time shorter for the traveler, but the math changes entirely.

Final Answer (Hypothetical):
If the rocket could sustain **1.28×10^9 m/s (4.27× light speed)** without accounting for relativity or expansion, it would take ~**21.8 billion years** to reach the edge of the observable universe. In reality, this is impossible—nothing can exceed the speed of light, and the universe's expansion would prevent such a journey.

In summary, this analogy suggests that.

If	You develop a rocket that can reach from Earth to the Moon within the blink of an eye.
Then	That rocket will take 21,800 million years to reach the end of the known universe after starting from one edge.

Eye blink (distance from Earth to the moon) vs 21.8 billion years (distance between two corners of the observable universe)
And then compare yourself against the distance from Earth to the moon. We are very, very, very minuscule against the universe.

Key Takeaway
Perhaps by now, your brain has begun to comprehend the smallness of Earth compared to the universe, considering the vastness of space. According to religions, this whole universe will come to an end on the day of judgment when God decides the eternal fate of Humans. According to religion, the fate of humanity and the universe is closely linked.

Although our Earth seems vast and complex to us, it is, in the grand scheme of things, an incredibly tiny speck. The universe is so enormous that it defies human comprehension, and Earth's size is almost negligible in comparison.

Objective Analysis of God

The Earth has a diameter of about 12,742 kilometers and a circumference of roughly 40,075 kilometers. While these numbers are impressive on a human scale, they pale compared to the cosmic scale. For instance:
- The Sun, our nearest star, is so large that 1.3 million Earths could fit inside it. Yet, the Sun is just one of an estimated 100 billion stars in the Milky Way galaxy, which spans about 100,000 light-years in diameter.
- Even our galaxy is just one of two trillion galaxies in the observable universe.
- As mentioned earlier, the observable universe is estimated to be 93 billion light-years across. To put this into perspective, if the entire universe were scaled down to the size of a football field, Earth would be smaller than a grain of sand. The distances between celestial objects are so vast that even light, which travels at about 300,000 kilometers per second, takes years to travel between stars and billions of years to cross the universe.

Earth's insignificance in size is matched by its isolation. The nearest star system, Alpha Centauri, is 4.37 light-years away, meaning light would take over four years to travel from there to Earth. The vast emptiness of space further emphasizes how small and alone our planet is.

Universe and Its Time

After considering the universe in terms of space and distance, we will now briefly analyze it in terms of time. The universe has been evolving and changing for approximately 13.8 billion years.
To understand this duration, let's take an example of seconds vs. years. If we reduce one second to one year, then 13.8 billion years will equal 437.6 years. Another way to comprehend it is to compare the human lifespan in this universe. Let's say that the average lifespan of humans is 70 years in 2025. Then, we will have lived for only one second in the life of the universe so far.

The entire age of the universe would be bout 6.25 years if a human lifespan (70 years) were just 1 second.

Section 2 - Understanding the Universe
Understanding the Scale of the Universe

This time, instead of doing the calculation, we will take advantage of some established analogies to help grasp the universe's lifetime compared to human time:

1. Cosmic Calendar (Carl Sagan's Analogy)
- Imagine the entire 13.8-billion-year history of the universe compressed into a single calendar year.
- The Big Bang happened on January 1st.
- The Milky Way forms in March.
- Our solar system appears in September.
- Dinosaurs roam the Earth on December 25th.
- Humans arrive late on December 31st, at 11:59:56 PM—just the last four seconds of the year.

2. A 24-Hour Clock
- If the universe's lifetime so far was a 24-hour day, humanity has existed for only the last fraction of a second before midnight.

3. A 1000-Page Book
- Imagine a book with 1000 pages, each representing 13.8 million years.
- The first few hundred pages describe stars and galaxies forming.
- The solar system appears around page 950.
- Dinosaurs show up on page 999.
- Human civilization will be the last word on the previous page.

4. A Football Field Timeline
- If the length of a football field (100 yards) represents the universe's age:
- The Big Bang is at the goal line (0 yards).
- The solar system forms around the 90-yard line.
- All human history? Just the thickness of a blade of grass at the end zone.

These analogies highlight how brief human existence is compared to the universe's timeline!

Objective Analysis of God

Universe and Its Complexity

Now comes the most challenging part, "complexity" at the cosmological and the atomic levels

At present, humans, in general, and particularly the scientific community, do not have enough knowledge to improve their understanding of the universe—let's say that as we learn more, it becomes more complex at both microscopic and telescopic levels.

Some food for thought is:
Let's start with micro things. Several microscopic structures have amazed and puzzled scientists due to their complexity and precision. Here are a few notable examples, starting with the microscopic level:

1. **DNA (Deoxyribonucleic Acid) – The Molecular Code of Life**
   a) DNA is a self-replicating molecule that stores genetic instructions for life.
   b) Scientists have been fascinated by its double-helix structure and ability to encode vast amounts of information in a tiny space.
   c) How it folds, repairs itself, and translates genetic code into proteins is still an area of deep research.
   d) Human DNA is only 2 meters long, but it contains every possible detail about a human. At the same time, it is so tightly packed that approximately **125 million human DNA molecules** could fit on the tip of a standard needle. This demonstrates the incredible complexity and compactness of biological molecules!

One thing to note about this example of DNA is how it can make each human so distinct – how much information should be stored in this small structure to detail a human? How can such a small thing make so many humans, who appear so similar but are simultaneously so different? Here is a food for Thought:

> *DNA uses just four building blocks to generate the immense diversity of life. Yet in the digital world, all the*

> *marvels of the last century—computers, the Internet, AI, robotics—emerge from only two digits: 0 and 1. Imagine the power of such simplicity and …..*

2. **Ribosomes – Nature's Molecular Machines**
   a) Ribosomes are microscopic factories that synthesize proteins from amino acids using instructions from DNA.
   b) Their highly organized, self-assembling structure has puzzled scientists, as they operate with machine-like precision.
   c) To understand their size, approximately 11 million to 44 million ribosomes could fit on the tip of a standard needle, and these are machine-like structures (this variation depends on the exact size of the type of ribosome (eukaryotic or prokaryotic).

3. **Neurons and Synapses – The Brain's Microscopic Network**
   a) A single neuron has thousands of connections (synapses) with other neurons, forming a hyper-complex network.
   b) Synaptic plasticity—how neurons rewire to learn and remember—is still not fully understood.

4. **The Cytoskeleton – A Cell's Intricate Scaffolding**
   a) The cytoskeleton is a microscopic framework inside cells, made of protein filaments and microtubules.
   b) It constantly rearranges itself to allow cell movement, division, and shape changes, acting like a construction crew inside the cell.

5. **Quantum Tunnelling in Enzymes**
   a) Some enzymes speed up chemical reactions using quantum effects, such as quantum tunnelling, in which particles "teleport" through energy barriers.
   b) This process defies classical physics and remains an active area of research in biochemistry and quantum biology.

6. **Bacterial Flagella – The Tiny Rotating Motor**

Objective Analysis of God

  a) Some bacteria move using flagella, which work like an engineered motor, spinning at speeds of up to 100,000 RPM.
  b) The structure consists of protein rings, a rotor, and a propeller, making it one of the most sophisticated molecular machines.
  c) The precise way these evolved step by step is still a matter of debate.

These microscopic structures demonstrate nature's incredible complexity and continue to push the boundaries of scientific understanding!

> *It is inconceivable that such a complex, interdependent mechanism could exist without deliberate intention. It must be the work of a capable, knowledgeable force—one possessing extraordinary intelligence to orchestrate such intricate design.*

At a high level, in Newtonian physics, we have a basic understanding of how things work, including gravity, forces, and energy. Outside this limited boundary, things are entirely unknown, or, as Albert Einstein said, "spooky." So, a few examples of spooky things are:

1. **Double slit experiment**
   - When the behavior of a particle changes based on whether you are looking at it or not, is it the impact of the light source or something else

2. **Quantum entanglement**
   - Where two particles are in a fuzzy or probabilistic state and can change their "shape/origin instantly " without having any connection, and the change process happens faster than the speed of light.
   - Does the phenomenon that helps migrating birds also help flocks of birds or schools of fish move in large quantities in a rhythm without colliding with one another

3. **Without a brain, intelligent slime**

- How a slime mold without any brain can replicate and optimize one of the most complicated system designs by humans - the Tokyo Subway station

4. **Where is solid matter in Atoms?**
   - Our perception of the material around us (physical, solid) is that it is solid as we touch it. Expecting that two solid bodies will come into contact with each other. However, as we delve into the depths of solid things, such as our fingers and the outside of a glass (while drinking water), there is no solid contact, as there is no solid material. All materials are made up of atoms, and atoms have vast empty space in them. When explored, all the particles of an atom exhibit a non-physical type of characteristic. The solid touching feeling we experience is the repulsion between two different atoms as they repel each other.

> *An atom is mostly empty space—about 99.9999999999996% of it is void!*
> *To put it in perspective, if a hydrogen atom were the size of Earth, its nucleus (the proton) would be only about 600 feet across. The vast majority of an atom consists of the space between the nucleus and the surrounding electrons.*

Furthermore, at the quantum level, even these particles, such as protons (made up of quarks), also lose their so-called solidity and become only vibration, according to string theory. Matter is composed of atoms, and upon closer examination at the microscopic scale inside an atom, all matter disappears, leaving us to wonder what matter or solid we are seeing and touching, but it is essentially nothing.

It is all strange and directly analogous to our earlier statement: the more we learn, the more we realize that we know nothing. The more we study solids, the more we find no solid material.

Alternatively, we can consider the planetary level.
At the mega-galactic level, the universe contains vast, complex structures that challenge our understanding of cosmology and physics. Here are some of the most mind-boggling ones:

Objective Analysis of God

The following examples demonstrate that, despite our so-called advancements in science, we are only scratching the surface of the vast universe's available knowledge.

1. **The Hercules–Corona Borealis Great Wall – Largest Structure in the Universe**
   a) A galactic superstructure spanning 10 billion light-years across.
   b) It consists of a massive collection of galaxies and galaxy clusters, defying expectations of how matter should be distributed on such a large scale.
   c) Its size challenges the Cosmological Principle, which states the universe should be homogeneous at large scales.

2. **The Giant Arc – A Cosmic Crescent of Galaxies**
   d) Discovered in 2021, this structure is 3.3 billion light-years across.
   e) It contains galaxies, galaxy clusters, and gas clouds that form a massive, curved shape.
   f) Its existence raises questions about how structures this large could have formed within the available time.

3. **The Sloan Great Wall – A Vast Filament of Galaxies**
   g) A supercluster of galaxies extending 1.4 billion light-years across.
   h) Challenges existing models of how quickly large-scale structures can form in the universe.

4. **The Bootes Void – An Enormous Empty Space**
   a) A cosmic void spanning 330 million light-years, containing very few galaxies.
   b) This extreme lack of matter is difficult to explain, as the universe should be more evenly distributed.
   c) Some speculate that it could result from the merging of multiple smaller voids.

5. **The Cold Spot – A Mystery in the Cosmic Microwave Background**
   a) A region in the cosmic microwave background (CMB) colder than expected.
   b) Some theories suggest it might be linked to a super void (a vast empty region of space).

Section 2 - Understanding the Universe
Understanding the Scale of the Universe

    c) Others propose more exotic explanations, like a remnant of a parallel universe collision.

6. **Galaxy Superclusters – The Universe's Gigantic Web**
   a) Galaxies are not randomly scattered but form a vast cosmic web of filaments, sheets, and knots.
   b) The Laniakea Supercluster, which includes the Milky Way, spans 520 million light-years and contains 100,000 galaxies.
   c) How these superclusters interact through gravity shapes the universe's evolution.

7. **Dark Matter and Dark Energy – The Invisible Architects of the Cosmos**
   a) Dark matter holds galaxies together despite their high rotation speeds, yet we cannot see or directly detect it.
   b) Dark energy is accelerating the universe's expansion, and its nature remains one of the biggest mysteries in physics.

8. **The Cosmic Web – The Largest-Scale Structure in the Universe**
   a) When viewed at massive scales, galaxies form a network of filaments and nodes, resembling a web or a neural network.
   b) This cosmic web is shaped by gravity and dark matter, but the details of how it formed are still being explored.
   c) How can a black hole's gravity be strong enough to even restrict light from escaping its force, but at the same time, a black hole could be the size of our solar system
   d) How supernovas create new materials, and how many materials will be in far galaxies.
   e) All the visible planetary bodies we talk about represent only 5% of the matter present in the universe; the remaining 95% is dark matter, and we have no clue about that
   f) What happened to all the antimatter?

These structures are so vast and mysterious that they challenge our fundamental understanding of physics, galaxy formation, and even the limits of the observable universe. However, they continue to transform and undergo changes that appear somewhat well-organized.

Objective Analysis of God

Summary:

The universe is a vast, intricate tapestry woven from matter and energy, spanning the subatomic scale of protons to immense galactic clusters. At its core, precise physical laws govern particles, stars, and cosmic expansion, creating an astonishing interplay of chaos and order. The staggering complexity of this system, where dying stars seed new worlds and forces bind atoms while accelerating the cosmos, raises profound questions.

Could such elegance be mere chance, or does it hint at a transcendent intelligence beyond human comprehension? If designed, it suggests a mind that surpasses time, physics, and imagination, leaving us humbled by the mysteries that science has yet to explain fully. Such a designer would possess unfathomable intelligence, capable of encoding the fabric of reality itself, from quantum mechanics to cosmic evolution. Their power would extend beyond space and time, shaping forces that govern galaxies, life, and the laws that hold existence together. The precision in nature's structure, from DNA to planetary motion, suggests immense intellect and an artistry so profound that it dwarfs human understanding.

> *Please keep this in mind as we navigate the concept of a religious God introduced in the holy texts written or dictated by the same entity.*

Probability & Statistics - The Law of Large Numbers

Probability and statistics, though essential in modern science, technology, and decision-making, are relatively recent branches in the history of mathematics. While basic ideas about chance existed in ancient times, such as in gambling, probability theory as a formal mathematical discipline didn't emerge until the 17th century. Statistics developed even later, gaining structure in the 18th and 19th centuries as a tool for analyzing data.

Despite its power and widespread use today, our brains struggle with probabilistic thinking. This is mainly because human intuition evolved for survival in environments where quick, rule-of-thumb decisions were more useful than rigorous mathematical reasoning. We are naturally drawn to patterns, even in randomness, and often misjudge risks and probabilities.

For example, many people find it hard to grasp why a 1-in-14 million chance of winning the lottery means it's almost sure they won't win. Similarly, we often fall victim to biases like the gambler's fallacy—the mistaken belief that past random events affect future ones.

In short, probability and statistics are recent tools for a modern, data-driven world, but our cognitive wiring hasn't caught up or aligned with them. We're trying to apply ancient mental habits to solve problems in a world increasingly relying on abstract, statistical truths.

In the earlier section, I attempted to lay the groundwork for you to grasp this vast and ancient universe in terms of its vastness and the enormous span of time that has passed. Perhaps your brain has begun to make sense of these huge numbers and relate them to the enormously vast universe in all its aspects — space, time, and complexity. Now, consider linking these gigantic numbers and realize that the massive number of planets, including those like Earth, actually increases the possibility of improbable events and the chances of life on numerous planets. Taking this thought to the religious God, according to which the whole universe was created only for testing Humans.

Objective Analysis of God

In statistics, probability, and the behaviour of large datasets reveal a fascinating truth:

> *As the population size or the number of events increases, the likelihood of encountering unusual or rare outcomes rises significantly. While considering the universe, for huge numbers (both in terms of space and time), unusual events become more probable.*
> *Then, we must multiply large numbers of space and time, further increasing the possibility of unusual happenings. For a lottery, there could be 1 to 14 million chances that you will not win, but at the same time, someone does win.*

This phenomenon, based on concepts such as the law of large numbers and probability scaling, demonstrates that events that appear improbable in a small sample size become more noticeable, or even certain, as the sample size increases.

In the following lines, I will explore how sample size, population size, and event frequency amplify the occurrence of unusual events, supported by examples and analogies, and extend the concept to the vast scale of the universe.

The Law of Large Numbers and Its Dual Role

The law of large numbers states that as the sample size grows, the sample mean approaches the actual population mean, providing a more reliable estimate of underlying parameters. However, this principle also influences the visibility of rare events. In small samples, randomness can dominate, producing seemingly unusual results. For instance, flipping a coin five times might yield four heads and one tail—a 4:1 ratio far from the expected 50/50 split. With 1,000 flips, the proportion stabilizes near 50%, aligning with the actual probability. Yet, in larger samples, rare phenomena become more apparent. A coin landing on its edge—perhaps a 1-in-10,000 chance—might never occur in five flips but could emerge in millions of trials. Thus, while small samples obscure rare events due to chance, large samples expose them by sheer volume.

This duality appears in practical scenarios. In a health study of 100 people, a rare side effect (e.g., a 1% probability) might affect one person, which seems anomalous. In a survey of 10,000, that same effect could impact 100 people, making it a noticeable trend despite the unchanged individual probability. As the sample size increases, the total count of unusual events rises, even if their relative rarity remains constant.

Population Size and Rare Events

Population size similarly affects the frequency of unusual outcomes. In a small group, opportunities for rare events are limited; in a larger one, they multiply. Consider a lottery: with 100 tickets, the chance of multiple winners or a jackpot is slim. With a million tickets, such outcomes become more plausible—not because the odds per ticket change, but because more tickets mean more chances for rare alignments.
Epidemiology offers another example. In a small town of 1,000, a rare disease (1-in-10,000 odds) might never appear. In a region of 10 million people, the same disease could strike 1,000 individuals, shifting it from a fluke to a pattern. Larger populations don't increase the inherent probability of an event but provide more instances where it can occur, making rare events more frequent in absolute terms.

Sample Size and Outliers

Outliers—data points that are far outside the norm—also become more detectable as the sample size increases. In a small dataset, extreme values might be missed due to limited observations. For example, if 10 students take an exam, one exceptional score (high or low) might be unusual. With 1,000 students, multiple extreme scores emerge, reflecting the natural spread of a larger sample. An analogy likens this to picking apples: from a handful, all might look similar, but from thousands, oddly shaped ones—outliers—surface more often.

In financial markets, analyzing 10 companies might reveal no crashes, but examining 1,000 could uncover several, simply because more data points increase the likelihood of capturing extremes. Larger samples don't create outliers; they expose the full range of possibilities inherent in the population.

Event Frequency and Unusual Results

The number of events or trials further amplifies this effect. Each trial is a chance for a rare outcome; the more trials, the greater the opportunities for a rare outcome to occur. Rolling a die once gives a 1-in-6 chance of rolling a 6, which seems unusual in isolation. Rolling it 100 times, however, makes at least one six likely (about a 99.5% chance of occurring at least once). An analogy of spinning a Wheel of Fortune reinforces this: one spin rarely lands on a grand prize, but 100 spins significantly boost the odds.
In clinical trials, a rare drug side effect (e.g., 1 in 1,000) might not be observed in a 50-person study but could emerge in a 10,000-person trial with repeated doses. More events—whether rolls, spins, or doses—multiply the chances of rare results manifesting.

Analogies for Clarity

Several analogies illustrate these principles:
1. Searching for Gems: Finding a rare gem in a small mine section is unlikely; exploring the whole mine increases the odds by expanding the search area (population size).
2. Weather Prediction: Observing a few days yields unreliable climate guesses, but many years of data refine accuracy (sample size and predictions).
3. Fish Behaviour: Unusual fish actions are rare in a small pond, but their vast population makes them more observable in an ocean.
4. Forest Diversity: Studying a few trees might suggest uniformity, but many reveal true variety (sample size and accuracy).
5. Treasure Hunt: A small search area might miss valuables, but a larger one uncovers rarities (outliers in bigger samples).

These analogies underscore a key takeaway: SCALE—whether in a population, sample, or event—enhances the detectability of the unusual.

Putting it together - The Universe as a Case Study.

This statistical lens applies dramatically to the universe's vast scale. Over billions of years and across immense space, the number of "events"—molecular collisions, cosmic interactions—reaches incomprehensible magnitudes. The origin of life exemplifies this. The odds of amino acids forming proteins by chance in one instance might be 1 in 10^{40}, yet Earth's primordial oceans hosted trillions of trials over eons. Each reaction built upon prior ones: simple elements formed carbon, then amino acids, then cells, and finally complex organisms. This cumulative process—layering events atop one another—turned the improbable into reality.

> *Such outcomes seem miraculous –*
> *on a minute human scale, but looking at the universal scale,*
> *they're statistically plausible on a cosmic scale.*

Examples of Scale and Improbability
1. Penicillin Discovery: A mould spore landing in Fleming's dish was a fluke (perhaps 1-in-10,000 odds), but countless global experiments ensured such a breakthrough eventually occurred.
2. Lottery Wins: A 1-in-292-million chance of winning Powerball seems impossible per ticket, but millions of tickets across repeated draws produce regular winners. Scale transforms rarity into routine
3. Chernobyl Disaster: A rare confluence of design flaws and errors (low individual odds) became likely with thousands of reactor years worldwide, demonstrating that scale can also yield disasters.
4. Social media: Individually, the odds of a viral post are rare, roughly 1 in 100,000. However, with billions of posts circulating on platforms like X, viral phenomena become almost inevitable.

Reflections: The Double-Edged Sword
Increasing events don't just unlock wonders—they also court risks. The same principle that explains the origin of life or the discovery of penicillin warns of rare catastrophes, such as nuclear meltdowns or market crashes (e.g., the 2008 crash). Rarity is relative:

Objective Analysis of God

impossible in isolation, expected in abundance. This challenges our intuition, which tends to focus on single trials rather than cumulative probabilities, and highlights the scale's ability to reveal the extraordinary, whether good or bad.

Conclusion

In statistics and beyond, increasing the number of events—whether through population, sample, or trials—increases the likelihood of unusual outcomes. The law of large numbers stabilizes averages but exposes rarities; larger populations and samples multiply opportunities; more trials ensure improbable alignments occur. From coin flips to cosmic evolution, this principle demonstrates that the unlikely becomes inevitable with enough opportunities.

In the universe's vast theatre, where time and space dwarf human perception, rare events stack upon one another, building complexity from simplicity. Whether in a lottery draw or life's genesis, scale and repetition tame improbability, proving the extraordinary is often just a matter of opportunity.

Section 3

Religions

Section 3 – Religions
Faith Over Facts: Why Belief Persists

This is a fundamental question—one that intrigues many, especially skeptics who seek to challenge believers with arguments they see as obvious and logical.

We will tackle this topic from two sides:
1. How the brain actually functions.
2. How the upbringing of a child in a believer's environment brainwashes them

How the Brain Functions

Before we delve into the complexities of religion and the paradox of liberal believers who claim to objectively analyze their faith while simultaneously adhering to traditions without scrutiny, we must first understand a more fundamental issue: the way our brain manipulates our perception and understanding of reality. This manipulation is not malicious or intentional in the way we typically think of deception. Instead, it is a deeply ingrained cognitive process — one that has evolved to help us navigate an overwhelming world of sensory input, social complexity, and existential uncertainty.

> *This may be the most critical discussion in the book—an inquiry into why followers often struggle to detect contradictions, falsehoods, and inconsistencies within their own faith, religious texts, and spiritual authorities. Paradoxically, the same individuals can use explicit logical analysis in their daily routine. Why does our perception become so selective—our eyes and minds seemingly locked—when it comes to the religion we follow?*

In recent years, this concept has become easier to discuss and more widely accepted, mainly because its application is now evident in the digital world. Social media platforms like Facebook, YouTube,

TikTok, and Instagram have built entire ecosystems around the principle of cognitive reinforcement. These platforms track what we watch, what we click, and what we linger on — and then they feed us more of the same. The algorithms are designed not to challenge us, but to comfort us with familiarity. They reinforce our existing preferences, beliefs, and biases, creating echo chambers that appear to be objective reality but are, in fact, highly curated illusions.

This phenomenon is not limited to digital media. It reflects how our brain has always functioned. Every moment of our lives, we are bombarded with sensory information — sights, sounds, smells, textures, and tastes. But what we perceive is not direct feed from our sensory organs. Our eyes, ears, nose, and skin are merely conduits. The real processing happens in the brain, which receives these signals and then interprets them based on prior experience, learned knowledge, emotional state, and subconscious bias.

In this process, the brain performs several critical functions:
- It filters out information and deems it irrelevant or unimportant.
- It prioritizes stimuli that align with our current goals, fears, or desires.
- It fills in gaps in perception with assumptions based on past experiences.
- It reconstructs reality in a way that feels coherent and meaningful to us.

This is why neuroscientists and psychologists often say, "We do not see with our eyes; we see through our brain." Our perception is not a mirror of the external world; it is a constructed narrative, shaped by numerous internal factors.

Religion does not just shape belief—it hijacks perception.

One of the most famous demonstrations of this principle is the "Invisible Gorilla" experiment, popularized by a BBC documentary. In the experiment, participants are asked to watch a video of people passing basketballs and count the number of passes. In the middle of the video, a person in a gorilla suit walks through the scene, beats their chest, and exits. Astonishingly, a significant portion of viewers

Objective Analysis of God

fail to notice the gorilla at all. Their brain, focused on the task of counting passes, filters out the unexpected and irrelevant stimulus — even one as absurd and conspicuous as a gorilla.

This exact filtering mechanism applies not only to sensory perception but also to cognitive understanding. When we read a book, listen to a lecture, or engage in a conversation, our brain is not passively absorbing information; it is actively processing it. It is actively evaluating, prioritizing, and — crucially — editing what we take in. If we have been conditioned to believe that a particular source is authoritative or sacred, our brain will often suppress critical analysis of that source. It will minimize doubt, reduce scrutiny, and amplify acceptance.

This is especially evident in religious contexts. A Christian reading the Bible or listening to a sermon from a respected priest may find it difficult to question the content, not because the ideas are flawless, but because the brain has been trained to treat them as such. Similarly, a Muslim reading the Quran or attending an Islamic lecture may experience a cognitive barrier to skepticism, even if they consider themselves liberal or open-minded. The reverence for the source creates a mental shortcut: "This is true because it comes from a trusted authority."

This phenomenon is not limited to religion. It applies to politics, education, relationships, and even personal identity. But religion presents a particularly potent example because it often involves deep emotional investment, community reinforcement, and existential significance. The stakes are higher, and the conditioning is stronger.

What complicates matters further is that the brain's manipulation is individualized. Each person's cognitive filters are shaped by their unique life experiences, cultural background, emotional history, and belief system. So while one person may interpret a religious text as metaphorical and symbolic, another may see it as literal and prescriptive — even if both consider themselves liberal thinkers. The spectrum of belief is not just external; it is internal, and it varies dramatically from one mind to another.

Your brain is not a seeker of truth. It is a loyal servant to your narrative.

This leads to a fascinating paradox: a person may genuinely believe they are analyzing their faith objectively, applying reason and critical thought. But their brain may still be operating within a framework of assumptions and biases that they are unaware of. They may be liberal in their social views, progressive in their politics, and open-minded in their interactions — yet still hold deeply traditional religious beliefs that they have never truly questioned. And when confronted with contradictions or challenges, their brain may instinctively defend those beliefs, not out of malice or ignorance, but out of cognitive habit.

> *The brain is a master of deception. It doesn't just filter reality—it reshapes it to fit what you're conditioned to believe. It blocks inconvenient thoughts, suppresses contradictions, and even manipulates your senses to deliver a version of truth that feels comfortable. You don't see what's there—you know what you're trained to see. You don't hear what's said—you listen to what aligns with your expectations. And you don't understand what's real—you know what reinforces your belief system. This isn't just bias—it's neurological self-preservation. The mind protects its narrative at all costs, even if that means distorting reality itself.*

It is essential to recognize that this is not a flaw or a failure. It is a feature of human cognition. Our brains are designed to create stability, coherence, and a sense of meaning. They resist chaos and ambiguity. They seek patterns and narratives. And in doing so, they often sacrifice objectivity for the sake of comfort.

Barin-washing a child

This understanding has deep implications for how we engage with religion, belief, and our own identities. It suggests that true objectivity is not a destination but a process — one that requires constant self-awareness, humility, and willingness to challenge our own assumptions. It also means that we must be cautious when

Objective Analysis of God

judging others. What appears to be blind faith or irrational tradition may, in fact, be the result of a deeply personal cognitive framework that we do not fully understand.

For example, a Muslim who considers themselves liberal may still adhere to practices or beliefs that seem rigid or conservative to others. This does not necessarily mean they are hypocritical or confused; it simply means they are not consistent. It may merely reflect the way their brain has reconciled different aspects of their identity. Similarly, a Christian who embraces progressive values may still hold traditional views on scripture or morality, not out of dogma, but rather due to cognitive alignment with their upbringing and emotional experiences.
In this light, the conversation about religion and liberalism becomes less about contradiction and more about complexity. It becomes a dialogue not just between beliefs, but between brains — each with its own filters, biases, and narratives.

So before we critique religious followers for mindlessly adhering to tradition, we must first examine the architecture of our own minds. We must ask: What assumptions am I making? What sources do I trust without question? What beliefs have I inherited rather than chosen? And how might my brain be shaping my perception in ways I do not even realize?
Only by engaging in this introspective process can we begin to approach accurate understanding — of ourselves, of others, and of the intricate dance between faith and cognition.

Many believers, even those who pride themselves on being open-minded, often hold firmly to the belief that it is their sacred duty to pass on their faith to their children. This conviction is deeply ingrained in religious teachings and reinforced by religious authorities, including priests, imams, and rabbis, as well as societal norms and expectations. Within many communities, the transmission of faith is viewed not only as tradition but also as a moral obligation. Parents who fail to instill religious beliefs in their children are frequently judged as irresponsible or neglectful, as though they've failed in one of the most fundamental aspects of parenting.

This pressure is not merely external. It is internalized by parents who genuinely believe they are acting in their children's best

Section 3 – Religions
Faith Over Facts: Why Belief Persists

interest. From a young age, children are exposed to religious rituals and practices—often not through explanation, but through observation. A child watches their parents pray, fast, attend religious services, and celebrate religious holidays. These rituals become part of the child's environment, absorbed passively but powerfully. The child sees these actions performed by the people they trust most—their parents—and naturally assumes their validity.

What makes this process even more potent is the reinforcement that often accompanies it. Children are praised for participating in religious rituals and may be rewarded for memorizing prayers or attending services. This creates a feedback loop: religious behavior is not only modeled but incentivized. By the time a child reaches an age where they can begin to think critically, their worldview has already been shaped by years of unexamined exposure. The beliefs and rituals have become deeply ingrained, making it difficult—if not impossible—for the child to question them without emotional or social consequences.

As Mr. Javed Akhtar once pointed out in a public debate, even the most liberal parents will ask their children what profession they wish to pursue, offering guidance and support. Yet, when it comes to religion, that same freedom of choice is rarely extended. Children are not given the Quran, the Bible, the Rig Veda, or other sacred texts and are encouraged to explore and decide for themselves. Instead, they are handed a belief system and expected to accept it without question.

This raises a critical question about the role of parenthood. Is it truly responsible to impose a belief system on a child before they are capable of understanding or evaluating it? Or is true parental responsibility found in nurturing a child's ability to think independently, to question, and to choose? Encouraging children to explore different philosophies, spiritual paths, or secular viewpoints does not mean abandoning moral guidance—it means trusting them to form their own conclusions.

When parents foster an environment of curiosity and open dialogue, they empower their children to become thoughtful, self-aware individuals. This doesn't mean shielding them from religion; it means presenting religion as one of many lenses through which to view the world. It means allowing space for doubt, for exploration,

Objective Analysis of God

and for personal conviction. Children raised in such environments may still choose to embrace their parents' faith—but they will do so with understanding, not blind adherence.

Unfortunately, this approach remains rare. Most children grow up in religious environments where questioning is discouraged and conformity is rewarded. The cycle continues: children become parents and pass on the same unexamined beliefs to the next generation. While there are exceptions—individuals who break free from this inherited framework—they are few and far between.

If we truly value open-mindedness and intellectual freedom, then we must reexamine the way religion is introduced to children. Parenthood should be about guiding, not dictating; about opening minds, not closing them. Only then can we hope to raise a generation capable of choosing their beliefs—not simply inheriting them

Trying to reshape beliefs built on bedrock is no small renovation; it is like redesigning a multi-floor building when the foundations are already set.

Premises of Analysis

Now, after understanding (to some extent) the foundational topics, we will move to religion and, in the following lines, take a deep dive into our approach.

Moses received the Torah around 1300 BCE, and the Vedas date back to approximately 1500 BCE, so our religions are only about 3500 years old. So, all recent known religions only existed for about:
- 0.0175% of human history
- 0.000077% of Earth's life
- 0.000025% of the universe's life

Please keep this in mind. We will address this topic while discussing the religious text, which suggests that the universe was created to test humans.

Moving on, on one side, we have a God who designs perfection at a microscopic level and a very complex galaxy level, and their interrelation. On the other side, we have God as told by (Yahweh, God, Trinity, or Allah), and we will try to relate and question how we can reconcile both Gods.

The following page reiterates the foundational premise of our work: that of reconciling the two concepts of God. It establishes the lens through which readers can interpret the insights that follow. We also provide a few high-level analytical examples—each chosen to illustrate the richness and complexity that will unfold in greater detail throughout the book. These examples are not exhaustive but rather serve as a guidepost for the type of rigorous, thought-provoking analysis readers can expect.

Objective Analysis of God

The entity that could have created the universe	Entity (God) informed by Religion
Having almost infinite special access – the whole universe of trillions of trillions of trillions... km	Only communicated with humans within a radius of 5,000 km.
Has been active for billions of years	Only communicated for 3000 years maximum
Extremely far-sighted in developing planning for billions of years	Cannot even foresee what will happen in the next few minutes
Extremely detail-oriented.	Extremely superficial, instructing humans to pray without explaining the steps
Highly organized and method-oriented – laws of the universe	Could not even develop simple ethical laws in which He plans to judge humans
Extremely capable and powerful – created the universe	Extremely whiny and weak - Cannot handle his minute creation – Satan - Cursing an old lady (Quran)
Incredibly imaginative and creative – diversity of creations	Cannot even come up with an idea on how to communicate religion – keep trying the same method again and again

Religion

Almost all religions' primary focus and purpose is guiding spiritual beliefs, ethical conduct, and personal and communal connection with the divine. The definition of religion typically focuses on spiritual, philosophical, and moral aspects of life. Religion itself is generally concerned with the following:

- Spiritual Purpose: Religion addresses questions about the meaning of life, the existence of a higher power, the afterlife, and the nature of the universe. It provides a framework for understanding human existence in terms of divine and moral conduct.
- Moral and Ethical Code: Religions typically guide personal behavior, virtues, and duties.
- Ritual and Worship: Religious rituals and practices are about connecting with the divine, expressing devotion, and seeking spiritual fulfillment. These practices are more concerned with personal and communal spirituality.

For reference, below is the distribution of the main religions in the world population:

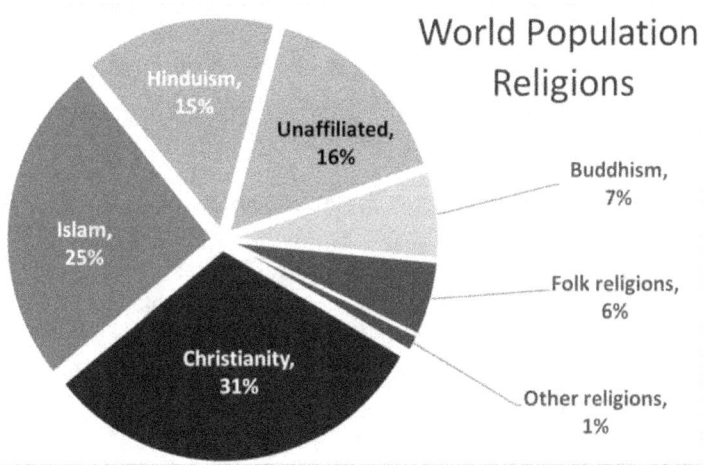

Source: - https://en.wikipedia.org/wiki/Major_religious_groups

Common themes:

Now, we will focus on the Abrahamic religions, which include Judaism, Christianity, and Islam. By covering Christianity and Islam, I will automatically cover Judaism. I will analyze religion through the primary holy text:

Objective Analysis of God

a) The Tanakh - Jews' holy text, also known as the Old Testament, is part of the Bible.
b) The Bible – Christians' holy text, and
c) The Quran – Muslims

Although all three religions acknowledge the influence of previous faiths to some extent, they share many commonalities. In the following few points, I will try not to highlight commonalities of faith, but rather how these are preached and enforced—basically, how these regions and their institutions promote and present their beliefs.

1. They force strictly that only their religion is THE correct one and the rest are entirely wrong, that is, they follow us or go to Hell – literally.
2. Mostly, the only way to receive a reward in the afterlife is to believe that your deeds are secondary; Christianity goes even further and says this is the only way to Heaven, and what you do in your life does not matter. Islam says that if you do good deeds, even then, you have to be a Muslim to attain Heaven (I will prove both with multiple verses), basically the same message in a different way.
3. There is not much questioning around religion allowed; questioning Christianity was not allowed till the mid-1800s, and for Islam, most Muslims consider the death penalty for questioning anything about Islam, even now.
4. They all direct you towards GOD, but they all provide a passage which goes through some supernatural entities (Saints or Imams like personalities), and they all put someone in between you and GOD
5. They all, one way or another, provide a way to perform financial sacrifices. By doing so, they all make you do things for those (supernatural entities between you and God), and these sacrifices involve money directly or indirectly—your time and efforts are your money.
6. So, you need to spend some money to please these intermediaries' entities to please GOD, and a large portion of financial sacrifices go to the so-called religious leaders/institutes, directly or indirectly.
7. All religions have worked hand in hand with the rulers of that time, sometimes directly by claiming the status of state religion or indirectly supporting the rulers.

Section 3 – Religions
Religion

8. All rulers have employed religious methods, such as interpreting religious scriptures and declaring by Priests, Mullas, and mujahideen, to enforce their rule and legitimacy.
9. All Religious texts are typically ambiguous and open to interpretation, which is why there are numerous sects within each religion.
10. Most of the religious scriptures are said to be coming from God for human guidance, but the majority of the text in these holy books has praises for God Himself or stories, not much direction or instructions on how to live a good life
11. Most religious texts were formalized many years after the death of the relevant prophets (the person on whom they were revealed). The Bible came into its established text form after about 300 years, and the Quran after 17.

> *12. God put so much effort into sending the message—even putting His son to death—but forgot to ensure that the message was preserved. God's message was "conserved" in the minds of followers and transmitted orally over at least 10-12 human generations. God let his most critical message be open to change, amendments, or loss.*

13. All holy books claim to be accurate and error-free. This claim has been passed down through the memories of the selected humans for many years. All religions claim to be completely authentic words, as revealed originally by God
14. All religions spread when associated with rulers and by taking the ruler's support, such as providing financial benefits to people following the state religion. This is very evident based on the world map and the percentage of religious followers
15. All Religious texts have contradictory statements, which religious scholars use in their arguments by selecting sentences that suit their argument at that time.
16. In all religions, the primary beneficiary is the institution spreading that religion, and it is, in fact, a huge beneficiary. Just consider the general lifestyle of these religious promoters or the expected amount of money flowing into their institutions.
17. Followers of all religions do not read/understand their holy book. In almost all religions, followers have been increasingly distanced from the main holy book. It is estimated that less than 1% of the followers have read and understood the book. I would

Objective Analysis of God

go one step further and note that fewer than 0.001% have read it critically.

18. Almost all religious people obtain their religious guidance and information by listening to spiritual leaders rather than reading. Providing ways for Priests and Mullahs to promote their own interpretation of the holy text, by quoting only what they want you to listen to
19. Most believers also have a steadfast belief that what is said to them from their religious platform is accurate and verified, with almost no critical thinking, questioning, or approach involved
20. Leaving religion is a BIG taboo, resulting in social isolation of the person or, in many cases, giving him the punishment of death. The primary reason is to prevent such behavior and serve as a significant deterrent for others.

We also must consider that thousands of books written as explanations of Holy books are challenging to verify. In my opinion, all those books were as good as today's social media. We have both genuine and manipulated information (correct and incorrect, biased or unbiased, accurate or completely fabricated) regarding those books.

All religions, with their various sects, validate the point that these alternative explanations and numerous interpretations of Holy books are not correct, as only one can truly convey faith and understanding. We will also see that even the sources and validation of all Holy books are more than questionable.

Religion's History:

The reason we will delve into the history of all religions is to show how, when, and where they have evolved, and to highlight the reasons behind their emergence and evolution in various geographical contexts.

> *My point here is that if there is only one God, then the origin of the religion in different geographies should also be the same, as coming from the same entity. Otherwise, it suggests that humans from diverse geographical backgrounds developed their religions.*

Below is a timeline and conceptual "tree" tracing the development of major religions from the oldest known practices to the emergence of Islam. This focuses on key religious traditions with significant historical influence, emphasizing their origins and interconnections. The tree structure highlights how some religions branched from or were influenced by earlier ones.

Timeline of Religions (Oldest to Islam)

1) Prehistoric/Animistic Traditions (c. 100,000 BCE and earlier)
   a) Origin: Evidence from burial sites (e.g., Neanderthal graves with offerings) suggests early humans practiced animism—belief in spirits inhabiting natural objects—or ancestor veneration.
   b) Key Features: No formal texts; rituals tied to nature and survival.
   c) Location: Global, predating the emergence of organized societies.
   d) Mentioned here as reference only, as we do not have enough information to do any analysis
2) Mesopotamian Religion (c. 3500 BCE)
   a) Origin: It merged with Sumer (modern Iraq) and city-states like Uruk.
   b) Key Features: Polytheism with gods like Anu (sky) and Enki (water); ziggurat temples; myths like the Epic of Gilgamesh.
   c) Influence: Early written religious traditions; impacted later Semitic religions.
3) Ancient Egyptian Religion (c. 3100 BCE)

Objective Analysis of God

   a) Origin: Alongside the unification of Upper and Lower Egypt.
   b) Key Features: Polytheism (e.g., Ra, Osiris); afterlife focus with mummification; pharaohs as divine.
   c) Influence: Distinct but paralleled other Near Eastern polytheistic systems.
4) Indus Valley Religion (c. 2500 BCE)
   a) Origin: In the Indus Valley Civilization (modern Pakistan/India).
   b) Key Features: Proto-Hindu elements inferred from seals (e.g., "Pashupati" figure); ritual bathing sites.
   c) Influence: Likely evolved into the Vedic religion.
5) Vedic Religion (c. 1500 BCE)
   a) Origin: Indo-Aryan migration into India; based on the Vedas (oral hymns).
   b) Key Features: Polytheism (e.g., Indra, Agni); fire sacrifices; caste system seeds.
   c) Evolution: Foundation of Hinduism.
6) Zoroastrianism (c. 1200–1000 BCE)
   a) Origin: Founded by Zoroaster (Zarathustra) in ancient Persia (modern Iran).
   b) Key Features: Monotheism or dualism (Ahura Mazda vs. Angra Mainyu); fire as purity symbol; eschatology.
   c) Influence: Later Abrahamic religions (e.g., concepts of heaven and hell) were influenced by these ideas.
7) Judaism (c. 1200 BCE)
   a) Origin: Traditionally dated to Abraham (c. 2000 BCE), codified with Moses and the Exodus (c. 1200 BCE).
   b) Key Features: Monotheism (Yahweh); Torah; covenant with God.
   c) Location: Ancient Israel/Canaan.
8) Hinduism (c. 1000 BCE – formalized over centuries)
   a) Origin: Evolved from the Vedic religion with the Upanishads and epics (Mahabharata, Ramayana).
   b) Key Features: Polytheism/monism; karma, dharma, reincarnation.
   c) Influence: Spawns later Indian traditions.
9) Jainism (c. 900–600 BCE)
   a) Origin: Attributed to Mahavira (c. 599–527 BCE), 24th Tirthankara, though earlier figures existed.
   b) Key Features: Non-violence (ahimsa); asceticism; soul liberation.

c) Connection: Emerged alongside Vedic/Hindu traditions, rejecting some aspects.
10) Buddhism (c. 500 BCE)
   a) Origin: Founded by Siddhartha Gautama (Buddha) in India (c. 563–483 BCE).
   b) Key Features: Four Noble Truths; Eightfold Path; rejection of Vedic rituals; nirvana.
   c) Connection: Branched from the Hindu philosophical context.
11) Taoism (c. 400 BCE)
   a) Origin: Attributed to Laozi in China; Tao Te Ching formalized ideas.
   b) Key Features: Harmony with the Tao (the Way); balance (yin-yang); simplicity.
   c) Location: Independent development in East Asia.
12) Confucianism (c. 500 BCE)
   a) Origin: Founded by Confucius (551–479 BCE) in China.
   b) Key Features: Ethical philosophy; filial piety; social harmony; less focus on metaphysics.
   c) Connection: Coexisted with Taoism, influencing Chinese culture.

We will not discuss the above two Chinese philosophies (mainly philosophies, with no formal introduction of any all-powerful and creator God or Deity). We will provide a high-level overview here:

Category	Taoism (Daoism)	Confucianism
Founder	Laozi (Lao Tzu)	Confucius (Kong Fuzi)
Main Texts	Tao Te Ching, Zhuangzi	Analects, Book of Rites, Five Classics
Focus	Harmony with nature and the Dao (the Way)	Order, morality, and social harmony
Said	The hippie mystic who wants to live in the mountains, write poetry, and meditate with the universe	The **wise elder statesman** who teaches ethics, rituals, and the importance of being a good son or citizen
Ultimate Principle	The Dao (impersonal natural force)	Tian (moral order / Heaven)
View of God(s)	Spiritual pantheon in religious Taoism, but	Not focused on gods; more ethical and social

Objective Analysis of God

	not central	
Creator God	No personal creator god	No personal creator god
Goal	Harmony with nature, immortality, balance	Moral development, social harmony, and ethical living
Worship/Ritual Focus	Harmony with nature/spirits, Daoist practices	Ancestor worship, social rituals
View on Society	Withdraw from artificial rules and hierarchy	Emphasize structure, roles, and responsibility
Key Virtue	Wu Wei (non-action / effortless action)	Ren (benevolence), Li (ritual, propriety)
Role of Government	Minimal intervention: let nature take its course	Strong ethical government led by virtuous rulers
Spiritual Focus	Individual spiritual harmony and immortality	Ethical behaviour and family/social duties
Attitude Toward Rules	Skeptical or dismissive of rigid rules	Deep respect for rules, rituals, and traditions

Some deities were later created but not part of the original concept.

> *You can see here that the religions or ways of life introduced in other parts of the world do not share any significant commonalities with the Abrahamic faiths. These two philosophies are somewhat aligned with Buddhism's original philosophy, which emphasizes living life without the concept of a supreme God and an afterlife, focusing on the Present.*

- Christianity (c. 30 CE)
    - Origin: Emerged from Judaism with Jesus of Nazareth (c. 4 BCE–30 CE).
    - Key Features: Monotheism; salvation through Christ; New Testament.
    - Connection: Direct offshoot of Judaism.
- Islam (610 CE)

- Origin: Founded by Muhammad in Mecca (610 CE, first revelation).
- Key Features: Monotheism (Allah); Quran; Five Pillars.
- Connection: Abrahamic tradition, claiming continuity with Judaism and Christianity.

Objective Analysis of God

Tree of Religions (Simplified):

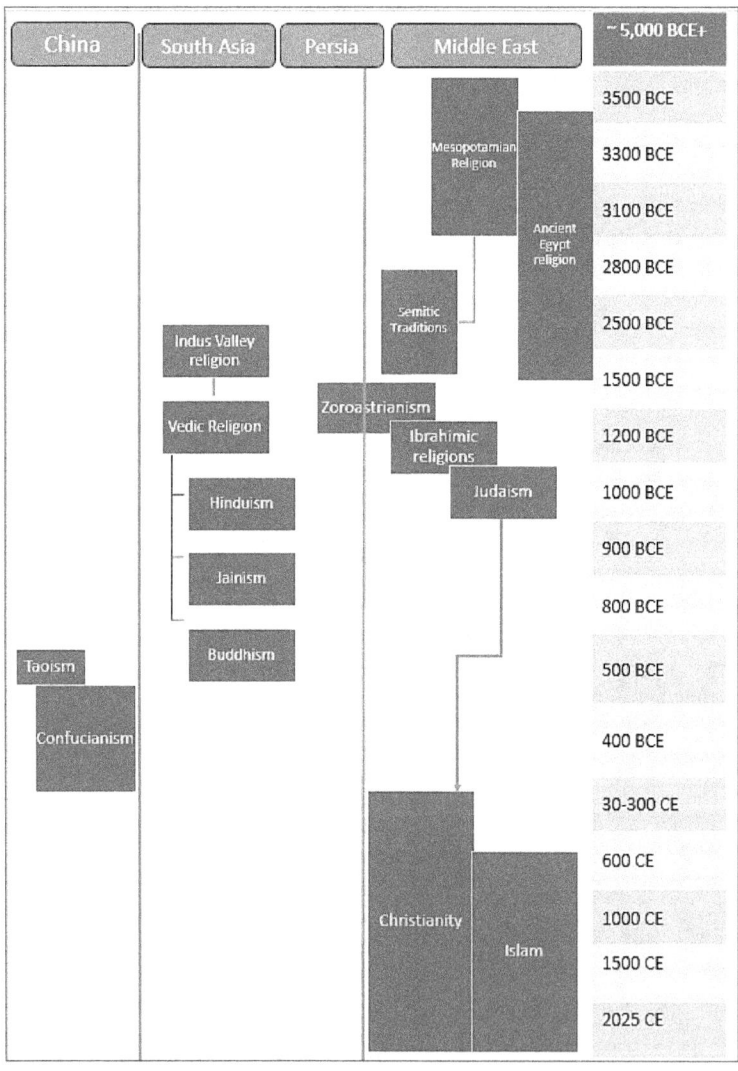

Section 3 – Religions
Religion's History:

Religions have continuously emerged for at least the last 5,000 years, with a notable surge around 3,500 years ago, as evidenced by the historical records that have been kept and unearthed. However, in the past 1,500 years, no significant new belief system has gained widespread adherence, and many older religions have seen a decline in influence. This trend aligns with the fact that, over the last 1,000 years, humanity's understanding of the universe has undergone significant evolution, providing answers to previously unknown mysteries that were initially attributed to an unknown force of God.

Here we can note that.

As mentioned earlier, there are two prominent families of known religions. These two families also have a very distinct geographical dividing line, as shown below:

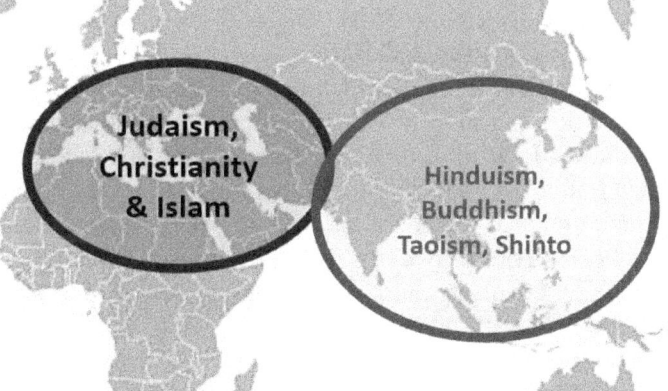

These two distinct sets of religions also indicate that if there is one God for the whole world, there would be some amalgamation of religions with traces of the True God in different parts of the world. In present-day geography, Islam and Christianity cover most of the world, mainly due to the influence of the colonial era and the rule of the Islamic caliphate.

Notes:
- **Roots**: Prehistoric animism represents humanity's earliest spiritual practices, influencing all subsequent traditions indirectly.
- Branches:
    - **Mesopotamian/Egyptian**: Early polytheistic systems; influenced Near Eastern cultures but faded as distinct religions.

Objective Analysis of God

- - Indian Traditions: The Indus Valley to Vedic religion gave birth to Hinduism, with Jainism and Buddhism as offshoots that reacted to or built upon it.
  - Abrahamic Line: Judaism serves as the trunk, with Christianity and Islam as its branches; Zoroastrianism has influenced their eschatology.
  - East Asian Traditions: Taoism and Confucianism developed independently in China, distinct from the Indian and Abrahamic traditions.
- Cross-Influence: Zoroastrianism had a significant impact on Judaism during the Persian period (e.g., the Babylonian Exile), indirectly influencing Christianity and Islam.

- Observations
- Chronological Spread: Religions evolved from animistic roots to organized systems by 3500 BCE, with monotheism emerging later (Zoroastrianism, Judaism).
- Interconnectivity: The Abrahamic religions (Judaism, Christianity, Islam) form a clear lineage, while Indian religions (Hinduism, Jainism, Buddhism) share a Vedic ancestry. East Asian traditions stand apart, focusing more on ways to conduct life and organize society rather than on belief systems.
- *End Point - Islam: By 610 CE, Islam synthesized earlier Abrahamic elements, marking it the last major religion in this timeline.*
- This framework simplifies a complex history—many smaller traditions (e.g., Greek, Roman, Shinto) are omitted for brevity.

> *This also suggests that different regions of the world, often isolated from one another, developed distinct philosophies on life and religion. If there were a single God, one might expect that the same religious beliefs would have been introduced universally and consistently throughout history.*

Abrahamic Religions:

- **Beliefs:**
- Abrahamic religions emphasize the existence of a GOD—an all-powerful, all-knowing creator and sustainer of this universe. Christianity has deviated slightly by introducing the concept of the Trinity, but its central idea remains the same. I will discuss later that Christianity's introduction of the Trinity is an afterthought, mainly intended to accommodate Jesus as the Son of God; some of the strange concepts were introduced while compiling the Bible from different sources.
- Religions provide some reward and punishment in the afterlife for deeds done in this world, again, a slight deviation in Christianity, which hints that belief in Jesus is the key.
- All holy scriptures (Bible and Quran) mainly talk about God, but have minimal information on how to conduct (moral and ethical values) in this world, which logically should be the main reason for those holy books.
- Considering the above in the background, these religions also mention that the whole universe was created for the test of Humans
- The Bible & Quran are full of stories, and people are asked to seek lessons from those stories, although stories in themselves can be interpreted in many ways
- Gives you an entity "EVIL/Satan" from which humans and their followers are supposed to protect themselves. This is a peculiar entity and a cornerstone of the entire human and heaven/hell narrative. However, stranger still is its relation and comparison with the all-mighty Creator - God, which we will discuss later.

- **Practices:**
- They all claim they have a complete way of life, but that way of life is not coming from God, as details are not part of the holy scriptures. So, God has not provided complete guidance, but details of guidance are coming from the so-called religious leaders, who are humans who have no connection with God or with even the prophet.

Objective Analysis of God

- All religions were divided into sects and belief systems within a few years of the advent of religion. Thus, the original religion did not survive even a few years after the death of the prophet or inventor of the faith.

> ***For Christianity, the original religion was formed about 3 centuries after the death of Jesus, and for Islam, the original religion was divided within 4-6 hours of the death of the Prophet.***

- For both religions, guidance and expectation were finalized many years, sometimes centuries, later, after the revelation
- Both religions have developed Imams / Saints, who are supposed to provide guidance.
- All such intermediary entities (Saints & Imams) were effectively and physically present only for 2-3 centuries, and even if we believe that they are essential, the instructions coming from them are human interpretation, so Human instructions.
- All three religions expect financial sacrifices, directly or indirectly, mainly given to the religious leaders in the name of God
- All three religions have primarily supported the power of the time and flourished by associating with administrative authorities

Introduction to Religions' Scriptures

The holy scriptures (Tanakh/Bible and Quran) are the primary source for understanding the God of the Abrahamic religions. We will primarily focus on and try to extract the image and characteristics of God as presented in these three (or two, as the Bible contains the Tanakh/Hebrew Bible).

> *The Bible is the holy scripture of the Christian faith. It also contains the five books of the primary Jewish scripture: the Tanakh/the Old Testament/the Hebrew Bible. Therefore, when covering teachings from holy scriptures, we will primarily treat Judaism under the heading of the Bible.*
> *However, while validating historically, I will treat the Old and New Testaments separately. The main reason for this approach is the sources of the book. In the Tanakh/Old Testament, God states, "I am saying it," and Scripture validates this approach. In contrast, the New Testament sources describe "these are the breath of God," without direct first-hand divine narration.*

Before we analyze their content, let's understand how the holy scriptures of the Bible and the Quran came into being. This discussion will be followed by high-level views on the concepts and teachings of three Abrahamic religions (Judaism, Christianity, and Islam), then moving into an object analysis of the respective religious sculptures.

All religions have either added to the so-called original writings or developed different interpretations, which is why there are so many sects within each religion. Limiting ourselves to the basic original scriptures helps us address each religion's fundamental foundation and will also limit the scope of this book.

- **Bible:** Old Testament and New Testament. I will treat these two sections separately and explain the reasoning later. As a preview, the New Testament cannot be historically verified as a direct revelation from God through a known prophet. Nowhere in the New Testament does it explicitly claim to be the direct word of God, nor is there historical evidence to prove its divine origin, especially considering its establishment around 300 AD as a sacred text. In my view,

Objective Analysis of God

Christianity's claim that the entire Bible constitutes the word of God is historically and textually unsubstantiated. While general followers of Christianity accept the Bible as divinely inspired, Christian scholars acknowledge that it does not explicitly claim to be dictated by God, unlike the Tanakh/Old Testament or the Quran. A significant portion of the New Testament states that it is not a direct revelation from God or His prophet, but a collection of communications among Jesus' followers, some of whom never even met Jesus personally.

- Later in this book, we will analyze numerous passages from the New Testament, examining whether they could be considered God's words and exploring contradictions among its various sources and writers.
- **Quran:** It appears now, about 17 years after the Prophet Mohammed's death, after its compilation. The story of the Quran is also similar, but is much controlled, in the following terms:
    - Formalized within 17 years vs 300+ years of the Bible
    - The people compiling it had seen and heard the Quran's verses directly from the Prophet Mohammed, unlike the Bible, which was compiled many generations after.
    - There were many persons to validate that what is written was, to some extent, said by Prophet Mohammed, whereas for the Bible, not a single person alive can validate the accounts.
    - One group mainly compiled the Quran from start to finish, whereas for the Bible, it took about 2-3 generations (about 80 years) of work before the Bible was finally compiled in its present form.

Summarizing the Scriptures:
Both the Bible and the Quran were supposed to be sent by an all-knowing God, who has created this universe for the sole purpose of placing humans into a test ground. So logically, these holy texts should be full of clear guidance for humans on how to live, but both books fail this logical test very miserably.

- For the Bible, only 30% is related to morals and living codes

- For the Quran, less than 10% of the text explains how to live on Earth, even though 10% is extremely vague. On the other hand, approximately 30% of the verses praise God Himself.
- We will see that a human-made Hammurabi's 282 codes provide a better approach and clear guidance in comparison, which were written about 2800 years before the first instruction from God (the Ten Commandments)

General Analysis of Abrahamic Religions

Before starting a detailed discussion on analyzing each religion, we will recap what we have discussed in earlier pages about the universe, specifically the one-dimensional aspect (left part) of our analysis.

Main points from previous discussion:

1. The universe is HUGE, so much so that it is almost incomprehensible for our brain to comprehend its vastness and its history (in terms of space and time)
2. The whole universe is extremely complex, even at the very minute level, and the entity that designed it and maintains it must have tremendous capability, knowledge, and wisdom.
3. The universe creator can go into minute details and consider all aspects of His design for long-term sustainability
4. Although all three religions consider Humans as the reason for the creation of this universe, humans have been in this universe for hardly 0.000027% of the time and on an even smaller part of the universe spatially.
5. Yes, humans have recently started understanding the universe and are at the very initial phase. At the same time, scientists/Humans admit that they do not know the complexity of the system in which we live. The more we know about it, the more complex and stranger it becomes
6. Considering humans' time and space in this universe, the stability we see is our misunderstanding, just like we took a screenshot of an action movie and admired the stability of a flying car (whereas the vehicle in the actual scene is plunging from a cliff into a deep valley.
7. We are like this child, who, for now, is enjoying the moment as a baseball-sized hailstorm has not hit his head as yet, but hail is falling everywhere, and in a few seconds, he may get hit by a falling hail and get injured, but at this moment, he looks pleased.

Section 3 – Religions
Main points from previous discussion:

Image generated by AI

We have also observed that the probability of an abnormal event occurring increases with the number of events that have occurred. If we consider the long life of the universe and the planets, every second on every planet, something happens. That is a huge number, so it also increases the probability of totally bizarre and unimaginable events.

Development of Moral Values - Religion or Society

Religion claims that throughout history, religions have played a pivotal role in shaping the moral frameworks of societies by developing systems of ethics, establishing norms for right and wrong, and offering guidance on how to live virtuously. However, despite the pervasive influence of religious teachings on moral values, religions have not been successful in enforcing or inculcating these values in human beings. There are several reasons why religion has struggled to foster universally moral behavior, and various examples throughout history serve as a testament to this limitation.

Religion – not the reason for Moral/Ethical Values

One aspect promoted by religions is that without religion, all moral values will be gone, and society will crumble. My submission to that is that if we look at history, ethical values were not introduced by religion. These values are the result of Humans realizing that to live in harmony in large groups, they must follow certain principles to sustain their existence. These values have evolved over centuries of practice and continue to update as human lifestyles change.

Many aspects of moral and ethical values were promoted by religion, which we now consider unethical. At the same time, we will see that after God stopped sending religions, humans continued to develop new ethical and moral standards and continue to evolve these.

1. One aspect is flawed values in the treatment of women in all big religions, as women are treated as the property of men, totally against the equality preached by the religions, but aligned with the culture of those days.
2. Another example is the use of religion to justify slavery. In the 18th and 19th centuries, Christian teachings were often cited to support the institution of slavery in the United States. Religious leaders and slave owners alike used biblical passages to justify the ownership of slaves, despite the core Christian principles of equality and love for one's neighbor. The same practices continued in Islam, where not a single word was mentioned, making slavery un-Islamic. Islam has instructions to treat slaves

better, but the same was written in Hammurabi's codes by a human about 2300 years earlier. The teachings of religions serve the interests of powerful groups, rather than cultivating the moral values of justice and equality.
3. The moral values of religions (especially Abrahamic religions) are derived from the 282 laws of Hammurabi (proven later-on), which were not introduced as religious principles but as social laws. Women's treatment is also derived from those laws, as at that time, women were controlled (and "owned") by men, and religion continued that practice.
4. One of the primary challenges in enforcing moral values through religion is the inconsistency between religious teachings and human actions. Many religious texts preach virtues such as compassion, kindness, honesty, and justice. Still, at the same time, they contain words that say otherwise — hypocrisy in the holy text (as captured in later pages in questions). In addition, throughout history, we have observed that individuals or groups employing religious rhetoric have often acted in ways that contradict the principles of equality and justice. For example, in the name of Christianity, during the Middle Ages, the Inquisition led to the torture and execution of thousands under the guise of religious purification. Similarly, the Crusades, which spanned several centuries, were wars fought with religious motivations, resulting in widespread death and suffering. Other worst examples in recent history are the Treatment of indigenous children in Canada – Sixty Scope, the Treatment of children in madrasas of Pakistan, and the Holocaust of Jews. This is a very long list. These events underscore the fact that religious teachings became tools for violence, intolerance, and aggression, rather than fostering moral behavior. The point here is that religion is not the reason moral values are introduced and practiced in humans, as we will see that religion has played a part in limiting or somehow derailing the growth of ethical values.
5. Lastly, the point is that these moral values evolved as Humans realized that they wanted to live in harmony. The best example of this is the traffic laws. No religion defines Traffic laws, but humans have developed, practiced, and enforced traffic "moral values" because they recognize that following this system is necessary.

Objective Analysis of God

> 6. *A few of the best examples of Humanity coming together and developing rules to ensure that moral values of equality and justice prevail are the development of Traffic laws and the Internet Protocol. These were designed out of nothing, based on sheer necessity – without any help or guidance from God.*

7. Even in modern times, religion has not been an absolute deterrent to immoral behavior. For instance, despite widespread religious teachings on the sanctity of life, the issue of abortion remains contentious, with individuals and groups from all faith backgrounds displaying diverging views. The violence perpetuated by extremist groups, such as Al-Qaeda or ISIS, and far-right Christianity, plus the war continuing in the Middle East, is fought indirectly in the name of religion. All these groups claim to uphold religious values, yet their actions reflect a stark violation of fundamental moral principles such as peace, compassion, and human dignity.
8. Religious organizations struggle to instill morality due to the diversity of interpretations within each faith. Different sects, denominations, or schools of thought within the same religion often have varying interpretations of moral behavior. In some cases, this leads to contradictions and confusion among followers. For example, in Islam, different interpretations of Sharia law can lead to vastly different practices of what is considered morally acceptable, from gender roles to punishment for crimes. The same applies to Christianity, where LGBTQ issues are handled differently between the United Church of Christ/Episcopal Church and the Southern Baptists/Catholics. This inconsistency weakens the ability of religious doctrines to provide a unified moral compass.

We will discuss and provide examples to show that moral behavior is often influenced more by societal, cultural, and psychological factors than by religious teachings. People may act kindly or justly due to a sense of empathy, a desire for community, or personal conviction, rather than strict adherence to religious rules.

> *As society evolves, moral values are shaped by human-made legal frameworks, scientific understanding, and philosophical discourse, often independent of religious dogma.*

In conclusion, religion has not been universally successful in enforcing or inculcating these values in human beings. Historical examples of violence, exploitation, and injustice committed in the name of religion highlight the limitations of faith in ensuring moral behavior. Furthermore, the diverse interpretations within religions and the influence of non-religious factors suggest that morality is a complex construct shaped by various forces beyond the realm of religion.

On the other hand, humans have done a remarkable job developing morals, values, and ethics. There are multiple examples of when humans need to build a code, primarily to ensure group survival and maintain justice. Humans' output has been remarkable, from the Hammurabi codes to the latest traffic laws.

Moral values are tied to social values:

Morality and ethics are fundamentally social constructs that have been developed through human interaction to ensure cooperation, stability, and order within societies. They provide frameworks for judging actions as right or wrong, based on how they affect others. Concepts like justice, honesty, and fairness have meaning only in relation to other people. For example, the rule "do not steal" exists to protect property rights in a community; it is irrelevant in isolation. A person living completely alone—disconnected from others—would face no moral or ethical dilemmas because their actions would impact no one but themselves.

> *The concept of morality and ethics comes when two entities/people interact, as these are social requirements.*

Without social interaction, there is no need for moral judgment. Ethics presuppose relationships, conflicts of interest, or shared values that only exist among groups. Even virtues like compassion or loyalty, which are directed at others, lose relevance in solitude. While an individual might maintain habits or personal codes, these do not constitute morality in the complete ethical sense; they are merely preferences or routines. Thus, morality and ethics are

Objective Analysis of God

inherently tied to human society. They emerge from the need to regulate interpersonal behavior and resolve conflicts, making them meaningless for a truly isolated individual. In essence, morality is a social necessity, not a universal constant.

> *Religions have failed humanity in providing any framework of equality. Religions have, in fact, reinforced the concept of inequality in the form of women's treatment, slavery, and the caste system in Islam (as discussed later in the question section)*

Try to imagine moral values and ethical standards for a person living alone and having no interaction with others.

Contribution of religions to building Moral values:

I will go one step further to say that Religion has hampered and obstructed the development of Moral values by assigning this task to God, rather than the collective society. Compare the Ten Commandments (which were given 400 years later) with the Hammurabi Code. Hammurabi's 282 codes (1700 BC), although far from any justice that we know now, are better than the 10 Commandments, in terms of:

- o Clarity & Preciseness,
- o Executability clarity
- o Social events and the width of scope

The Ten Commandments, traditionally listed in the Hebrew Bible (Exodus 20:1–17 and Deuteronomy 5:4–21), are ethical and religious principles central to Judaism and Christianity. Here's a simplified list of their core prohibitions and directives:

1. You shall have no other gods before Me.
2. You should not make a carved idol or worship any image for yourself.
3. You shall not take the name of the Lord your God in vain.
4. Remember the Sabbath day, to keep it holy (rest and refrain from work).
5. Honor your father and mother.
6. You shall not murder.
7. You shall not commit adultery.
8. You shall not steal.

Section 3 – Religions
Development of Moral Values - Religion or Society

9. You shall not bear false witness against your neighbor (lie or perjury).
10. You shall not covet your neighbor's spouse, house, servants, animals, or possessions.

I will rest my case by comparing these with the following, which were developed through human efforts over hundreds of years.

https://avalon.law.yale.edu/ancient/hamframe.asp

A more detailed section on Hammurabi's codes is presented later.

> *A side note: if we assume, as some scholars suggest, that these codes also came from the same God, it might explain why the laws were reduced from 282 to 10. Among the above 10 commandments, four are not directly related to moral guidance, which suggests that the sources may not be the same.*
>
> *Religion has struggled to provide clear moral ethics from the start, while humans have developed more practical laws to ensure social well-being. Religious scriptures have traditionally placed greater emphasis on praising God than on providing moral guidelines.*

Objective Analysis of God

Moral fallacies of the Bible / New Testament

Often celebrated as a cornerstone of Christian ethics, the New Testament contains numerous passages that seem to contradict established equality and moral standards, arguably undermining established ethical values. For example, its text endorses slavery, misogyny, killing completely innocent people and babies, even animals, and intolerance, which have historically perpetuated immorality among adherents.

> *Although we will explore more examples later, I want to highlight a few here to emphasize that, contrary to the claims of religious institutions and their promoters, their core scriptures have often undermined the moral values of followers. In many cases, the teachings attributed to God appear more aligned with the cultural practices of the time than with universal ethical standards.*

- Slavery: Ephesians 6:5 (NIV) commands, "*Slaves, obey your earthly masters... with respect and fear,*" legitimizing oppression. Similarly, Colossians 3:22 and 1 Timothy 6:1-2 instruct slaves to obey masters "*wholeheartedly,*" even "*those who are harsh*" (1 Peter 2:18, NIV). These verses were cited to justify slavery, delaying abolition.

- Misogyny: Women are subjugated in 1 Timothy 2:12 (NIV): "*I do not permit a woman to teach or assume authority over a man.*" 1 Corinthians 14:34-35 silences women in churches, while Ephesians 5:22-24 demands wives "*submit to your husbands as to the Lord.*" Such texts have entrenched gender inequality.

- Violence and Intolerance: Jesus states, "*I did not come to bring peace, but a sword*" (Matthew 10:34, NIV), and Luke 19:27 (NIV) allegorically urges killing enemies: "*Bring them here and slaughter them.*" Revelation 21:8 condemns diverse groups to "*the fiery lake of burning sulfur,*" fostering exclusion. John 14:6 and 3:18 assert salvation solely through Christ, marginalizing non-Christians.

- Ethical Extremes: Matthew 5:29-30 (NIV) advocates self-mutilation to avoid sin: "*If your right eye causes you to stumble, gouge it out.*" Luke 14:26 demands followers "hate" family, promoting division. Romans 13:1-2 commands submission to oppressive authorities, discouraging dissent.

- Harsh Judgments: Acts 5:1-11 depicts divine execution for dishonesty, while 1 Corinthians 6:9-10 excludes "the wicked" from God's kingdom. Matthew 15:4 (NIV) invokes death for cursing parents, and 2 Thessalonians 3:10 denies food to the unemployed.

- Though interpretations vary, literal adherence to these verses has justified slavery, patriarchy, and violence, eroding moral progress. By enshrining such ethics, the New Testament has often lowered, rather than elevated, the moral consciousness of its followers.

Moral fallacies of the Quran

Like the Bible, the Quran is also subject to interpretation, and scholars, philosophers, and critics have debated its moral teachings over the centuries. Some critics argue that the Quran contains moral contradictions or fallacies, while believers maintain its divine coherence. Critics also argue that certain Quranic teachings appear contradictory when compared to one another or universal ethical principles.

Below are some commonly cited points of contention:

As a foundational religious text, the Quran presents a complex tapestry of moral teachings that have sparked debate over their alignment with equality and ethical principles. Below is an exploration of key moral values and ethical issues derived from Quranic verses, highlighting tensions between divine commandments and humanistic ethics.

The following are a few points highlighting contradictions between Quranic teachings and equality/ethical standards, particularly on issues like gender equality, violence, slavery, and justice. Defenders argue for historical context; my submission to that is that the

Objective Analysis of God

primary purpose of Islam was to change the culture and behavior of humans, so saying that it was practiced at that time itself negates the reason for introducing Islam.

We have also discussed these from other angles later on.

Divine Justice vs. Retributive Punishment

- Quran 39:53: "*Say, 'O My servants who have transgressed... do not despair of Allah's mercy. He forgives all sins.*" At the same time, Allah is saying
- Quran 4:14: "*He will put them into the Fire to abide eternally.*" Here, Allah's seemingly unjust justice comes to light: He metes out disproportionate justice, where infinite punishment is inflicted for finite sins (e.g., disbelief), which contradicts the ethical principle of proportionality and thereby challenges the balance between mercy and retribution.

Human Agency vs. Divine Predestination

- Quran 18:29: "*Whoever wills—let them believe; whoever wills—let them disbelieve.*" Quran 14:4: "Allah leaves astray whom He wills."

  This has been repeated multiple times in the Quran and is one of the primary points of discussion regarding the extent of human free will. If there is even a slight intervention from Allah, the actions of humans are subject to the amount of free will given by Allah to that Human. In this case, can Allah justify the punishment, as actions done by humans are a result of what attributes Allah has given, whether small or large, does not matter? This negates Allah's fairness and Humans' accountability.

Permitting Wife-Beating

- Quran (4:34): "*...[If wives] persist in defiance, strike them.*" This verse is explicitly addressed to husbands towards their wives. From the equality principle of Islam, the same instruction should have been given to wives as to husbands. Believers argue that certain conditions and prerequisites must be met before reaching this point. My submission is that, to ensure the principles of equality, the same could have been applied to wives, allowing them to strike their husbands after similar prerequisites and conditions.

Section 3 – Religions
Development of Moral Values - Religion or Society

Slavery & Sexual Exploitation
- Quran (4:24): "*Also [forbidden are] married women except those your right hands possess...*"
The wording "Your right hands possess" is commonly translated as referring to the women they received or captured after defeating the enemy in war. Here, the Quran is promoting the slavery of women and allowing free sexual relations with them without their consent and will. This is sexual slavery, although it was a norm of that time, but it is totally against any standard of human moral standards and is a main moral failing stated in the Quran.

Death / severe punishments for Apostasy (Indirectly Supported)
- Quran 2:217: "*And whoever of you reverts from his religion and dies while a disbeliever—for those, their deeds have become worthless in this world and the Hereafter, and those are the companions of the Fire; they will abide therein eternally*". Also, similar verse 30:90-01
Although the punishment of death for Apostasy – leaving Islam is not explicitly mentioned in Quran, apostasy has been associated with severe punishment. I fail to understand why the punishment for not accepting Islam is less than the punishment for leaving Islam. This raises ethical concerns about religious freedom. I see it more as forcibly ensuring that the person remains in Islam and continues to follow rituals, and continues to enforce Islamic institutions financially and with efforts. However, their mind are not accepting it. Another point is that it contradicts Verse 2:256 ("No compulsion in religion"); what more compulsion can Allah give than eternal punishment and the removal of all benefits attained previously for good deeds? Lastly, why is Allah closing the door for that person to come back and join the Islamic ranks? These are all against any standards of fairness and justice.

Allowing polygamy while negating it
- Quran (4:3): "Marry women of your choice, two, three, or four...", and in the same Chapter (4:129): "*And you will never be able to be just between wives, even if you should strive [to do so].*" It allows injustice to be done to wives, as men cannot provide similar justice to multiple wives. Strangely, Allah allows for the grounds for injustice to happen, whereas there is

Objective Analysis of God

no reason to allow polygamy. Here, Allah is supposed to be the creator of humans and knows humans the most, but He still allows injustice to be done to women/wives. The Irony is that it is permitted knowingly and with complete understanding that injustice will happen.

Women's Testimony Worth Half a Man's
- Quran (2:282)"...*And if there are not two men, then a man and two women...*"
  This verse says that women's testimony is inherently less reliable, reinforcing that both genders are not equal, and further that all humans are not equal. Whereas Allah also says that all humans are equal, Allah only considers men as humans and gives lesser importance to women. Although Allah mentioned about human equality multiple times, but such verses (also when He say that Israelites (Banu Isra'il) were favored by Allah or Allah Favorable/chosen nation– 2:47, 2:122, 45:16, 44:32) reaffirm that Allah do not believe in gender equality and also that He cannot do justice and cannot treat all human ethically in just manner.

Allowing Child Marriage
- Quran (65:4)"*For those who have not menstruated [due to youth]...*"
  The phrase "those who have not menstruated" points to prepubescent girls, clearly implying that child marriage is allowed; otherwise, there is no value in using this condition. Allowing Child Marriage is against any norm of moral and ethical standards, as a child who cannot understand the implications of marriage cannot give proper consent. Believers argue that it is related to divorce law. Still, divorce only comes after marriage, and if the Quran is referring to prepubescent girls' divorce, then girls' marriage has to happen at a younger age, even before/the "prepubescent" period.

Animal Welfare vs. Ritual Sacrifice
- Quran (6:38): "*Animals are communities like you,*" but it still asks for animal sacrifices. Quran (22:36): "*Sacrifice camels as symbols of Allah.*"

Mass ritual slaughter conflicts with the Quran's emphasis on animal dignity and the moral and ethical standard of preserving food and not being wasteful. Remember that during the Hajj season, thousands of animals are sacrificed in accordance with Islamic instructions. All that animal killing is only to make Allah Happy. Note that for centuries, as close to the 1980s, when the Saudi Govt was not rich and organized thousands of animals to be killed/sacrificed to please GOD, and their meat was burnt and buried, while millions around the world cannot afford to have a meat meal for months. This is contrary to the moral principle of preserving food.

Conclusion

The Quran's ethical teachings remain a subject of profound debate. While it advocates mercy, justice, and charity, its alignment with general human rights, equality, and justice is contested. The Quran's moral framework, rooted in 7th-century Arabian norms, often conflicts with broader ethical paradigms, including human equality and rights, gender equality, human dignity, and the pursuit of justice. A morally perfect text coming from an all-just and loving God should not require such moral fallacies, especially when the message is applicable till the end of humanity.

Outside religion -Historical Moral development:

The development of morality is intrinsically linked to the emergence and evolution of human societies, driven by practical needs for cooperation, conflict resolution, and collective survival. This argument is supported by secular moral frameworks and societal structures across diverse regions, as illustrated in some examples below:

Asia: Confucianism and Legalism
In ancient China, Confucianism (5th century BCE) emphasized social harmony, filial piety, and ethical governance without invoking deities. Confucius framed morality as a product of human relationships and societal roles, advocating for virtues like benevolence (ren) and righteousness (yi) to stabilize hierarchical structures. Later, the Legalist tradition (Qin Dynasty, 221–206 BCE) codified strict laws and punishments to enforce order, prioritizing societal stability over spiritual doctrines.

Indian Subcontinent: Arthashastra and Secular Governance
The Arthashastra (4th century BCE), a treatise by Kautilya (also known as Chanakya), outlined secular principles for statecraft, economics, and justice. It emphasized the ruler's duty to ensure welfare (\) through pragmatic policies, including fair taxation and disaster management. This reflected a moral system tied to societal well-being rather than religious mandates.

Africa: Ubuntu and the Gada System
The Ubuntu philosophy in Southern Africa ("I am because we are") centers on communal interdependence, promoting empathy and collective responsibility. Similarly, the Gada system of the Oromo people (Ethiopia) established a democratic, age-based governance structure that emphasized egalitarianism, environmental stewardship, and conflict resolution through consensus—a moral framework rooted in societal cohesion.

Middle East: Code of Hammurabi and Pre-Islamic Trade Ethics
The Code of Hammurabi (c. 1754 BCE, Babylon) primarily addressed practical societal needs through laws governing property, trade, and justice (e.g., principle of "eye for an eye", in code 197 – *"If he breaks another man's bone, they shall break his bone."*, and code 200 - *"If a man knocks out the teeth of his equal, his teeth shall*

be knocked out."). Its focus on deterrence and fairness aimed to maintain order in a complex urban society. Pre-Islamic Mecca's trade networks also relied on secular ethics, such as honoring contracts and equitable dealings, to foster trust among diverse merchants.

Europe: Greco-Roman Philosophy and Enlightenment Thought
Ancient Greek philosophers, such as Aristotle (384–322 BCE), grounded morality in human flourishing (eudaimonia) and virtue ethics, arguing that ethical behavior arises from the rational pursuit of the common good. The Roman Twelve Tables (451 BCE) codified secular laws to resolve class conflicts. Unlike earlier religious or unwritten customs, the Twelve Tables were written laws displayed publicly in the Roman Forum, ensuring transparency and accountability. They aimed to reduce disputes between patricians (elites) and plebeians (commoners) by codifying rights and procedures. Like Hammurabi's Code, punishments were strict, but procedures (trials, evidence) were formalized. These include:

Legal Procedures (Table I–II)
- Right to a trial: Defendants must be summoned before a magistrate.
- Evidence & witnesses: Required for convictions.
- Failure to appear: If a witness refused to testify, they could be branded an outlaw.

Debt & Slavery (Table III)
- **Debt bondage (*nexum*)**: Creditors could enslave debtors after a 30-day grace period.
- **Execution for unpaid debts**: If debts remained unpaid, creditors could kill or sell the debtor.

Property & Inheritance (Tables IV–V)
- **Paterfamilias rule**: A father had absolute power (*patria potestas*) over his family, including selling children into slavery.
- **Inheritance**: If no will existed, property went to the nearest male relative.

Torts & Injuries (Tables VII–VIII)
- **"Eye for an eye" retaliation**: Allowed for physical injuries (*talio*), similar to Hammurabi.

Objective Analysis of God

  - *"If one has broken another's limb, let there be retaliation in kind, unless a compromise is made."* (Table VIII.2)
- **Fines for injuries**:
  - Breaking a bone: 300 *asses* (if the victim was free), 150 asses (if the victim was a slave).
  - Verbal insults: Heavy penalties.

Public & Sacred Law (Tables IX–XII)

- **Ban on special privileges**: *"Privileges, or statutes favoring individuals, are forbidden."* (Table IX.1)
- **Burial restrictions**: No excessive funeral rites or burying gold with the dead (except dental gold).
Later legal systems (e.g., *the Corpus Juris Civilis under Justinian) were built on these principles. This influence even continued into modern legal processes and has an Impact on modern law.* Concepts such as due process, property rights, and public legal codes can be traced back to the Twelve Tables.

All these were developed without divine guidance and direction, indicating that Humanity was well on course to establish an adequate moral and social justice system. I am reiterating here what I said earlier: after examining this evidence, I conclude that the introduction and enforcement of religious moral standards have obstructed the organic development within society.

Later, Enlightenment thinkers like Immanuel Kant (categorical imperative) and John Stuart Mill (utilitarianism) derived morality from reason and societal welfare, rejecting religious authority.

Modern Secular Morality
Contemporary examples include Scandinavian social democracies, where high trust, egalitarianism, and welfare are rooted in secular Humanism.

> *Scandinavia (Denmark, Sweden, Norway) has some of the highest percentages of non-religious and atheist/agnostic populations in the world, but is considered one of the better moral societies.. Approximately 70% of the population is non-religious. This figure indicates that religious moral values have failed humanity.*

The Universal Declaration of Human Rights (1948) exemplifies a global moral framework based on dignity and equality, one that transcends religious justification.

These examples show morality evolves through reason, experience, and social struggle, not divine revelation. If religious morality were truly "innate," it would align with universal human rights. Instead, its rigid doctrines often clash with modern ethics, suggesting that religious morality is artificial rather than divinely inspired.

Why Religious Morality has failed

One argument presented by believers is that they do not practice it.

> *My point is that religious moral values are not inherently unpracticed, but rather that they are man-made and serve the interests of religious institutions. These institutions have historically shaped moral codes selectively to secure compliance and favor in the name of religion. After studying the holy scriptures, I would even say, 'Thank God' that these religious morals are not thoroughly followed.*

If religious morality were truly beneficial, its positive effects would be visible in the behavior of its adherents. Yet, widespread hypocrisy, corruption, and violence among religious groups suggest that religious teachings do not translate into real-world moral superiority. Here's why:

No Empirical Evidence That Religious People Are More Moral
Studies show little to no moral advantage: Research (e.g., Zuckerman, 2008; Galen, 2012) finds that secular societies often have lower crime rates, better social welfare, and higher happiness indices than highly religious ones.
Example: Scandinavian countries (mostly secular) rank highest in trust, equality, and low corruption, while more religious nations (e.g., some in Latin America, Africa) struggle with violence and inequality.

Religious Texts Are Often Ignored or Selectively Followed
Cherry-picking morality: Believers frequently disregard inconvenient teachings (e.g., "love thy enemy," prohibitions on greed) while enforcing others
Example: Many self-identified Christians support policies contrary to Jesus' teachings (e.g., wealth inequality, militarism), proving religion doesn't dictate their ethics.

Religion Doesn't Prevent—and Often Justifies—Immoral Acts
Atrocities in God's name: Crusades, slavery, terrorism, and persecution (e.g., witch trials, blasphemy laws) were/are justified using religious doctrine.

Modern scandals: Systemic child abuse in churches, megachurch fraud, and extremist violence demonstrate that religion doesn't guarantee goodness.

Secular Systems Produce Ethical Behavior Without Religion
Human rights, democracy, and science—not religion—have driven the abolition of slavery, the pursuit of gender equality, and the development of medical ethics.
Example: The most peaceful and prosperous societies today (e.g., New Zealand, Canada, Japan) are highly secular, relying on humanist principles rather than divine command.

Subjective "Moral Benefits" Are Just Cultural Habits
Charity? Atheists donate blood at equal/higher rates than believers (AAPOR, 2019). Community? Secular mutual-aid networks (e.g., Food Not Bombs) thrive without faith. Meaning? Philosophy, art, and relationships can offer a sense of purpose without requiring a belief in God.

Religion's Moral Influence Is a Myth
If religious morality worked, devout societies would be objectively more just, peaceful, and compassionate, but they aren't. Moral progress occurs despite religion, not because of it, as secular systems demonstrate that ethics don't require faith.

Conclusion
From ancient legal codes to modern human rights, morality has evolved as a pragmatic response to the complexities of society. Whether through Confucian ethics, Ubuntu communalism, or Enlightenment rationality, to present-day traffic laws and internet protocol, all these systems demonstrate that moral principles arise from the need to regulate human interactions, foster cooperation, and ensure survival, independent of religious influence. Societies codify morality not through divine mandate, but through collective experience and adaptive governance.

General Question from Believers

Section 3 – Religions
General Question from Believers

Question: Why does God go through such a big hassle	**G1**

Analysis and background:
By now, you may have some idea of the universe's vastness, and all Abrahamic religions consider that this entire universe was created so that God can test humans.

The notion that an omnipotent God created the vast universe solely to test humans, as posited by some Abrahamic interpretations, raises profound questions about divine intent and efficiency Taking the analogy that the Earth is just one spoonful of all the water available in all water bodies (oceans, rivers, lakes), like creating first oceans, lakes, and rivers, and associated systems, then take out and use one spoonful of water.

Creation of such an immense cosmos for the sole purpose of testing humanity seems disproportionate. Why would an all-powerful deity undertake such a grandiose endeavor when a simpler, self-contained Earth could suffice?

Alternatively, the universe might not be exclusively for human testing; some theological views suggest it hosts other purposes or beings, perhaps angels or extraterrestrial life, although this contradicts the narrative of Abrahamic religions.
An omnipotent God could have tested humans in a simpler system. Still, the universe's grandeur might instead suggest a purpose beyond human understanding, keeping in mind that when the omnipotent already knows the answer, an all-knowing God seems to defy simple logic.

Creating the notion that the God of religion is not the God, but man-made God

Conclusion: We fail to see the logic in building and maintaining the entire universe over billions of years to test Humans in a very tiny portion of it.	**Please rate this Conclusion:**

Objective Analysis of God

Question: Why wait that long	**G2**

Analysis and background:
Having explored the vastness of the universe in terms of space, it's now essential to shift our focus to its temporal dimension. To grasp the scale of cosmic time, let's revisit a simple analogy: if we compress time so that one second represents one year, then the universe's age of approximately 13.8 billion years would translate to just 437.6 years. Within this scaled framework, the span during which divine religious teachings were actively delivered—roughly 2,000 years—would amount to a mere 30 minutes. This striking comparison highlights how brief the period of direct religious instruction has been in the grand timeline of existence.

Such brevity raises fundamental questions. If the purpose of humanity's existence involves a divine test or spiritual development, one might expect a more sustained or evenly distributed engagement. Yet, the disproportionate timing and known gap of about 1500 years (since Islam) open up the mind about the validity of the ever-living God of religion and His efforts to communicate with Humans.

This fleeting half-hour of divine communication—when viewed against the backdrop of 437.6 compressed years of cosmic history—raises a deeper skepticism. The so-called revelations from God, encapsulated in religious texts, appear not only brief but profoundly questionable in their authenticity. If these messages were truly divine, one would expect clarity, consistency, and universality across time and cultures. Instead, what we find are fragmented doctrines, conflicting narratives, and human interpretations masquerading as sacred truth. The brevity of this "communication" and its ambiguous nature suggest that it may not have been a genuine transmission from a higher power, but rather a product of human imagination and sociopolitical evolution. In this context, waiting for further divine instruction seems not only unnecessary but also misguided.

Conclusion: It appears completely ridiculous for God to wait for 437 years and conduct a test for half an hour by introducing religion.	Please rate this Conclusion:

Section 3 – Religions
General Question from Believers

Question: Universe complexity	**G3**

Analysis and background:

Humans have only taken the first few steps in understanding the universe's complexity, and as we learn more, it becomes increasingly complex.

So, God, who has created this complex, vast universe and has been maintaining and managing its complexity for such an extended period, cannot even find a proper way to implement His religion on this earth. He cannot develop a system to communicate his will, at least, and ask humans; he cannot even maintain continuity in his message. How can such an omnipotent, all-knowing, and all-intelligent entity make such simple mistakes, and on top of that, continue to make mistakes, as some religions argue that He has sent about 250,000 messengers?

To me, such an entity cannot design and develop this complex universe where even tiny things fit into the environment and the vast universe continues.

Or He does not want Humans to pass. If this is the case, then who are we humans to confront or deny His will?

Conclusion: For an extremely competent entity like God, it seems highly illogical that He cannot develop a system to implement his religion or his ask.	**Please rate this Conclusion:**

Objective Analysis of God

Question:
GOD and what He is asking

G4

Analysis and background:
God's capabilities are immense; consider what He has created and continues to maintain. On the other hand, all religions promote prayer and sacrifice, which He demands, such as the sacrifice of animals, rituals of praise, and asking Him for forgiveness.

Why does the creator of this universe want animals to be sacrificed to please Him? Why is such a vast and potent entity so hungry for his praying and asking for the sacrifices of animals in His name?

Another argument is that God wants us to make these kinds of sacrifices to teach us to love Him more than anything else. This is completely illogical, as no matter what is said, most sacrifices in today's world happen where there is no connection between humans and animals. So, humans do not have any feelings about those sacrificed and subsequently show no love and devotion towards God. All-knowing God should have known this "future" that about 90% of the sacrifices would not fulfill His aim. The worst part is that if followers do not perform these rituals, they will face the most severe kind of punishment.

Why does a God who does not want anything, does not need anything, still end up asking such minuscule efforts, in such a small portion of the universe, and such a small amount of time?

He will not gain anything from these rituals. Still, animals will be killed, and money will come out of the pockets of followers and indirectly go into the religious institutes…. This represents a self-centered God.

Conclusion:"
It is illogical for God to ask humans to pray and sacrifice such minute things, and with no apparent reason to fulfill his objective.

Please rate this Conclusion:

Section 3 – Religions
General Question from Believers

Question:
Unstable universe

G5

Analysis and background:

A common argument put forth by religious proponents is that the Earth and the universe exhibit a remarkable degree of stability and order—suggesting, perhaps, a divine hand in their design. However, this perception is deeply skewed by the brevity of human existence. When measured against the vast timeline of the cosmos or even the geological age of Earth, our lifespan is but a fleeting moment. What appears stable and harmonious to us during this narrow window is, in reality, a snapshot of ongoing chaos and transformation.

To illustrate this, imagine watching a 24-hour action-packed film but only glimpsing a single pixel for a fraction of a second. That pixel might seem calm, even static, but the whole movie is anything but. Earth's tectonic activity alone reshapes continents, forms mountains, and triggers devastating events such as earthquakes and tsunamis. These are not anomalies—they are part of a continuous, dynamic process.

If we could observe the universe at its true pace and scale, we'd witness a relentless churn of energy, matter, and motion. Stars explode, galaxies collide, and planetary systems evolve or collapse. Even Earth has faced countless existential threats—mass extinctions, the Ice Age, climate shifts, and possibly dozens of near-misses from celestial bodies capable of wiping out entire species. The idea that our environment is inherently stable is a comforting illusion born from a limited perspective. In truth, the cosmos is anything but tranquil.

Conclusion:
Earth only appears stable as we watch and analyze it at a very micro level. The entire universe and the Earth are constantly changing and volatile.

Please rate this Conclusion:

Objective Analysis of God

| **Question:** What is so special about humans | **G6** |

Analysis and background:
Many religious teachings claim that God has specially selected humans to undergo a divine test, which determines their fate in either heaven or hell for eternity. But this claim becomes increasingly complex to justify when viewed against the staggering diversity of life on Earth. Scientists estimate that over 8.7 million species currently exist, and more than 99% of all species that have ever lived—roughly 5 billion—are now extinct. Among this vast biological tapestry, humans represent just one branch, emerging only in the last few hundred thousand years. Suppose God's intention was to create life with purpose. Why would that purpose be reserved exclusively for a single species, while billions of others lived, evolved, and vanished without any spiritual significance? Moreover, many of these species exhibit complex behaviors, intelligence, and social structures. Dolphins, elephants, and certain primates exhibit empathy, problem-solving abilities, and even mournful rituals. If moral awareness or consciousness is the criterion for divine testing, then excluding these beings seems arbitrary. The idea that humans were created with a "special plan" also clashes with evolutionary evidence, which shows that Homo sapiens are the product of gradual biological processes—not a sudden divine intervention.

If God's communication and judgment are honest, why would they be confined to such a narrow slice of life's history and diversity? The exclusivity of human-centered theology appears more like a projection of human ego than a reflection of cosmic design. In light of the numbers and the broader biological context, the claim of divine favoritism toward humans lacks both logical and fair grounds.

| **Conclusion:** It would be irrational of God to develop 875 million living species and task only one to pray to him and make sacrifices, and then punish or reward that one. | Please rate this Conclusion: |

Section 3 – Religions
General Question from Believers

Question: Deploy religion in less than 2% time and in 0.003% of the area	**G7**

Analysis and background:

When we examine the historical footprint of the Abrahamic religions—Judaism, Christianity, and Islam—it becomes evident that their geographic and temporal scope is surprisingly narrow. The entire sequence of prophetic activity, from Adam to Muhammad, occurred within a region spanning less than 5,000 kilometers, primarily concentrated in the Middle East. This area represents a mere 0.003% of the Earth's total landmass, raising questions about the universality of these teachings. If a divine message were truly meant for all of humanity, why would it be confined to such a minuscule portion of the planet?

Temporally, the span of prophetic revelation is equally limited. From roughly 1500 BCE, marking the emergence of Judaism, to around 650 CE with the rise of Islam, the active period of religious instruction lasted no more than 2,000 years. When compared to the estimated 250,000-year existence of Homo sapiens, this accounts for less than 1% of human history. Such a brief window of divine engagement seems disproportionate if the goal was to guide all of humanity across time.

Even demographically, the focus appears misaligned. Throughout recorded history, regions such as China and South Asia have consistently had the most significant human populations. Yet, these areas remained largely untouched by Abrahamic prophets during their formative periods. This raises a critical question: if these religions were intended as universal truths, why were they delivered in such a geographically and demographically limited context? The evidence suggests a human-centered narrative shaped by regional history, rather than a truly global divine plan.

Conclusion: God's judgment appears questionable in implementing His wishes over such a short period and in such a limited location, particularly among a small group of people.	**Please rate this Conclusion:**

Objective Analysis of God

Question: Where is God Now	**G8**

Analysis and background:
When viewed through the lens of demographic history, the claim that God chose humanity for a divine test—yet only revealed His message to a tiny fraction of people—raises serious questions about fairness, scope, and intent. According to estimates from the Population Reference Bureau and other demographic sources, approximately 117 billion humans have ever been born on Earth. Of these, only about 2.5 to 3 billion were born before or during the lifetimes of Jesus and Muhammad, whose ministries spanned roughly from 4 BCE to 632 CE.

This means that less than 2.6% of all humans who have ever lived were alive when God's supposed revelations were actively delivered through prophets. Even if we generously include those who lived in the centuries immediately before and after these figures, the percentage remains virtually unchanged. The remaining 97%+ of humanity, those born before the Abrahamic revelations or after their initial spread, either never received the message or inherited it through layers of interpretation, translation, & institutional control. If divine judgment hinges on exposure to these teachings, then the overwhelming majority of humans were excluded from direct access. This undermines the idea of a universal and just divine plan. Why would an omnipotent God choose to communicate with such a narrow slice of humanity, both in time and geography, while leaving billions without firsthand guidance?

The numbers don't just challenge theological assumptions—they expose a deep asymmetry in the supposed divine outreach. If salvation depends on receiving the message, then God's approval appears to have been extended to less than 2% of all humans—a figure that calls into question the very premise of divine justice.

Conclusion: It is unreasonable that God went through the efforts of creating the Universe and humans in such detail, and decided not to contact humans at all for the 1,400 years in which 98% of Humans are born (religious)	Please rate this Conclusion:

Section 3 – Religions
General Question from Believers

Question: Was God experimenting	G9

Analysis and background:
Fossil evidence and evolutionary biology offer a compelling narrative that challenges traditional religious claims about the sudden creation of humans. The Earth has supported life for approximately 3.4 billion years, while the universe itself spans 13.8 billion years. Yet Homo sapiens only emerged around 250,000 years ago, representing a mere 0.00000025% of the universe's lifespan. This timeline suggests that humans arrived at the very end of a long and complex biological history, rather than being its central focus.

Throughout those billions of years, Earth was home to an extraordinary diversity of species and ecosystems. If one were to argue that God was actively shaping life, then it appears this process involved extensive experimentation, creating and destroying countless species. In fact, over 99% of all species that have ever lived are now extinct. The species we see today represent less than 1% of life's historical diversity. This pattern of creation & extinction raises questions about the logic, capability, and intent, especially if the ultimate goal was to test humans.

Some religious scholars attempt to reconcile this by suggesting that Adam was selected from among already existing Homo sapiens. But this view introduces a theological contradiction: if God is truly omniscient, then Adam's selection was not a spontaneous act—it was known from the beginning. Why, then, would an all-knowing deity create billions of species and allow nearly all to perish before initiating a human-centered divine narrative? If Adam was always part of the plan, the preceding biological history seems unnecessary and wasteful. These inconsistencies suggest that the story of divine selection may be more symbolic than literal.

Conclusion: It is illogical for God, with His wisdom and capabilities, to experiment and arrive at the final stage after extensive testing. He is all-knowing, and He should know what and how to create.	Please rate this Conclusion:

Objective Analysis of God

Question: God's experiments with Humans	**G10**

Analysis and background:

On the previous page, we discussed why God created so many species and experimented with them before creating humans. An all-knowing God should know what he wants and go directly there. Now we will delve even further.

Again, based upon the fossil evidence we have, the evolutionary journey of Homo sapiens is far more complex and gradual than religious narratives often suggest. Fossil and genetic evidence reveal that modern humans are just one branch of a broader hominin family tree, which includes species like *Homo habilis*, *Homo erectus*, *Homo neanderthalensis*, and *Homo heidelbergensis*. These species lived and evolved over millions of years, with overlapping timelines and geographic dispersals across Africa, Europe, and Asia. *Homo sapiens* emerged roughly 250,000 years ago, but we were not the first, nor the only, intelligent hominins to walk the Earth.

If we accept the religious argument that God selected Adam from among existing Homo sapiens, then we must also confront the implications of divine foreknowledge. An all-knowing God would have been aware from the beginning that Adam would be chosen. Yet, the evolutionary record reveals a lengthy, trial-and-error process of hominin development, with many species living, adapting, and eventually becoming extinct. Why would a divine plan involve the creation and destruction of so many intelligent beings before selecting one for spiritual significance?

Moreover, if Adam was chosen from a population of Homo sapiens, what distinguished him from the rest? Were the others not worthy of divine communication? This selective approach raises troubling questions about fairness and purpose.

In light of this, the narrative of a sudden, purposeful creation of humans appears inconsistent with the evidence. All these Human versions had something close to our present form, clearly showing God's progress through His experiments.

Conclusion: God seemed uncertain in shaping humanity, despite humans being the very reason for the universe's creation. One would expect clarity in choosing whom to create and test.	Please rate this Conclusion:

Section 3 – Religions
General Question from Believers

Question: So self-centric God	**G11**

Analysis and background:
When we examine the overarching themes of the Quran and the Bible, a consistent portrayal of God emerges—an entity who desires worship, praise, gratitude, and obedience, across both texts, we find repeated assertions that God created all beings to worship Him, that followers must seek His forgiveness, thank Him for their blessings, and adhere to His commands to avoid severe punishment. Meanwhile, it is emphasized that angels, jinn, and all of creation already worship and glorify Him continuously. Much of the sacred literature is devoted to affirming God's greatness, power, and omniscience.

This raises a deep but simple question: what is the need for God to be worshiped and praised? If God is truly omnipotent, omniscient, and self-sufficient, then He would not require validation, adoration, or emotional reinforcement from His creations. The concept of a being who demands constant recognition and submission—despite already being surrounded by countless entities that worship Him—suggests a paradox. Why would a perfect, all-knowing deity need praise from imperfect beings?

One possible interpretation is that worship serves the worshiper more than the worshiped—that it's a tool for spiritual discipline, humility, and moral alignment. Yet, the framing in religious texts often implies that God's favor or wrath hinges on whether humans comply with this demand. If all of creation already praises Him, and He is beyond need, then the insistence on human worship seems less about divine necessity and more about theological control.

Ultimately, the question challenges us to reconsider whether divine worship is truly for God—or for the institutions and narratives that have been built around Him.

Conclusion: Considering the Holy text, the entity God comes across as very self-centric, someone who only wants others to praise him and beg Him for forgiveness	Please rate this Conclusion:

Objective Analysis of God

Question: Flaws in God's Creations - Humans	**G12**

Analysis and background:

Human birth is often accompanied by a broad spectrum of physical and mental conditions, some of which significantly impair an individual's ability to comprehend, communicate, or engage with abstract concepts, such as religion. Mental disorders such as severe ADHD, autism spectrum disorder, or intellectual disabilities can limit a person's capacity to understand religious teachings, participate in rituals, or make moral decisions in the way religious frameworks typically demand. This reality raises a profound theological question: why would an all-powerful, all-knowing God create individuals with such limitations if the ultimate goal is to test them or reward their worship?

Religious believers often respond by saying that these individuals are part of a divine test—not for themselves, but for their caretakers or parents. Yet this explanation seems ethically and logically strained. If God truly possesses infinite wisdom and creativity, why would He choose to inflict lifelong suffering on one person merely to test another? Surely, an omniscient deity could devise countless other ways to challenge human compassion and responsibility without condemning someone to a life of pain, isolation, or cognitive impairment.

Moreover, if religious salvation hinges on understanding & worship, then individuals with mental disabilities are excluded from the very system that claims to be universal and just. They cannot praise, repent, or choose belief—yet they are still subject to the same existential framework. This contradiction raises questions about the coherence of divine justice. It suggests that either the system is flawed or that the narrative of purposeful creation & testing is a human construct struggling to explain the complexities of real life.

Conclusion: All-capable and all-powerful God cannot make humans with mental deficiencies, considering the object of creating humans is to test them, and the object of creating the universe is to put humans to the test.	Please rate this Conclusion:

Section 3 – Religions
General Question from Believers

Question:
Flaws in God's Creations - Animals

G13

Analysis and background:
When non-believers raise the issue of birth defects and suffering in humans, religious adherents often respond by framing these conditions as a divine test—intended for the individual, their caretakers, or society at large. However, this explanation quickly falters when extended to the animal kingdom. Animals, unlike humans, are not considered moral agents in religious doctrine. They are not subject to divine commandments, nor are they promised rewards or punishments in an afterlife. Yet, they too experience immense suffering: congenital deformities, predation, starvation, and disease. If animals are not being tested, then what purpose does their pain serve in a universe supposedly governed by a merciful and omnipotent God?

This contradiction becomes even more glaring when we consider the nature of these flaws. The randomness and frequency of biological defects—both in humans and animals—mirror the imperfections of a human-designed system, like a factory prone to errors. But if God is all-powerful and all-knowing, why would such flaws be so common in His creation? Why would a perfect designer allow for such widespread and seemingly purposeless suffering?

The presence of these flaws challenges the coherence of religious claims about divine perfection and intentionality. Either no deity is overseeing the intricate workings of life, or the God described in religious texts is not as omnipotent and benevolent as claimed. The evidence points toward a universe shaped by natural processes—evolution, chance, and entropy—rather than one meticulously managed by a flawless divine being. This invites a reevaluation of theological assumptions in light of observable reality.

Conclusion:
By-birth flaws in animals do not align with any God's merciful nature and overall divine intent.

Please rate this Conclusion:

Objective Analysis of God

Question: God vs devil /Satan	**G14**

Analysis and background:

The narrative of God taking a stand against Satan raises profound theological contradictions when examined closely. According to religious texts, God is all-powerful, all-knowing, and the creator of everything—humans, angels, jinn, and the vast universe itself. Among these creations is Satan, a jinn, one of countless beings brought into existence by God. Yet, despite this divine supremacy, the story unfolds as a cosmic struggle between God and Satan, with Satan positioned as a persistent adversary. This premise alone challenges the logic of omnipotence: why would an all-powerful deity need to oppose a being He created and could eliminate at will?

The contradiction deepens when we consider the outcomes described in scripture. Both the Bible and the Quran suggest that the majority of humanity will ultimately be led astray and end up in Hell. Verses such as Matthew 7:13–14, Luke 13:23–24, and Matthew 22:14 in the Bible, as well as Quranic passages like 7:179, 32:13, 56:7–14, and 11:119, all point to a grim conclusion: most people will fail the divine test. If Satan's role is to misguide, and he succeeds in doing so for the majority, then by the logic of the narrative, Satan is winning—and fulfilling the very function he was allowed to play.

This raises unsettling questions: Is Satan truly an enemy, or an instrument of divine design? If God knew the outcome from the beginning, why create a system where suffering and damnation are the default for most? The story, when stripped of its theological framing, appears less like a battle of good versus evil and more like a paradoxical drama authored by the very being who claims to oppose its antagonist.

God is demanding Humans to take a stand against Satan, but with all his power, He did not do it by himself ??????

Conclusion: This confrontation between God and Devil/Satan seems illogical, considering the stature of both, as told by religion.	Please rate this Conclusion:

Section 3 – Religions
General Question from Believers

Question:
Devil, Satan, Iblees - will go to Heaven

G15

Analysis and background:

The story of Adam and the Devil, central to both Christianity and Islam, presents a series of theological paradoxes that challenge conventional religious narratives. According to scripture, God created the universe as a testing ground for humans, with the Devil—also known as Satan—serving as the primary agent of misguidance. Yet, if God is truly omniscient and omnipotent, then the Devil's role was neither accidental nor rebellious in the ultimate sense—it was foreseen, permitted, and arguably essential to the divine plan.

This leads to a provocative implication: without Satan's influence, there would be no meaningful test, no moral struggle, and thus no need for heaven or hell. In this framework, Satan is not merely a rogue antagonist but a necessary component of the system God designed. His actions, while portrayed as evil, are instrumental in fulfilling the very purpose for which the universe was created. If Satan had refused to mislead, the entire structure of divine judgment would collapse.

Such reasoning raises further questions about divine justice and consistency. If Satan is fulfilling a role that aligns with God's expectations—however dark that role may be—then is he truly condemned? Or is he, paradoxically, a servant of divine will? This opens the door to the unsettling possibility that Satan, having played his part in the cosmic drama, could be entitled to the same divine rewards promised to obedient agents. Upon close examination, the narrative blurs the lines between villainy and holy purpose, necessitating a reevaluation of theological assumptions regarding good and evil, as well as the nature of divine intent.

Conclusion:
Considering the above, Devil /Satan should be given Heaven as the reward for making God's efforts worthwhile.

Please rate this Conclusion:

Objective Analysis of God

Question: God is missing the central teaching	G16

Analysis and background:
The foundational premise of the relationship between God and humans, as presented in religious doctrine, is that God seeks to guide humanity—teaching people how to live, what moral standards to uphold, and ultimately preparing them for judgment in the afterlife. This relationship is framed as a divine test, where obedience leads to reward and disobedience results in punishment. However, when we examine the content of the holy texts said to originate from God—namely, the Bible and the Quran—a striking contradiction emerges.

If the primary purpose of creation is to test humans, one would expect these scriptures to be rich in precise, detailed instructions outlining what is expected of them. Yet, only a small fraction—estimated between 5% to 15%—of these texts directly address human conduct and obligations. In contrast, a disproportionately large portion, often 30% or more, is devoted to praising God, recounting historical narratives, and emphasizing His power, mercy, and greatness.

This imbalance raises a critical question: if the divine objective is to test human behavior, why are the guidelines so sparse and indirect? Instead of offering comprehensive moral and behavioral frameworks, the texts often rely on parables, symbolic language, and fragmented commandments. As a result, religious leaders and scholars are left to interpret, expand, and codify the remaining 85–95% of doctrine—effectively constructing the practical religion that followers adhere to.

This disconnect between stated divine purpose and scriptural content suggests either a misalignment in the transmission of divine intent or a human-centered reinterpretation of religious texts to fill in the gaps left by vague or incomplete guidance.

Conclusion:
If God wants humans to follow a path, logically, He should have included it in His main text and not have it mediated (by saints and Imams) to explain it.

Please rate this Conclusion:

Section 3 – Religions
General Question from Believers

Question: Even less Morals and Ethics	**G17**

Analysis and background:
It is widely observed that moral and ethical teachings make up only a small fraction—roughly 5%—of the total content in sacred texts such as the Bible and the Quran. Yet, these basic principles, including treating others with respect, refraining from theft, and upholding justice, are universally recognized as the core values upon which human society can exist, even before the emergence of these religions. Religious life is meant to be built. If God intended to guide humanity toward righteous living and ultimately judge them based on their moral conduct, then one would expect these teachings to be presented with clarity, depth, and consistency.

Instead, the bulk of religious scripture is devoted to historical narratives, divine self-praise, and metaphysical assertions, while the practical guidance for daily life is sparse and often ambiguous. Crucially, the responsibility for interpreting these limited moral instructions has been left to religious scholars and leaders who emerged centuries after the prophets. Their interpretations vary widely, resulting in conflicting doctrines, sectarian divisions, and ongoing theological disputes that persist to this day.

If this fragmented and indirect method of communication is indeed God's chosen approach, it raises a troubling implication: that confusion is part of the design. And if confusion is divinely intended, then how can humans be held fully accountable for failing to follow a path that was never clearly laid out? The burden of understanding falls on fallible minds interpreting ancient texts through cultural and historical filters. In such a system, the line between divine guidance and human invention becomes blurred, raising questions about the fairness of divine judgment itself.

Conclusion: God's revelation of His true path and guidance to humans falls short of His intentions and plans.	**Please rate this Conclusion:**

My-OAG.com

Objective Analysis of God

Question: Human moral values	**G18**

Analysis and background:
As explored earlier, moral values did not originate from divine revelation but emerged organically through human social development. When early humans began living in groups, they quickly recognized the need for cooperation, mutual respect, and shared norms to ensure survival and harmony. These understandings—such as fairness, empathy, and reciprocity—formed the foundation of moral values, which have continued to evolve alongside human civilization.

Religions later adopted and codified many of these values, often retrofitting them into theological frameworks. However, because human societies shaped these moral systems, they also carried the biases, inequalities, and power structures of their time. This is evident in religious endorsements of practices like slavery and the subjugation of women—norms that served the interests of the powerful and were later sanctified as divine will. Such contradictions between religious teachings and ethical principles highlight the human origins of these moral codes.

A compelling example is the Code of Hammurabi, a set of 282 laws created around 1750 BCE in ancient Mesopotamia. These laws addressed justice, property rights, and social order long before the emergence of Abrahamic religions, demonstrating that structured moral systems existed independently of divine instruction. Similarly, the evolution of traffic laws in modern society illustrates how moral and practical norms continue to develop through human reasoning and collective need.

These examples underscore that morality is a human construct—adaptive, imperfect, and constantly refined—not a fixed set of divine commands. Religion may have preserved and propagated specific values, but it did not invent them.

Conclusion: If all moral values originate from God, they can't have flaws, and they remain constant over time. Like, why was slavery good earlier, not so good later on, as per religious institutions	Please rate this Conclusion:

Section 3 – Religions
General Question from Believers

Question:
God designed the Cruel world of animals

G19

Analysis and background:
The natural world is filled with scenes of cruelty and suffering, particularly among animal beings that, according to religious doctrine, are not subject to divine testing, judgment, or reward in the afterlife. Yet they exist within a system that is said to be designed and sustained by an all-powerful, all-loving God. This raises a troubling contradiction: if animals are not moral agents and are excluded from spiritual accountability, why are they subjected to such brutal conditions?

Carnivorous animals, by design, must kill and consume other creatures to survive. This includes acts that, from a human perspective, are deeply disturbing—such as predators tearing apart the young of prey species in front of their parents. In many cases, animal parents risk their own lives to protect their offspring, only to witness them being violently killed. These events are not rare; they occur in millions of locations worldwide every second. And yet, this system is said to be divinely crafted and maintained.

If God is truly all-loving and all-capable, why would such a system be necessary? Why would survival depend on suffering, and why would empathy and parental instinct be built into animals only to be rendered futile? Carnivores are not cruel by choice—they are cruel by necessity. The design itself demands it.

This reality challenges the coherence of the theological claim that a benevolent and omnipotent deity governs the universe. If suffering is embedded into the very fabric of life, and no spiritual purpose is assigned to those who endure it, then the system appears indifferent at best—or deeply flawed.

Conclusion:
An all-loving and all-capable God will not design a system as cruel and unjust in the animal kingdom.

Please rate this Conclusion:

Objective Analysis of God

| Question: Why Intermediaries and not direct communications | G20 |

Analysis and background:
Religions worldwide rely heavily on intermediaries—such as saints, priests, mullahs, imams, and other spiritual authorities—to interpret and communicate the supposed will of God. These figures serve as the gatekeepers of divine knowledge, translating ancient texts and shaping doctrine for the masses. Yet, a closer examination of the holy books reveals a striking deficiency: they contain limited practical guidance on how to live daily life and are riddled with contradictions. This leaves interpretive gaps, which religious leaders fill with their own perspectives and agendas.

In effect, these intermediaries wield enormous influence. Their interpretations—often subjective & unregulated—become the basis for religious law, ritual, and belief. Over time, countless practices have been added to religious traditions that were never part of the original scriptures. This fluidity allows religion to evolve, but it also opens the door to manipulation, confusion, and division.

Many of these religious authorities claim a direct or indirect connection to God, presenting themselves as chosen vessels of divine insight. Yet, in reality, most are products of indoctrination—individuals shaped by centuries of theological conditioning rather than objective understanding. Their authority is not derived from divine clarity but from institutional power & inherited belief systems.

This structure ultimately serves the religious establishment, preserving its dominance over general followers. By controlling interpretation and ritual, religious institutions maintain a monopoly on spiritual truth, discouraging independent thought and reinforcing obedience. The result is a system where divine communication is filtered through human agendas, often obscuring the very message it claims to uphold.

And it all stems from the Holy Text and its inabilities.

| **Conclusion:** A capable God cannot just leave the whole system in the hands of ordinary humans, who have been committing atrocities in the name of religion and God, and even then, there is no check and punishment from God. | Please rate this Conclusion: |

Section 3 – Religions
General Question from Believers

Question: Aggression against other religious beliefs	**G21**

Analysis and background:
Religious doctrines across major faiths share a striking commonality: a strong resistance to apostasy, or the act of leaving one's religion. Historically, religious institutions have enforced severe consequences for those who abandon their faith, ranging from social ostracism to threats of death. In many cases, these punishments were not just cultural but were justified as divine mandates, promoted by religious leaders in the name of God. Apostasy was seen not merely as a personal choice but as a betrayal of divine truth—an offense warranting the harshest retribution.

At the same time, these doctrines promise extraordinary rewards to those who remain faithful until death. Eternal paradise, divine favor, and spiritual elevation are offered as incentives for unwavering belief. This dual structure—punishment for leaving and reward for staying—creates a powerful mechanism of control, discouraging doubt and dissent.

While modern societies have seen some relaxation of these rigid stances, especially in more secular or pluralistic environments, this shift is primarily due to the rise of critical thinking and increased access to knowledge. As people began to question inherited beliefs and explore alternative worldviews, the grip of religious authority began to weaken.

Islamic texts, like Quran 3:86–90, describe apostates as cursed by Allah, angels, and all people, destined to remain in Hell eternally. Similarly, the Bible 6:4–6 that those who fall away are "crucifying the Son of God all over again" and subjecting Him to public disgrace. These verses reflect the resounding theological condemnation of apostasy, reinforcing the idea that faith must be preserved at all costs, even if that cost is the loss of free will.

Conclusion: On one side, God encourages people to explore and find the correct God, but on the other hand, God curses that same person. This contradicts God's intention to allow humans to make decisions using their free will.	**Please rate this Conclusion:**

Objective Analysis of God

Question: Sacrifices - Life or Money	**G22**

Analysis and background:
Religion often demands sacrifices from its followers—whether in the form of time, effort, or money. This expectation is deeply ingrained in religious practice, where adherents are taught to donate a portion of their earnings in the name of God. These offerings are framed as acts of devotion, meant to demonstrate faith and earn divine favor. However, the mechanics of this system reveal a more complex reality.

Religious institutions frequently request small tokens of money or material gifts, especially during visits to places of worship or participation in rituals. These contributions are often indirect—through the purchase of items such as candles, prayer beads, or offerings that are produced and sold by the spiritual leaders or affiliated groups within the Church, Mosque, Temple, or other religious centers. Although individually modest, these repeated donations reinforce an influential psychological association: that blessings and divine approval are linked to financial giving.

This dynamic subtly conditions followers to believe that spiritual rewards are transactional in nature. The more one gives, the more one is seen as faithful or deserving of divine grace. Yet, it is evident that none of these funds or sacrifices reach any divine entity. Instead, they are collected and managed by the religious authorities who oversee the institution. In practice, this system sustains the financial and social power of religious leadership, while cloaking it in the language of spiritual duty. The result is a structure where devotion is monetized, and faith becomes intertwined with economic exchange—raising questions about the true nature of sacrifice and the intentions behind institutionalized religion.

Conclusion: God, who created and manages the whole universe, would not be interested in small donations or money to favor His followers.	Please rate this Conclusion:

Question: Direct or indirect money	**G23**

Analysis and background:
Rituals form the backbone of religious practice across cultures and faiths, consistently emphasized by religious scholars as essential acts of devotion. These rituals—ranging from grand pilgrimages like the Hajj to routine worship services—often require significant financial and personal investment. Followers are expected to contribute through donations, travel expenses, lodging, ceremonial offerings, and time-consuming preparations. While these acts are framed as spiritual obligations, they also serve to sustain the infrastructure and influence of religious institutions.

The structure of these practices increasingly resembles a business model, where participation is not only encouraged but often portrayed as necessary for divine favor, spiritual cleansing, or communal belonging. This creates an inherent disparity: those with financial means can engage fully in these rituals. In contrast, others may be excluded or feel spiritually inadequate due to their inability to afford participation. The commercialization of religious experience—whether through fees, merchandise, or donation-based access—raises a critical concern about equity and authenticity in spiritual life.

This raises a deeper philosophical question: has access to spiritual rewards been monetized? Sacred texts across traditions emphasize inner faith, righteous deeds, and moral integrity as the true path to divine approval. Yet, the institutionalized rituals often suggest that material contributions are a gateway to favor or favoritism. If spiritual merit is tied to financial capacity, then the message of universal accessibility and divine justice becomes blurred. The tension between scripture and practice invites reflection on whether religion, in its institutional form, has drifted from its foundational principles toward a model shaped by economics and exclusivism.

Conclusion: A rational and just God should not ask his followers to come to a place and spend money to receive His favors and to remove their sins.	Please rate this Conclusion:

Objective Analysis of God

Question: Can a free man and a slave be equal	**G24**

Analysis and background:
Religions often proclaim universality—that their teachings are meant for all of humanity, regardless of background or status. Yet, when examined closely, many religious doctrines have historically reinforced social hierarchies and divisions, offering preferential treatment based on birth, class, or lineage. This contradiction is especially evident in the way Abrahamic religions have addressed slavery.

Rather than condemning slavery outright, both the Bible and the Quran acknowledge its existence and offer guidelines for its regulation. In the biblical texts, verses such as Ephesians 6:9, Colossians 4:1, and Philemon 1:16 speak to the treatment of slaves, urging masters to be fair—but never questioning the institution itself. Similarly, the Quran discusses slavery in the context of warfare and social norms of the time, with verses like 8:67–71, 47:4, and 2:177 outlining conditions under which slaves may be taken or freed.

This approach reflects the socio-economic realities of ancient civilizations, where slavery was deeply entrenched and provided essential labor for the elite. By accommodating these norms rather than challenging them, religious texts appear to have favored the interests of influential individuals—effectively legitimizing a system of exploitation. While some argue that these scriptures aimed to improve the conditions of slaves, the absence of a clear moral stance against slavery suggests tacit endorsement.

The broader implication is troubling: if divine guidance is meant to uplift all humans equally, why does it accommodate systems that inherently degrade and divide? This tension between proclaimed universality and historical inequality invites a deeper reexamination of religious ethics and their alignment with justice.

Conclusion: God, who created all humans as equal, cannot endorse and allow slavery to continue.	Please rate this Conclusion:

Section 3 – Religions
General Question from Believers

Question:
Politicians/Rulers and Religion

G25

Analysis and background:
Throughout history, religious leaders and political rulers have often formed powerful alliances to consolidate control over populations, particularly within Christian and Islamic societies. These collaborations were not merely coincidental—they were strategic, designed to intertwine spiritual authority with political power, creating systems where questioning one meant challenging both.

In Christian history, the fusion of church and state was most evident during the medieval period. The Catholic Church wielded immense influence over monarchs, often legitimizing their rule through divine sanction. In return, kings and emperors enforced religious orthodoxy, suppressing dissent through inquisitions, excommunications, and public punishments. The Church's endorsement of rulers gave them moral authority, while rulers protected the Church's wealth and dominance. This mutual reinforcement allowed both institutions to maintain control over education, law, and social norms.

Similarly, in Islamic history, caliphates and sultanates often relied on religious scholars (ulama) and clerics to justify their governance. The concept of sharia law became a tool not only for spiritual guidance but also for political enforcement. Religious leaders issued fatwas that aligned with the interests of rulers, while political authorities funded religious institutions and granted them judicial power. This alliance enabled the suppression of reformist voices and maintained rigid hierarchies that favored the elite.

In both traditions, the union of religious and political power created a climate where obedience was framed as piety, and dissent was viewed as heresy or rebellion. The result was centuries of control over thought, behavior, and belief—where faith was not just a personal journey, but a mechanism of institutional dominance.

Conclusion:
Rulers have long used religion to legitimize control, while religious institutions gain protection and privileges in return.

Please rate this Conclusion:

Objective Analysis of God

Question: The Great Flood – Whole World?	**G26**

Analysis and background:

The Great Flood during Noah's time covered the entire world, destroying all living things and leading to the reintroduction of the human race. Earth's water is finite and recycled, meaning the same water molecules have been present on the planet throughout its history. Even if all the water on Earth melted and entered the oceans,

Earth's water is finite, yet it is also replenished through recycling. The same water molecules that dinosaurs drank, filled ancient oceans, or fueled Roman aqueducts are still here today. So, today's water will be in similar quantities to that present at the time of Noah.

Now, let's assume that if all the Earth's ice melted, sea levels would rise approximately 70 meters (230 feet), drastically altering the planet's geography, particularly since humans often live near water sources. Those water sources would shift slightly inward, but the total land area would be reduced by only 10%.

Current Land Area: ~29% of Earth's surface (148 million km²).

Lost Land: Approximately 7–10% of the current land area (10–15 million km²) would be flooded, primarily in low-lying regions.

New Land Area: ~20–22% of Earth's surface (~102–114 million km²) would remain, concentrated in continental interiors and high-altitude regions.

https://www.nationalgeographic.com/magazine/article/rising-seas-ice-melt-new-shoreline-maps

https://earthscience.stackexchange.com/questions/14814/how-would-earth-map-look-like-if-all-ice-melts

https://www.youtube.com/watch?v=VbiRNT_gWUQ

How can a creator not know and see that?

Conclusion: It is impossible to cover all land area on earth with water, which we have currently (or at the time of Noah), so Noah's great flood for the whole world is only a story.	Please rate this Conclusion:

Section 3 – Religions
General Question from Believers

Question: The Great Flood – regeneration of humans.	**G27**

Analysis and background:
The story of Noah's flood, central to Abrahamic religions, claims that a divine deluge wiped out all land-based life on Earth, sparing only those aboard Noah's ark. According to this narrative, humanity was meant to restart from the survivors who landed on Mount Ararat. However, historical and archaeological evidence present a different picture—one that challenges the global scope of this event.

Regions such as present-day China and India have long been among the most populous and culturally rich areas in the world. Civilizations such as the Indus Valley and early Chinese societies were thriving during the period traditionally associated with Noah's flood. These cultures have their own records of significant floods, but none suggest a complete annihilation of life. Instead, they document natural disasters and their responses—often leading to advancements in water management and agriculture. For example, ancient Chinese societies developed sophisticated irrigation systems, reflecting a practical and adaptive approach to recurring floods.

Moreover, global flood myths are not exclusive to the Bible. Similar stories appear in Sumerian, Greek, and Hindu traditions, each rooted in regional experiences of natural catastrophes. These myths likely originated from collective memories of post-Ice Age flooding, when the melting of glaciers caused sea levels to rise and reshape landscapes worldwide.

Given this broader context, the Noah story appears less as a literal historical account and more as a theological narrative shaped by cultural and environmental experiences. While it holds symbolic meaning within religious frameworks, its claim of a global reset of humanity is not supported by historical evidence or the continuity of ancient civilizations outside the Middle East.

Conclusion: The great flood, as described in the holy texts, could not have happened. The great flood only occurs in a limited space and does not affect all humans.	Please rate this Conclusion:

Objective Analysis of God

Question: Disobedience → disappointment → Punishment	**G28**

Analysis and background:
Genesis 6:6–7: *"The LORD regretted that He had made human beings on the earth, and His heart was deeply troubled. So the LORD said, 'I will wipe from the face of the earth the human race I have created...'"*

This passage suggests a profound emotional response from God—regret and sorrow over humanity's corruption. It implies that despite His omniscience, God experienced disappointment, prompting a drastic act of judgment: the Great Flood.
In the Quran, a similar flood narrative unfolds, though the language differs. Allah does not express regret; instead, the emphasis is on divine justice and the consequences of disobedience. Both texts agree that humanity's refusal to follow divine instruction led to punishment. Some interpretations even mention a race of "giants" whose wickedness contributed to divine wrath.

The flood, however, raises troubling ethical and theological questions. If God is all-knowing and all-powerful, why create beings destined to fail? Why respond with mass destruction, including the deaths of countless innocent animals? The command to Noah—to grow trees, build an ark, and gather select humans and animals—suggests a long, deliberate process. Could a more merciful or constructive solution not have been devised?

While the Quran avoids the term "regret," the outcomes in both scriptures are nearly identical. This leads to a deeper inquiry: can an omniscient God truly regret? If He knew the outcome from the beginning, then regret implies a change of heart—something incompatible with divine perfection. The tension between justice, foreknowledge, and emotional response remains unresolved.

Conclusion: Experiencing disappointment implies that an all-knowing God did not foresee the outcome.	Please rate this Conclusion:

Section 3 – Religions
General Question from Believers

Question: The Great Flood – big ships existed at that time	**G29**

Analysis and background:
The earliest archaeological evidence of large ships, dating from roughly 5,000 to 2,500 BCE, demonstrates that ancient civilizations were capable of constructing impressive river and coastal vessels. According to scripture, the Ark was approximately 450 feet / 140 meters long and featured three decks.

By the time Noah's Ark is said to have sailed (estimated between 3,000 and 2,300 BCE), shipbuilding had advanced enough to support regional trade and navigation. Civilizations such as the Egyptians, Mesopotamians, and the people of the Indus Valley were constructing sizable vessels for commerce and transportation. For example, the Abydos Boats of Egypt (~3,000 BCE), found near the tomb of Pharaoh Khasekhemwy, measured up to 82 feet / 25 meters and were likely used for ceremonial or riverine purposes. The Khufu Solar Ship (~2,500 BCE), a 140 feet / 43-meter-long cedarwood vessel buried near the Great Pyramid, showcases remarkable craftsmanship but was not seaworthy in the modern sense of the term.

Mesopotamian clay models from the Ubaid period (~5,000 BCE) depict large reed boats used for trade along rivers and coastal routes. Similarly, the dockyards at Lothal in the Indus Valley (c. 2500 BCE) suggest maritime trade with distant regions, such as Mesopotamia and Oman.

All those ancient ships—crafted by skilled civilizations in Egypt, Mesopotamia, and the Indus Valley—could have offered refuge to countless disobedient humans during the flood, had they been given the chance. Instead, the narrative centers solely on Noah's Ark, excluding the possibility that others might have survived through their own ingenuity. This omission underscores the symbolic nature of the story, where salvation is reserved not for capability, but for divine favor...

Conclusion: When Noah built the ark, there were hundreds of big ships in the world, and people in that region could have easily survived, making God's claim incorrect.	Please rate this Conclusion:

Objective Analysis of God

Question: Life on Noah's ark – time, size, and survival	**G30**

Analysis and background:
The story of Noah's Ark presents numerous logistical and biological challenges when examined through a rational lens. One major issue is the survival of animals during and after the flood. Even if we assume divine intervention allowed animals to suppress their hunger, it's challenging to imagine carnivores like lions resisting the urge to eat prey animals such as goats for many days. If God could perform such a miracle, one might ask why He didn't simply eliminate the non-righteous humans or giants directly, rather than orchestrating a global flood that also devastated innocent animal life.

Beyond behavior, the physical constraints of the Ark pose another problem. The sheer diversity of species—millions across the globe—could not realistically fit into a single vessel, regardless of its size. After the flood, repopulation would have taken decades or centuries, especially for species with low reproduction rates. During this time, carnivores would have had no sustainable food sources, and herbivores would have faced a barren landscape. A flood that lasted months would have destroyed most vegetation, leaving no immediate food supply for plant-eating animals.

Additionally, the current geographic distribution of species contradicts the idea of a single point of repopulation. Unique species, such as pandas in China or kangaroos in Australia, suggest continuous, localized evolution rather than a global reset. If all animals had perished except those on the Ark, how did such region-specific biodiversity reemerge?

Conclusion: Noah's story has many inconsistencies, which indicate that it is not factual.	Please rate this Conclusion:

Section 3 – Religions
General Question from Believers

Calculating the size required for Noah's Ark to hold "all animal species of that time" involves massive assumptions, as the biblical narrative (Genesis 6–9) lacks scientific specificity. Below is a simplified analysis based on hypothetical parameters:

Key Assumptions

Scope of "Animals": *Only land-dwelling vertebrates (mammals, birds, reptiles, amphibians) are included (no insects, fish, or marine life).*

"Species" are defined as modern taxonomic species, though some creationists argue for broader "kinds" (e.g., "dog kind" instead of individual dog breeds).

Time frame: *Assume the flood occurred ~4,300 years ago. This excludes extinct species (e.g., dinosaurs), unless you assume they coexisted with humans.*

Animal Volume: *The average animal size is sheep-sized. Juveniles are used to minimize space and food needs. Modern land vertebrates: ~35,000 species (mammals: 6,500, birds: 11,000, reptiles: 12,000, amphibians: 5,500). Pairs required: 2 of each, totaling 70,000 animals.*

Space Requirements": Average space per animal: A sheep occupies ~1 m^2 or 10 ft^3.

Final Answer:

So, 70,000 animals would need ~9 football/soccer fields of space. (70,000 X1 =70,000 m2 → 110x75(soccer field) x9 = 74,250 m2 This does not consider logistics, feeding needs, or behavior incompatibility.

Noah's ark should have a deck size of about nine soccer fields – now, even if we consider three floors, then it should have been as big as three soccer fields.

For comparison, today's largest ship in operation, in terms of deck area, is the "Pioneering Spirit" (382 x 124 m^2), which is approximately equivalent to 6.63 soccer fields.

Objective Analysis of God
Abrahamic Religions

Section 3 – Religions
Abrahamic Religions

Judaism

Judaism is one of the oldest monotheistic religions, with a rich and complex history spanning 3,000 years. Here's a brief overview of its historical development based on archaeological, biblical, and scholarly sources:

1. Origins (c. 2000–1200 BCE)
- Patriarchal Period: According to the Hebrew Bible, Judaism traces its roots to Abraham, who made a covenant with God (Yahweh) in the land of Canaan (modern-day Israel and Palestine). His descendants, Isaac and Jacob (later named Israel), became the ancestors of the Twelve Tribes of Israel.
- Exodus & Moses (c. 13th–12th century BCE): The biblical narrative describes the Israelites enslaved in Egypt before being freed by Moses, who received the Torah (including the Ten Commandments) at Mount Sinai. Scholars debate the historicity of the Exodus, but it remains a central aspect of Jewish identity.

2. Israelite Kingdoms (c. 1200–586 BCE)
- Settlement in Canaan: After wandering in the desert, the Israelites (led by Joshua) supposedly conquered Canaan (though archaeology suggests a more gradual settlement).
- United Monarchy (c. 1020–930 BCE): The Bible describes Saul, David, and Solomon ruling a United Kingdom of Israel, with Jerusalem as its capital (though evidence outside the Bible is limited).
- Divided Kingdoms (Israel & Judah): After Solomon's death, the kingdom split:
  - Northern Kingdom (Israel): Fell to the Assyrians (722 BCE).
  - Southern Kingdom (Judah): Survived until the Babylonian conquest (586 BCE), when the First Temple was destroyed and Jews were exiled to Babylon.

3. Babylonian Exile & Second Temple Period (586 BCE–70 CE)
- Babylonian Exile (586–538 BCE): Jews developed key religious practices (synagogues, Torah study) while in exile.
- Return & Second Temple (538 BCE–70 CE):
  - Persian Period (538–332 BCE): Jews returned under Cyrus the Great and rebuilt the Second Temple.

Objective Analysis of God

- - Hellenistic Period (332–63 BCE): Greek rule led to cultural clashes (Maccabean Revolt, 167–160 BCE → Hanukkah).
  - Roman Period (63 BCE–70 CE): Rome took control; Jewish revolts (e.g., Great Revolt, 66–73 CE) led to the destruction of the Second Temple (70 CE).

4. Rabbinic Judaism (70–600 CE)
- After the Temple's destruction, Pharisees (precursors to rabbis) reshaped Judaism:
  - Oral Torah compiled into the Mishnah (c. 200 CE).
  - Talmud (Jerusalem, c. 400 CE; Babylonian, c. 500 CE) became a central text.
- Diaspora: Jews spread across the Roman Empire, Persia, and beyond.

5. Medieval Judaism (600–1700 CE)
- Islamic & Christian Worlds: Jews lived under Muslim rule (Golden Age in Spain, 900–1200s) or faced persecution in Christian Europe (Crusades, Inquisition, expulsions).
- Kabbalah (Jewish mysticism) emerged (e.g., Zohar, 13th century).
- Ashkenazi & Sephardi traditions developed.

6. Modern Judaism (1700–Present)
- Emancipation & Enlightenment (Haskalah): Jews gained European rights but faced assimilation pressures.
- Reform, Orthodox, Conservative, & Other Movements emerged in the 1800s.
- Zionism (late 1800s): Movement for Jewish return to Israel → State of Israel (1948).
- Holocaust (Shoah, 1939–1945): Nazi genocide killed 6 million Jews, reshaping global Jewry.

Key Historical Facts:
- First monotheistic religion (influenced Christianity & Islam).
- No centralized authority after Temple destruction → rabbis guided practice.
- Diaspora led to diverse Jewish communities (Mizrahi, Ashkenazi, Sephardi, etc.).

Judaism:

Although Judaism is the main religion that provided the basis for Christianity and Islam, I will not critically analyze it separately for the following reason:
- Its central holy scripture is part of the Bible (the first five books of the Bible), and I will be analyzing it along with the Bible (and I am only critically analyzing the main holy text of each religion)
- In today's world, its followers are minimal, and there is no reason it can be a major religion in terms of the number of followers
- We do not have an authentic history of the initial days of Judaism; all we have is what is recorded in the Bible and the Quran. So, by evaluating the Bible and the Quran, we can determine Judaism as well

Section 4

Christianity

Section 4 – Christianity

Christianity

My Argument:

Here, I will argue the following main points:
- Christianity was the brainchild and necessity of the Roman Empire at that time
- The Bible (New Testament portion) is not God's spoken/delivered message, but a completely human-made text, and can be proven by The Bible itself
- The concept of the Trinity in itself deviates from Monoletheism and was created to accommodate the idea of Jesus as the Son of God
- Whole Christianity is standing on very weak grounds in terms of historical facts, holy scripture, and logical build-up, with no direct and strong connection with Jesus, the prophet or Son of God

The Bible consists of two main parts: the Old Testament (also known as the Torah or the Hebrew Bible) and the New Testament. The Old Testament was already in existence and followed by the Jews, meaning it is not a new "message" from God. The New Testament, however, can be considered a new message for the Christian religion, as it was communicated to the followers of this new faith. Therefore, I will treat the Old and New Testaments separately.

> *Christianity rests on extremely shaky and weak ground among the three major religions considered to originate from God. This assessment considers several factors: its historical development, formalized only about 300 years after Jesus; the authenticity of its holy texts, with roughly half of the New Testament written by authors who never knew Jesus; and its connection to the preceding religion, Judaism, while carrying the serious theological complication of the Trinity, which challenges monotheism.*

Christianity - Main concepts:

Main concepts and teachings:

Objective Analysis of God

Christianity is one of the world's largest religions, centred on the life, teachings, death, and resurrection of Jesus Christ. Its core beliefs and teachings are derived from the Bible, particularly the New Testament. Here are the main concepts and teachings of Christianity:

1. God

- **Monotheism**: Christians believe in one God, the creator and sustainer of the universe.
- **Trinity**: God is understood as three distinct entities or persons in one: the Father, the Son (Jesus Christ), and the Holy Spirit. The Trinity is a Christian doctrine that describes God as three distinct entities—God the Father, God the Son (Jesus Christ), and God the Holy Spirit—one in essence. It is the cornerstone of modern Christianity - the Trinity teaches that God is one and three simultaneously (one essence but three distinct entities). This is known as the Trinity. This is a strange concept, considering it to be Monoletheism, and we will explore it

2. Jesus Christ

- **Incarnation**: Jesus is believed to be the Son of God and the Messiah (Christ) prophesied in the Old Testament. He is both fully divine and fully human.
- **Teachings**: Jesus emphasizes love, forgiveness, humility, and service to others. Key teachings include the Sermon on the Mount (Matthew 5-7) and the Great Commandment (to love God and love your neighbor).
- **Death and Resurrection**: Jesus was crucified, died, and rose from the dead on the third day. His resurrection is central to Christian faith, symbolizing victory over sin and death.

3. Salvation

- **Sin**: Humanity is born with original sin (inherited from Adam and Eve) and is separated from God due to sin.
- **Grace**: Salvation is a gift from God, received mainly through faith in Jesus Christ, not by works/deeds performed on earth (Ephesians 2:8-9). We will explore some contradictory verses from the Bible.
- **Atonement**: Jesus' death on the cross atoned for humanity's sins, reconciling people with God.
- **Eternal Life**: Believers are promised eternal life with God in heaven.

4. The Bible
- **Sacred Scripture**: The Bible is the "inspired" Word of God, consisting of the Old Testament (Hebrew Scriptures – revelation to Moses – 5 books) and the New Testament (life and teachings of Jesus and the early church). Please note the word "inspired" here; we will discuss it.
- **Authority**: It is the ultimate authority for Christian faith and practice.

5. The Church
- **Body of Christ**: The church is the community of believers, described as the body of Christ (1 Corinthians 12:27).
- **Sacraments**: Baptism and Communion (Eucharist) are central to Christian worship and symbolize spiritual truths.
- **Mission**: The church is called to spread the Gospel (good news of Jesus) and serve others.

6. Ethics and Morality
- **Love and Compassion**: Jesus taught love for God and neighbour, including enemies (Matthew 22:37-39, Matthew 5:44).
- **The Ten Commandments**: These provide moral guidelines, such as honouring God, respecting life, and practicing honesty. They are a continuity of Judaism and will be the subject of our discussion.
- **Social Justice**: Christians are called to care for the poor, oppressed, and marginalized (James 1:27, Matthew 25:35-40).

7. Eschatology (End Times)
- **Second Coming**: Christians believe Jesus will return to judge the living and the dead and establish God's kingdom fully.
- **Heaven and Hell**: Eternal life with God in heaven is promised to believers, while separation from God (hell) is the consequence of rejecting salvation.

8. Key Practices
- **Prayer**: Communication with God, both individually and collectively.
- **Worship**: Gathering to praise God, often through singing, prayer, and preaching.
- **Service**: Helping others through acts of charity and justice.

Objective Analysis of God

Christianity's core teachings center on the nature of God, the redemptive work of Jesus Christ, and the call to live a life of love, faith, and service. Its emphasis on grace, salvation, and eternal life offers hope and guidance to millions of believers worldwide.

History before Christianity

The religious landscape of the ancient Mediterranean was shaped by the Greeks and Romans, with Judaism coexisting as an early monotheistic faith alongside them. Christianity later emerged as a radical departure from both of these. Let's explore the distinctions between Greek and Roman religion, the role of Judaism, the persecution of early Christians, and the factors that led to Christianity's eventual dominance in the Roman Empire.

Geographic Differences: Greece was a collection of independent city-states with localized religious variations, while Rome expanded into a vast empire, systematizing the religions of conquered peoples.

Cultural Distinctions: Greek religion was characterized by its mythological elements and philosophical influences, with oracles and festivals playing a central role in religious life. Roman religion was state-centered and practical, adopting foreign gods and blending religion with political loyalty through the imperial cult.

Historical Development: Greek religion was decentralized, with each city-state having its patron deity. Roman religion became a tool of state control, with the Pontifex Maximus overseeing official rites.

Law and Philosophy: Greece had no unified legal code, and dominated abstract philosophy with great names like Socrates, Plato, and Aristotle. At the same time, Rome developed civil law, which underpins modern Europe, and focused on practical ethics, as contributed by Cicero and Seneca.

Judaism: A Monotheistic Counterpoint
Judaism stood apart from Greco-Roman polytheism with its strict monotheism, covenantal theology, and emphasis on ethical law. Originating among the ancient Hebrews, Judaism's key elements included the Torah, the Temple in Jerusalem, and synagogues.

Under Roman rule, Jews were granted religious tolerance but faced periodic repression due to their refusal to participate in emperor worship. Significant events included the Maccabean Revolt and the destruction of the Second Temple.

Christianity: Persecution and Rise to Power
Christianity emerged as a Jewish messianic movement centered on Jesus of Nazareth, who was crucified under the Roman governor Pontius Pilate. His followers disseminated his teachings across the empire, sparking conflict with Roman authorities. Christians were persecuted for rejecting Roman gods and emperor worship, arousing suspicions of conspiracy, and being scapegoated for disasters.

Why Did Christianity Spread Despite Persecution?
Several factors contributed to Christianity's rapid growth:
- **Inclusive Message and Universal Appeal**: Christianity offered salvation to all, spreading through Paul's missionary journeys.
- **Strong Community Networks**: Early Christians formed tight-knit communities that provided charity and support.
- **Roman Infrastructure**: The Pax Romana and extensive roads allowed missionaries to travel safely, with Greek as the common language.
- **Decline of Traditional Roman Religion**: Many Romans turned to mystery cults and philosophy, while Christianity offered a personal relationship with God.
- **Imperial Support Under Constantine**: Emperor Constantine's conversion and the Edict of Milan legalized Christianity, with the Council of Nicaea unifying Christian doctrine.

Conclusion
Greek religion was rich in myths and city-focused, while Roman religion was pragmatic and served the empire. Judaism maintained its monotheistic identity under foreign rule, surviving despite periodic repression. Christianity, emerging from this complex religious landscape, faced brutal persecution but ultimately triumphed through its inclusive message, strong communities, and strategic use of Roman infrastructure and the Romans' needs. With Constantine's endorsement, Christianity transitioned from a persecuted sect to the empire's dominant faith, reshaping Western civilization and, at the same time, making it easier for the Roman emperor to manage and control his vast kingdom. The interplay of these religious traditions highlights one of history's most profound

cultural transformations—the shift from pagan diversity to Christian unity in the ancient Mediterranean world.

While both Greek and Roman civilizations influenced Christianity, the Roman Empire had the most profound impact on the development of the Christian faith. The Roman Empire's infrastructure, legal system, and eventual imperial support under Constantine were crucial to the spread and establishment of Christianity as the state religion of the Roman Empire.

> *As discussed later, Roman authorities leveraged the power of religion to enforce their rule, especially as traditional Roman faiths were in decline. Furthermore, the vast conquered empire encompassed diverse religious practices and regulations, which complicated the enforcement of uniform laws.*

The synthesis of Roman governance with Christian doctrine created enduring institutions that shaped Western civilization.

Christianity - History

There is a significant gap between when Jesus was crucified and when Christianity became an established religion; this considerable period spans approximately 300 Years. During those 300 years, Christian leaders tried to propagate the teachings of Jesus. Still, there was no holy scripture, "The Bible," no organized and consolidated message on Christianity, no concept of Christianity or Trinity, etc. So, effectively, there was no Christianity, but only the teachings of Jesus spread using oral or "unofficial" written codes. This is a crucial fact. For 300 years, the teachings and descriptions of Jesus' sayings and incidents were communicated through oral and written letters and documents, primarily as a means of communication between Christian leaders of that time.

> *For 300 years, we can say that the New Testament—"the words of God"—was kept "alive" while playing the Chinese Whispers / Telephone game. The result expected will also be similar to what is expected at the end of the game.*

The words "Christianity" or "Trinity" are not mentioned in the Bible once. The word "Christian" appears three times in Acts 11:26, Acts 26:28, and 1 Peter 4:16, referring to its followers, which is how this religion is known as "Christianity." We will explore it further.

Below is an overview of how Christianity has changed and adopted influences over time:

1. Spreading Jesus Message (1st & 2nd Century CE):

- **Origins in Judaism:** Christianity emerged within a Jewish context in the 1st century CE in the Roman province of Judea. Jesus of Nazareth, whom Christians regard as the Son of God and Messiah, preached a message of love, repentance, forgiveness, and the coming of the Kingdom of God.
- **The Apostles and Early Christianity:** After Jesus' crucifixion and believed resurrection, his followers (the Apostles) spread his teachings throughout the Roman Empire. Early Christians were predominantly Jewish, but over time, the movement grew to include Gentiles (non-Jews).
- **The teachings of Paul of Tarsus** (one of the most influential figures in early Christianity) were instrumental in spreading Christianity beyond its Jewish roots. He emphasized faith in Jesus as the Christ (the Anointed One) and the importance of grace rather than adherence to the Mosaic Law.
- **Early Persecutions:** Christianity initially faced persecution by Roman authorities, who viewed the new religion as a threat to the established order. Despite this, Christianity continued to spread across the Roman Empire, primarily through the efforts of missionaries and the establishment of Christian communities.

2. The Early Church and Theological Development (3rd–5th Century CE):

- **The Roman Empire and Constantine:** In 313 CE, Emperor Constantine issued the Edict of Milan, granting religious tolerance to Christianity and marking the beginning of its shift from a persecuted minority religion to an officially recognized one. Constantine himself converted to Christianity, and in 380 CE, Emperor Theodosius I declared Christianity the official religion of the Roman Empire.

Objective Analysis of God

- **Bible formed**: The Bible, as we know it today, was "solidified" and "formalized" in part by the work of the First Council of Nicaea in 325 CE, though the whole canon of the New Testament was not universally agreed upon until later councils (like the Council of Carthage in 397 CE). By that account, we can say that the 300 years mentioned earlier, as the time it took to have the Bible, can be extended to 400 Years.
- **The Formation of Christian Doctrine:** During this period, the Bible was compiled, with the New Testament canon being formally established. Key Christian doctrines such as the Trinity (God as Father, Son, and Holy Spirit) and the Incarnation (Jesus as both fully divine and fully human) became central to Christian belief.

3. Medieval Christianity and the Rise of the Catholic Church (5th–15th Century):

- After the fall of the Western Roman Empire (476 CE), Christianity spread across Europe. The Papacy gained power, and monastic orders preserved knowledge and spread the faith. The Crusades (1096–1291) aimed to reclaim the Holy Land, while the Great Schism (1054 CE) divided Christianity into the Roman Catholic and Eastern Orthodox branches.

Protestant Reformation and Denominational Rise (16th Century):

- Martin Luther's 95 Theses (1517) sparked the Protestant Reformation, challenging Catholic practices and leading to denominations like Lutheranism, Calvinism, and Anglicanism. The Catholic Counter-Reformation, encompassing the Council of Trent (1545–1563), aimed at internal reform.

Colonialism and Global Spread (16th–19th Century):

- European colonial powers spread Christianity to the Americas, Africa, and Asia. Missionaries blended Christian teachings with local cultures, leading to syncretic forms of Christianity.

Christianity as used by the Roman Empire

The Roman Empire's relationship with Christianity evolved significantly over time, and in many ways, the adoption of Christianity helped the Roman emperors consolidate power and strengthen their rule.

Background:

After Alexander the Great's death in 323 BCE, the Roman Empire (then a republic) faced significant challenges as it expanded into the fragmented Hellenistic world. Key issues included:

1. **Fragmentation of Alexander's Empire**: His empire split into rival Hellenistic kingdoms (Ptolemaic, Seleucid, Antigonid), creating instability in the eastern Mediterranean. Rome clashed with these kingdoms, notably in the Macedonian Wars (214–148 BCE) and Syrian Wars (192–188 BCE).
2. **Piracy and Mediterranean Instability**: The collapse of centralized authority led to an increase in piracy, prompting Rome to secure its trade routes, as seen in Pompey's Pirate Wars (67 BCE).
3. **Internal Political Struggles**: Rome faced class conflicts (patricians vs. plebeians), highlighted by the Gracchi reforms (133–121 BCE) and the Social War (91–88 BCE), weakening its ability to handle external threats.
4. **Rise of Rival Powers**: Rome contended with the Parthian Empire in the east and Carthage in the west, leading to the Punic Wars (264–146 BCE), which drained resources.
5. **Cultural and Religious Shifts**: Hellenistic culture and foreign religions (e.g., cult of Isis) challenged Roman traditions, creating social tensions.
6. **Economic Strain**: Expansion brought wealth but also inflation, land disputes, and reliance on slave labour, disrupting local economies.
7. **Military Overextension**: Administering distant territories strained Rome's resources, making it vulnerable.
8. The adoption of Christianity under Emperor Constantine the Great (reigned 306–337 CE) was driven by challenges faced by the Roman Empire, both before and during his rule:

Challenges Before Constantine:

Objective Analysis of God

- **Political Instability**: The Crisis of the Third Century (235–284 CE) was marked by civil wars, invasions, and economic decline, which weakened the traditional Roman state religion.
- **Economic Decline**: Inflation, heavy taxation, and currency debasement caused widespread dissatisfaction, making traditional religion less appealing.
- **Military Threats**: Barbarian invasions and Persian attacks strained the empire, undermining faith in traditional gods.
- **Religious Pluralism**: Many turned to mystery religions and Eastern cults, while Christianity offered hope and salvation.

Challenges During Constantine's Reign:
- **Division of the Empire**: Constantine fought civil wars to reunite the empire, winning the Battle of the Milvian Bridge (312 CE) after a vision of the Christian Chi-Rho symbol.
- **Need for Unity**: Christianity's growing popularity and organization made it a unifying force for the empire's diverse populations.
- **Edict of Milan (313 CE)**: Constantine granted religious tolerance to Christians, thereby ending the persecution of Christians.
- **Council of Nicaea (325 CE)**: Constantine convened to resolve theological disputes, produce the Nicene Creed, and strengthen church unity.

We can say that Emperor Constantine's adoption of Christianity was a political move rather than a religious one. It unified diverse populations, offered moral and spiritual appeal, had organizational strength, and was seen as securing divine favour, as explained below. Facing political, economic, and military crises, Constantine adopted Christianity to unify the empire, legitimize his rule, and secure divine support, which ultimately led to its rise as the dominant religion in the Roman Empire. This provided both the Greek Empire and Christianity with great benefits.

The Mutual Benefits of Christianity and the Roman Empire

The rise of Christianity within the Roman Empire brought significant advantages to both the empire and the faith itself. Roman rulers strategically adopted and promoted Christianity to strengthen governance, unify diverse populations, and consolidate imperial authority. Below are key aspects of how Christianity was utilized to support Roman rule:

1. Unifying the Empire Under a Single Faith

Before Christianity, the Roman Empire was religiously fragmented, with a vast array of gods and cults worshipped across its territories. The shift to a monotheistic religion provided a cohesive spiritual framework, helping to bridge cultural and regional divides.
Roman emperors had long relied on the Imperial Cult to reinforce their divine status, but as Christianity gained influence, this practice waned. Instead, Christian doctrine was adapted to support centralized authority, with emperors like Constantine positioning themselves as both political and spiritual leaders. By aligning imperial rule with Christian teachings, the empire fostered a shared identity that strengthened its unity and cohesion.

2. Legalization and Imperial Protection of Christianity

A turning point came in 313 CE with the Edict of Milan, issued by Constantine and Licinius, which legalized Christianity and granted religious tolerance across the empire. This decree ended centuries of persecution, allowing Christians to worship openly.
Beyond mere tolerance, Constantine actively promoted Christianity by:
- Funding the construction of grand churches, such as Rome's original St. Peter's Basilica.
- Granting the Church land, wealth, and legal privileges.
- Integrating Christian leaders into the imperial administration.

These measures not only secured Christian support for the emperor but also established the Church as a key institution within the empire.

3. Christianity as a Tool for Social Control

Christian teachings emphasized moral values such as charity, obedience to authority, and the sanctity of family—principles that reinforced social stability. Roman rulers recognized the Church's potential to influence public behavior and utilized it to maintain social order.
Emperors like Constantine presented themselves as **God-appointed rulers**, blending political and religious authority. By associating

Objective Analysis of God

their reign with divine will, they strengthened their legitimacy and discouraged dissent. Over time, the Church became a vital partner in governance, helping to shape societal norms and reinforce imperial authority.

4. Managing Religious Disputes and Suppressing Rival Cults

Early Christianity was marked by theological divisions, such as the **Arian Controversy**, which threatened to fracture the faith. Roman emperors intervened in these disputes to prevent the development of destabilizing schisms.
Key actions included:
- Convening the Council of Nicaea (325 CE) to establish orthodox doctrine.
- Gradually suppressing pagan worship, culminating in Theodosius I's ban on pagan rituals (391 CE).

By endorsing an official version of Christianity and eliminating competing religions, emperors ensured that the Church remained a unifying force, rather than a divisive one.

5. Imperial Patronage and Christian Symbolism
Constantine's conversion marked a turning point in imperial policy. He actively promoted Christianity through:
- Adopting the Chi-Rho symbol and the cross as emblems of divine favor.
- Sponsoring Christian art and architecture to legitimize his rule.
- Aligning military victories with Christian providence.

Subsequent emperors followed this model, using Christian imagery and rhetoric to reinforce their authority. The Church, in turn, gained unprecedented influence, becoming deeply embedded in imperial governance.

6. The Establishment of a State Church
By the late 4th century, Christianity had become the official state religion under Theodosius I. The empire institutionalized the Church by:
- Granting bishops legal and financial privileges.
- Involving clergy in administrative functions.
- Elevating the Bishop of Rome (the Pope) as a key political and spiritual figure.

This merger of church and state ensured that Christianity remained a pillar of imperial authority long after Rome's political decline.

7. Christian Diplomacy and Barbarian Alliances
As the Western Roman Empire faced invasions from Germanic tribes, Christianity became a tool for diplomacy. Many barbarian groups, such as the Visigoths and Franks, converted to Christianity, easing their integration into Roman society.
Notable examples include:
- Clovis, King of the Franks, whose conversion strengthened ties with Rome.
- The use of Christian missionaries to spread Roman influence among barbarian nations.

These alliances helped preserve Roman cultural and religious dominance even as the empire began to fragment.

The Enduring Legacy of Christianity in the Roman Empire
Christianity played a pivotal role in shaping the late Roman Empire by:
- Providing a unifying religious identity.
- Reinforcing imperial authority through moral and theological legitimacy.
- Serving as a mechanism for social control and conflict resolution.
- Facilitating political alliances with neighboring tribes.

As the empire transitioned into a Christian state, the Church's power grew, ensuring that Christianity remained central to Europe's political and cultural development long after the fall of the Roman Empire. The symbiotic relationship between the Roman Empire and Christianity laid the foundation for the medieval world, where the Church would continue to wield immense influence.

Objective Analysis of God

In this work, I have used the following three names of sacred books interchangeably; ideally, they are distinct, and the differences are explained in more detail below. The reason for adopting this approach was that the scope of my work does not delve into the details of the differences between these three and encompasses various audiences.

These terms are often used interchangeably, but they carry distinct meanings depending on the religious tradition and context. Here's a clear breakdown:

1. **Tanakh**
   - **Jewish term** for the Hebrew Bible
   - Acronym for:
     - **T**orah (Law or Teaching)
     - **N**evi'im (Prophets)
     - **K**etuvim (Writings)
   - **Canonical order and emphasis** are specific to Jewish tradition
   - Written in **Hebrew and Aramaic**, preserved in the **Masoretic Text**
   - No New Testament—this is the complete Jewish Bible

2. **Hebrew Bible**
   - **Academic term** used to refer to the Tanakh in a neutral way
   - Avoids Christian framing like "Old Testament"
   - Used in **interfaith and scholarly settings** to discuss the shared scriptures without theological bias
   - Content is the same as the Tanakh, but the term is more inclusive and less religiously loaded

3. **Old Testament**
   - **Christian term** for the first part of the Christian Bible
   - Includes the same core books as the Tanakh, but:
     - **Different order** and **grouping**
     - **Additional books** in Catholic and Orthodox versions (e.g., Tobit, Maccabees, Wisdom of Solomon)
     - Often based on the **Greek Septuagint**, not the Hebrew Masoretic Text

Interpreted through a **Christological lens**, with many passages seen as foreshadowing Jesus.

Term	Tradition	Content	Language	Extras / Notes
Tanakh	Jewish	Torah, prophets' writings	Hebrew	Original Jewish canon
Hebrew Bible	Academic	Same as Tanakh	Hebrew	Neutral term for interfaith dialogue
Old Testament	Christaian	Similar Core, reordered	Greek / Hebrew	May include extra books (apocrypha)

Objective Analysis of God

Holy Books - Tanakh & Bible

Before we delve into the content of these books, let's consider a few historical facts about how and when these holy scriptures were created and formalized. I believe it is an important aspect to provide the basis for analyzing the contents, or I must say, the sayings and words of the Supreme, all-knowing and all-powerful God.

First: Bible (Old Testament + New Testament)

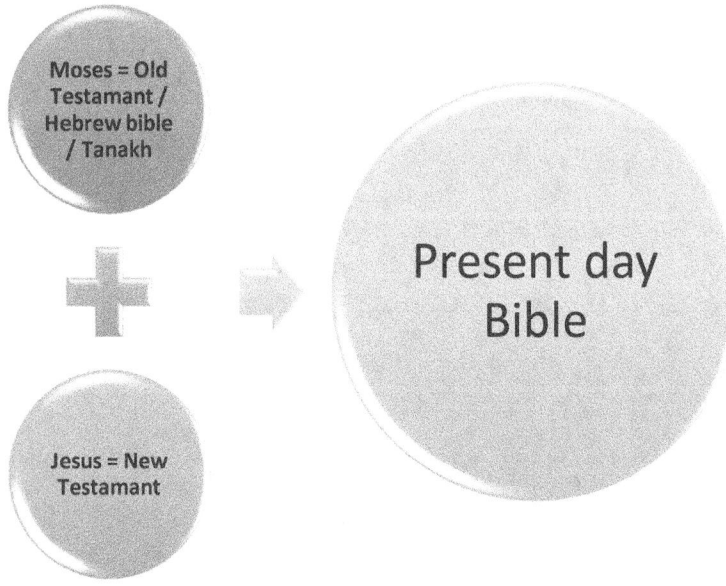

Tanakh - Old Testament or Hebrew bible
History:
The Old Testament, also known as the Tanakh, is the foundational text of Judaism, revealed to the Prophet Moses around 1200-1300 BC. It does not have a verifiable account of its origin; we will consider the following accounts and then analyze them. The Tanakh is the canonical collection of Jewish scriptures, which Christians refer to as the Old Testament. While the Tanakh and the Christian Old Testament share much of the duplicate content, their structures, groupings, and interpretations differ. Here's a breakdown:
The Tanakh is divided into three main sections and contains 24 books (though some are combined in Jewish tradition):
Torah ("Law" or "Instruction")
    1.   Genesis (Bereshit)

2. Exodus (Shemot)
3. Leviticus (Vayikra)
4. Numbers (Bamidbar)
5. Deuteronomy (Devarim)

Focus: Creation, the patriarchs, the Exodus, and the laws given to Israel.

Nevi'im ("Prophets")
1. Former Prophets: Joshua, Judges, Samuel (1–2), Kings (1–2).
2. Latter Prophets: Isaiah, Jeremiah, Ezekiel, and the Twelve Minor Prophets (Hosea, Joel, Amos, Obadiah, Jonah, Micah, Nahum, Habakkuk, Zephaniah, Haggai, Zechariah, Malachi).

Focus: The History of Israel and Prophetic Messages.

Ketuvim ("Writings")
- Psalms, Proverbs, Job, Song of Songs, Ruth, Lamentations, Ecclesiastes, Esther, Daniel, Ezra-Nehemiah (combined), Chronicles (1–2).

Focus: Poetry, wisdom literature, and historical reflections.

Total: 24 books (e.g., Samuel, Kings, Chronicles, Ezra-Nehemiah, and the Twelve Minor Prophets are each counted as one book in Jewish tradition).

It is debatable what constitutes the Old Testament, as different sects have their interpretations of the Old Testament (although there is general agreement on the 27 books of the New Testament), resulting in variations in the Bible's content among different Christian sects.

- Protestant: 39 (OT) + 27 (NT) = 66 books. - about 37% of the Christian Population
- Catholic: 46 (OT) + 27 (NT) = 73 books. – about 50%
- Orthodox: ~49–51 (OT) + 27 (NT) = 76–78 books. – about 12%

Scholars have extensively studied the origins of the Tanakh through textual criticism, archaeology, linguistics, and historical analysis. While absolute verification of every detail is impossible due to the ancient nature of the texts, we can utilize the following references to support their historical and literary development. Here's a breakdown of key findings:

1. Textual Evidence
- Dead Sea Scrolls (3rd century BCE–1st century CE): Discovered in the 1940s–50s, these manuscripts include

Objective Analysis of God

fragments of nearly every Old Testament book (except Esther). They demonstrate the remarkable preservation of the Hebrew text over time, though with minor variations.
- Septuagint (3rd–2nd century BCE): The Greek translation of the Hebrew Bible provides early textual evidence and shows how Jewish communities outside Palestine interpreted the texts.

The consistency between the Dead Sea Scrolls and later manuscripts lends credibility to the transmission process, though earlier oral or written sources are lost to time.

2. Archaeological Evidence
- Ancient Near Eastern Context: Many Old Testament events and customs align with archaeological findings from Mesopotamia, Egypt, and Canaan (e.g., the Code of Hammurabi parallels Mosaic Law, and the Merneptah Stele [1208 BCE] mentions "Israel" as a people in Canaan).
- City of David: Excavations in Jerusalem confirm the existence of a Judahite kingdom by the 10th–9th centuries BCE, though debates persist about the extent of David and Solomon's reigns.
- Babylonian Exile: Archaeological records (e.g., the Babylonian Chronicles) corroborate the conquest of Judah and the destruction of Jerusalem (586 BCE), aligning with accounts in 2 Kings and Jeremiah.

Some events (e.g., the Exodus) lack direct evidence, likely due to the perishable nature of records from nomadic or oppressed groups.

3. Literary and Historical Criticism
- Documentary Hypothesis: Scholars like Julius Wellhausen proposed that the Torah (Pentateuch) was compiled from multiple sources (J, E, D, P) between the 10th and 5th centuries BCE, reflecting evolving theological and political contexts.
- Prophetic Books: Texts like Isaiah and Amos reflect known historical crises (e.g., Assyrian and Babylonian invasions), though some prophecies may have been edited later.
- Royal Annals: Books like Kings cite lost sources (e.g., "the Book of the Annals of the Kings of Israel"), suggesting reliance on earlier records.

4. Linguistic Analysis

- Hebrew vocabulary, grammar, and writing styles in the Old Testament match other Northwest Semitic texts from the same period (e.g., the Moabite Mesha Stele).
- Aramaic influences in later books (e.g., Daniel) align with the post-exilic period (6th century BCE onward).

5. Challenges and Debates
- Patriarchs and Exodus: No direct evidence confirms Abraham or the Exodus as described, though some argue for a smaller-scale migration or oral traditions rooted in broader Semitic migrations.
- Conquest of Canaan: The Book of Joshua's account conflicts with archaeological evidence (e.g., Jericho was uninhabited at the time of its supposed fall). Some scholars suggest a gradual infiltration rather than a military conquest.
- Dating of Texts: Conservative scholars date parts of the Torah to Moses (~13th century BCE), while critical scholars argue for later compilation (e.g., during the Babylonian exile or Persian period).

The Old Testament's origins are partially verifiable through archaeology, textual analysis, and historical context, but gaps remain. It is a composite work, shaped over centuries by oral traditions, written sources, and theological revisions.

Religious viewpoint:
According to Jewish tradition, the Torah was revealed by God to Moses on Mount Sinai during the Israelites' exodus from Egypt (around 13th–12th century BCE). The Torah is considered the literal word of God, written by Moses under divine inspiration. This view is based on passages like Exodus 24:12, where God gives Moses the tablets of the law. The Oral Torah, which interprets and expands on the written Torah, is also believed to have been revealed to Moses and passed down through generations.

Non-religious viewpoint:
Modern biblical scholarship, employing methods such as source criticism, suggests that the Torah was composed over centuries by multiple authors and editors. This theory is known as the Documentary Hypothesis. The primary sources identified are:

Objective Analysis of God

- J (Yahwist): Uses the name Yahweh for God; emphasizes anthropomorphic descriptions of God.
- E (Elohist): Uses the name Elohim for God; focuses on moral and prophetic themes.
- D (Deuteronomist): Associated with the book of Deuteronomy; emphasizes law and covenant.
- P (Priestly): Focuses on rituals, laws, and genealogies; uses formal, structured language.

Most scholars agree that the Torah was compiled from multiple sources (e.g., J, E, D, P) over centuries, likely finalized during the Babylonian exile (6th century BCE) or the Persian period, long after the traditional lifespan of Moses (13th century BCE). Dead Sea Scrolls (3rd century BCE–1st century CE): Include the oldest surviving Torah manuscripts, confirming its antiquity but not Mosaic authorship.

Contents:

1. Law (Torah) - 35-40%
- The Torah (first five books: Genesis, Exodus, Leviticus, Numbers, Deuteronomy) contains laws, commandments, and instructions.
- Key themes:
    - Creation and the origins of humanity (Genesis)
    - The covenant between God and Israel (e.g., Abrahamic and Mosaic covenants)
    - Laws governing ritual, morality, and society (e.g., the Ten Commandments, dietary laws, sacrifices)

2. Prophecy (Nevi'im) - 20-25%
- The Nevi'im contains the writings of the prophets, who conveyed God's messages of judgment, hope, and restoration.
- Key themes:
    - Call to repentance, social justice, and righteousness (e.g., Isaiah, Amos, Micah)
    - Predictions of the coming Messiah and future restoration
    - God's judgment on Israel and other nations

3. Wisdom Literature (Ketuvim) - 15-20%

- This section includes philosophical and poetic writings that offer reflections on life, suffering, and faith.
- Key themes:
    - Wisdom, understanding, and human nature (e.g., Proverbs, Ecclesiastes)
    - The problem of suffering and the search for meaning (e.g., Job, Ecclesiastes)
    - Praise of God, love, and faith (e.g., Psalms, Song of Songs)

4. History and Narrative - 10-15%
- Historical narratives detailing the rise, fall, and restoration of Israel as a people.
- Key themes:
    - The conquest of Canaan and establishment of Israel (e.g., Joshua, Judges)
    - The monarchy of Israel (e.g., David, Solomon, Kings)
    - The exile and return from Babylonian captivity (e.g., Ezra, Nehemiah)

5. Creation and the Beginning of the World - 5-10%
- The opening chapters of Genesis tell the story of creation and the origins of humanity.
- Key themes:
    - God's creation of the world and humanity (Genesis 1-2)
    - The fall of humanity through Adam and Eve
    - The flood and the covenant with Noah

6. Covenant and Relationship with God - 5-10%
- The relationship between God and Israel is foundational, with covenant as the central theme.
- Key themes:
    - The Abrahamic and Mosaic covenants and God's promises
    - Obedience to God's laws and the consequences of breaking the covenant
    - God's faithfulness despite Israel's disobedience

7. Morals and Ethics - 5-10%
- The Hebrew Bible emphasizes moral behavior, justice, and ethical living by God's will.

Objective Analysis of God

- Key themes:
    - Ethical commandments, such as the Ten Commandments and laws of justice (e.g., honesty, kindness, charity)
    - Moral conduct in daily life, emphasizing justice, compassion, and fairness (e.g., the laws on gleaning for the poor, treating strangers with kindness)
    - Ethical teachings from wisdom literature (e.g., Proverbs, Micah, and parts of the Torah)
    - Social justice, care for the marginalized, and a call to love one's neighbor

8. Messianic Hope and Future Redemption - 5%
- Prophecies and hopes for a future Messiah and the restoration of Israel.
- Key themes:
    - Messianic prophecies, especially in Isaiah, Jeremiah, and Daniel
    - The anticipated arrival of a saviour to bring peace and restore justice

9. Ritual and Sacrifice - 5%
- The Hebrew Bible outlines religious rituals, sacrifices, and festivals that bind Israel's worship practices.
- Key themes:
    - Instructions for sacrifices, offerings, and atonement (e.g., Leviticus, Exodus)
    - Religious festivals and holy days (e.g., Passover, Yom Kippur, Sukkot)
    - Role of the priesthood and temple worship

These themes, along with their respective percentages, provide an overall view of the diverse content and teachings in the Hebrew Bible, with **Morals and Ethics** being an essential part of the broader framework of laws and social justice. The percentages are estimates and may overlap, as many of these themes are interwoven throughout the text.

Topic	Percentage	Description
Law (Torah)	35-40%	Laws, commandments, and instructions for Israel; includes creation, covenant, and rituals.
Prophecy (Nevi'im)	20-25%	Writings of prophets, including calls for repentance, justice, and future hope.
Wisdom Literature (Ketuvim)	15-20%	Poetic and philosophical writings reflecting on life, wisdom, suffering, and faith.
History and Narrative	10-15%	Historical accounts of Israel's rise, kings, exile, and return.
Creation and the Beginning of the World	5-10%	The story of creation, Adam and Eve, and the early history of humanity and Israel.
Covenant and Relationship with God	5-10%	The central theme of God's covenant with Israel and the consequences of keeping or breaking it.
Morals and Ethics	5-10%	Ethical teachings on justice, social responsibility, love, and righteous conduct.
Messianic Hope and Future Redemption	5%	Prophecies about the future Messiah and the restoration of Israel.
Ritual and Sacrifice	5%	Instructions on religious rituals, sacrifices, festivals, and temple worship.

Objective Analysis of God

This table gives a clear overview of the main topics and their relative importance in the Hebrew Bible.

The Hebrew bible and the Hammurabi codes

There is a connection between the **Hebrew Bible (~1300 BCE)** (specifically the Old Testament or Tanakh) and the **Code of Hammurabi (~1700 BCE)**, though they are distinct legal systems. Both reflect the ancient Near Eastern context in which they were created, and scholars have identified both similarities and differences between the two. As the Hammurabi codes were documented about 400 years before the Hebrew Bible, it is safe to say that any similarities are likely due to the Hebrew Bible adopting laws from the Hammurabi Codes, rather than the other way around.

Here's a breakdown of how they are related:

1. Context and period
- **The Code of Hammurabi** is one of the oldest known legal codes, dating back to around 1754 BCE. It was written by the Babylonian king **Hammurabi** and comprises 282 laws that cover various aspects of society, including family, property, commerce, and punishment.
- The **Hebrew Bible** contains various laws, most notably in the **Torah** (the first five books of the Bible), traditionally attributed to Moses. The laws found in books like **Exodus**, **Leviticus**, **Numbers**, and **Deuteronomy** were likely compiled and written down over several centuries, with most of the legal content probably taking shape between the 13th and 6th centuries BCE.

The Hebrew Bible and the Code of Hammurabi originate from the ancient Near Eastern region, specifically Mesopotamia and the Levant, indicating that they share specific cultural and legal influences.

1. **Lex Talionis (Law of Retaliation)**

One of Hammurabi's Code's most famous elements is the lex talionis principle — "*an eye for an eye.*" This concept of proportional justice, where the punishment fits the crime, is found in the Code of Hammurabi and the Hebrew Bible.
- In Hammurabi's Code, Code #196 states: "*If a man puts out the eye of another man, his eye shall be put out.*"
- Similarly, in Exodus 21:24 of the Hebrew Bible, the law reads: "*Eye for eye, tooth for tooth, hand for hand, foot for foot.*"

While both codes promote proportional punishment, the Hebrew Bible includes additional provisions that emphasize mercy and

Objective Analysis of God

fairness, suggesting that this was intended to limit excessive retribution, rather than absolute retaliation.

2. Property Laws and Theft
Both the Code of Hammurabi and the Hebrew Bible include laws related to the protection of property and the restitution for theft.
- Code #6 of Hammurabi deals with theft: "*If anyone steals the property of a temple or palace, that thief shall be put to death.*"
- In Exodus 22:1, the Hebrew Bible similarly addresses theft and restitution: "*If a man steals an ox or a sheep and slaughters or sells it, he shall repay five oxen for an ox and four sheep for a sheep.*"

Both legal systems emphasize the importance of restoring stolen goods; however, Hammurabi's Code prescribes the death penalty in some cases, whereas the Hebrew Bible provides a more proportional approach to restitution.

3. Family and Inheritance Laws
Both the Code of Hammurabi and the Hebrew Bible contain laws governing marriage, divorce, and inheritance, illustrating the significance of family and property structures in society.
- Code #128 of Hammurabi states:
- "*If a man gives his wife a divorce because she has borne him no children, he must return the dowry to her.*"
- In Deuteronomy 25:5-10, the Hebrew Bible presents the law of levirate marriage (marriage of a widow to her deceased husband's brother): "*If brothers dwell together, and one of them dies and has no son, the wife of the dead man shall not be married outside the family...her husband's brother shall go in to her and take her as his wife.*"

Both codes reflect concerns about family inheritance and the preservation of lineage; however, the Hebrew Bible also includes additional protections for women, such as specific laws regarding inheritance rights (e.g., Numbers 27:8-11 and Deuteronomy 21:15-17).

4. Slavery Laws
Slavery was a common institution in the ancient Near East, and both the Code of Hammurabi and the Hebrew Bible include provisions related to the treatment of slaves.
- Code #15 of Hammurabi provides:

- "*If a man has hired a slave and the slave dies because of his negligence, the master shall pay for the loss of the slave.*"
- Similarly, Exodus 21:20-21 in the Hebrew Bible states: "*If a man strikes a servant or a maid with a rod, and he dies under his hand, he shall be surely punished. Notwithstanding, if he continues a day or two, he shall not be punished: for he is his money.*"

Both codes recognize the ownership of slaves and set guidelines for their treatment. Still, the Hebrew Bible provides specific protections, including the release of slaves after a certain period (e.g., Exodus 21:2).

5. Punishments and Justice

Both Hammurabi's Code and the Hebrew Bible lay out specific punishments for various crimes, including false accusations, bodily injury, and crimes against others. The punishments can be severe, reflecting the importance of maintaining order and justice in society.

- Code #2 of Hammurabi addresses false accusations: "*If a man accuses another man of a crime and cannot prove it, the accuser shall be put to death.*"
- Similarly, in Deuteronomy 19:16-19, the Hebrew Bible states: "*If a false witness rises against any man to testify against him that which is wrong, then both the men...shall stand before the Lord, before the priests and the judges...and the judge shall make diligent inquiry.*"

Both codes emphasize the importance of preventing false accusations and ensuring justice is served. However, while the Code of Hammurabi prescribes the death penalty for false accusations, the Hebrew Bible requires a thorough investigation to ensure fairness in judgment.

6. Laws Regarding Wages and Labor

Both legal systems emphasize fair wages for workers and regulate the treatment of laborers.

- Code #282 of Hammurabi: "*If a man hires an ox or a donkey, and the animal is damaged or dies, the owner of the ox or donkey must pay the hire.*"
- Leviticus 19:13 in the Hebrew Bible: "*You shall not oppress your neighbor or rob him. The wages of a hired servant shall not remain with you all night until the morning.*"

Objective Analysis of God

Both sets of laws demonstrate a concern for the fair treatment of workers and emphasize the importance of prompt payment for labor. The Code of Hammurabi regulates the treatment of hired animals, while the Hebrew Bible focuses on human laborers, ensuring they are paid fairly and promptly.

7.   Laws Concerning Adultery and Marital Fidelity
Both the Code of Hammurabi and the Hebrew Bible address the issue of adultery, especially in the context of family honor and social order.
- Code #129 of Hammurabi: "*If a woman hates her husband and says, 'You shall not marry,' and he takes another woman, the first wife shall not be abandoned, but the second wife must be given a gift.*"
- Leviticus 20:10 in the Hebrew Bible: "*The man who commits adultery with another man's wife, even he who commits adultery with his neighbor's wife, the adulterer and the adulteress shall surely be put to death.*"

Both sets of laws place strong emphasis on the sanctity of marriage and the importance of faithfulness. While the Code of Hammurabi focuses on the consequences for wives in the case of marital disputes, the Hebrew Bible has strict punishments for adultery, showing a similar concern for the family unit.

8.   Compensation for Personal Injury
Both legal codes include provisions for compensating individuals who suffer personal injury, as well as guidelines for restitution.
- Code #199 of Hammurabi: "*If a man knocks out the teeth of another man, his teeth shall be knocked out.*"
- Exodus 21:24 in the Hebrew Bible: "*Eye for eye, tooth for tooth, hand for hand, foot for foot.*"

The principle of proportionality is evident in both laws. While the Code of Hammurabi specifies specific injuries, the Hebrew Bible articulates the broader principle of equal retribution (lex talionis), ensuring justice is proportional to the harm done.

9.   Laws Regarding the Care of the Poor and Vulnerable
Both the Code of Hammurabi and the Hebrew Bible contain provisions designed to protect society's most vulnerable members, such as widows, orphans, and the poor.

- Code #117 of Hammurabi: "*If a man takes a poor woman to be his wife and does not treat her properly, he shall be punished.*"
- Deuteronomy 10:18 in the Hebrew Bible: "*He executes justice for the fatherless and the widow, and loves the stranger, giving him food and clothing.*"

Both legal systems emphasize the importance of caring for society's most vulnerable members. The Code of Hammurabi protects women in marriage, while the Hebrew Bible advocates caring for orphans, widows, and strangers, showing a similar concern for social justice.

10. Protection of Life and Punishments for Murder

Both legal systems prescribe severe penalties for murder and unlawful killing, underscoring the value of human life in society.
- Code #210 of Hammurabi: "*If a man commits murder, that man shall be put to death.*"
- Exodus 21:12 in the Hebrew Bible: "*Anyone who kidnaps a person and sells them, or still has them when caught, must be put to death.*"

Both the Code of Hammurabi and the Hebrew Bible prescribe the death penalty for serious offences like murder and kidnapping, signalling the gravity of taking a life or violating someone's freedom. However, the Hebrew Bible also contains more detailed instructions regarding manslaughter and cities of refuge (Numbers 35:9-34), showing a more nuanced approach to justice in some instances.

11. Laws Concerning False Witnesses

Both the Code of Hammurabi and the Hebrew Bible treat false accusations seriously, emphasizing the need for truthfulness in legal proceedings.
- Code #5 of Hammurabi: "*If a man has falsely accused someone and the accused person has been put to death, then the accuser shall be put to death.*"
- Deuteronomy 19:16-19 in the Hebrew Bible: "*If a false witness rises against any man to testify against him of wrongdoing, then both the men in the controversy shall stand before the Lord, before the priests and the judges, who shall inquire diligently.*"

Both codes seek to protect individuals from false accusations and emphasize the importance of integrity in legal proceedings. Hammurabi's Code prescribes the death penalty for false

Objective Analysis of God

accusations that lead to execution, while the Hebrew Bible emphasizes a thorough investigation to ensure justice is served.

12. Laws Regarding Contracts and Debt

Both legal systems include regulations governing contracts, loans, and debt repayment.

- Code #48 of Hammurabi: "*If a man borrows money from a merchant and cannot repay the loan, the borrower shall become a slave until the debt is paid.*"
- Leviticus 25:39-40 in the Hebrew Bible: "*If your brother becomes poor and sells himself to you, you shall not make him serve as a slave... but as a hired servant, as a sojourner, he shall be with you.*"

Both the Code of Hammurabi and the Hebrew Bible contain laws designed to protect individuals from falling into financial ruin, particularly regarding debt and servitude. The Code of Hammurabi allows for enslavement in cases of unpaid debts, while the Hebrew Bible provides protections, ensuring that debtors are treated fairly and released after a specific period (Leviticus 25:10).

> *The Old Testament is the oldest record of God's words. It serves as the foundation for the laws and punishments in all Abrahamic religions, including the moral and ethical principles that continue, in basic form, into Islamic Shariah. As noted above, many of these laws were derived from Hammurabi's Code—a human-made system designed to establish moral and ethical standards in his kingdom—demonstrating that the claim that religion alone created or introduced morality in humans is mistaken.*

The above facts demonstrate that humans can develop more effective moral values and laws. It appears that it was religion or God who created these laws from Humans and published them with His name, not once, not twice, but at least three times—until the Quran /Islam (Sharia Law).

Another aspect is that if humans had continued to develop from the Hammurabi Codes and this activity had not been overtaken by "God" and religious institutions, but instead continued to evolve under humans' social will to improve life, there would have been better moral codes than those imposed by Religion.

Different Applications
However, the two systems differ in their approach to justice and law. Hammurabi's Code is secular, emphasizing social order and the king's authority. At the same time, the Hebrew Bible integrates law with religious and moral teachings, reflecting the covenantal relationship between God and the Israelites. This makes Hammurabi's code more just and aligned with Human innate moral values.

--- This we will discuss in more detail while discussing Islam

Analysis of Tanakh/Torah – brief:

I will give a detailed analysis of the contents of the Old Testament and the complete Bible, but to indicate that these words cannot come directly from the Creator of the universe, who is all-knowing and all-powerful. We see numerous contradictions and inaccurate scientific facts from the God who should be highly accurate and correct. The following are only a few points to prove my point:

1. Creation Accounts
- Contradiction: Genesis 1:24–27 (animals before humans) vs. Genesis 2:18–19 (humans before animals).
    - Genesis 1:24–27: *"And God said, 'Let the earth bring forth living creatures according to their kinds...' Then God said, 'Let us make man in our image...'"*
    - Genesis 2:18–19: *"Then the Lord God said, 'It is not good that the man should be alone; I will make him a helper fit for him.'... Now out of the ground the Lord God had formed every beast of the field..."*

2. Age of the Earth
- Scientific Issue: The genealogies in Genesis 5 and 11 suggest the Earth is only a few thousand years old.
    - Genesis 5:3–32: Lists genealogies from Adam to Noah, implying a young Earth.
    - Genesis 11:10–26: Lists genealogies from Shem to Abraham, further supporting a young Earth.

3. Global Flood
- Scientific Issue: Genesis 6–9 describes a global flood.
    - Genesis 7:19–20: "And the waters prevailed so mightily on the earth that all the high mountains under the whole

Objective Analysis of God

heaven were covered. *The waters prevailed above the mountains, covering them fifteen cubits deep."*

4. Tower of Babel
- Scientific Issue: Genesis 11:1–9 claims all languages originated from a single event.
  - Genesis 11:7–9: *"Come, let us go down and there confuse their language, so that they may not understand one another's speech... Therefore, its name was called Babel because the Lord confused the language of all the earth."*

5. Sun Standing Still
- Scientific Issue: Joshua 10:12–14 describes the sun standing still.
  - Joshua 10:13: *"And the sun stood still, and the moon stopped, until the nation took vengeance on their enemies... The sun stopped amid heaven and did not hurry to set for about a whole day."*

6. Firmament
- Scientific Issue: Genesis 1:6–8 describes a solid "firmament."
  - Genesis 1:6–8: *"And God said, 'Let there be a firmament amid the waters, and let it separate the waters from the waters.'... And God called the firmament Heaven."*

7. Flat Earth
- Scientific Issue: Isaiah 40:22 and Job 38:13 suggest a flat Earth.
  - Isaiah 40:22: *"It is he who sits above the circle of the earth..."*
  - Job 38:13: *"That it might take hold of the skirts of the earth, and the wicked be shaken out of it?"*

8. Contradictory Census Numbers
- Contradiction: Exodus 12:37 vs. Numbers 1:46.
  - Exodus 12:37: *"And the people of Israel journeyed from Rameses to Succoth, about six hundred thousand men on foot, besides women and children."*
  - Numbers 1:46: *"All those listed were 603,550."*
  - No archaeological evidence of this mass movement

9. Contradictory Genealogies
- Contradiction: Matthew 1:1–17 vs. Luke 3:23–38.
  - Matthew 1:6–16: Lists Solomon as David's heir.
  - Luke 3:23–31: Lists Nathan as David's heir.

10. Contradictory Commandments

- Contradiction: Exodus 20:8–11 vs. Deuteronomy 5:12–15.
  - Exodus 20:11 grounds the Sabbath command in creation (God resting on the seventh day).
  - Deuteronomy 5:15 ties it to Israel's deliverance from Egypt (liberation from slavery).

11. Contradictory Accounts of Saul's Death
- Contradiction: 1 Samuel 31:4–6 vs. 2 Samuel 1:6–10.
  - 1 Samuel 31:4: *"Saul took his sword and fell upon it."*
  - 2 Samuel 1:10: *"So I stood beside him and killed him, because I was sure that he could not live after he had fallen."*

12. Contradictory Numbers in Battles
- Contradiction: 2 Samuel 10:18 vs. 1 Chronicles 19:18.
  - 2 Samuel 10:18: *"And the Syrians fled before Israel, and David killed 700 charioteers..."*
  - 1 Chronicles **19:18**: *"And the Syrians fled before Israel, and David killed 7,000 charioteers..."*

13. Contradictory Ages of Ahaziah
- Contradiction: 2 Kings 8:26 vs. 2 Chronicles 22:2.
  - 2 Kings 8:26: *"Ahaziah was twenty-two years old when he began to reign..."*
  - **2 Chronicles 22:2**: *"Ahaziah was forty-two years old when he began to reign..."*

14. Contradictory Accounts of David's Census
- Contradiction: 2 Samuel 24:1 vs. 1 Chronicles 21:1.
  - 2 Samuel 24:1: *"Again the anger of the Lord was kindled against Israel, and he incited David against them, saying, 'Go, number Israel and Judah.'"*
  - 1 Chronicles 21:1: *"Then Satan stood against Israel and incited David to number Israel."*

15. Contradictory Numbers in Solomon's Stables
- Contradiction: 1 Kings 4:26 vs. 2 Chronicles 9:25.
  - 1 Kings 4:26: *"Solomon also had 40,000 stalls of horses for his chariots..."*
  - 2 Chronicles 9:25: *"Solomon had 4,000 stalls for horses and chariots..."*

16. Contradictory Accounts of the Exodus Timeline
- Contradiction: Exodus 12:40-41 vs. Genesis 15:13.
  - Exodus 12:40: *"The time that the people of Israel lived in Egypt was 430 years."*
  - Genesis 15:13: *"Then the Lord said to Abram, 'Know for certain that your offspring will be sojourners in a*

Objective Analysis of God

land that is not theirs and will be servants there, and they will be afflicted for 400 years.'"

17. Slavery
- Moral Issue: Exodus 21:20–21 permits beating slaves.
    - Exodus 21:20–21: *"When a man strikes his slave... with a rod and the slave dies under his hand, he shall be avenged. But if the slave survives a day or two, he is not to be avenged..."*

18. Treatment of Women
- Moral Issue: Numbers 31:17–18 allows keeping virgin girls as spoils of war.
    - Numbers 31:17–18: *"Now therefore, kill every male among the little ones, and kill every woman who has known a man by lying with him. But all the young girls who have not known a man by lying with him, keep alive for yourselves."*

19. Genocide
- Moral Issue: 1 Samuel 15:3 commands the destruction of entire populations.
    - 1 Samuel 15:3: *"Now go and strike Amalek and devote to destruction all that they have. Do not spare them, but kill both man and woman, child and infant..."*

20. Animal Sacrifices
- Moral Issue: Leviticus 1–7 prescribes animal sacrifices.
    - Leviticus 1:3: *"If his offering is a burnt offering from the herd, he shall offer a male without blemish..."*

21. Contradictory Laws on Slavery
- Contradiction: Exodus 21:2–6 vs. Leviticus 25:44–46.
    - Exodus 21:2: *"When you buy a Hebrew slave, he shall serve six years..."*
    - Leviticus **25:46**: *"You may bequeath them to your sons after you to inherit as a possession forever."*

22. Contradictory Laws on Blasphemy
- Contradiction: Leviticus 24:16 vs. Exodus 20:7.
    - Leviticus 24:16: *"Whoever blasphemes the name of the Lord shall surely be put to death."*
    - Exodus 20:7: *"You shall not take the name of the Lord your God in vain, for the Lord will not hold him guiltless who takes his name in vain."*

23. Contradictory Accounts of Hezekiah's Reign
- Contradiction: 2 Kings 18:13–16 vs. 2 Chronicles 32:1–8.

- 2 Kings 18:13: *"In the fourteenth year of King Hezekiah, Sennacherib king of Assyria came up against all the fortified cities of Judah and took them."*
- 2 Chronicles 32:1: *"After these things and these acts of faithfulness, Sennacherib king of Assyria came and invaded Judah..."*

24. Contradictory Accounts of Goliath's Death
- Contradiction: 1 Samuel 17:50 vs. 2 Samuel 21:19.
    - 1 Samuel 17:50: *"So David prevailed over the Philistine with a sling and a stone..."*
    - 2 Samuel 21:19: *"And there was again war with the Philistines at Gob, and Elhanan... struck down Goliath the Gittite..."*

I will let you decide if these could be the words of God, which were men to guide Humans for at least 15,000 years. Are they clear enough to provide explicit instructions to Humans? These issues reflect the diverse origins, historical contexts, and literary styles of the Old Testament. Including verse translations helps identify and analyze these passages more precisely. While they may challenge literal interpretations, many believe these texts convey spiritual and moral truths rather than scientific or historical accuracy.

"Development" of the Bible:

Christians build the Bible by taking the Tanakh (plus a few other books) as the Old Testament and adding Jesus' part as the New Testament. Christians adopted the Tanakh into the Old Testament, splitting some books and adding others (the Deuterocanon) depending on their tradition. Both share core texts (Torah, Prophets, Psalms), but their structures and theological emphases differ. Different sects of Christianity have varying versions of the Old Testament, but the exact text and books are the same as those in the New Testament.

- **Protestant Old Testament (39 Books)**
  Includes all 24 books of the Tanakh, but splits combined books (e.g., Samuel → 1–2 Samuel, Kings → 1–2 Kings, Chronicles → 1–2 Chronicles, Ezra-Nehemiah → Ezra + Nehemiah, Twelve Minor Prophets → 12 separate books). Order: Group books by genre (Law, History, Poetry, Prophets).
  Excludes: Deuterocanonical books (e.g., Tobit, Maccabees), which are included in the Catholic and Orthodox Bibles.
- **Catholic Old Testament (46 Books)**
  All Protestant and Deuterocanonical books (e.g., Tobit, Judith, Wisdom of Solomon, Sirach, Baruch, 1–2 Maccabees).
  These additional books were written during the Second Temple period (c. 3rd–1st century BCE) and are not part of the Jewish Tanakh.
- **Orthodox Old Testament (~49-51 Books)**
  This includes all Catholic books and additional texts, such as 1 Esdras, 3 Maccabees, Psalm 151, and 4 Maccabees (as an appendix), totalling 49–51 books.

Old Testament (Tanakh in the Bible)

All three sections of the Tanakh are included in some form in the Old Testament of the Christian Bible:
- **Torah (Law) – Included**
  Genesis, Exodus, Leviticus, Numbers, Deuteronomy

These are identical in Jewish and Christian traditions (though arranged differently, the interpretation may differ).
- **Nevi'im (Prophets) – Included, but rearranged**
Books like Joshua, Judges, Samuel, Kings, Isaiah, Jeremiah, Ezekiel, and the Twelve Minor Prophets are included.
Some Christian Bibles are split (e.g., 1 & 2 Samuel), and the order differs.
- **Ketuvim (Writings) – Mostly included, with some differences**
Books such as Psalms, Proverbs, Job, Ruth, Esther, Daniel, Ezra, Nehemiah, and Chronicles are included.

Some differences exist:
> Daniel and Esther have extra sections in Catholic and Orthodox Bibles (called the deuterocanonical books).

Some books are grouped or ordered differently.

Key Differences:
The Christian Old Testament order is topical (Law → History → Wisdom → Prophets), while the Tanakh order is thematic and ends with Chronicles.
Catholic and Orthodox Bibles include books not found in the Jewish Tanakh or Protestant Old Testament. These are known as the Deuterocanonical books (e.g., Tobit, Judith, 1 and 2 Maccabees). Protestant Bibles include only the books in the Jewish Tanakh but follow the Christian order.

Objective Analysis of God

Analysis of the New Testament

We will examine the New Testament in more detail, having already conducted a critical review of the history of Christianity. We need to explore this topic more to fully understand and support my previous comments on "New Testaments as having no history of coming directly from God or His prophet—Jesus." Some points will be repeated, but they are essential to a complete understanding of my argument.

Starting with the process of how the Bible took 300 + years to take its form:

The "canon finalization of the Bible" refers to the historical process by which the books included in the Bible—both the Old Testament and New Testament—were officially recognized and accepted as authoritative, inspired scripture by religious communities, forming a fixed collection or "canon." The term "canon" comes from the Greek word "Kanon", meaning "rule" or "measuring stick," implying a standard list of texts considered divinely inspired and normative for faith and practice.

For the New Testament specifically, canon finalization refers to the process by which the 27 books of the Bible were selected, debated, and eventually agreed upon by Christian and church leaders after approximately 300-400 years of Jesus' ministry. They performed an exercise and distinguished these selected texts from other writings of the time. Here's a breakdown of what this process entailed:

What It Means

Early Christians produced and circulated numerous writings, including gospels, letters, and apocalypses. Canon finalization involved determining which were genuinely inspired by God and suitable for use in worship, teaching, and doctrine. Writings deemed non-inspired, heretical, or of lesser authority (e.g., Gospel of Thomas, Shepherd of Hermas) were excluded from the canon, though some were still valued for devotional reading. Establishing Authority: The finalized canon became the authoritative basis for Christian theology, liturgy, and identity, setting it apart from competing religious movements. It was a gradual process in the 300s CE to collect oral and written texts over the last 300-400 years, and church leaders, like all humans, decided which to take and which to discard.

New Testament Canon Finalization Timeline
The process for the New Testament unfolded roughly as follows:
- **1st-2nd Century**: Early Christian communities circulated texts like the Gospels and Paul's letters. No fixed canon existed yet; different regions used different collections.
- **2nd Century Challenges**: Figures like Marcion (c. 140 CE) proposed a limited canon (Luke + 10 Pauline epistles), prompting orthodox leaders to clarify which books were authoritative. Documents like the Muratorian Fragment (c. 170 CE) list the 27 most current books, though some were still disputed.
- **3rd-Century Debate: Books like Hebrews, James, 2 Peter, 2 and 3 John, Jude, and Revelation faced scrutiny over authorship, theology, and** widespread use. Origen (c. 185-254 CE) distinguished between "universally accepted" and "disputed" books.
- **4th Century Consensus**: Key milestones solidified the 27-book canon:
    - Athanasius's Easter Letter (367 CE): The Bishop of Alexandria listed the 27 books we know today as the New Testament, the first surviving list to match the modern canon precisely.
    - Councils of Hippo (393 CE) and Carthage (397 CE): These local church councils in North Africa affirmed the same 27 books, reflecting broader agreement.
    - Post-4th Century: While minor debates lingered (e.g., the acceptance of Revelation in the Eastern Church), the 27-book canon became standard across most of Christianity by the 5th century.

Even today, with resources we take for granted—access to the Internet, PDFs, printed texts, and easy travel—this would be a mammoth undertaking. Now imagine attempting the same in 300–400 AD and claiming to produce the authentic Word of God.

Objective Analysis of God

Bible - Content

A significant (about 46% by chapter counts) portion of the New Testament comprises letters (also called epistles). These letters were written by early Christian leaders, such as Paul, Peter, James, John, and Jude, to various churches, individuals, or broader audiences. They provide theological teachings, practical advice, and encouragement for Christian living.

Before we move on to some definitions:

Category	Topics / Covers	By
Gospel	Accounts of Jesus' life, teachings, death, and resurrection.	Matthew, Mark, Luke, John
Epistles	Letters written by early Christian leaders to churches or individuals.	Pauline Epistles (13) + General Epistles (8)
Revelation	Apocalyptic book with visions of the end times and God's ultimate victory.	John - book

Contributors:
The Bible is built on the writings of the following authors:

Leader	Estimated Birth	Place of Birth	Estimated Death	Place of Death	Most Active Period
Paul	5–10 AD	Tarsus (modern Turkey)	64–67 AD	Rome (Italy)	30s–60s AD
Peter	1 BC–1 AD	Bethsaida (Galilee)	64–68 AD	Rome (Italy)	30s–60s AD
James	1 BC–1 AD	Nazareth or Galilee	62 AD	Jerusalem (Israel)	30s–60s AD
John	6–10 AD	Bethsaida (Galilee)	98–100 AD	Ephesus (modern Turkey)	30s–90s AD
Jude	1 BC–1 AD	Nazareth or Galilee	65–80 AD	Persia or Armenia	30s–60s AD
Matthew	~1 BC–1 AD	Capernaum or Galilee	~60–70 AD	Ethiopia	30s–60s AD
Mark	~5–10 AD	Jerusalem or Cyrene	~68 AD	Alexandria	40s–60s AD
Luke	~10–15 AD	Antioch (modern Turkey)	~84 AD	Greece	50s–80s AD

> *It is essential to note that there is no direct mention of Jesus or God in firsthand sources—all contributors to the Bible, as defined within the text itself, relied on second or third-hand accounts of events and sayings. As we will discuss later, none of these original authors were alive when the Bible was compiled and formalized, having died roughly 300 years earlier.*
> *Thus, the Bible does not contain an original, verified narrative, and its so-called authors could not confirm the accounts at the time of compilation..*

Breakdown of the New Testament
The New Testament consists of 27 books, which can be divided into the following categories:
1. The Gospels (4 books):
   - Matthew, Mark, Luke, and John
   - These books focus on the life, teachings, death, and resurrection of Jesus Christ.
2. The Acts of the Apostles (1 book):
   - Acts
   - This book describes the early history of the Christian church and the spread of the gospel after Jesus' ascension.
3. The Letters/Epistles (21 books):
   - These are divided into two groups:
     - Pauline Letters (13 books): Written by the Apostle Paul.
     - General Letters (8 books): Written by other apostles or early Christian leaders.
4. The Book of Revelation (1 book):
   - Revelation
   - A prophetic book about the end times and the ultimate victory of God.

Letters in the New Testament
The 21 letters comprise a substantial portion (about 46% by chapter count) of the New Testament. Here's a breakdown:
Pauline Letters (13 books):
   1. Romans
   2. 1 Corinthians
   3. 2 Corinthians
   4. Galatians

Objective Analysis of God

5. Ephesians
6. Philippians
7. Colossians
8. 1 Thessalonians
9. 2 Thessalonians
10. 1 Timothy
11. 2 Timothy
12. Titus
13. Philemon

General Letters (8 books):
1. Hebrews (author uncertain)
2. James
3. 1 Peter
4. 2 Peter
5. 1 John
6. 2 John
7. 3 John
8. Jude

Percentage of the New Testament that Is Letters
By chapter count, the New Testament letters (epistles) comprise roughly 46% of the total. Here's the breakdown:
Total New Testament: 260 chapters.
- Letters (Epistles): 121 chapters.
- Pauline Epistles (Romans to Philemon): 87 chapters.
- General Epistles (Hebrews to Jude): 34 chapters.

Remaining Books:
- Gospels (Matthew–John): 89 chapters.
- Acts: 28 chapters.
- Revelation: 22 chapters.

Here we have to note a few things:
a) More than half of the New Testament (about 48% by book and 33% by chapters) is written by Paul, who never saw or met Jesus, nor had a native language common to Jesus. His influence is disproportionately large relative to his contribution, as his words build the foundation of Christianity, a person who never met Jesus.
b) The Bible was first compiled and formed into a Holy book in Greek after approximately 300 years, not in Hebrew.

c) All content of the Bible (not as the Bible but as letters of books) was written at least 50 years after Jesus
d) We will see later that it will take another 300-400 years to be compiled in the form of the Bible; at that time, none of the authors were present to validate the content

Objective Analysis of God

Leader	Interaction with Jesus	Native language	Contribution
Paul	Never saw or met Jesus Wrote 13 epistles Romans, 1 & 2 Corinthians, Galatians, Ephesians, Philippians, Colossians, 1 & 2 Thessalonians, 1 & 2 Timothy, Titus, Philemon	Greek (primary), Aramaic, Hebrew	~ 30%
Peter	Saw and met Jesus closely, but denied Jesus before the crucifixion. 2 epistles.1 & 2 Peter	Aramaic (primary), some Greek	~ 4%
James	Saw and met Jesus closely, but denied Jesus before the crucifixion. Wrote one epistle. James	Aramaic, some Greek, and Hebrew	~ 1%
John	Saw and met Jesus closely, but denied Jesus before the crucifixion. Gospel, three epistles, and Revelation. spell of John, 1 John, 2 John, 3 John, Revelation	Aramaic some Greek	~ 20%
Jude	It may have been present during Jesus' time. 1 epistle; emphasized defending the faith. Jude	Aramaic some Greek	~ 0.5%
Mathew	Saw and met Jesus closely. 1 Gospel focusing on Jesus as the Jewish Messiah. Gospel of Matthew	Aramaic, some Greek, and Hebrew	~ 10%
Mark	Never saw or met Jesus. 1 Gospel emphasizing Jesus' actions. Gospel of Mark	Greek some Aramaic	~ 7%
Luke	Never saw or met Jesus. 1 Gospel and Acts. Gospel of Luke, Acts	Greek	~25%
Unknown Authors	Authorship of some book- Hebrews (author uncertain)	Greek	~2%

Historical Variations

However, in the early centuries of Christianity (before the canon was finalized), there were debates about which books should be included, leading to temporary "versions" of the New Testament with different book counts:

1. **Early Collections**: Some early Christian communities used smaller collections, like only the Gospels or Paul's letters (e.g., Marcion's canon in the 2nd century included just a modified Luke and 10 Pauline epistles, totalling **11 books**).
2. **Disputed Books**: Certain books, like Hebrews, James, 2 Peter, 2 and 3 John, Jude, and Revelation, were debated for inclusion. Some early lists, such as the Muratorian Fragment (c. 170 CE), omit a few of these, suggesting a canon of around 22-24 books, depending on the community.
3. **Additional Texts**: Some groups, like the Gnostics, included apocryphal works (e.g., the Gospel of Thomas and the Gospel of Mary), but these were never widely accepted as canonical. In fringe traditions, these could inflate the count beyond 27, though no standard number emerged.

Non-Canonical Traditions

Certain smaller or historical Christian sects have occasionally recognized different texts, but they don't constitute a "version" of the New Testament with a fixed number of books.

- **Ethiopian Orthodox Tewahedo Church**: While their *Old Testament* canon is broader (81 books total for the Bible), their New Testament remains the standard 27 books.
- **Syriac Peshitta**: Early versions of this translation initially excluded 2 Peter, 2 and 3 John, Jude, and Revelation (totalling **22 books**), but later editions aligned with the 27-book canon.

Why did it take so much time?

Once the Church began compiling the Bible, it took approximately 100 years to formalize it in its present form, comprising 27 books for the New Testament; however, it still has issues with the Old Testament. Several factors shaped the finalization:
- Criteria for Inclusion: Books were evaluated based on:
- Apostolic Origin: Written by an apostle or their close associate (e.g., Mark with Peter, Luke with Paul).
- Orthodoxy: Consistency with core Christian teachings.
- Widespread Use: Acceptance and use in liturgy across churches.

Objective Analysis of God

- Communication Limits: Early Christianity spanned a vast empire with slow communication, so consensus took time to emerge.
- Competing Texts: Apocryphal works and heretical writings (e.g., Gnostic texts) required discernment to reject.

Outcome
By the end of the 4th century, the New Testament canon was "finalized" because the 27 books were widely recognized as scripture. This didn't mean an absolute, universal decree—no single "Council of the Bible"—but rather a growing consensus ratified by tradition and church practice. The Old Testament canon, by contrast, varies slightly between traditions (e.g., Protestant vs. Catholic), but the New Testament's 27 books have remained consistent across major Christian branches.

In short, "canon finalization" refers to the process of sifting, affirming, and settling on the books that comprise the Bible as we know it—a dynamic journey from a fluid collection of writings to a fixed, sacred library. Many people firmly believe that these are coming directly from God..........

Standard New Testament Canon
In most Christian traditions today—Protestant, Roman Catholic, and Eastern Orthodox—the New Testament comprises **27 books**. These books were largely settled upon by the 4th century and include:
- 4 Gospels (Matthew, Mark, Luke, John)
- Acts of the Apostles
- 21 Epistles (letters from Paul, James, Peter, John, Jude, and Hebrews)
- Revelation

This 27-book canon is universally accepted across mainstream Christianity, so the number of books considered part of the New Testament typically remains consistent in these traditions.

Related Historical facts around the New Testament "selection"
Before we proceed, please note that the Quran also underwent similar stages of development. Still, its timeframe was limited to approximately 17 years, and the selected wording and approach were far superior to be called the Book of God.

The Bible, a cornerstone of religious and cultural history, owes much of its development to the pervasive influence of Greek culture following Alexander the Great's conquests (336–323 BCE). The Hellenists were Jews who were raised outside of Israel. They spoke Greek and used the Greek translation of the Old Testament. The Hellenist era is considered to be between the death of Alexander the Great in 323 BC and the death of Cleopatra VII in 30 BC, and Hellenism represents a body of humanistic and classical ideals associated with ancient Greece and including reason, the pursuit of knowledge and the arts, moderation, civic responsibility, and bodily development. The spread of Hellenism reshaped the ancient world, creating a linguistic, intellectual, and political environment that facilitated the translation of the Hebrew Scriptures into Greek (the Septuagint) and the composition of the New Testament in Koine Greek. This essay examines the multifaceted Greek influence on the Bible, the reasons behind its development, and the unique role Greek rulers played in utilizing it to reinforce their authority in the post-Alexander era.

Alexander the Great and the Hellenistic Framework
Alexander the Great's empire, stretching from Greece to India, united diverse peoples under a shared Hellenistic culture. After he died in 323 BCE, his generals, the Diadochi, divided the empire into successor states, including the Ptolemaic Kingdom in Egypt and the Seleucid Empire in Syria and Mesopotamia. These rulers promoted the Greek language, philosophy, and governance, establishing Koine Greek as the lingua franca of the eastern Mediterranean. This cultural unification had profound implications for religious communities, particularly the Jewish diaspora, which adapted to Greek-speaking environments in cities such as Alexandria and Antioch.

For Jews scattered across these Hellenistic realms, the shift from Hebrew and Aramaic to Greek necessitated new methods for preserving their sacred traditions. Meanwhile, Greek intellectual traditions—most notably exemplified by philosophers such as Plato and Aristotle—began to influence Jewish thought, setting the stage for a synthesis that would shape the biblical texts. The post-Alexander era thus provided both the tools (language) and the context (cultural exchange) for the Bible's evolution.

Objective Analysis of God

The Septuagint: Bridging Cultures

A pivotal moment in this process was the creation of the Septuagint (LXX), the Greek translation of the Hebrew Scriptures. According to the "Letter of Aristeas", this effort began under Ptolemy II Philadelphus (r. 283–246 BCE), who reportedly commissioned 70 Jewish scholars to translate the Torah for the Library of Alexandria. While the account may be legendary, it reflects a historical truth: by the 3rd century BCE, the Septuagint emerged in Alexandria, a center of Hellenistic learning, to meet the needs of Greek-speaking Jews.

The Septuagint's development had several drivers. Primarily, it addressed the linguistic reality of the Jewish diaspora, whose fluency in Hebrew had waned. It also served a cultural purpose, enabling Jews to maintain their identity while engaging with Hellenistic society. Additionally, it offered an apologetic tool, presenting Jewish theology to Greek audiences familiar with philosophical discourse. Koine Greek, a widely accessible dialect, ensured its reach across the Mediterranean.

The translation process subtly adapted Hebrew concepts to Greek frameworks. For instance, "Torah," meaning instruction or teaching, became *nomos* (law), aligning it with Greco-Roman legal traditions. Such shifts made the text more intelligible to Hellenistic readers, reflecting the influence of Greek culture on its presentation.

Why Greek Rulers Needed the Bible

Greek rulers, particularly the Ptolemies and Seleucids, had strategic reasons for supporting the development of the Bible, especially the Septuagint, in their diverse empires. Maintaining stability required managing subject populations with distinct religious identities, such as the Jews. The Septuagint offered a means to integrate these communities into the Hellenistic order without erasing their traditions. For the Ptolemies in Egypt, sponsoring the translation enhanced their legitimacy as enlightened rulers, aligning with their patronage of the Library of Alexandria as a symbol of universal knowledge.

Moreover, Greek rulers utilized the Septuagint to consolidate their rule by fostering a shared cultural framework. In Egypt, where Jews formed a significant minority, a Greek-language scripture allowed the Ptolemies to monitor and influence Jewish religious life, ensuring it aligned with state interests. Under Seleucid rule, the situation differed: the Maccabean Revolt (167–160 BCE) erupted partly due to Antiochus IV's aggressive Hellenization policies, including attempts to suppress Jewish practices. However, even here, the Septuagint—already in circulation—served as a point of negotiation. After the revolt, the Hasmonean rulers retained Greek influences while resisting Seleucid dominance, and the Septuagint remained a key text for diaspora Jews under the influence of Hellenism.

By supporting or tolerating the Septuagint, Greek rulers could co-opt Jewish loyalty. They presented themselves as protectors of local traditions while subtly reshaping them to fit Hellenistic norms. This dual strategy—cultural preservation and control—helped maintain order in multiethnic empires.

The New Testament in a Hellenistic World

By the 1st century CE, when the New Testament emerged, the Hellenistic world had been fully integrated into the Roman Empire; yet, Greek remained the dominant language of the eastern provinces. Written in Koine Greek, the New Testament reflects this context. Its authors, including Paul of Tarsus—a Jew trained in Greek rhetoric—crafted texts for audiences that spanned both Jews and Gentiles, using Greek literary forms such as biographies ("bioi") and epistles ("epistulae").

The spread of Christianity drove the development of the New Testament after Jesus' death (circa 30–33 CE). Early Christians needed to record their teachings, unify their communities, and evangelize diverse populations. Greek, as the common tongue, was essential for this mission. The Gospel of John, for example, uses *Logos*—a term rooted in Greek philosophy—to describe Jesus, bridging Jewish theology with Hellenistic thought. This adaptability made the New Testament a powerful tool for outreach in cities like Corinth and Ephesus.

The text also addressed internal needs, including the establishment of doctrine, countering heresies such as Gnosticism, and distinguishing Christianity from Judaism. Greek facilitated rapid dissemination, enabling the faith to transcend its Jewish origins and appeal to a broader Hellenistic audience.

Political and Religious Dynamics Post-Alexander and the need for the "Bible"

Objective Analysis of God

The post-Alexander era's political upheavals further shaped the Bible. The Seleucid push for Hellenization sparked the Maccabean Revolt, reinforcing Jewish attachment to their scriptures as a symbol of resistance against foreign influence. The Septuagint, already in use, became a lifeline for diaspora Jews under such pressures. Later, the Roman conquest (63 BCE) and the destruction of the Second Temple (70 CE) intensified the need to codify Jewish and Christian texts. For Christians, the New Testament became a portable foundation for a faith no longer tied to a physical temple, while Greeks ensured its accessibility across the empire.

Was the Bible politically motivated?
The Greek influence on the Bible, catalyzed by Alexander the Great's legacy, was a dynamic interplay of language, culture, and power. The Septuagint emerged from the practical needs of the diaspora and the political strategies of its rulers, while the New Testament reflected Christianity's Hellenistic expansion. Greek rulers, from the Ptolemies to the Seleucids, relied on the Bible to navigate the complexities of ruling diverse empires, utilizing it to integrate and control subject peoples. The reasons for its development—preserving faith, evangelizing, and asserting identity—were inseparable from this Hellenistic context, ensuring the Bible's enduring impact through the medium of Greek thought and controlling a vast and diverse empire.

Analysis of the Bible's content
I will conduct separate analyses for the New and Old Testaments, in line with my initial argument. The percentages below are rough estimates, as they account for factors such as a single verse covering multiple topics. Still, here, I want to adopt a general approach and utilize the content of the Bible to build my argument.

Topic	Old Testament	New Testament	Complete Bible
Praising God	9%	8%	8%
Law	17%	4%	14%
Prophecy	18%	7%	14%
Wisdom Literature	9%	4%	7%
History and Narrative	19%	29%	22%
Creation and the Beginning	2%	2%	2%

Topic	Old Testament	New Testament	Complete Bible
Covenant and Relationship	8%	13%	9%
Morals and Ethics	**8%**	**8%**	**8%**
Messianic Hope and Redemption	5%	21%	10%
Ritual and Sacrifice	5%	4%	6%

Objective Analysis of God

Questions from Christians

Section 4 – Christianity
Questions from Christians

Question: Concept of Trinity	**C1**

Analysis and background:

The selected verses from the Bible present a compelling theological puzzle regarding the nature of God as understood in Christian doctrine, particularly the concept of the Trinity. These passages suggest distinct roles and interactions among the Father, the Son (Jesus), and the Holy Spirit—raising questions about whether they are genuinely one entity or three separate beings.

John 14:26: *"the Helper, whom the Father will send in my name."* This verse implies a clear distinction between the Father, the Son, and the Holy Spirit, each with a unique function: the Father sends, the Son authorizes, and the Spirit teaches.

Luke 23:34: *"Father, forgive them, for they know not what they do."* This moment of intercession suggests a relational dynamic, as if Jesus is appealing to another conscious entity.

Matthew 27:46 and Mark 15:34: *"My God, my God, why have you forsaken me?"*—a deeply emotional plea that implies separation or abandonment, which seems paradoxical if Jesus and God are the same being.

Luke 23:46: *"Father, into your hands I commit my spirit!"* Again, a direct communication that reinforces the sense of distinct identities.

Taken together, these verses portray a dialogue and emotional exchange between entities traditionally understood as one unified God. This raises a question: How can one entity speak to, plead with, or feel forsaken by itself? The complexity of these interactions continues to fuel centuries of debate about the nature of divine unity and distinction within Christian theology.

Conclusion: The basic concept of the Trinity is unusual, considering it is a Monolithic religion. As God and His Son cannot be one entity, we also have "the Spirit".	Please rate this Conclusion:

Objective Analysis of God

Question: God communicates through the Spirit	C2

Analysis and background:
The Bible presents a complex picture of divine communication, especially concerning the role of the Holy Spirit. In the New Testament, the Spirit is shown speaking directly to individuals, seemingly outside the traditional prophetic framework. For instance, Acts 8:29 states, "*And the Spirit said to Philip, 'Go over and join this chariot.'*" Similarly, Acts 10:19–20 reads, "*And while Peter pondered the vision, the Spirit said to him, 'Behold, three men are looking for you. Rise and go down and accompany them without hesitation, for I have sent them.'*" In Acts 13:2, the Spirit commands, "*Set apart for me Barnabas and Saul for the work to which I have called them.*" These verses suggest that the Spirit actively communicates with believers, lending divine authority to their actions.

However, this seems to contradict earlier biblical teachings where God emphasizes that He communicates only through His prophets. Verses such as Numbers 12:6–8, Amos 3:7, Hebrews 1:1–2, Deuteronomy 18:18–19, 2 Chronicles 36:15–16, Jeremiah 7:25–26, and 1 Samuel 3:1 reinforce this idea. If God can speak to non-prophets, why not to all humans?

Additionally, the Bible alternates between God communicating to the Holy Spirit and through it, further complicating the Spirit's role. This ambiguity raises concerns about consistency and control over divine messages, particularly when multiple authors claim to be inspired by the same source. It challenges the clarity of divine communication and the theological coherence of the Spirit's function.

Conclusion: God communicating directly to non-prophets is contrary to what is written in the Bible, indicating that the Holy Spirit's roles contradict the Rules set by God Himself.	Please rate this Conclusion:

Section 4 – Christianity
Questions from Christians

Question: Jesus as a Savior	**C3**

Analysis and background:
All of Jesus's accounts were documented at least 30-60 years after his "Death," so they are accounts of an oral transfer of history, which cannot be without bias.
Secondly, Christianity teaches that salvation is through faith in Jesus Christ alone:
John 14:6 -- *"Jesus said to him, 'I am the way, the truth, and the life. No one comes to the Father except through me."*
Acts 4:12 -- *"And there is salvation in no one else, for there is no other name under heaven given among men by which we must be saved."*
John 10:9 - *"I am the door. If anyone enters by me, he will be saved and will go in and out and find pasture."*

Meaning Christianity attached belief in Jesus and his resurrection as the sole means of being a saviour and obtaining salvation, as well as the reward of Heaven. If God let his son be murdered so brutally just to cleanse the sins of humanity, then why does He not just remove all the sins? Surely, He can do that. God should be able to cleanse all sins, as He is the one who defines sins – it makes no sense. This has raised objections from people of other faiths (e.g., Judaism, Islam, Hinduism, etc.), who see this claim as exclusionary and intolerant.

Critics argue that this teaching creates division and disregards the validity of other religious traditions and their paths to God or enlightenment... Where is God's Justice? I do all the evils, but have faith in Jesus; he will cleanse all my sins. A person performing all the Goods but does not have faith in Jesus will go to hell.

Conclusion: Jesus taking all sins of humans is against the plans of God, as it destroyed the foundation of reward and punishment against good and bad deeds.	Please rate this Conclusion:

Objective Analysis of God

| **Question:** Resurrection of Jesus | **C4** |

Analysis and background:
The doctrine of the Incarnation—central to Christian theology—asserts that Jesus Christ is both fully human and fully divine. While this belief is foundational to many Christian traditions, it presents a basic logical challenge. Critics often question how a single individual can simultaneously embody two natures that appear fundamentally incompatible.

To be divine is to possess supernatural attributes: eternal existence, omnipotence, omniscience, and the ability to transcend physical limitations. A divine being is not subject to suffering, death, or the constraints of time and space. In contrast, to be human is to be finite, mortal, and bound by physical laws. Humans experience pain, ignorance, emotional vulnerability, and ultimately death. These qualities are not just different from divinity—they are its opposite.

This raises a central paradox: if Jesus was truly divine, how could He suffer, feel hunger, experience fear, and die on the cross? And if He was truly human, how could He perform miracles, forgive sins, and claim unity with God? The coexistence of these two natures in one person seems to defy the principle of non-contradiction, leading some to view the Incarnation as a theological mystery rather than a rational doctrine.

Christian theologians have long grappled with this tension, often invoking the concept of a "hypostatic union"—a mystical fusion of divine and human natures. Yet for many outside the faith, this explanation remains unsatisfying. The Incarnation continues to provoke debate, not only about Jesus's identity, but about the very nature of divinity and humanity itself.

| **Conclusion:** These two properties of Jesus are opposite of each other and difficult to coexist in one entity. | Please rate this Conclusion: |

Question: The Bible as a word of God	**C5**

Analysis and background:
The New Testament, which forms the central portion of the Christian Bible, is primarily a compilation of letters—epistles—exchanged between early Christian figures, often referred to as saints. Depending on the denomination, the Bible contains varying numbers of books: the Protestant Bible includes 66, while the Catholic Bible has 73, incorporating the Deuterocanonical texts. Of these, more than 22 New Testament books are letters, many of which were authored by Paul and other apostles, addressing theological issues, moral guidance, and community concerns. Notably, none of the biblical authors claims to be God. Their writings reflect personal experiences, spiritual insights, and teachings attributed to Jesus, but they do not present themselves as divine. Paul, in his letters to Timothy and others, acknowledges that the recognition of these texts as sacred scripture occurred centuries after Jesus' death. While many of the letters were written in the 1st century CE, the formal compilation and canonization of the New Testament did not take place until the 4th century CE—raising questions about historical accuracy and editorial influence over time.

Furthermore, the original texts were not written in Jesus' native language, Aramaic, but primarily in Greek, with Latin translations emerging later. The Old Testament, by contrast, was written over many centuries, mainly in Hebrew, and gradually came to be regarded as sacred by the 1st century CE.

This long and complex process of transmission, translation, and canonization invites scrutiny. The gap between authorship and official recognition, along with linguistic and cultural shifts, complicates the claim of divine origin and challenges the Bible's reliability as a direct and unaltered message from God.

Conclusion: The Bible, which is primarily the New Testament for Christians, is not a direct link to God, nor is it from Jesus.	Please rate this Conclusion:

Objective Analysis of God

Question: Is Salvation Through Faith or Conduct?	**C6**

Analysis and background:
The concept of Jesus as the Saviour, central to Christian theology, is often critiqued for its focus on spiritual salvation while seemingly overlooking the immediate, tangible needs of humanity—such as poverty, inequality, and systemic injustice. Critics argue that emphasizing faith in Jesus as the sole path to salvation may detract from addressing pressing social issues like racism, economic disparity, and political oppression. They question whether a spiritual savior alone is sufficient to confront the material struggles that define much of human existence.

The historical reach of Christianity compounds this concern. For much of history, vast regions—including Africa, China, and India—remained largely untouched by Christian teachings. These areas have been among the most densely populated since the dawn of civilization; yet, Christianity was geographically confined to a relatively small region around the Middle East, spanning approximately 5,000 kilometers. This raises a profound theological question: how will God judge those who never had access to Christian doctrine? Is it to hold them accountable for not believing in a faith they were never exposed to?

The Bible itself presents differing views on salvation. Ephesians 2:8–9 (NWT) states, "*By this undeserved kindness you have been saved through faith, and this is not of your own doing; rather, it is God's gift. No, it is not a result of works, so that no one should have grounds for boasting.*" Yet James 2:14–17 (NWT) counters, "*Of what benefit is it, my brothers, if someone says he has faith but he does not have works? That faith cannot save him, can it? ... Faith by itself, without works, is dead.*"

This tension between faith and works, combined with the limited historical spread of Christianity, raises questions about the fairness and universality of salvation through Jesus alone.

Conclusion: The concept that one only needs to admit to Christian faith for salvation is flawed and against the foundations of the religious idea of sins, righteous life, etc.	Please rate this Conclusion:

Section 4 – Christianity
Questions from Christians

Question: Where is the holy Spirit	**C7**

Analysis and background:

The concept of the Trinity—Father, Son, and Holy Spirit as coequal and coeternal persons within one Godhead—is a cornerstone of mainstream Christian theology. However, this doctrine does not appear explicitly in the Bible. The term "Trinity" itself is never mentioned in any biblical text. Instead, the idea seems to have developed over time as a theological framework to reconcile the Old Testament's strict monotheism with the New Testament's portrayal of Jesus as the Son of God and the active presence of the Holy Spirit.

Scriptural passages suggest a hierarchy or distinction among these entities. In John 14:16–17, Jesus says, *"And I will ask the Father, and he will give you another Helper, to be with you forever, even the Spirit of truth, whom the world cannot receive, because it neither sees him nor knows him. You know him, for he dwells with you and will be in you."* This implies that Jesus requests the Father to send the Spirit, indicating a chain of authority. Likewise, John 14:26 states, *"But the Helper, the Holy Spirit, whom the Father will send in my name, will teach you all things and bring to your remembrance all that I have said to you."* Again, the Father initiates the action, the Spirit carries it out, and the Son's name authorizes it.

These verses suggest that the Father holds primary authority, the Son acts in obedience, and the Spirit functions as a messenger or teacher. Therefore, the notion of all three being equal in status and power is not directly supported by the biblical text, but rather inferred through later doctrinal development.

Conclusion: The concept of the Holy Spirit in the presence of Father God appears as the Helper of God, having a lower stature than God. Therefore, it cannot be equal to God; consequently, it cannot be God.	Please rate this Conclusion:

Objective Analysis of God

Question: Timings of Jesus' return	**C8**

Analysis and background:
The earliest Christian communities, as depicted in the New Testament, were marked by an intense expectation of Jesus' imminent return and the fulfillment of history.
Apostles like Paul, Peter, and John expressed this hope with urgency, using language that suggested it would occur within their generation, shaping a theology of immediacy.
1 Thessalonians 4:15-17: *"For this we declare to you by a word from the Lord, that we who are alive, who are left until the coming of the Lord, will not precede those who have fallen asleep. For the Lord himself will descend from heaven... then we who are alive, who are left, will be caught up together with them in the clouds to meet the Lord in the air."*
1 Corinthians 7:29-31: *"What I mean, brothers and sisters, is that the time is short... For this world in its present form is passing away."*
1 Corinthians 15:51-52: *"Listen, I tell you a mystery: We will not all sleep, but we will all be changed— in a flash, in the twinkling of an eye, at the last trumpet."*
Romans 13:11-12: *"And do this, understanding the present time: The hour has already come for you to wake up from your slumber, because our salvation is nearer now than when we first believed. The night is nearly over; the day is almost here."*
1 Peter 4:7: *"The end of all things is near. Therefore, be alert and of sober mind so that you may pray."*
Revelation 1:3: *"Blessed is the one who reads aloud the words of this prophecy, and blessed are those who hear it and take to heart what is written in it, because the time is near."*
Revelation 22:7, 12, 20: *"Look, I am coming soon! Blessed is the one who keeps the words of the prophecy in this scroll."*
However, two thousand years have elapsed, creating a striking contrast with their initial anticipation.

Conclusion: These lines were clearly from a wishful follower, not the words of God, now that 2025 years have passed & still no sign.	Please rate this Conclusion:

Section 4 – Christianity
Questions from Christians

Question: Jesus' resurrection was not alone	**C9**

Analysis and background:
When a story is developed by a group of contributors over time, it often results in variations, inconsistencies, and a lack of narrative control. This seems to be the case with the Bible, which contains numerous accounts that sometimes contradict or omit significant events. One striking example is found in Matthew 27:52–53 (NWT): *"And the tombs were opened, and many bodies of the holy ones who had fallen asleep were raised. (And coming out of the tombs after his resurrection, they entered into the holy city and appeared to many people.)"*
This passage describes an extraordinary event following Jesus' death—an earthquake, the tearing of the temple veil, and the resurrection of many saints who then entered Jerusalem and appeared to its inhabitants. Such a miraculous occurrence would presumably have had a profound impact on the city and its people. Yet, curiously, this event is not mentioned by any other Gospel writer, nor is it referenced in Acts or the epistles, which detail the early Christian movement.
Given the magnitude of the event—resurrected individuals walking among the living—it raises questions about historical consistency and theological emphasis. Why would such a significant miracle be recorded only in Matthew? Was it symbolic, allegorical, or simply overlooked by other authors?
This example illustrates the broader issue of multiple contributors shaping a sacred text over the course of centuries. With diverse perspectives, theological agendas, and regional influences, maintaining a unified narrative becomes difficult. As a result, readers encounter passages that challenge coherence and invite deeper scrutiny into the Bible's composition and historical reliability.

Conclusion: Such anomalies and illogical elements captured in the Bible confirm that it is not from an all-knowing God, but rather a human creation.	**Please rate this Conclusion:**

Objective Analysis of God

Question: Bible – "3rd hand" books	C10

Analysis and background:
The New Testament is composed mainly of letters—epistles—written by apostles such as Paul, Peter, and John to guide and instruct early Christian communities. These writings, along with the Gospels and other texts, were not compiled into a formal canon until approximately 300 years after Jesus' death. This process of transmission involved multiple generations of followers, church leaders, and scribes, reflecting evolving theological interpretations and historical contexts.

In terms of scale, the King James Version (KJV) of the New Testament contains roughly 138,000 words. Of these, nearly half are found in the epistles, which were personal and communal letters addressing specific issues, beliefs, and moral teachings. While many of these letters claim divine inspiration—often referred to as "the Breath of God"—they are nonetheless authored by individuals who interpreted and communicated their understanding of Jesus' message.

This raises important questions about the nature of biblical authority. A critical examination reveals that the New Testament is not a direct transcript from God or a prophet, but rather a third-hand compilation shaped by human voices. Furthermore, for the first three centuries, these texts existed in scattered, uncontrolled forms—copied, circulated, and debated among various communities—before being officially recognized as scripture.

This long and complex journey from oral tradition to canonized text underscores the human element in the Bible's formation. While it remains sacred to millions, its origins reflect a layered history of belief, interpretation, and institutional influence rather than a single, uninterrupted divine revelation.

Conclusion: Considering what is in the New Testament, how it was compiled, when it was compiled, who wrote it, and the authors' direct contact with Jesus, all point to the fact that the Bible cannot be God's words.	Please rate this Conclusion:

Section 4 – Christianity
Questions from Christians

Question: Christianity is a Polytheistic religion	# C11

Analysis and background:
I keep bringing this thing back, considering that it is the foundational issue of a so-called monotheistic region.
One of the most defining theological distinctions between Christianity and the monotheistic traditions of Judaism and Islam is the Christian doctrine of the Trinity. Christianity teaches that Jesus is both the Son of God and God Himself, alongside the Holy Spirit and God the Father. This raises a fundamental question: how can Christianity claim to be monotheistic while presenting three distinct entities with divine status?

The Trinity is often described as one God in three persons, yet biblical passages suggest clear distinctions in identity, authority, and function. For instance, John 14:28 states, "*You heard me say, 'I am going away and I am coming back to you.' If you loved me, you would be glad that I am going to the Father, for the Father is greater than I.*" This verse implies a hierarchy, with the Father being superior to the Son. Similarly, Matthew 26:39 recounts Jesus praying, "*My Father, if it is possible, may this cup be taken from me. Yet not as I will, but as you will,*" showing submission and separate will. Revelation 1:1–2 further distinguishes Jesus from God, stating that the revelation was given by God to Jesus, who then passed it on to the reader.

While the Holy Spirit is often interpreted symbolically or variably by clergy, the Father and Son are consistently portrayed as distinct beings with different roles and levels of authority. These scriptural references challenge the coherence of the Trinity as three equal persons in one God, and raise valid questions about the nature of divine unity in Christian theology.

Conclusion: The Bible states that the Father and Son are distinct personalities, with the Father holding more power and authority over the Son. Therefore, they cannot represent a single God.	Please rate this Conclusion:

Objective Analysis of God

Question: The Doctrine of Inerrancy	**C12**

Analysis and background:
The doctrine of inerrancy in Christianity is the belief that the Bible, in its original manuscripts, is without error or contradiction in all matters it addresses, similar to the stance of Islam regarding the Quran. Religious institutions promote and enforce this belief to prevent anyone from pointing out issues and inaccuracies, thereby challenging their authority. This is why criticism of the Bible was met with severe punishment and was not allowed until about the mid-1800s.

How can the Bible be considered the actual words of God and without error when it was written, selected, and compiled by humans? Rituals, preaching, laws, and beliefs were aligned with the practices of the time, such as slavery and the treatment of women. These writings were intended to provide hope for the future (afterlife) while ensuring the powerful continued to enjoy their privileges. On the other hand, the Bible encourages examination and questioning:

Acts 17:11: *"Now the Berean Jews were of more noble character than those in Thessalonica, for they received the message with great eagerness and examined the Scriptures every day to see if what Paul said was true."*
1 John 4:1: *"Dear friends, do not believe every spirit, but test the spirits to see whether they are from God, because many false prophets have gone out into the world."*

Therefore, the doctrine of inerrancy does not hold merit, and even the Bible itself negates it.

Conclusion: The doctrine of Inerrancy does not hold merit, and even the Bible negates it.	Please rate this Conclusion:

Section 4 – Christianity
Questions from Christians

Question: The Ten Commandments and Hammurabi's rules	**C13**

Analysis and background:
Both the Ten Commandments and the Code of Hammurabi reflect foundational moral and legal principles that shaped ancient societies, despite their origins in distinct cultural and historical contexts. The Code of Hammurabi, originating in Babylon around 1750 BCE, is one of the earliest known legal systems, inscribed on stone and detailing laws governing civil, criminal, and economic behavior. The Ten Commandments, central to the Hebrew Bible and traditionally dated to around the 13th century BCE, serve as a concise moral code delivered to Moses on Mount Sinai.

Despite their different purposes—Hammurabi's code serving as a comprehensive legal framework and the Ten Commandments as divine moral imperatives—their content overlaps strikingly. Both texts prohibit theft, murder, and bearing false witness, emphasizing the importance of justice, personal responsibility, and social order. These shared themes suggest a common ethical foundation among ancient Near Eastern civilizations.

Given the chronological precedence of Hammurabi's code, some scholars argue that the Hebrew Bible may have drawn inspiration from it, adapting its legal concepts into a theological framework. While the Ten Commandments are more spiritual in tone, focusing on divine authority and covenantal obedience, the underlying behavioral expectations mirror those found in Hammurabi's secular laws.

Examples of Common Lines in the Two Texts (this is discussed in detail earlier) :
- The Ten Commandments: "*You shall not murder.*" (Exodus 20:13)
  The Code of Hammurabi: "*If a man has struck another man and caused his death, he shall be put to death.*" (Law 1)
- The Ten Commandments: "*You shall not steal.*" (Exodus 20:15)
  The Code of Hammurabi: "*If a man steals an ox, he shall pay thirty times its value.*" (Law 8)
- The Ten Commandments: "*You shall not commit adultery.*" (Exodus 20:14)

The Code of Hammurabi: "*If a man's wife is caught committing adultery, both she and her lover shall be bound and thrown into the water.*" (Law 129)

The similarities are too pronounced to ignore, raising the possibility that the biblical authors were influenced by existing legal traditions when shaping their own moral code. This does not diminish the religious significance of the Ten Commandments, but it does highlight the interconnectedness of ancient legal thought and the evolution of ethical systems across civilizations.

Conclusion: The codes of Hammurabi, written approximately 400 years earlier, in 1750 BCE, by a human and enforced as secular laws, are simpler, straightforward, and more executable than the laws provided by God.	Please rate this Conclusion:

Section 4 – Christianity
Questions from Christians

| **Question:** God's Name – known or unknown | **C14** |

Analysis and background:
The Bible contains passages that appear to contradict one another, raising questions about consistency in divine communication. A notable example is found in Exodus 6:2–3, where God tells Moses, *"I appeared to Abraham, Isaac, and Jacob as El Shaddai, but by my name Yahweh (YHWH) I did not make myself known to them."* This statement suggests that the patriarchs were unaware of the name Yahweh. However, this claim is challenged by earlier verses in Genesis, where Abraham explicitly uses the name YHWH. For instance, Genesis 12:8, 15:7, and 22:14 include references such as "Abraham called the place YHWH-Yireh," indicating familiarity with the divine name.

This contradiction raises theological and historical concerns, particularly given the foundational role of the patriarchs in the Israelite tradition. According to Genesis, these figures had direct relationships with God and used His name:

- **Abraham:** The first patriarch, chosen by God and the recipient of the covenant.
- **Isaac:** Abraham's son, who inherited and continued the covenantal promise.
- **Jacob** (Israel): Isaac's son, whose twelve sons became the twelve tribes of Israel.
- **Joseph:** Jacob's son, whose leadership in Egypt preserved the family during famine.

If these founding figures knew and used the name YHWH, then the statement in Exodus appears to negate earlier revelations. This inconsistency suggests either a shift in theological emphasis or a layering of redaction within the biblical text, reflecting evolving understandings of God's identity across generations.

| **Conclusion:** God is making a wrong claim that the name YHWH was not known, as many generations continue to worship God as YHWH. | **Please rate this Conclusion:** |

Objective Analysis of God

| Question: Moses' Father-in-Law's Name | C15 |

Analysis and background:
In the Bible, there are multiple references to Moses' father-in-law, but different names are used in various passages to refer to him. In Exodus 2:18, he is referred to as Reuel, the father of Zipporah, Moses' wife. However, in Exodus 3:1 and Numbers 10:29, he is referred to as Jethro, Moses' father-in-law. Additionally, Judges 4:11 implies that Hobab, the son of Reuel, might also be Moses' father-in-law.

This raises the question: Why are multiple names (Reuel, Jethro, Hobab) used for the same person?

How can God make such a mistake by giving three different names to the same person and creating confusion? Religious scholars argue that one is a name and the other is a title. However, an all-knowing God would be aware that an objective mind would question this and seek the correct answer, potentially challenging the validity of the entire book. So, why would God intentionally seed doubts in the minds of His followers?

This contradiction is more likely to stem from the fact that the Bible was written by different authors, rather than from a single, all-knowing source, God.

This inconsistency suggests that the Bible may have been compiled from various sources and traditions, leading to the use of different names for the same individual. This raises questions about the reliability and divine inspiration of the text, as an all-knowing God would not create such confusion.

| **Conclusion:** This contradiction is more likely to come from the fact that there were different writers of the Bible than from one All-knowing source, God. | Please rate this Conclusion: |

Section 4 – Christianity
Questions from Christians

Question: Death of Nadab and Abihu	**C16**

Analysis and background:
Leviticus 10:1–2 recounts a dramatic and unsettling episode involving Nadab and Abihu, the sons of Aaron, who were struck dead by divine fire for offering "unauthorized fire" before the Lord. The passage states that they presented fire "which He had not commanded them," but it does not clarify the exact nature of their transgression. Scholars and theologians have speculated that they may have used common fire instead of the sacred fire from the altar, entered the sanctuary at an improper time, or acted with irreverence or carelessness.

This incident is frequently cited as an example of the perceived severity—or even cruelty—of divine punishment in the Hebrew Bible. The idea that God would respond with death by fire for what appears to be a procedural error raises questions about justice, mercy, and the role of fear in religious obedience. It suggests that even minor deviations from divine instruction can provoke extreme consequences.

Such narratives often serve a broader theological and institutional purpose: to reinforce the necessity of absolute obedience to God's commands and, by extension, to religious authority. By portraying divine punishment as swift and unforgiving, these stories instill a deep sense of caution and compliance among believers. The message is clear—faith is not a matter of me, but relies on belief, about precise adherence to ritual and law.

In this context, Nadab and Abihu's fate serves as a cautionary tale, emphasizing that sacred duties must be performed with exactness and reverence, and that divine holiness tolerates no error, however well-intentioned or small.

Conclusion: All Merciful God would not perform just cruel and barbaric acts; either God is not merciful, or this section of the bible is incorrect.	**Please rate this Conclusion:**

Objective Analysis of God

Question: Jesus' parents migrated to Egypt?	C17

Analysis and background:
The accounts of Jesus' early childhood in the Gospels of Matthew and Luke contain significant narrative divergences or even contradictions regarding the migration of his parents, a focal point of biblical scholarship.

In Matthew's Gospel, after Jesus is born in Bethlehem, an angel warns Joseph about King Herod's plot to kill the child. Obedient to the divine message, Joseph takes Mary and Jesus and flees to Egypt (Matthew 2:13-15). Matthew emphasizes the danger from Herod and the subsequent return to Israel only after Herod's death. Even then, due to concerns over Herod's son Archelaus, the family settled in Nazareth, Galilee, rather than returning to Bethlehem or Judea (Matthew 2:19-23).

Luke, by contrast, makes no mention of any flight to Egypt. He describes Mary and Joseph living in Nazareth before Jesus' birth, traveling to Bethlehem for a census, and after Jesus is born, returning to Nazareth via Jerusalem following religious rites such as the presentation in the Temple (Luke 2:1-7, 2:22-39). There is no hint of persecution by Herod or the urgent need for refuge in Egypt.

This divergence reveals that the Gospel writers—not God—shaped their narratives to suit different audiences and theological goals. Each author emphasized distinct aspects of Jesus' life and message, reflecting personal interpretation and cultural context. These variations suggest the Gospels are curated reflections by human authors, not direct divine transcripts.

Conclusion: The precision, accuracy, and consistency we expect from a God capable of designing, creating, and managing this vast universe and its minute atoms are not evident in the above example.	Please rate this Conclusion:

Section 4 – Christianity
Questions from Christians

Question: God's complete will to decide	**C18**

Analysis and background:

Romans 9:16: "*So then it depends not on human will or exertion, but on God, who has mercy.*" Also Ephesians 2:8-9 and 2 Timothy 1:9

This verse has sparked significant controversy, primarily due to the tension it creates between God's sovereignty and human free will. It raises the fundamental question of whether salvation is entirely dependent on God's mercy, as the verse suggests, or if human actions, such as faith and choice, play a role in the process of salvation.

The verse emphasizes that salvation comes solely from God's mercy, not from human effort or desire. This perspective implies that humans cannot question God or change their destiny, as God's will predetermines everything. If this verse is taken to be 100% from God, it undermines the entire concept of Heaven and Hell based on human deeds. This concept is foundational to almost all religions, including Christianity, which teaches that human actions and choices determine one's eternal fate.

By leaving this concept behind, the idea that humans are superior creatures due to their free will is removed. It challenges the traditional notions of human instruction, judgment day, Heaven, and Hell, as well as the purpose behind creating the entire universe. Essentially, it suggests that humans have no control over their salvation, and it is entirely in the hands of God's mercy.

This raises profound questions about the nature of free will, human responsibility, and the justice of God in determining the eternal fate of individuals.

Conclusion: This concept cannot come from God, as it negates all things related to God and religion.	**Please rate this Conclusion:**

Pg. 211
My-OAG.com

Objective Analysis of God

Question: Brutally killed children – God wishing/permitting Genocide.	C19

Analysis and background:
Isaiah 13:16 states, "*Their infants will be dashed to pieces before their eyes; their houses will be looted, and their wives violated.*" Similarly, Jeremiah 51:20–24

This reflects a brutal response to the atrocities committed by the Babylonians against the Israelites. In Psalm 137:9, the anguish of exile is expressed with chilling words: *"Happy is the one who seizes your infants and dashes them against the rocks."* These passages echo the horrors of ancient warfare, where such acts were tragically common and used to instill terror.

However, the inclusion of such violent imagery in sacred scripture raises profound moral and theological questions. The notion of divine retribution—where God commands or permits the destruction of entire generations—appears to promote genocide. The idea that infants and mothers, who bear no personal guilt, should suffer such fates is deeply unsettling. It challenges the concept of God as all-merciful and compassionate.

If God is the creator of all people, including both Israelites and Babylonians, how can He endorse or decree such cruelty? The "eye for an eye" principle may reflect human justice systems of the time, but when attributed to a divine being, it becomes ethically problematic. These verses evoke a visceral reaction, forcing readers to confront the tension between divine justice and mercy.

Ultimately, passages like Isaiah 13:16 compel believers and scholars alike to wrestle with the nature of divine morality. Can such extreme violence be reconciled with the image of a loving God, or do these texts reflect human interpretations of divine will shaped by the brutal realities of their era?

Conclusion: God, who is all merciful, cannot say this about his creations; these cannot be words coming out of God.	Please rate this Conclusion:

Section 4 – Christianity
Questions from Christians

Question: Rapist to buy the victim and marry her	**C20**

Analysis and background:
Deuteronomy 22:28-29 (NIV):
28 *"If a man finds a young woman who is a virgin, who is not pledged to be married, and he rapes her and they are discovered,*
29 *he shall pay her father fifty shekels of silver. He must marry the woman, for he has violated her. He can never divorce her as long as he lives."*

This passage has long sparked debate on ethical and theological grounds due to its disturbing implications. It mandates that a rape victim must marry her attacker, with financial compensation paid not to her, but to her father—treating the woman as property rather than a person with agency or dignity.

The phrase "and they are discovered" adds another troubling layer, implying that justice is conditional on visibility. If the crime goes unnoticed, the perpetrator faces no consequence, leaving the victim without protection or recourse.

In contrast, Hammurabi's Code—specifically Law 156—offers a more humane approach. If a man defiles a woman betrothed to his son, he must pay compensation, and she is free to marry the man of her choosing. While still rooted in patriarchal norms, this law acknowledges the woman's autonomy and offers restitution directly to her.

This comparison raises a profound question: how can a divine law, believed to be perfect and merciful, prescribe a punishment that seems harsher and less just than a human legal code from ancient Mesopotamia? It challenges the assumption that all biblical laws reflect divine justice, inviting deeper reflection on the historical, cultural, and moral contexts in which these texts were written.

Conclusion: Hammurabi's Code has more justice for a woman who is raped than God's law	Please rate this Conclusion:

Pg. 213
My-OAG.com

Objective Analysis of God

Question: Destroy cities when captured	**C21**

Analysis and background:
See the following verses not taught by the church and ask yourself, can the God you worship, as portrayed by the church?

Deuteronomy 20:10 *When you march up to attack a city, make its people an offer of peace.*
20:11 *If they accept and open their gates, all the people in it shall be subject to forced labor and shall work for you.*
20:12 *If they refuse to make peace and they engage you in battle, lay siege to that city.*
20:13 *When the Lord your God delivers it into your hand, put to the sword all the men in it.*
20:14 *As for the women, the children, the livestock, and everything else in the city, you may take these as plunder for yourselves. And you may use the plunder the Lord your God gives you from your enemies.*
20:15 *This is how you are to treat all the cities that are far from you and do not belong to the nearby nations.*
20:16 *However, in the cities of the nations the Lord your God is giving you as an inheritance, do not leave alive anything that breathes.*
20:17 *destroy[a] them—the Hittites, Amorites, Canaanites, Perizzites, Hivites, and Jebusites—as the Lord your God has commanded you.*
20:18 *Otherwise, they will teach you to follow all the detestable things they do in worshiping their gods, and you will sin against the Lord your God.*

I will not even comment on this.

Conclusion: God is highly biased towards all and favors one generation. Such a God cannot do Justice on the day of Judgement.	Please rate this Conclusion:

Section 4 – Christianity
Questions from Christians

Question:
Why not just place all in Heaven

C22

Analysis and background:
John 3:16 – *"For God so loved the world, that he gave his only begotten Son, that whosoever believeth in him should not perish, but have everlasting life."*

The concept of salvation through belief in Jesus raises several profound theological and philosophical questions. While it is central to Christian doctrine, Multiple arguments emerge from this single verse that challenge the coherence and fairness of the salvation narrative:

- If God intended to grant everlasting life, why create such an elaborate framework—an entire universe, Earth, heaven, hell, and human history—only to hinge salvation on a single act of belief? Why did God need to subject His son to immense suffering and crucifixion to achieve redemption? If God is omnipotent, could He not have offered salvation without resorting to such extreme measures? This raises questions about divine justice and necessity.
- If belief in Jesus is the sole path to eternal life, what happens to the billions of people throughout history who never had access to this message? Entire civilizations have lived and died without encountering Christianity—does that make them undeserving of salvation?
- This doctrine appears to undermine the moral weight of human actions. If faith alone secures eternal life, regardless of one's deeds, then the concepts of justice, accountability, and ethical behavior lose their significance. It challenges the idea of divine fairness if good and bad deeds are rendered irrelevant by belief.

These questions highlight the tension between faith-based salvation and broader notions of justice, inclusivity, and moral responsibility. Many religious critics say that "I have to sin; otherwise, Jesus' death will go in vain."

Conclusion:
These words cannot be from God but appear to be coming out of some human wish to propagate Christianity.

Please rate this Conclusion:

Objective Analysis of God

Question: Punish only if Salve dies after beating	**C23**

Analysis and background:

Exodus 21:20–21 - *"Anyone who beats their male or female slave with a rod must be punished if the slave dies as a direct result, but they are not to be punished if the slave recovers after a day or two, since the slave is their property."*

What about the slaves' injuries and trauma? The verse focuses solely on punishing the owner if he kills a slave, but what if the slave is severely injured, permanently disabled, or left unable to work or live a dignified life? In those cases, the owner faces no consequences whatsoever.

Look at the enormous gap between a slave recovering after "a day or two" (Exodus 21:21) and the extreme case of death. There is no law addressing intermediate harm—no protection if a slave loses a limb, suffers organ damage, or endures lifelong disability.

This effectively gives owners a free pass to brutalize slaves within the bounds of avoiding outright murder. And the final clause—"*for the slave is their property*" (Exodus 21:21)—only reinforces this injustice, reducing human beings to disposable commodities.

If God is the creator of all people, then both slave and master are His children. Why, then, would divine instruction appear to favor one over the other, especially when that favor results in continued oppression? These contradictions challenge the moral coherence of divine law and invite deeper reflection on whether such laws reflect eternal justice—or the limitations of human societies projecting their norms onto the holy.

Conclusion: These words can only come from a cruel person who wants to give powerful legal or religious rights to do what every owner wants with their slave.	Please rate this Conclusion:

Section 4 – *Christianity*
Questions from Christians

Question:
Obedient Women

C24

Analysis and background:
Timothy 2:11–12 - *"A woman should learn in quietness and full submission. I do not permit a woman to teach or to assume authority over a man; she must be quiet."*

The parallels between the oppression of slaves and the subjugation of women are deeply embedded in the texts and traditions of all Abrahamic religions. Across centuries, sacred scriptures have often portrayed women as subordinate, relegated to roles of silence, obedience, and domesticity. Their autonomy, voice, and leadership potential are frequently diminished or denied. This raises a profound theological question: Is this truly the voice of a just and compassionate God who claims to value all His creations equally? Or are these interpretations shaped by patriarchal societies seeking to preserve power and enforce hierarchies that benefit men?

If divine law is meant to reflect eternal justice, why does it so often replicate the cultural biases of its time rather than rise above them? Why are women—like slaves—treated as second-class citizens, their worth and dignity contingent on the authority of others?

The contradiction is stark. In Galatians 3:28, it is written: "There is neither male nor female… for you are all one in Christ." Yet this same divine figure is frequently cited to justify the silencing of women in religious spaces. Such selective application of scripture reveals a troubling inconsistency. It begs the question: who truly benefits from these interpretations? The answer often points not to divine will, but to human agendas—where theology becomes a tool for control rather than liberation.

Conclusion:
These words can only come from a human who wants to grant powerful legal or religious rights to men over women, perpetuating the status quo of society.

Please rate this Conclusion:

Objective Analysis of God

Question: Lot offers his daughters to save angels	C25

Analysis and background:
GEN 19:8 – *"Look, I have two daughters who have never slept with a man. Let me bring them out to you, and you can do what you like with them. But don't do anything to these men, for they have come under the protection of my roof."*

This verse is part of the story of Lot in the city of Sodom. When two angels visit Lot, the men of Sodom surround his house and demand to have sex with the visitors. In response, Lot offers his two virgin daughters to the mob instead, to protect his guests.

This verse raises several moral issues:
- Treatment of Women: Lot's offer to give his daughters to the mob highlights the low status and value of women in this context. It suggests that women were seen as property to be used and sacrificed for the protection of male guests.
- Strange to protect Angels: Angels are supposed to have capabilities to fly, why could they not do the obvious thing, or their and Lot's God help angels (as God does not interfere in humans)
- Divine Approval: The story is part of the biblical narrative, and Lot is later saved by the angels, which could be interpreted as divine approval of his actions. This raises concerns about the moral messages conveyed by the Bible and whether it endorses such behavior.

This verse raises significant moral issues regarding the treatment of women and the interpretation of divine approval in biblical narratives.

Conclusion: God does not seem to care about women and their emotions, enforcing the idea that women are mere men's property.	Please rate this Conclusion:

Section 4 – **Christianity**
Questions from Christians

Question: War slaves – God's justice or practice of the time	**C26**

Analysis and background:

Deuteronomy 21:10-14 - 10 *"When you go out to war against your enemies, and the Lord your God gives them into your hand and you take them captive, 11 and you see among the captives a beautiful woman, and you desire to take her to be your wife, 12 and you bring her home to your house, she shall shave her head and pare her nails. 13 And she shall take off the clothes in which she was captured and shall remain in your house and lament her father and her mother a whole month. After that, you may go in to her and be her husband, and she shall be your wife. 14 But if you no longer delight in her, you shall let her go where she wants. But you shall not sell her for money, nor shall you treat her as a slave, since you have humiliated her."*

Here god is permitting an Israelite soldier to take a captive woman as his wife after giving her one month to mourn her family. The passage reflects a continuation of patriarchal norms that prioritize male desire and authority over female autonomy and emotional well-being. Just imagine the trauma this woman would endure—her family killed in war, her freedom stripped, and her grief confined to a brief mourning period before being forced into marriage with the very man responsible for her suffering.

This law fails to acknowledge the depth of human emotion, particularly the anguish and psychological devastation such a woman would experience. It treats her as property, rather than as a person with agency and dignity. The absence of divine empathy in this context is striking. If God is all-knowing and merciful, why are such laws so heavily skewed in favor of men, with little regard for the emotional and moral complexity of women's experiences?

Conclusion: God is creating an unjust and cruel system, providing separate standards for Slaves and their owners, which aligned with practices of that time, and also pleasing the wealthy and powerful of that time.	**Please rate this Conclusion:**

Objective Analysis of God

Question: Was it for a particular incident	C27

Analysis and background:
Deuteronomy 25:11-12 - "*If men get into a fight with one another, and the wife of one intervenes to rescue her husband from the grip of his opponent by reaching out and seizing his genitals, you shall cut off her hand; show no pity.*"

This is a particular law. In all situations, God decided to take this one example and allowed the necessary action to be taken afterward.
When I come across this and cannot even find a law about how to treat a person who steals bread for their family, I find it confusing and irrational for God to have included it in the Bible and forgotten to state a law for more general occurrences.

Plus, compare it with the Middle Assyrian Laws (A 8). The Middle Assyrian Laws (MAL) are a set of legal codes developed during the Middle Assyrian Empire, roughly between 1450 and 1250 BCE, with surviving copies dating to the reign of Tiglath-Pileser I (circa 1114–1076 BCE). These laws were written in Akkadian, using the cuneiform script, and preserved on clay tablets discovered in northern Iraq during early 20th-century excavations.

The Law Itself (Tablet A, 8): "*If a woman has crushed a man's testicle in a quarrel, they shall cut off one finger of hers. If the other testicle becomes infected (or is damaged) because of the blow, or if she crushes the second testicle in another quarrel—they shall tear out both her [eyes].*"

The Assyrian Empire conquered Israel (722 BCE) and influenced the Near Eastern legal tradition—a clear case of God copying things from past texts and Laws.

Conclusion: God has not done justice by placing just unimportant verses in the Bible and leaving out more common occurrences. These words are more Human than Gods.	Please rate this Conclusion:

Section 4 – Christianity
Questions from Christians

Question: Keep women like slaves	**C28**

Analysis and background:
Timothy 2:9-12
9 I also want the women to dress modestly, with decency and propriety, adorning themselves, not with elaborate hairstyles or gold or pearls or expensive clothes,
10 but with good deeds, appropriate for women who profess to worship God.
11 A woman should learn in quietness and full submission.
12 I do not permit a woman to teach or to assume authority over a man; she must be quiet.- "I do not permit a woman to teach or to assume authority over a man; she must be quiet."

It clarifies how God instructs women to behave. Women are often expected to have a lower status and be subject to, or in some respects, considered property of men. And these sentences made Timothy continue enforcing these types of norms with women.

On sides, if you go back to previous on and start from 1:18 onwards you will see that it is Paul instructing Timothy by clearly mentioning that *"Timothy, my son, I am giving you this command"*, what is said is not coming from God or his prophet but coming from a person who has not even seen the prophet and then claiming that his words are words of God.

Repeatedly, God comes across and proves Himself as God for Men and not for women.

Conclusion: These words do not portray God (the Protector of universal equality), in both aspects 1. Their nature is to make women entirely submissive to men. And 2. How these words are documented in the Bible	Please rate this Conclusion:

Objective Analysis of God

Question: King 2:24 – 2 bears and 42 boys	**C29**

Analysis and background:
King 2:24 – *"Elisha turned around and looked at them, and he cursed them in the name of the LORD. Then two bears came out of the woods and mauled forty-two of them."*
Here, what happens is that as Elisha (**Elisha** was a mighty **prophet of Israel** in the 9th century BC) travels to **Bethel**, a group of **young men (or boys)** jeer at him, shouting, *"Go on up, you baldhead!"*. God got angry and mauled all 42 boys by two bears.
This incident has several different aspects to consider. Firstly, it represents a very harsh and severe punishment for mere teasing or mocking. A prophet represents God, and this is how God is often perceived in this world and throughout history—not by what He says about Himself, but by His actions. It is important to note that it was not the prophet who carried out the punishment, but God Himself, as such miracles cannot occur without His will and actions. Secondly, religious institutions often employ such stories to instill a deep sense of fear regarding divine punishment, reinforcing obedience through the threat of severe consequences. These narratives serve as cautionary tales, warning followers that any deviation from prescribed behavior—whether moral, ritualistic, or doctrinal—could result in catastrophic outcomes. By emphasizing divine wrath and retribution, institutions can maintain control and ensure compliance, not necessarily through love or understanding, but through fear of divine judgment.
Thirdly, the idea that two bears could simultaneously attack and kill 42 individuals is far-fetched and invites skepticism. Was this meant to be taken literally, or was it symbolic—a hyperbolic warning against disrespecting religious authority? Regardless of interpretation, the underlying message is clear: challenge sacred figures or divine order, and face dire consequences.

Conclusion: This is contrary to the merciful nature of God, as promoted by the Church—the concepts of what God says about Himself and what He does … appear to be two opposing sides.	Please rate this Conclusion:

Section 4 – Christianity
Questions from Christians

Question:
Baptism Heals Diseases

C30

Analysis and background:
James 5:14 – Anointing with oil cures sickness.
James 5:14 (NWT): "*Is there anyone sick among you? Let him call the elders of the congregation to him, and let them pray over him, applying oil to him in the name of Jehovah.*"

This verse embodies a spiritual approach to healing, emphasizing the power of prayer and the importance of communal support. However, it's essential to acknowledge that the Bible does not portray this as a rejection of medical treatment. Instead, it encourages a holistic view—one that integrates faith with practical care.

Here are key interpretations and parallels:
- Faith and Medicine: The Bible acknowledges the role of physicians. For example, Colossians 4:14 refers to "Luke, the beloved physician," showing that medical professionals were respected and valued in early Christian communities. Prayer and medicine are not mutually exclusive; they can work in tandem.
- Comfort in Suffering: Even when physical healing doesn't occur, the ritual of anointing and prayer provides emotional and spiritual comfort. It fosters a sense of connection, hope, and peace during times of illness.
- Church's Role: This verse calls on religious communities to actively care for the sick, reminding congregations of their pastoral responsibility. It's a challenge to prioritize compassion and presence over passive belief.

And as a modern reference, when the Pope had the flu, he didn't rely solely on prayer. He visited a hospital and consulted with medical professionals. Faith may guide healing, but it often walks hand in hand with science.

Conclusion:
Pope using medical facilities even for minor sickness negates what the Bible is saying. So, even the Pope does not follow the Bible, as they know what will work.

Please rate this Conclusion:

Objective Analysis of God

| Question: Even more Barbaric instruction | C31 |

Analysis and background:
Judges 21:10 *"So the assembly sent twelve thousand of their best warriors with instructions to go to the town of Jabesh Gilead and put to the sword those living there, including the women and children. 11 This is what you are to do: completely destroy all the men and every woman who is not a virgin. 12 They found among the inhabitants of Jabesh Gilead four hundred young women who had never slept with a man, and they took them to the camp at Shiloh in Canaan. 13 Then the whole assembly sent an offer of peace to the Benjamites at the rock of Rimmon. 14 So the Benjamites returned at that time and were given the women of Jabesh Gilead, who had been spared. And they were all married to them. But there were not enough women for all of them.*

Once again, we encounter a recurring pattern in specific biblical passages—one that reflects cruelty, harsh punishments, and deeply troubling social norms, all while God is described as "most merciful." This contradiction is difficult to reconcile. The texts often present solutions to societal issues that involve violence, forced marriages, and the objectification of women, rather than compassion, justice, or empathy.

Women are frequently portrayed not as individuals with emotions but as property to be exchanged, conquered, or subdued. In some cases, they are forcibly married to their captors, as seen in Deuteronomy 21:10–14, or treated as compensation for crimes committed against them, as in Deuteronomy 22:28–29. These laws institutionalize suffering and strip victims of dignity, offering no real justice or healing.

Such instructions reflect the values of ancient patriarchal societies, where dominance and control were often exercised through divine order. Yet attributing these norms to a merciful deity raises questions. If God is truly compassionate and just, why do these texts endorse systems that perpetuate trauma and inequality? Are these laws divine mandates, or human constructs shaped by the limitations of their time?

Conclusion: With passages like these, it is challenging to portray God as a symbol of love, justice, and mercy.	Please rate this Conclusion:

Objective Analysis of God

Question: Kill all but leave one, as she helped you	C32

Analysis and background:
Joshua 6: - 17 "The city and all that is in it are to be devoted to the Lord. Only Rahab the prostitute and all who are with her in her house shall be spared, because she hid the spies we sent.
18 But keep away from the devoted things, so that you will not bring about your own destruction by taking any of them. Otherwise, you will make the camp of Israel liable to destruction and bring trouble on it.
19 All the silver and gold and the articles of bronze and iron are sacred to the Lord and must go into his treasury."
20 When the trumpets sounded, the army shouted, and at the sound of the trumpet, when the men gave a loud shout, the wall collapsed; so, everyone charged straight in, and they took the city.
21 They devoted the city to the Lord and destroyed with the sword every living thing in it—men and women, young and old, cattle, sheep, and donkeys.
22 Joshua said to the two men who had spied out the land, "Go into the prostitute's house and bring her out and all who belong to her, in accordance with your oath to her."
23 So the young men who had done the spying went in and brought out Rahab, her father and mother, her brothers and sisters, and all who belonged to her. They brought her out of the city and placed her outside the camp of Israel.
24 Then they burned the whole city and everything in it, but they put the silver and gold and the articles of bronze and iron into the treasury of the Lord's house.
25 But Joshua spared Rahab the prostitute, with her family and all who belonged to her, because she hid the men Joshua had sent as spies to Jericho—and she lives among the Israelites to this day. – **NO COMMENTS**

Conclusion: These appear to have come out of a barbaric movie script and dialogue of a ruthless ruler, rather than will and instruction coming from God.	Please rate this Conclusion:

Section 4 – Christianity
Questions from Christians

| **Question:** Coming from "all-loving God" | **C33** |

Analysis and background:

Samuel 15:3 – *"Now go and attack the Amalekites and devote to destruction all that belongs to them. Do not spare them, but put to death men and women, children and infants, oxen and sheep, camels and donkeys."*

God commands King Saul, through the prophet Samuel, to completely destroy the Amalekites as judgment for their past sins (Exodus 17:8–16; Deuteronomy 25:17–19). The Amalekites had attacked Israel during their Exodus from Egypt, targeting the weak and helpless. This was a holy war in ancient Israel, where certain enemies and their possessions were to be wholly devoted to God as an act of judgment and punishment. The command was specific to this situation and not a general biblical principle.

I struggle to comprehend the rationale behind the killing of women, children, and even animals in specific biblical passages. What wrongdoing could these innocents possibly have committed? These acts are often portrayed as divine punishment for the "sins" of others—yet the victims themselves bear no guilt. In many cases, such violence occurred during wartime, reflecting the brutal norms of ancient conflict rather than any moral transgression on the part of those who suffered.

If God, who is described as all-knowing and merciful, commands or condones such actions, then how is that nature distinguishable from the flawed and vengeful tendencies of humans? The idea of collective punishment—where entire populations are wiped out for the actions of a few—feels deeply unjust and incompatible with the notion of divine compassion.

This leads to a difficult but necessary reflection: perhaps these words were not spoken by God but written by humans—humans shaped by the violence, tribalism, and survival instincts of their time.

| **Conclusion:** These words of God show the exact nature and mindset of the people of that age. | Please rate this Conclusion: |

Objective Analysis of God

Question: Slaves be Slave	C34

Analysis and background:
Ephesians 6:5- "*Slaves, obey your earthly masters with fear and trembling, in singleness of heart, as you follow Christ...*"
The Bible continues to support and enforce slavery. This creates two versions of life and two levels of humanity: the enslaved and the free, while still adhering to the doctrine and promoting the idea of equality.
This contradiction is evident as the Bible simultaneously endorses the subjugation of specific individuals while preaching that all humans are equal in the eyes of God.
This pattern of religion supporting powerful elites and validating cruel and unjust practices has persisted throughout history. Religious institutions often align themselves with those in power, using their influence to maintain the status quo and justify the exploitation of the vulnerable. This relationship between religion and power ensures that the elites continue to enjoy their privileges while the oppressed remain subjugated.
The Bible's acceptance of slavery exposes deep contradictions within the doctrine of equality. While religious teachings often proclaim that all people are created equal in the eyes of God, the presence of laws and narratives that normalize human ownership undermines that very principle and promotes the idea that the Bible is shaped more by human influence than by divine justice.
When institutions emphasize certain verses while ignoring others that condone inequality, it suggests a curated theology designed to serve specific social or political agendas. If divine revelation truly upholds universal dignity, then its message should be consistent and uncompromising in its defense of human rights. The fact that it does not invite serious reflection on whether these texts represent timeless moral truths or the cultural biases of the societies that produced them.

Conclusion: Such verses and the claim that God treats all humans equally or teaches that all humans are equal cannot both be true simultaneously.	Please rate this Conclusion:

Section 4 – Christianity
Questions from Christians

Question: Priest appointed by God	**C35**

Analysis and background:

Deuteronomy 17:12 - "*As for anyone who presumes to disobey the priest appointed to minister there to the Lord your God, or the judge, that person shall die. So, you shall purge the evil from Israel.*".. Two Key Issues to Consider:

Consequences of Challenging Religious Authority: Throughout history, questioning or opposing a priest or religious leader has often resulted in severe punishment, including death. From inquisitions and excommunications to public executions, dissent was usually treated as heresy or rebellion against divine order. This fear-based control mechanism ensured that religious figures remained beyond reproach, protected by both spiritual doctrine and political power.

Divine Appointment: A Modern Dilemma. In contemporary Christianity, the claim that priests are divinely appointed raises serious questions. What verifiable evidence exists to confirm that God has chosen a specific individual for spiritual leadership? Without clear, universal criteria or divine signs, the appointment process often relies on institutional endorsement rather than divine revelation. This ambiguity opens the door to manipulation, favoritism, and the perpetuation of hierarchical control.

Broader Implications Religious institutions frequently position themselves as the ultimate authority, discouraging critical thought and fostering dependence. This creates a form of intellectual and spiritual servitude, where questioning is equated with sin and obedience is rewarded. The pattern is unmistakable: conditioning minds for submission, legitimizing gender inequality, and ensuring that men remain loyal to power structures they do not control. Meanwhile, alliances between religious elites and political or economic powers consolidate influence, allowing a select few to dominate the many.

Conclusion: Considering that God has not appointed any priests in known history, this wording appears to be coming from a Priest who does not want to be questioned, rather than from God.	Please rate this Conclusion:

Objective Analysis of God

| **Question:** One solution - Kill | **C36** |

Analysis and background:
Leviticus 20:27 - *"A man or a woman who is a medium or a wizard shall be put to death; they shall be stoned to death; their blood is upon them."*

Just like today's computer users have one easy solution for any computer issue. --- Reboot.

The portrayal of God's response to human error or disobedience in many religious texts often centers around one recurring theme: "Kill". Whether through divine wrath, plagues, floods, or eternal damnation, the solution seems to be elimination rather than restoration. Unlike a computer that can be rebooted and given a fresh start, human souls—according to some doctrines—are condemned to hell after enduring a lifetime of suffering. This raises profound questions about the nature of divine mercy and justice. If God is omnipotent and compassionate, why is annihilation so frequently the chosen path?

Another troubling issue is religion's historical fear and condemnation of "magic"—a term often used to describe knowledge or phenomena that defied conventional understanding. In earlier times, scientific discoveries such as predicting eclipses or understanding disease were labeled as sorcery. Those who pursued such knowledge were persecuted, silenced, or even executed. This suppression wasn't about protecting truth—it was about preserving authority. By branding curiosity as heresy, religious institutions maintained control and stifled intellectual progress.

The irony is striking, religion itself claims to reveal hidden truths and attract followers through divine insight—precisely what it accuses magic of doing. If God truly understands the mysteries behind what we call "magic," why not enlighten humanity rather than punish those who seek answers? This tension between revelation and repression invites us to reconsider whether divine wisdom is being shared—or strategically withheld to serve human power structures.

| **Conclusion:** Organized religion opposes magic—and later, science—because it threatens the monopoly on narrative that keeps the powerful in control. | Please rate this Conclusion: |

Objective Analysis of God

Question: Women's submission continues	C37

Analysis and background:
Deuteronomy 25:5-6 - 5 *"If brothers dwell together, and one of them dies and has no son, the wife of the dead man shall not be married outside the family to a stranger. Her husband's brother shall go in to her and take her as his wife and perform the duty of a husband's brother to her."* 6 - *"And the first son whom she bears shall succeed to the name of his dead brother, that his name may not be blotted out of Israel."*

Such a rigid and unjust rule raises a fundamental concern: where is the woman's voice, her will, her choice? Once again, we see the continuation of systemic oppression, where women are treated as passive recipients of decisions made by men or divine decree, rather than as autonomous individuals with agency.

It's difficult to imagine that any thoughtful woman, upon deeply engaging with religious texts like the Bible or the Quran, would not question the fairness of doctrines that perpetuate such persistent and complex discrimination. These scriptures often reflect cultural norms that bars women of their freedom, dignity, and autonomy in decision-making. What's even more perplexing is the logic behind laws that compel a woman to marry her deceased husband's brother, as seen in the practice of levirate marriage. Why should God, who is described as all-wise and compassionate, enforce such arrangements without regard for the woman's emotional reality or personal desires?

Interestingly, this very issue was raised during Jesus' time by the Sadducees, who challenged the concept in a theological debate. Yet the biblical narrative seems to sidestep the ethical dilemma. This pattern suggests that many religious laws may reflect human constructs more than divine compassion, crafted to preserve social order.

Conclusion: Rules created by God are very general, lacking respect or consideration for women's nature.	Please rate this Conclusion:

Section 4 – Christianity
Questions from Christians

Question: Again - All problems one solution - Kill	C38

Analysis and background:
Leviticus 20:10 - "*If a man commits adultery with the wife of his neighbor, both the adulterer and the adulteress shall be put to death.*"

This verse delivers a stark and uncompromising punishment for adultery—death for both parties involved. But even beyond the severity of the penalty, the phrasing raises a curious question: why specify "the wife of his neighbor"? Does proximity determine the gravity of the sin? Would the punishment differ if the woman lived farther away, or belonged to a different tribe or region?

This specificity suggests a cultural context in which community boundaries and property, including women, were tightly guarded. The term "neighbor" may reflect a tribal or social structure where violations within the community were seen as direct threats to cohesion and honor. Still, the punishment—death—feels extreme, and it reflects a broader pattern in the Hebrew Bible where divine justice often equates sin with execution.

Yet this harshness is challenged in John 8:7, where Jesus responds to the crowd seeking to stone a woman caught in adultery: "Let the one who is without sin among you be the first to throw a stone at her." With this statement, Jesus reframes justice—not as blind punishment, but as a call for introspection and mercy. His words effectively halt the execution, rendering the law unenforceable in practice.

This raises a dilemma: if Jesus, considered divine in Christian belief, overrides Mosaic law, does that imply such laws are no longer binding? And if divine figures themselves challenge these laws, what does that mean for human obedience to them? Are these laws timeless moral truths—or historical constructs intended to evolve with human understanding?

Conclusion: This is another indication that the Bible was written by different individuals, with their own agendas and perspectives, rather than by a single, all-knowing being.	Please rate this Conclusion:

Objective Analysis of God

| **Question:** Kill – Kill and only Death as punishment | **C39** |

Analysis and background:
Death is a widespread punishment in the Bible, especially in the Old Testament, and in total, there are about 36 sins worthy of death (in God's eyes). Some examples are:
- Murder – Exodus 21:12
- Kidnapping – Exodus 21:16, Deuteronomy 24:7
- Adultery – Leviticus 20:10, Deuteronomy 22:22
- Incest – Leviticus 20:11-14
- Bestiality – Exodus 22:19, Leviticus 20:15-16
- Homosexuality (same-sex relations between men) – Leviticus 20:13
- Blasphemy – Leviticus 24:16
- Breaking the Sabbath – Exodus 31:14-15, Numbers 15:32-36
- False Prophecy – Deuteronomy 13:1-5, Deuteronomy 18:20
- Idolatry – Deuteronomy 17:2-5, Deuteronomy 13:6-10
- Rebellious Children – Deuteronomy 21:18-21
- Witchcraft, Sorcery, or Spiritism – Exodus 22:18, Leviticus 20:27
- False Witness in Capital Cases – Deuteronomy 19:16-21
- Sacrificing Unauthorized Fire (Nadab and Abihu) – Leviticus 10:1-2
- Profaning the Temple or Sanctuary – Leviticus 24:10-16

Out of a total of 613 commandments, about 55 have punishments, and out of 55, 36 have the death penalty, including stoning to death.

| **Conclusion:** This does not reflect a God who is very intelligent, resourceful, or merciful, when about 65% of his punishments in the Bible are gruesome deaths. | **Please rate this Conclusion:** |

Section 4 – Christianity
Questions from Christians

Question:
Menstruation as "Unclean"

C40

Analysis and background:
Leviticus 15:19-30 – Calls menstruation sinful; anyone who touches her or she touches will be unclean, needs to sacrifice two birds (doves/pigeons)
Science: Natural biological process; not harmful
Only quoting 19, 20, and 30 here:

19 "When a woman has her regular flow of blood, the impurity of her monthly period will last seven days, and anyone who touches her will be unclean till evening.
20 Anything she lies on during her period will be unclean, and anything she sits on will be unclean……
30 The priest is to sacrifice one for a sin offering and the other for a burnt offering. In this way, he will make atonement for her before the Lord for the uncleanness of her discharge.

Period is a natural process; one can say that anything that touches the blood needs to be cleaned, but why do such women become unclean, and even if anything or anyone touches her, will she also become unclean?

There is also an illogical duration of cleanliness, as it will remain unclean till evening. Cleaning yourself after touching such a woman is one thing, but for that person to remain unclean till evening is strange, and it becomes more so when there is no mention of the start time. He will be unclean till evening if he touches in the morning or a few minutes before evening.

Conclusion:
These irrational instructions cannot be the words of the creator, the all-knowing God.

Please rate this Conclusion:

Pg. 235
My-OAG.com

Objective Analysis of God

Question: Creation process in Genesis	**C41**

Analysis and background:

Genesis 1:25-27 - 25 *"God made the wild animals according to their kinds, the livestock according to their kinds, and all the creatures that move along the ground according to their kinds. And God saw that it was good.*
26 *Then God said, "Let us make mankind in our image, in our likeness, so that they may rule over the fish in the sea and the birds in the sky, over the livestock and all the wild animals, and over all the creatures that move along the ground."*
27 *So God created humanity in his image, in the image of God he created them; male and female he created them.*

Genesis 2:18-19: 18 *The Lord God said, "It is not good for the man to be alone. I will make a helper suitable for him."*
19 *Now the Lord God had formed out of the ground all the wild animals and all the birds in the sky. He brought them to the man to see what he would name them; and whatever the man called each living creature, that was its name.*

A notable difference is how God can be perceived as confused in the order of creation.

Additionally, what about all the animals and creatures that have become extinct, and we only see their fossils, such as dinosaurs, which were created millions of years ago?

Conclusion: A contradiction, which can only come from a human author and not from the creator of the universe	Please rate this Conclusion:

Section 4 – Christianity
Questions from Christians

Question: Who has seen God	**C42**

Analysis and background:

John 1:18 - 18 *No one has ever seen God, but the one and only Son, who is himself God and is in closest relationship with the Father, has made him known*

1 Timothy 6:16 - 16 *Who alone is immortal and who lives in unapproachable light, whom no one has seen or can see. To him be honor and might forever. Amen.*

Genesis 32:30 - So Jacob called the place Peniel, saying, "*It is because I saw God face to face, and yet my life was spared.*" This is referring to an event of wrestling with God, an event which God did not deny in the Bible

Exodus 33:11: "*The Lord spoke to Moses face to face.*" –
The phrase "face-to-face" carries a particular and powerful meaning—it implies direct, visible, and personal interaction. In everyday language, it suggests a literal encounter where both parties see and engage with one another without barriers. So when scripture uses this term to describe a meeting between God and a human, it naturally evokes the image of a physical, visual exchange. If, however, the intended meaning was symbolic—representing spiritual closeness or deep communication without actual visual contact—then the choice of words becomes problematic. Why would a divine text, believed to be perfect and precise, use language that so easily leads to misunderstanding? It raises the question: could God, who is said to be omniscient, be careless in selecting such a loaded term?

Such contradictions reveal a deeper tension: the effort to reconcile human language with divine mystery often leads to strained explanations. If the text requires constant reinterpretation to avoid conflict, one must ask whether it reflects divine perfection—or human authorship trying to express the ineffable with limited tools.

Conclusion: There is an apparent contradiction between the holy book and the church's explanation, which is also unreasonable and bizarre. Humans are trying to cover up errors in God's selection of words.	**Please rate this Conclusion:**

Objective Analysis of God

Question: Number of Animals on the Ark	**C43**

Analysis and background:
Genesis 6:19-20 (NWT): "*You are to bring into the ark two of every sort of living creature to preserve them alive with you, a male and a female... two of each will go in to you to preserve them alive.*"
Genesis 7:2-3 (NWT): "*You are to take with you seven pairs of every clean animal, a male and its mate; and one pair of every unclean animal, a male and its mate; and seven pairs of the flying creatures of the heavens, male and female, to preserve offspring alive on the entire earth.*"

Beyond the obvious contradiction, the story of the Global Flood presents numerous logistical and conceptual challenges:

Noah's role in preserving life: Was Noah truly capable of keeping every species alive? The task seems far beyond human ability, especially without modern tools or knowledge.
"Throughout the Earth": The command to gather animals from across the globe raises serious concerns about feasibility. How could one man, in a pre-industrial age, locate and transport creatures from every continent?
Housing all land animals in a single vessel: With tens of millions of land species potentially existing, fitting them into one boat—while preventing predation and ensuring survival—is biologically and physically implausible.
Gender-changing species: Some animals, particularly sea creatures, can change gender—a fact highlighted even in pop culture (e.g., Finding Nemo). While sea life might survive a flood without boarding the ark, this biological complexity adds another layer of difficulty to the idea of preserving "male and female" pairs. The Global Flood event has many issues and has been discussed earlier.

Conclusion: This whole event, as an act of an all-powerful God, is illogical, as God could have created all animals back again.	Please rate this Conclusion:

Section 4 – Christianity
Questions from Christians

Question: God or Satan	**C44**

Analysis and background:

2 Samuel 24:1 (NIV) - 1 *"Again the anger of the Lord burned against Israel, and he incited David against them, saying, 'Go and take a census of Israel and Judah."*

1 Chronicles 21:1 (NIV) - 1 *"Satan rose against Israel and incited David to take a census of Israel."*

Even if we consider the Church's defense that sometimes God uses Satan to do what He does not want to do directly, this introduces several paradoxes.

Firstly, asking Satan to perform his work contradicts the story of the omnipotent God, as it implies that God is indirectly responsible for actions that are typically attributed to Satan. This raises questions about the nature of God's intentions and the consistency of His actions.

Secondly, if this defense is valid, it supports the idea that Satan is a vital part of God's overall scheme. This suggests that God is manipulating humans while still calling it judgment. If God is using Satan to influence human actions, it undermines the concept of free will and human accountability. How can humans be expected to control and act against God if their actions are being manipulated by Satan, who is ultimately carrying out God's will?

This contradiction challenges the traditional understanding of the relationship between God and Satan and raises doubts about the fairness and justice of divine judgment.

Conclusion: It shows that the Bible is a work of many humans, not an all-knowing God	Please rate this Conclusion:

Objective Analysis of God

Question: Punishment for Ancestors'	C45

Analysis and background:
Exodus 20:5 (NIV) - 5 *"You shall not bow down to them or worship them; for I, the Lord your God, am a jealous God, punishing the children for the sin of the parents to the third and fourth generation of those who hate me."*
Ezekiel 18:20 (NIV) - 20 *"The one who sins is the one who will die. The child will not share the guilt of the parent, nor will the parent share the guilt of the child. The righteousness of the righteous will be credited to them, and the wickedness of the wicked will be charged against them."*

Multiple issues here:
- Contradiction on who will be punished for sins
- Church explanation that the verse is not referring to the punishment, but considering the impact of sinful patterns, like the consequences of idolatry on families, suggesting that a society's sin can have effects on descendants. So, where does it stop? It is not a non-stop cycle. So, it will never stop.
- This explanation also indicates that it does matter where you are born, which is out of human control, thus impacting the concept of complete justice and free will.
- God being Jealous, can we associate the emotions of Jealousy with God? How could God be jealous, and if He can become Jealous, which is a sign of insecurity and will lead to a **negative** attitude and **destructive outcomes**

Such verses in the Holy text portray a very narrow-minded God with minimal imagination and control over His own justice system.

Conclusion: These words cannot come from God; these are totally against His characteristics and also go against His Justice.	Please rate this Conclusion:

Section 4 – Christianity
Questions from Christians

| Question: Timing of Jesus' Crucifixion | C46 |

Analysis and background:
Mark 15:25 (NIV)- 25 *"It was nine in the morning when they crucified him."*
John 19:14-16 (NIV) - *14 "It was the day of Preparation of the Passover; it was about noon. 15 "Here is your king," Pilate said to the Jews. But they shouted, "Take him away! Take him away! Crucify him!" 16 Finally, Pilate handed him over to them to be crucified. So, the soldiers took Jesus away."*

The issue of conflicting timelines in the Gospel accounts, regarding the crucifixion of Jesus. This discrepancy has led to confusion about the actual timing of key events.

In response, the Church often intervenes with interpretive explanations, suggesting that the difference stems from varying cultural conventions or narrative techniques. Some argue that John may have been speaking more generally, using symbolic structure to advance theological themes rather than precise chronology. However, this very act of clarification reveals something deeper: it acknowledges that the Bible contains human elements—variations in perspective, cultural context, and literary style. If the Bible were the literal and unaltered word of God, such inconsistencies would presumably not exist. The need to reconcile contradictions through human reasoning suggests that the text is a compilation of human reflections, shaped by the authors' intentions, audiences, and limitations.

Thus, while the Church's explanations aim to preserve theological coherence, they inadvertently highlight the Bible's human origins—raising essential questions about divine authorship, historical accuracy, and the nature of sacred scripture itself.

| **Conclusion:** Either an apparent contradiction around the time of the most important event of Christianity, or confirmation that the Bible is not coming from God. Both provide proof that the Bible is not the word of God. | Please rate this Conclusion: |

Objective Analysis of God

Question: Changing basic moral values	**C47**

Analysis and background:

Genesis 20:12: *"Besides, she really is my sister, the daughter of my father, but not the daughter of my mother, and she became my wife."*

Deuteronomy 27:22: *"Cursed is the one who lies down with his sister, the daughter of his father or the daughter of his mother."*

This is a fundamental moral value; how can God change it over time? Practices allowed in earlier eras (e.g., polygamy, concubinage) were later restricted or condemned. It is also said that marrying a sister was culturally accepted in some societies. We are not discussing the culture of the time; here, we are talking about something directed by God, which should be time-independent.

Church says that it is a reflection of changing socio-religious standards across biblical eras. The text shows development—not inconsistency—in ethical understanding. Abraham's era predated Sinai; Deuteronomy reflects a codified theocracy, but here God is defining Moral values.

It appears that God's moral values have evolved - God's thinking & standards for holiness have become clearer over time. What was culturally tolerated in the patriarchal era was later forbidden under the Law.

Additionally, the Prophet's use of this to save his own life seems a bit off as well. This event occurred twice, as seen in Genesis 12:10–20 in Egypt. Would you be comfortable doing it to save your life, knowing that you have complete faith in God controlling your life?

Conclusion: God, who is all-knowing and the ultimate proponent of moral values, would not have a system where He experiments and changes moral values & expectations over time.	Please rate this Conclusion:

Question:
Leprosy Cured by Bird Blood

C48

Analysis and background:
Leviticus 14:1-7: *The Lord said to Moses, 2 "These are the regulations for any diseased person at the time of their ceremonial cleansing, when they are brought to the priest: 3 The priest is to go outside the camp and examine them. If they have been healed of their defiling skin disease, the priest shall order that two live clean birds, cedar wood, scarlet yarn, and hyssop be brought for the person to be cleansed. 5 Then the priest shall order that one of the birds be killed over fresh water in a clay pot. 6 He is to take the live bird and dip it, together with the cedar wood, the scarlet yarn, and the hyssop, into the blood of the bird that was killed over the fresh water. 7 Seven times he shall sprinkle the one to be cleansed of the defiling disease, and then pronounce them clean. After that, he is to release the live bird in the open field."*

The Bible describes a ritual purification process involving bird blood for individuals who have recovered from a "defiling skin disease," commonly interpreted as leprosy. This practice is detailed in Leviticus 14, where the priest performs a ceremonial cleansing using two birds—one sacrificed and the other released—alongside cedar wood, scarlet yarn, and hyssop.

The symbolism is rich, yet the literal elements are striking. The use of bird blood as part of a healing ritual may seem archaic or unsettling by modern standards, especially when viewed through the lens of contemporary medicine and ethics.

Frankly, the passage speaks for itself. Its complexity, its ritualistic nature, and its reliance on symbolic acts over scientific understanding leave little need for commentary. It stands as a reflection of ancient beliefs about purity, illness, and divine intervention—offering insight into how early societies sought to reconcile physical affliction with spiritual restoration.

Conclusion:
God is asking to continue what the age-old rituals for healing, which have no relation whatsoever with the actual sickness or its cure, showing a complete lack of knowledge of the "all-knowing" God.

Please rate this Conclusion:

Objective Analysis of God

| Question: Can God Lie? | C49 |

Analysis and background:
Titus 1:2: "*In hope of eternal life, which God, who never lies, promised before the ages began.*"
2 Thessalonians 2:11: "*For this reason God sends them a powerful delusion so that they will believe the lie*"

Let's approach this from a different angle: If God possesses infinite power and wisdom, why would He choose to send "powerful delusions" to people, as described in 2 Thessalonians 2:10–11? If the goal is to test human faith and moral integrity, then fairness demands that individuals be allowed to make choices freely, without divine interference that clouds judgment. A delusion—especially one originating from God—undermines the very foundation of free will, leaving people with no genuine path to truth.

The Church's explanation, much like the concept of "hardened hearts" in Islamic theology, attempts to justify this by claiming it's a judicial act—a consequence for those who repeatedly reject the truth. But this reasoning feels circular and unsatisfying. If God already knows who will reject Him, why intervene in a way that ensures their condemnation?
This raises a deeper philosophical dilemma: If God is truly impartial and omniscient, why not allow each soul to navigate its own journey without manipulation? Sending delusions or hardening hearts seems to contradict the principle of divine justice. It implies that some are doomed not by their own choices, but by divine orchestration.

In that light, the entire framework appears flawed. If God already knows the final outcome, why not assign souls to heaven or hell directly? Why create a complex system of trials and punishments if the conclusion is predetermined? It challenges the coherence of divine fairness and the authenticity of human freedom.

Conclusion:
The all-powerful Goad does not need to lie or deceive people; these are traits of a weak entity.

Please rate this Conclusion:

Question: All Languages from Babel	**C50**

Analysis and background:
Genesis 11:1-9 – All languages split at Babel.
Science: Languages evolved independently.
Genesis 11:1: "*Now all the earth continued to be of one language and one set of words.*"
This verse introduces the **Tower of Babel narrative** (Genesis 11:1–9), explaining humanity's shift from linguistic unity to diversity. After the Flood, humanity settles in Shinar (Babylon) and arrogantly seeks to build a city and tower "to make a name for themselves," defying God's command to "fill the earth" (Genesis 9:1). God confuses their language, scattering them across the globe. Babylonians' goal to build a tower "with its top in the heavens" (11:4) reflects defiance of God's sovereignty and rejection of His mandate to spread across the earth (Genesis 9:1). God's intervention (11:7–9) disrupts their rebellion, forcing them to scatter—fulfilling His original command.

Noah's flood story is supposed to have happened around 2300 BCE. At that time, civilizations were thriving in other parts of the world:
Mesopotamia
Sumerians: Cities include Uruk, Ur, and Lagash.
Achievements: Cuneiform writing, ziggurats, and advanced agriculture.
Flood Myths: The Epic of Gilgamesh (similar to Noah's story) emerged here.
Indus Valley Civilization
Cities: Harappa, Mohenjo-Daro (peak ~2600–1900 BCE). Achievements include urban planning, sewage systems, and trade networks.
Egypt
Early Dynastic Period (~3150–2686 BCE): Unification of Upper and Lower Egypt.

Old Kingdom (~2686–2181 BCE): Pyramid-building era (e.g., Djoser's Step Pyramid, Great Pyramid of Giza).
China
Hongshan Culture (~4700–2900 BCE): Known for jade artifacts

Objective Analysis of God

and ritual sites.
Liangzhu Culture (~3300–2300 BCE): Advanced rice cultivation, water management.

Peru (Andes)
Norte Chico Civilization (~3500–1800 BCE): Among the oldest complex societies in the Americas, with monumental architecture (e.g., Caral).

Europe
Minoans (Crete, ~3500–1100 BCE): Early maritime culture.
Megalithic Cultures (e.g., Stonehenge, ~3000 BCE): Built stone circles and burial mounds.

Mesoamerica
Olmec Predecessors (~2500–400 BCE): Early villages and ceremonial centers.

These were not due to the spreading out of survivors from Noah's ark. These civilizations existed and continued to develop independently of the flood of Noah.

Conclusion: There is ample evidence that multiple languages existed, which were not derived from or had no contact with the Abrahamic religion. Proving that whoever wrote the Bible was not aware of what was going on the earth	Please rate this Conclusion:

Question: Is God's Power Limited?	C51

Analysis and background:
Judges 1:19: "*Jehovah was with Judah, and he took possession of the mountainous region, but they could not drive out the inhabitants of the low plain because they had war chariots with iron scythes.*"
Matthew 19:26: "*With God all things are possible.*"
Scripture consistently affirms God's unlimited power (e.g., Psalm 115:3; Jeremiah 32:27). Iron chariots pose no inherent obstacle to Him (Exodus 14:23–28; Joshua 11:4–9).

The Lord's presence is affirmed ("The Lord was with Judah"), yet Judah's inability to conquer the plains highlights a tension between divine promise and human action. Here, Church attempts to twist the narrative by suggesting that the failure indicates Judah relied on their own strength rather than trusting God fully.

The Church says that the Israelites' failure reflects their lack of faith or obedience, not God's weakness. However, here God is clearly stating that the failure to conquer the plains is attributed to the inhabitants' iron chariots, the advanced military technology of the time, and it has nothing to do with their faith. If they had had the faith and conquered the hill country, that would have given them more faith to continue.

According to logic and biblical narration, both sources suggest that it was a combined failure of God's omnipotent characteristics.

Conclusion:	Please rate this Conclusion:
God is saying that although God was with Judah, Judah still failed, and NOT God. God seems powerless against other Humans, which is unsound.	

Objective Analysis of God

Question: Is Scripture Perfect or Corrupted?	C52

Analysis and background:
John 10:35: "*The scripture cannot be nullified.*"
Jeremiah 8:8: "*Look! The lying pen of the scribes has made it into a lie.*"

What we're faced with here is a striking scenario: God appears to acknowledge that His own message has been distorted—either in its interpretation or its delivery. This raises serious concerns about the integrity of divine communication. Religious leaders, entrusted with the sacred duty of preserving and conveying God's Word, bear immense responsibility. Yet history shows that their misrepresentations have misled countless followers. The use of the word "Look:" signals that this distortion is not hypothetical—it's actively happening.

But that leads to a deeper question: what is God doing to safeguard His message? A mere acknowledgment isn't enough. If God is truly omnipotent, then ensuring that His guidance reaches humanity clearly and uncorrupted should be a divine priority. Otherwise, it suggests a troubling possibility—has God failed in this responsibility?

How can humans be judged fairly if they've never received accurate instruction? It's akin to being tested at the end of the year without ever being taught the material. The fairness of divine judgment hinges on the clarity and accessibility of divine guidance.

This very contradiction is what compelled me to begin this journey—to seek truth beyond inherited doctrine, to question what has been passed down, and to understand whether divine justice truly aligns with human experience.

Conclusion: God has admitted that His message got corrupted and He did nothing about it; then how come He can be just in judging humans and deciding their fate on judgment day?	Please rate this Conclusion:

Section 4 – Christianity
Questions from Christians

Question: Is God Consistent?	**C53**

Analysis and background:
1 Corinthians 14:33: *"God is not a God of confusion but of peace."* Genesis 11:7: *"Come! Let us go down and there confuse their language so that they may not understand one another's speech."* This verse presents a puzzling narrative. To understand its context: after the Flood, God instructed Noah's descendants to "fill the earth" (Genesis 9:1). Yet instead of dispersing, they settled in Babel (Babylon) and began constructing a city and a tower "to make a name for themselves" (Genesis 11:4). Their unified language and collective ambition were directed toward self-glorification rather than fulfilling God's command. Observing this, God concluded that such unity would lead to unchecked rebellion (Genesis 11:6), and so He intervened by introducing multiple languages to disrupt their plans.

Beyond the theological implications, several critical issues emerge:

Geographical inconsistency: According to the narrative, all of humanity was concentrated in Babylon. This contradicts historical and anthropological evidence, which shows human populations were already spread across various regions.

Divine intervention through division: Rather than guiding humanity back to its intended path, God chooses to fragment human communication—effectively planting the roots of confusion, conflict, and cultural division.

Moral contradiction: This act echoes earlier concerns, such as in "C49 – Can God Lie?", where divine actions appear deceptive. If God deliberately misleads or confuses humanity, it raises questions about divine transparency and fairness.

Altogether, this passage challenges the coherence of divine justice and invites reflection on whether such stories reflect divine will—or human attempts to explain the complexities of civilization and control.

Conclusion: Again, a similar argument is that the all-powerful God does not need to lie or deceive people; these are traits of a weak entity.	**Please rate this Conclusion:**

> *If the Bible is God's perfect word, why does it disagree with itself on fundamental questions?*
>
> *Indeed, an all-knowing and all-perfect God cannot make such mistakes; these mistakes provide evidence that these words cannot be the words of God, but rather are written by humans with a hidden agenda.*

Section 4 – Christianity
Questions from Christians

Question: Earth on Pillar	# C54

Analysis and background:

Samuel 2:8 - *"He raises the poor from the dust; He lifts the needy from the ash heap to seat them with nobles and inherit a seat of honor. For the foundations of the earth are the Lord's, and He has set the world upon them."*

Psalm 75:3 - *"When the earth totters, and all its inhabitants, it is I who keep steady its pillars."*

To begin with, interpreting the Earth's "pillars" and "foundations" as literal, physical structures is scientifically inaccurate. These descriptions, often found in scripture, are sometimes explained by religious institutions as architectural metaphors—symbolic language meant to highlight God's role as the Creator and Sustainer of the universe. In this view, phrases like "the earth totters" are said to represent moral or societal instability. At the same time, "I keep its pillars steady" is interpreted to mean that God maintains order and justice amidst chaos. However, even with metaphorical interpretations, several critical concerns arise:

Linguistic ambiguity: The use of metaphorical language in sacred texts that are translated across cultures and languages can lead to confusion, misinterpretation, and doctrinal inconsistency.

Moral contradiction: If God is actively upholding moral values, why do we witness a persistent decline in ethical behavior and social justice across the world?

Free will vs. divine control: God's direct intervention in stabilizing moral order raises questions about human free will. If divine influence overrides human choices, how can individuals be held accountable for their actions?

These tensions suggest that while metaphor may soften literal inconsistencies, it doesn't resolve deeper theological dilemmas about divine justice, human freedom, and the clarity of sacred communication.

Conclusion: God's message needs to be simple and should be easily translated into many languages without losing its meaning. All-knowing God should know this basic requirement.	Please rate this Conclusion:

Objective Analysis of God

Question: Stars Can Fall to Earth	C55

Analysis and background:
Revelation 6:13 – *"And the stars of the sky fell to the earth as the fig tree sheds its winter fruit when shaken by a gale"*.
Science: Stars are massive suns; impossible

God's apocalyptic revelations often depict sweeping cosmic disturbances—symbolic of divine judgment and the end of the current age. These dramatic events are said to usher in the final restoration of creation under Christ's reign. Yet, while scripture uses vivid celestial imagery, it's essential to recognize that stars are colossal entities, millions of times larger than the Earth. In reality, it is Earth—not the stars—that serves as the stage for this divine culmination.

Historically, people have interpreted natural disasters, like meteorite impacts, as manifestations of divine wrath. One example is the asteroid believed to have caused the extinction of the dinosaurs—an object roughly the size of Mount Everest (10–15 km wide) that struck Earth at a velocity of 20 km per second, unleashing energy beyond comprehension. However, this was merely a lifeless rock, not a radiant star fueled by nuclear fusion like our Sun, which emits energy comparable to countless atomic explosions.

While ancient interpretations linked such phenomena to divine anger, they were shaped by limited scientific understanding. The Creator of the cosmos, who fashioned stars and galaxies, surely comprehends their true nature. These symbolic portrayals reflect humanity's attempt to grasp the divine through the lens of their time—an effort that is both poetic and constrained by the boundaries of early knowledge.

Conclusion: These words cannot come from the creator of the stars and the earth	Please rate this Conclusion:

Section 4 – Christianity
Questions from Christians

| **Question:** Earth Created Before Sun | **C56** |

Analysis and background:
Genesis 1:14-19 – The Sun made after the Earth.
14 And God said, *"Let there be lights in the vault of the sky to separate the day from the night, and let them serve as signs to mark sacred times, and days and years,*
15 *and let them be lights in the vault of the sky to give light on the earth."* And it was so.
16 *God made two great lights—the greater light to govern the day and the lesser light to govern the night. He also made the stars.*
17 *God set them in the vault of the sky to give light on the earth,*
18 *to govern the day and the night, and to separate light from darkness. And God saw that it was good.*
19 *And there was evening, and there was morning—the fourth day*

The Bible presents a creation sequence in which Earth is formed before the Sun. This order reflects the understanding of the world held by people in ancient times, but it diverges significantly from what modern science has revealed.

- The narrative mirrors the worldview of its era, rooted in limited observational knowledge rather than astronomical accuracy.
- The text assumes Earth as the central focus of creation, consistent with the belief that the universe revolved around it—a view later overturned by heliocentric models.
- The account does not distinguish between the light of the Sun and that of the Moon, treating both as similar entities despite their vastly different natures—one a luminous star, the other a reflective satellite.

This portrayal underscores how ancient cosmology shaped scriptural descriptions, offering insight into the cultural lens through which divine creation was once interpreted.

| **Conclusion:** God, the creator of the Sun and Earth, cannot say this | **Please rate this Conclusion:** |

Objective Analysis of God

Question: Four Corners of the Earth	**C57**

Analysis and background:

Revelation 7:1: *"After this I saw four angels standing at the four corners of the earth, holding tight the four winds of the earth, so that no wind could blow on the earth or the sea or on any tree."*

This verse appears to reflect a geocentric worldview, suggesting that the Earth has "four corners"—a concept rooted in ancient beliefs about a flat, square Earth rather than the scientifically established spherical shape. The imagery of angels holding back the winds further reveals a limited understanding of natural forces, as atmospheric dynamics drive wind and cannot be physically restrained by sentient beings.

Such descriptions raise essential questions about the origin and accuracy of the text. If this were truly a statement from the creator of the universe—one presumed to possess perfect knowledge of Earth's structure and natural laws—why would it contain imagery that contradicts observable reality?

The Church often interprets these verses metaphorically, claiming they symbolize God's protection over humanity. Yet this explanation invites deeper scrutiny. If God is all-powerful, why rely on such obscure and convoluted metaphors to convey divine care? And more importantly, where is the tangible evidence of this protection and justice, especially in a world marked by natural disasters, suffering, and injustice?

These inconsistencies challenge the coherence of divine communication and raise the possibility that such verses may reflect human attempts to understand the sacred through the lens of limited knowledge, rather than direct revelation from an omniscient source.

Conclusion: Again, can you believe that the creator of the Earth and the universe would say such a thing? It has to come from a person who is getting his knowledge from other humans from that time.	Please rate this Conclusion:

Question: Storehouses for Snow	**C58**

Analysis and background:
Job 38:22 (NWT):
"Have you entered into the storehouses of the snow, or have you seen the storehouses of the hail?"

This verse, found in God's response to Job (Job 38–41), is intended to emphasize God's supreme authority over creation. After Job's anguished questioning of God's justice throughout chapters 3–37, God replies with a barrage of rhetorical questions meant to assert His unmatched wisdom and control over the natural world.

However, the descriptions used—particularly those involving weather phenomena—reflect a scientifically outdated worldview. Ancient Near Eastern cultures often portrayed elements like wind, rain, and lightning as divine instruments or weapons, and this passage continues that tradition. God is depicted as personally directing these forces, yet modern science explains weather through atmospheric pressure, temperature gradients, and planetary rotation—not divine manipulation.

This raises a troubling inconsistency: if God is truly omniscient, why does His explanation rely on mythological imagery rather than accurate natural principles? The appeal to divine wisdom rooted in ancient cosmology may have resonated in its time, but today it exposes a gap between theological claims and scientific understanding.

In that light, God's "wisdom of yesterday" seems less like timeless truth and more like a reflection of human limitations—suggesting that the divine voice in this passage may be shaped more by cultural context than by universal knowledge.

Conclusion: Once more, these are the common understandings of that time, but not the creator of all animals, the all-knowing.	Please rate this Conclusion:

Objective Analysis of God

Question: Snakes Eat Dust	C59

Analysis and background:
Genesis 3:14 – " *So the Lord God said to the serpent, 'Because you have done this, cursed are you above all livestock and all wild animals! You will crawl on your belly and you will eat dust all the days of your life.*"
Fact: Snakes eat prey, not dirt.

This verse marks God's judgment on the serpent after it tempted Eve to eat the forbidden fruit. Yet snakes continue to prey on other animals. Does this imply the serpent has bypassed God's divine will, despite God being all-powerful and all-knowing?

If "eating dust" is a metaphor for crawling on its belly, then what sets the snake apart from other creatures like rodents? In many ways, the snake is remarkably adaptable to its environment, sometimes even more so than other animals. Its stealth, resilience, and ability to thrive in hostile conditions suggest a lifestyle shaped by nature's design rather than divine disgrace.

Furthermore, if everyone is judged separately on their appointed day, why was punishment pronounced on the entire "race" of serpents? This universal judgment raises similar questions about the consequences faced by humanity in the story of Adam. Is there room to interpret these judgments as symbolic, meant to illuminate broader truths about temptation, consequence, and spiritual inheritance?

Conclusion: We could not translate the "punishment" given to the snake here. Snake life is, like that of other animals, somewhat better.	Please rate this Conclusion:

Section 4 – Christianity
Questions from Christians

Question : One medicine for all sicknesses	**C60**

Analysis and background:

James 5:14 (NWT): "*Is there anyone sick among you? Let him call the elders of the congregation to him, and let them pray over him, applying oil to him in the name of Jehovah.*"

This verse outlines a spiritual approach to healing, emphasizing the power of prayer and communal support during times of illness. It reflects a tradition where physical ailments are met not only with medical care but also with spiritual intervention—anointing with oil and invoking divine presence through prayer.

This practice is echoed in other parts of scripture and interpreted in various ways:

Faith and Medicine: The passage does not reject medical treatment. Instead, it encourages believers to seek divine help in conjunction with professional care. For instance, Colossians 4:14 refers to "Luke, the beloved physician," showing that early Christians valued medical expertise and saw no conflict between faith and science.

Comfort in Suffering: Even when physical healing isn't guaranteed, the ritual of anointing and prayer provides emotional and spiritual support. It fosters a sense of hope, solidarity, and peace, reminding the sick that they are not alone.

Church's Role: This verse calls on religious communities to take an active role in caring for the vulnerable. It challenges congregations to prioritize compassion, presence, and pastoral care—not just preaching or ritual.

And as a modern example, even the Pope—spiritual leader to millions—relied on medical professionals when he contracted the flu. This underscores a simple truth: faith and medicine are not adversaries. They can coexist, each offering healing in its own way.

Conclusion: Pope using medical facilities even for minor sickness negates what the Bible is saying. So, even the Pope does not follow the Bible, as they know that the Bible's recommendations are wrong.	**Please rate this Conclusion:**

Objective Analysis of God

Bible - Order of Universe Creation

In the following lines, we will narrate the Bible version of how the universe was created. There are many logical and scientific issues and inconsistencies, which I will let you explore and decide if this can be the recipe and order of events. Does this order make any logical or scientific sense?

Analysis and background:
This will be a long one, as this is the premise of this book
Genesis 1:1-2:3:
1. In the beginning, God created the heavens and the earth.
2. Now the earth was formless and desolate, and there was darkness upon the surface of the watery deep, and God's active force was moving about over the surface of the waters.
3. And God said, "Let there be light." Then there was light.
4. And God saw that the light was good, and God began to divide the light from the darkness.
5. God called the light Day, and the darkness he called Night. And there was evening, and there was morning —the first day.
6. Then God said, "Let there be an expanse between the waters, and let there be a division between the waters and the waters.
7. Then God made the expanse and divided the waters beneath the expanse from the waters above the expanse. And it was so.
8. God called the expanse Heaven. And there was evening and there was morning, the second day.
9. Then God said, "Let the waters under the heavens be collected together into one place, and let the dry land appear." And it was so.
10. God called the dry land Earth, and the collection of the waters he called Seas. And God saw that it was good.
11. Then God said, "Let the earth bring forth grass, seed-bearing plants, and trees yielding fruit according to their kinds, the fruit having its seed in it on the earth." And it was so.
12. The earth began to produce grass, seed-bearing plants, and trees yielding fruit, the fruit having its seed in it according to their kinds. Then God saw that it was good
13. And there was evening and there was morning, the third day.
14. Then God said: "Let there be luminaries in the expanse of the heavens to divide the day from the night, and they will serve as signs for seasons and for days and years.

15. They will serve as luminaries in the expanse of the heavens to shine upon the earth." And it was so.
16. God made the two great luminaries, the greater luminary for dominating the day and the lesser luminary for dominating the night, and also the stars.
17. God put them in the expanse of the heavens to shine upon the earth
18. and to dominate by day and by night and to divide the light from the darkness. Then God saw that it was good.
19. And there was evening and there was morning, the fourth day.
20. Then God said, "Let the waters swarm with living creatures, and let flying creatures fly above the earth across the expanse of the heavens."
21. So, God created the great sea creatures and every living creature that moves and swarms in the waters according to their kinds and every winged flying creature according to its kind. And God saw that it was good.
22. Then God blessed them, saying: "Be fruitful and become many and fill the waters of the sea, and let the flying creatures become many on the earth."
23. And there was evening and there was morning, the fifth day.
24. Then God said, "Let the earth bring forth living creatures according to their kinds: domestic animals and creeping animals and wild animals of the earth according to their kinds." And it was so.
25. God made the wild animals of the earth according to their kinds, the domestic animals according to their kinds, and all the creeping animals of the ground according to their kinds. And God saw that it was good.
26. Then God said, "Let us make man in our image, according to our likeness, and let them have in subjection the fish of the sea and the flying creatures of the heavens and the domestic animals and all the earth and every creeping animal that moves on the earth."
27. And God went on to create the man in his image, in God's image he created him; male and female he created them.
28. Further, God blessed them, and God said to them: "Be fruitful and become many, fill the earth and subdue it, and have in subjection the fish of the sea and the flying creatures of the heavens and every living creature that moves on the earth."

Objective Analysis of God

29. Then God said, "Here I have given to you all vegetation bearing seed that is on the entire earth, and every tree on which there is the fruit of a tree bearing seed. Let them serve as food for you
30. And to every wild animal of the earth and every flying creature of the heavens and to everything moving on the planet in which there is life, I have given all green vegetation for food." And it was so.

Converting into days' order:
1. Day 1: Light and darkness were separated.
2. Day 2: The sky (expanse) was created, separating the waters.
3. Day 3: Land, seas, and vegetation established.
4. Day 4: Sun, moon, and stars set to govern time and seasons. Day 4 (v. 17–19): God positions the sun, moon, and stars in the sky to govern time (seasons, days, years) and illuminate the earth.
5. Day 5 (v. 20): God creates marine life (fish, sea creatures) and birds, filling the waters and skies (v. 21–23): Creation of aquatic life (fish, sea creatures) and birds. God's first blessing commands them to multiply and fill their domains.
6. Day 6 (v. 24–25): Creation of land animals (wild animals, livestock, insects). Each creature is made "according to their kinds," highlighting biodiversity and divine order. (v. 26–30) Creation of Humanity:

Humans are uniquely made "in God's image" (Imago Dei), reflecting His rationality, morality, and relational capacity (Genesis 9:6; Ephesians 4:24).

These are aligned with the knowledge of the time. I will only highlight the main discrepancies; you can go on to identify many more:

Discussion points
1. Order of Creation
   a. Genesis: Vegetation (Day 3) → Sun (Day 4).
   b. Science: The sun (4.5 billion years ago) existed long before Earth's vegetation (~470 million years ago). Photosynthesis requires sunlight, making this sequence scientifically implausible.
2. First creation
   c. Genesis: First heaven and earth were created; Heaven refers typically to anything we see upward.

Section 4 – Christianity
Questions from Christians

    d. Science: Geocentric approach. Universe: ~13.8 billion years; Earth: ~4.5 billion years; life: ~3.7 billion years. Evolutionary processes span millions of years.
3. Celestial Bodies
    e. Genesis: Sun, moon, and stars created on Day 4 after Earth.
    f. Science: Sun and stars formed before Earth. Solar system formation began with the sun's ignition, followed by planetary accretion.
4. Life Development
    g. Genesis: Marine life and birds (Day 5) → Land animals and humans (Day 6).
    h. Science: Marine life (~500 million years ago) → Land plants (~470 million years ago) → Land animals (~370 million years ago) → Birds (~150 million years ago) → Humans (~300,000 years ago).
5. Biological Diversity
    i. Genesis: Fixed "kinds" created separately.
    j. Science: Evolution via common descent, with species diverging over time through natural selection and genetic mutation.
6. Human Origins
    k. Genesis: Humans were created entirely in God's image (Day 6).
    l. Science: Humans evolved from hominids, sharing ancestry with apes (diverging ~6–7 million years ago).
7. Cosmology
    m. Genesis: Earth-centred universe with a "firmament" (solid dome) holding back celestial waters.
    n. Science: Earth orbits the sun; the universe expands within a space-time continuum; no physical "dome" exists.
8. Death and Suffering
    o. Genesis: Some interpretations suggest no death before Adam's sin.
    p. Science: The Fossil record shows predation, disease, and extinction long before humans existed.
9. Green vegetation for all living
    q. Genesis: Every living being has green vegetation
    r. Science: Many fish and thus many birds do not consume green vegetation directly or indirectly (eating animals that have eaten green vegetation)

Objective Analysis of God

10. No Vegetation on vast areas of Earth
    s. surfaceGenesis: Vegetation on all parts of Earth
    t. Science: NASA and the FAO estimate that ~33% of land is "barren or sparsely vegetated," but only about 15–20% is entirely devoid of vegetation.
11. Story of Adam
    u. No mention of Adam. Not sure how the story of Adam will come here

Christian God's Moral Values

The Bible presents high moral standards to guide humanity toward justice, compassion, and spiritual growth. In biblical tradition, failing to meet God's standards invites consequences both temporal and eternal, symbolizing a breach in the divine-human relationship and a drift away from truth, grace, and redemption.
But,

What we see in the Bible is that God Himself not only breaks these standards but also goes well below any standard, as seen in the lines below. This hypocrisy from the God who sets the standards and will be the sole judge on judgment day is again mind-boggling. How can Humans accept these two faces of God, where His words are not aligned with what He has been teaching and for which He has set up this whole universe? This is one of the places where the entire castle of God and religion began to break up, brick by brick.

Few examples are below, for ref only:

1. **God's Contradiction to Moral Standards**
   - 1 Kings 22:23 – "*The Lord has put a lying spirit...*"
   - Isaiah 13:16 – "*Infants will be dashed in pieces...*"
   - 2 Samuel 12:14-15 – Infant death as divine punishment
   - Deuteronomy 4:24 – "*God is a jealous God.*"
   - Joshua 24:19-20 – "*He will not forgive...*"
   - Psalm 94:1 – "*God of vengeance...*"
   - Leviticus 26:25 – "*Execute vengeance...*"
   - Romans 12:19 – "*It is mine to avenge.*"
2. **Genocide and Mass Violence**
   - 1 Samuel 15:2-3 – "*Kill... child and infant*"
   - Deuteronomy 2:34, Joshua 6:21, Numbers 25:4-5 – Destruction of all ages
   - Exodus 23:23 – "*Blot out nations...*"
   - 1 Samuel 15:3, Psalm 137:9, Joshua 6:21 – Violent commands
   - 2 Kings 2:23-24 – Bears maul youths
3. **Slavery and Sexual Exploitation**
   - Leviticus 25:44-46, Exodus 21:20-21 – Slaves as property
   - Numbers 31:17-18 – Virgin girls kept as war spoils

Objective Analysis of God

- Exodus 21:7, Deuteronomy 22:28-29 – Selling daughters, forced marriage
- Numbers 5:11-31 – Adultery test causing abortion

4. **Gender Inequality**
   - Leviticus 27:3-4 – Female vow valued less
   - Exodus 21:10-11 – Reduced marital rights for first wife
   - 1 Corinthians 14:34-35, 1 Timothy 2:12 – Women silenced
   - Leviticus 21:9 – Priest's daughter burned for prostitution
   - 1 Timothy 2:12, 2 Samuel 12:8 – Subjugation and polygamy

5. **Harsh Punishments for Minor Offenses**
   - Leviticus 24:16 – Death for blasphemy
   - Numbers 15:32-36 – Stoned for gathering sticks

6. **Tribalism and Favoritism**
   - Deuteronomy 7:6 – Chosen people narrative
   - Genesis 9:25 – Curse on Canaan
   - Nehemiah 13:23-27 – Interracial marriage punished

7. **Eternal Punishment and Predestination**
   - Matthew 25:46 – Eternal punishment for finite sins
   - Romans 9:16-18 – God hardens whom He chooses

8. **Conditional Forgiveness and Blood Atonement**
   - Matthew 6:14-15 – Forgiveness withheld conditionally
   - Hebrews 9:22 – No forgiveness without blood

9. **Free Will Undermined**
   - 1 Kings 22:23 – Lying spirit sent to prophets

10. **Hypocrisy in Justice and Forgiveness**
    - Malachi 3:6 – "*I the Lord do not change.*"
    - Romans 3:5-6 – "*Is God unjust? By no means.*"
    - Romans 1:20 – Accountability for invisible qualities

11. **Lack of Moral Clarity**
    - Proverbs 25:2 – "*It is the glory of God to conceal...*"
    - Matthew 5:17, Luke 24:44 – Affirming past laws without condemnation

12. **Collective Punishment**
    - Exodus 20:5 – Children punished for parents' sins
    - 2 Samuel 24:15 – 70,000 Israelites killed for David's actions

Conclusion

Here you can see that the Bible's **shifting moral standards** (e.g., on slavery, women's rights, and violence) disprove the claim of **objective divine morality**. If morality is based *solely* on God's commands, then acts like genocide or slavery could be deemed "moral" if God ordered them. **Deuteronomy 20:16-17:** *"But in the cities of these peoples that the Lord your God is giving you for an inheritance, you shall save alive nothing that breathes, but you shall devote them to destruction..."*

This raises the question: Is killing innocent children moral *because God commands it*, or is there an independent standard?

These contradictions challenge the claim that God's morality is **objective, unchanging, or perfect**. If morality requires divine authority, God's actions undermine His own standard.

Can objective morality exist if its source (God) violates it?

Section 5

Islam

Section 5 – Islam

Islam:

My main arguments against Islam are:
1. How can God say that He has completed the region as last communication to humans for ages to come (at least 1500 years), but Islam cannot even survive 4-5 hours after the death of the Prophet Mohammed?
2. Why was the last written message and instruction to the Human not even documented, given in complicated language (in terms of how it can be manipulated and interpreted)?
3. Why does the last book have about 30% text dedicated to the praise of Allah, instead of providing clear instructions on how to fulfill His desires

An all-knowing God would not make illogical decisions or deliberately mislead His followers. If Prophet Muhammad's companions struggled to understand the valid message and fell into internal conflicts within hours of his passing, then how can I, 1,500 years later, confidently follow Islam? Nowadays, when interpretations of the Quran and Islamic faith have become so fragmented. The Quran does not explicitly outline any details on a specific topic, including how to perform Namaz, which adds to the uncertainty.

Islam – Main Concepts:

Islam was built upon the lessons of its previous religions - Judaism and Christianity, resulting in a more refined sacred text. However, despite this refinement, it does not introduce groundbreaking new concepts. From the concept and name of Allah to rituals like Ramadan, Namaz, and fasting, most religious practices predate Islam; Islam primarily modified their implementation rather than creating them anew. Additionally, Islam continued the practice of slavery, upheld certain limitations on women's rights, and retained harsh legal punishments rooted in Hammurabi's code.

Islam is a monotheistic religion founded in the 7th century CE by the Prophet Muhammad in the city of Mecca. It is based on the teachings of the Quran, which Muslims believe to be the word of God (Allah) as revealed to Muhammad, and the Hadith, which are

Objective Analysis of God

the recorded sayings and actions of the Prophet. The main concepts and teachings of Islam can be summarized as follows:

1. The Five Pillars of Islam
These are the core practices that define a Muslim's faith and actions:
1. **Shahada (Declaration of Faith):**
    a. The testimony that "*There is no god but Allah, and Muhammad is His messenger.*"
    b. This is the foundational belief in Islam.
2. **Salah (Prayer):**
    a. Muslims perform five daily prayers facing Mecca.
    b. Prayer is a direct connection between the worshipper and Allah.
3. **Zakat (Charity):**
    a. Obligatory giving of a portion of one's wealth (usually 2.5%) to the poor and needy.
    b. It emphasizes social justice and community welfare.
4. **Sawm (Fasting during Ramadan):**
    a. Fasting from dawn to sunset during the month of Ramadan.
    b. It teaches self-discipline, empathy for those in low-income situations, and spiritual reflection.
5. **Hajj (Pilgrimage to Mecca):**
    a. Muslims who are physically and financially able must perform the Hajj at least once in their lifetime.
    b. It symbolizes unity and equality among Muslims.

2. The Six Articles of Faith
These are the core beliefs in Islam:
1. **Belief in Allah (God):**
    a. Allah is the one and only God, omnipotent, merciful, and without partners or associates.
2. **Belief in Angels:**
    a. Allah creates angels to carry out His commands and act as messengers.
3. **Belief in the Prophets:**
    a. Muslims believe in all the prophets sent by Allah, including Adam, Noah, Abraham, Moses, Jesus, and Muhammad (the final prophet).
4. **Belief in the Scriptures:**

a. Muslims believe in the divine books revealed to prophets, including the Torah, Psalms, Gospel, and the Quran (the final and most complete revelation).
5. **Belief in the Day of Judgment:**
   a. The belief in an afterlife where all individuals will be resurrected and judged by Allah based on their deeds.
6. **Belief in Divine Decree (Qadar):**
   a. Everything that happens is by the will of Allah, though humans have free will to choose their actions.

In Shia Islam, the articles of faith often center on Tawḥīd, Adl (divine justice), Nubuwwah (prophethood), Imāmah (leadership of infallible Imams), and Qiyāmah, reflecting theological nuances.

3. The Quran
- The Quran is the holy book of Islam, believed to be the literal word of Allah as revealed to Muhammad over 23 years.
- It covers guidance on worship, morality, law, and the purpose of life.
- It is written in Arabic and is considered untranslatable in its whole meaning, though translations exist for understanding.

4. The Sunnah and Hadith
- The Sunnah refers to the practices and traditions of the Prophet Muhammad.
- The Hadith are collections of his sayings, actions, and approvals, which provide practical examples of how to live according to Islamic principles.
- For Shia and Ismaili sects, the teaching of Imams takes similar importance, and Hadiths

5. Tawhid (Oneness of God)
- The central concept of Islam is the absolute oneness of Allah.
- Associating partners with Allah (shirk) is considered the gravest sin.

6. Akhirah (Afterlife)
- Muslims believe in life after death, where individuals will be rewarded with Paradise (Jannah) or punished in Hell (Jahannam) based on their faith and deeds.

7. Sharia (Islamic Law)
- Sharia is the moral and legal framework derived from the Quran, Hadith, and scholarly consensus.

Objective Analysis of God

- It covers aspects of daily life, including worship, family, business, and criminal law.
- The interpretation and application of Shariah vary across cultures and schools of thought.
- Note that the term "Shariya" is not explicitly used in the Quran (sometimes words used: 1. **"shir'atan"** (شِرْعَةً) (45:18) or **"shara'a"** (42:13) (شَرَعَ) or **"shir'atan"** (5:48) (شِرْعَةً), but the divine laws are mentioned at an extremely high level, without going into any details.
- Here, we have to make a distinction between Shariah and Fiqh:
    - **Shariah** refers to Islam's divine, unchanging principles (Quran and Sunnah).
    - **Fiqh** (فقه) is the human interpretation and application of Shariah through jurisprudence.
- The Quran provides the core legal framework of Shariah, while the Sunnah, scholarly consensus, and analogical reasoning (Qiyas) fill in practical details. Like "Give Zakat", but how, when, how much, etc, have been left with Scholars to define
- Even these verses are only about 1% of the Quran

It is like Allah is making the law to "Go North," but without any SMART targets, such as how much, when, by what time, etc. So, a person taking one step has achieved the target, or a person walking for all of life will fall short of achieving it.

8. Moral and Ethical Teachings
- Islam emphasizes honesty, justice, compassion, humility, and generosity.
- It prohibits harmful behaviours like lying, stealing, backbiting, and oppression.
- Family and community are highly valued, emphasizing caring for parents, neighbours, and the poor.

9. Jihad
- Often misunderstood, jihad means "struggle" or "striving."
- It can refer to an internal struggle for self-improvement (greater jihad) or, in specific contexts, a physical battle to defend Islam (lesser jihad).

- It is not synonymous with "holy war."

10. Equality and Brotherhood
- Islam teaches that all humans are equal before Allah, regardless of race, ethnicity, or social status.
- The concept of Ummah (global Muslim community) emphasizes unity and solidarity among Muslims.

11. Respect for Other Religions
- Islam recognizes the validity of previous Abrahamic religions (Judaism and Christianity) and their prophets.

12. Modesty and Conduct
- Modesty in behaviour, dress, and speech is highly emphasized.
- For example, hijab (modest clothing) is prescribed for men and women, with slightly specific guidelines for women.

These teachings form the foundation of Islamic belief and practice, guiding Muslims in their spiritual, moral, and social lives.

Objective Analysis of God

History:

Like other religions, Islam has evolved, adapting to various historical, cultural, and social contexts while remaining true to its core principles. Over the centuries, Islam has interacted with multiple civilizations, philosophies, and other religions, shaping the development of Islamic thought and practices. Below is a broad overview of how Islam has evolved and adopted influences from different religions and cultures:

1. The Foundation of Islam (610–632 CE):
- Islam originated in the 7th century CE with the life and teachings of the Prophet **Muhammad** in Mecca (modern-day Saudi Arabia). The foundational text of Islam, the **Quran**, was revealed to Muhammad by the archangel **Jibril (Gabriel)** over a period of 23 years, beginning in 610 CE. The message emphasized the oneness of God (Allah), the importance of monotheism, and guidance for personal conduct, ethics, and social justice.
- Muhammad's teachings also emphasized **submission to the will of God**, which is the central concept in Islam (Islam means "submission" or "surrender").
- Early Islam was shaped by the teachings of Muhammad and the Quran, along with the **Hadiths** (sayings and actions of Muhammad), which provided additional guidance for Muslims.

Major conflicts emerged in the Muslim world within a few hours of Prophet Mohammed's death. When it was divided into two groups over who should be the successor, two claimed Ali or Abu Bakr—both the closest and most faithful followers of the Prophet, but one had to be wrong. This difference gave rise to the Sunni and Shia sects, which have continued to evolve and adopt numerous additional differences in their beliefs, rituals, and teachings.

As mentioned earlier, Allah, who sent His final message to earth and His teaching messages, was so feeble/ill communicated that his lifetime direct follower could not understand or remember these within hours of the Messenger's demise, and started denying it within 4-5 hours of his death.

Then, how can Allah expect His message to reach me correctly, and I can follow it after 1400+ years, considering the enormous amount of misinformation that has been injected into the message over the years?

Objective Analysis of God

In the following lines, we will follow Sunni history, as that is the majority of Muslims.

2. The Rashidun Caliphate (632–661 CE):
- After Muhammad's death, Islam spread rapidly across the Arabian Peninsula and beyond. The **Rashidun Caliphate** (632–661 CE), led by the first four caliphs, focused on expanding the Muslim community and establishing Islamic governance based on the Quran and Hadiths.
- During this period, Islam spread through military conquest, trade, and missionary activity into North Africa, Persia, and the Byzantine Empire.
- The **Sunni** and **Shia** split, which remains a significant division within Islam, began to emerge due to differing views on leadership succession after Muhammad's death. Sunnis believed that the leader (caliph) should be chosen by consensus. In contrast, Shia Muslims believed leadership should stay within Muhammad's family, specifically with his cousin and son-in-law, **Ali**.

3. The Umayyad and Abbasid Dynasties (661–1258 CE):
- The **Umayyad Caliphate** (661–750 CE) expanded the Islamic empire further into Spain, Central Asia, and India. The Umayyads made Arabic the official language of administration and contributed to the spread of Islam in these regions. However, the Umayyad dynasty was criticized for its focus on worldly power and wealth, leading to a backlash and the eventual rise of the **Abbasid Caliphate** (750–1258 CE).
- The **Abbasid period** is often regarded as the "Golden Age" of Islam, marked by a flourishing of culture, science, philosophy, and art, particularly in cities such as Baghdad, Damascus, and Cairo. Islamic scholars translated works from Greek, Persian, and Indian scholars, preserving and expanding upon knowledge in fields like mathematics, medicine, astronomy, and philosophy.
- The spread of **Islamic mysticism (Sufism)** also occurred during this period. Sufism emphasized the direct personal experience of God, often through practices such as meditation, chanting (dhikr), and asceticism. The **Sufi orders** became a central part of Islamic spirituality.

4. Islamic Golden Age and Interactions with Other Cultures (8th–15th Century):

- During the Islamic Golden Age, Islam interacted significantly with other cultures and religions. Muslim scholars made advancements in a wide variety of fields, influencing the development of both Islamic and Western thought. Although considered the DARK AGES for Europe, this period was the golden age for Islam and provided the foundation for Europe to build upon.

> - *This period (8th to the 14th century CE) is considered the time when Islam took the baton from the Greeks and, after dashing, passed it on to Europe and the West.*

- **Persian, Greek, and Indian influences** were absorbed into Islamic intellectual life. For example, Persian literature, art, and architecture had a lasting impact on Islamic culture. The translation movement in the **House of Wisdom** in Baghdad preserved and transmitted Greek philosophy, particularly the works of **Aristotle**, **Plato**, and **Pythagoras**.
- Islam also interacted with Christianity and Judaism. Both Christianity and Judaism share common roots with Islam, as they are all Abrahamic **religions**. Islamic theology developed in tandem with Christian and Jewish thought, as scholars from these traditions interacted and debated theological issues.
- The influence of **Christianity** on Islamic art, architecture, and science is evident, particularly in regions such as Spain during the Al-Andalus period (711–1492 CE), where Muslims, Jews, and Christians coexisted and interacted, resulting in a rich exchange of ideas.

5. The Crusades and the Ottoman Empire (11th–17th Century):

- The **Crusades** (1096–1291) were a series of military campaigns launched by Christian powers in Europe to reclaim Jerusalem and the Holy Land from Muslim rule. The Crusades had a profound impact on Christian-Muslim relations, creating tensions, but also leading to the exchange of knowledge and trade between Europe and the Islamic world.
- The **Ottoman Empire** (1299–1922) lasted for over 600 years and was one of the most influential Islamic empires in history. The Ottomans united large parts of the Middle East, North

Africa, and Southeastern Europe under Islamic rule. The empire was a melting pot of cultures and religions, with Muslims, Christians, and Jews coexisting in a system known as **Dhimmi**, where non-Muslims were granted protection in exchange for paying special taxes.
- The 13th to 14th centuries were marked by i) The Rise of the Mamluks, ii) Rise of the Mamluk s, and iii) Isolated but great Muslim Delhi sultanate.
- The Ottoman Empire contributed significantly to Islamic architecture, particularly with structures like **Istanbul's Süleymaniye Mosque and Hagia Sophia**. The Ottomans also played a key role in the spread of Islam into Eastern Europe and the Balkans.

6. Colonialism and Modern Influence (19th–20th Century):
- The **colonial period** saw many Muslim-majority regions come under European control, which had a significant impact on Islamic societies. Western powers imposed their political, social, and cultural systems, leading to resistance movements and the emergence of modernist Islamic thought.
- The spread of **Western ideas** such as democracy, secularism, and human rights led to debates within the Muslim world. Islamic reformers such as Jamal al-Din al-Afghani and Muhammad Abduh advocated for a return to Islamic principles while also seeking to modernize and reconcile Islamic teachings with the challenges of the modern world.
- The **rise of nationalist movements** in the Muslim world in the 19th and 20th centuries, particularly in the Middle East and South Asia, led to the formation of independent nation-states. **Islamic modernism** sought to address issues such as colonialism, education, and political reform, while **Islamic fundamentalism** emphasized a return to traditional Islamic practices and governance.

7. Islam in the Contemporary World (20th–21st Century):
- In the 20th and 21st centuries, Islam has continued to adapt to modern global challenges. The rise of **Islamic fundamentalism** and the emergence of groups like **Al-Qaeda** and **ISIS** have created tensions, as they challenge Western political systems and promote strict interpretations of Islam.
- However, there are also movements within Islam promoting **Islamic democracy**, **gender equality**, and **interfaith dialogue**.

Scholars like **Abdulaziz Sachedina** and **Amina Wadud** have advocated for gender equality within Islamic practice, particularly regarding women's rights and leadership roles.
- Islam has become a global religion, with significant Muslim populations in regions such as Europe, North America, and Southeast Asia. This has led to the development of a worldwide Muslim identity that balances traditional Islamic values with the realities of living in diverse societies.

8. Islam's Influence on and Interaction with Other Religions:
- Islam has influenced and been influenced by other religious traditions, particularly **Christianity** and **Judaism**. As an Ibrahamic faith, Islam shares many similarities with these religions, such as the belief in one God and the recognition of figures like **Ibraham, Moses**, and **Jesus** as prophets.
- **Sufism**, Islam's mystical dimension, has interacted with **Christian mysticism** and **Jewish Kabbalah** in various ways. Sufi practices, such as poetry (e.g., **Rumi**) and music (e.g., the **whirling dervishes**), have influenced other spiritual traditions and have been embraced by people outside the Islamic world.
- Modernity's interaction has led to discussions about secularism, human rights, and democracy in many Muslim-majority countries, often resulting in diverse interpretations of Islamic teachings in modern life.

Conclusion:
Like other major world religions, Islamic practices have evolved over the centuries, adapting to different cultural, political, and intellectual currents. It has been shaped by the rise of Islamic empires, the spread of European colonialism, interactions with other religions, and the challenges posed by modernity. Throughout its history, Islam has absorbed and integrated influences from various cultures while maintaining a steadfast commitment to its core beliefs, including the oneness of God and the teachings of the Prophet Muhammad. Today, Islam is a dynamic and global religion, with diverse interpretations and practices that continue to evolve in response to the challenges of the contemporary world.

Objective Analysis of God

Central Claim of Islam:

Islam is Deen-e-Fitrat (Natural Religion)?

Islam claims to be the most natural and logical way of life for humanity.
The claim that "Islam is Deen-e-Fitrat" (Islam is the religion of human nature) means that Islamic teachings align with the innate disposition (fitrah) that Allah has instilled in every human being. "Fitrah" refers to the natural inclination towards recognizing Allah, truth, and morality. The Islamic concept that "Islam is Deen-e-Fitrat" (the religion of innate human nature) is based on the belief that Allah created humans with an inherent disposition (fitrah) that naturally inclines them toward the path of Islam.

Also refer to my submission earlier under the heading of "Moral values - Religion or Society development", especially "Moral values are tied to Social values"

First, to understand why this claim is being promoted, Islamic teachings—such as monotheism, justice, compassion, and moderation—resonate with inherent human instincts. They avoid extremes, promoting balance in spirituality, social life, and personal conduct, as indicated in the Quran and the teachings of the Prophet Mohammed.

1. **Innate Recognition of Good and Evil**
    - Allah embedded in human nature the ability to distinguish between fundamental good (ma'ruf) and evil (munkar).
    - The Quran supports this:
    - *"By the soul and He who proportioned it And inspired it [with discernment of] its wickedness and its righteousness."* (Quran 91:7-8)
    - Conscience (al-nafs al-lawwama—the self-reproaching soul) is an internal moral guide (Quran 75:2).

2. **Natural Belief in Allah (Tawhid)**
    - Every child is born in a pure state (fitrah), instinctively inclined toward monotheism.
    - Even in hardship, humans naturally turn to a higher power (Quran 30:30).

3. **Innate Moral Values**
- Humans are born with an inherent sense of justice, compassion, honesty, and dignity.
- Islam reinforces these natural virtues rather than imposing foreign ethics.
- Evil arises from the corruption of fitrah by external influences (society, desires, Satan).

4. **Balance Between Body and Soul**
- Islam acknowledges natural human needs (food, marriage, emotions) and regulates them without extreme asceticism or indulgence.
- It aligns with human instincts while elevating them through divine guidance.

Islam claims to be Deen-e-Fitrat because its teachings harmonize with the innate good that Allah has placed in humanity, while providing a corrective framework for corrupted tendencies. It does not suppress natural human inclinations but purifies and channels them toward righteousness.

In the following lines, we will try to develop a counterargument to the above and try to prove that Islamic teaching is not the human "Fitrah" nature and the so-called innate moral values, and not "innate", built into human nature by birth.

First approach will be the straight teachings of Islam, and then introducing the counter-narrative of Mullahs about Free will over-taking natural innate "Fitrah"

Counterargument:
The claim that Islam is the "religion of innate human nature" (Deen-e-Fitrat) suggests that its teachings perfectly align with humanity's inherent moral and spiritual disposition. However, several theological and empirical observations challenge this assertion. Below is a structured critique:

1. Innate Morality vs. Divine Commandments
    - Quran 91:7–8 — If humans naturally recognize good and evil, why does Islam impose rigid commandments (e.g., hudud punishments, apostasy laws, gender rulings) instead of trusting human conscience?

Objective Analysis of God

- Punishments like stoning for adultery contradict modern ethical intuitions about justice and rehabilitation.
- If morality is truly innate, why does Islam rely on fear of hell and strict legalism rather than natural ethical reasoning?

2. Slavery and Human Dignity
   - Quran 24:33 — Slavery is permitted despite regulated treatment, conflicting with the innate human revulsion toward forced servitude.
3. Gender Inequality and Fairness
   - Quran 2:282, 4:11 — Inequality in inheritance and testimony clashes with the innate human sense of fairness and gender equity.
4. Flawed Human Nature in the Quran
   - While Islam speaks of fitrah (natural disposition), the Quran also describes humans as:
     - "Hasty" (17:11)
     - "Ungrateful" (17:67)
     - "Disputative" (18:54)
     - "Prone to oppression and ignorance" (33:72)
   - Raises the question: Does the Quran acknowledge that human nature is flawed, and if so, how does that reconcile with the concept of fitrah?
5. Original Sin vs. Fitrah
   - Christianity acknowledges a fallen human nature, which arguably explains moral failures more effectively than Islam's concept of innate purity.
6. Contradictions in Human Purity
   - If humans are born pure, why does the Quran state:
   - "*Man is in loss*" (103:2)
   - "The soul is inclined to evil" (12:53)
7. Need for Prophethood
   - If humans naturally know right from wrong, why does Islam require prophethood and divine legislation?
8. Moral Intuitions vs. Islamic Commandments
   - Many Islamic rulings conflict with widely accepted moral instincts and progressive ethical reasoning.
9. Freedom of Belief
   - Severe punishments for apostasy contradict the innate human desire for intellectual freedom:
     - Quran 2:217, 4:137, 3:86–91, 47:25–27
   - Yet the Quran also encourages exploration and reasoning:

Section 5 – Islam
Central Claim of Islam:

   o   Quran 2:164, 2:256, 39:17–18, 8:22, 17:36, 3:190–191
10. Animal Rights
   • Islam permits ritual slaughter (dhabihah) without stunning, which conflicts with modern standards for ethical treatment of animals.

Question

If Islam aligns with fitrah, why do so many of its laws contradict moral reasoning and intuitive ethics?

> *This contradiction within the Quranic approach reveals an inconsistency with the concept of innate moral values.*
>
> *On one hand, Allah praises reason and condemns those who fail to use it— "Indeed, the worst of living creatures in the sight of Allah are the deaf and dumb who do not use reason" (Quran 8:22).*
>
> *Yet on the other hand, the text prescribes severe punishments for those who arrive at conclusions outside of divine prescriptions, effectively reducing moral reasoning to a constrained choice.*
>
> *Like saying, "You can have the car in any color, as long as it's black."*
>
> *(Henry Ford)*

Objective Analysis of God

The Problem of Cultural Relativism in Morality
- If morality is innate, why do Muslim-majority societies differ on issues like democracy, women's rights, and free speech?

Examples:
- Honor Killings: Some cultures justify them using Islam, while others reject them, proving morality is shaped by society, not just fitrah.
- Slavery in History: Many early Muslims owned slaves despite Islam's "soft" reforms. If morality is innate, why was abolition not immediate?

Question: Why does Islamic morality appear to be flexible across time and cultures if it is genuinely rooted in an unchanging fitrah?

Does the Quran Suggest That Morality Is Taught, Not Innate?
- The Quran repeatedly emphasizes guidance (huda) as something given to prophets, implying humans need external teaching.

Examples:
- Quran 16:78 - "And Allah brought you forth from the wombs of your mothers knowing nothing, and gave you hearing and sight and hearts that you might give thanks."– This suggests moral understanding is developed, not pre-installed.
- Quran 16:93 -"*Had Allah willed, He would have made you one nation, but He leaves to stray whom He wills and guides whom He wills.*"– If morality were innate, why would people need divine guidance to avoid misguidance?

Conclusion: Is Islam Really "Deen-e-Fitrat"?

While Islam claims to align with human nature, many of its laws conflict with evolving moral intuitions, suggesting that:
- Either human fitrah is not as clear-cut as Islam claims, or
- Islamic rulings are more culturally conditioned than divinely aligned with innate morality.

Final Question: If Islam is the "natural" religion, why do so many humans, including those raised in Muslim families, reject or question its teachings? Does this not prove that morality is more complex than fitrah alone?

Human morality develops through reason, experience, and social progress, rather than solely through an unchanging "natural religion." If Islam were truly Deen-e-Fitrat, its moral framework would be universally intuitive, which it is not. We will discuss this in more depth in the following few lines.

If Islam were truly Deen-e-Fitrat (the "natural religion" or innate faith), its moral framework would align with universally intuitive human values. However, many Islamic moral injunctions—such as gender inequality, harsh punishments, slavery, and religious exclusivism—are not self-evidently moral to most humans today. Instead, morality evolves through:
- Reason – Ethical progress comes from critical thinking, debate, and philosophical refinement (e.g., abolition of slavery, women's rights, secular governance).
- Experience – Societies learn from historical mistakes (e.g., theocracies often lead to oppression; polygamy creates social strife).
- Social Progress – As cultures interact and knowledge expands, moral frameworks improve (e.g., democracy, human rights, and pluralism are now widely accepted as superior to rigid religious absolutism).

If Islam's morality were truly "natural," it would not require theological enforcement or severe punishments to sustain it. The fact that many of its doctrines (e.g., apostasy laws, child marriage, jihad) conflict with modern ethical intuitions proves that morality is not divinely fixed but evolves with human civilization. Thus, Islam, like all religions, is a product of its historical context, not an eternal, universal moral truth.

Even if we take this innate argument and Mulla's claim that the innate information given by Allah is overtaken by the lust and desire of money and power, which comes as part of the Free Will, my submission to that is:

> *Even if we accept the claim that Islam is the 'innate religion' (Deen-e-Fitrat) and that people's moral confusion comes from greed and power, things allowed by free will, there's still a problem/question.*
>
> **Allah created humans from nothing, meaning every ability (including free will) comes from Him. If a person can override their 'innate' morality due**

> *to free will, which Allah gave them, then that's not the person's fault—it's Allah's design flaw.*
>
> *He made some humans capable of rejecting the morals He supposedly ingrained in them.*

The following are some examples of moral values developing differently across geographies and historical periods, demonstrating that morality is shaped by culture, reason, and social progress, not a fixed "innate" code:

1. Viking Honor Culture vs. Christian Morality (Scandinavia, 8th–12th Century)
Pre-Christian Norse Ethics:
- Blood feuds were a moral obligation—failure to avenge a slain kinsman was dishonorable.
- Piracy and raiding were glorified (e.g., Lindisfarne raid, 793 CE).
- Slavery (thralls) was economically and socially normalized.

Post-Christianization (11th–12th Century):
- Church imposed forgiveness, pacifism, and monogamy, clashing with Viking warrior ethos.

Moral shift was forced, not "innate"—showing ethics are imposed, not divinely ingrained.

2. Japanese Bushido vs. Confucian Ethics (Feudal Japan, 16th–19th Century)
Samurai Bushido (Pre-Tokugawa):
- Seppuku (ritual suicide) was morally obligatory for failure or dishonor.
- Loyalty to lord & family—betraying one's "daimyo (大名)" was worse than patricide.
- Tokugawa-era Confucianism (1603–1868):
- The Shogunate (Shogun) imposed family piety, scholar-bureaucrat ideals, and suppressed warrior violence.

Moral conflict: Samurai torn between feudal violence and Confucian harmony.

3. Aztec Human Sacrifice vs. Spanish Catholic Morality (Mesoamerica, 15th–16th Century)
Aztec Empire (Pre-1521):
- Mass human sacrifice (e.g., Templo Mayor) was a sacred duty to sustain the cosmos.
- Cannibalism (ritual consumption of victims) was religiously sanctioned.

Spanish Conquest (1521 onwards):
- Catholicism framed sacrifice as "evil"—but replaced it with Inquisition executions.

Moral reversal was colonial imposition, not natural intuition.

4. Pashtunwali Tribal Code vs. Islamic Sharia (Afghanistan/Pakistan, Ongoing)
Pashtun Tribal Ethics (Pre-Islamic & Modern):
- Badal (blood vengeance) obligates endless generational feuds.
- Honor killings prioritized over Quranic due process.

5. Roman Family vs. Christian Family Ethics (Ancient Rome, 1st–4th Century CE)
Pagan Roman Morality:
- Father had vitae necisque potestas—legal right to kill disobedient children/wives.
- Infanticide (intentionally killing an infant / unwanted baby) was routine.

Christianization (4th Century Onwards):
- The church banned infanticide and weakened the paternal power of death.

Change came from imperial decree (Theodosius), not "innate" morality.

6. Trobriand Islanders' Sexual Morality vs. Victorian Ethics (Melanesia, 20th Century)
Trobriand Culture (Anthropologist Malinowski's Studies):
- Pre-marital sex encouraged, no concept of illegitimacy.
- Sexual freedom for teens, unlike Puritan/Victorian repression.

Colonial Christianization:

Objective Analysis of God

- o Missionaries imposed shame, monogamy, and modesty, clashing with native norms.

Shows "morality" is cultural, not universal.

Conclusion:

These examples demonstrate that morality is shaped by geography, power, and historical context, rather than an unchanging "natural religion." Even if one cause of change were some religious enforcements, if Islam's morality were truly innate, it would align seamlessly with the morals of all human societies. Instead, it clashes with tribal codes, warrior ethics, and indigenous values, proving that morality is constructed, not revealed.

> *If Allah has given us moral innate values and free will, to overcome them, then why does He need to go back and impose harsh punishment to restrict free will?*
>
> *A morality that must be imposed through dogma and fear cannot claim to be innate. Actual ethical progress stems from human reason and collective experience, rather than unchanging religious doctrines.*

Free will vs Fate

The debate between free will and divine fate remains a cornerstone of theological inquiry, particularly within Islamic thought. Numerous verses in the Quran affirm that everything in existence unfolds by Allah's command, which raises the challenging question: if every human act—even sin—is foreseen and allowed by Allah, why then are individuals held accountable and punished for those very actions?

Believers and scholars commonly explain that Allah's knowledge of the future does not force human behavior. Just as anticipating the sunrise doesn't cause it to rise, knowing future sins doesn't mean Allah compels them. They argue that humans sin voluntarily, and Allah's omniscience merely reflects this inevitability without interfering.

Yet this explanation struggles under philosophical scrutiny. If Allah already knows each individual's choices and final destination, the necessity of earthly trials becomes questionable. Why put humans—especially innocent children—through suffering and complexity if their fate is already sealed? The standard response is that life is a test, allowing us to exercise our free will and earn our place in the afterlife. But this logic feels circular: if Judgment Day is a replay of our choices, Allah could implant that knowledge in our minds without putting us through life.

Here are a few illustrative examples that highlight the disconnect:

- **Gods "locking" the hearts**

The question of Allah sealing the hearts of individuals presents a profound challenge to reconciling divine omniscience with human free will. The Quran frequently refers to this phenomenon—where Allah places veils over the hearts, hearing, and sight of certain people—making them seemingly incapable of recognizing divine truth. Believers often argue that such sealing is not arbitrary but rather a consequence of persistent rejection of faith; Allah, in His infinite knowledge, knows who will never embrace the truth, and thus confirms their path through divine intervention.

Objective Analysis of God

However, this explanation introduces a troubling paradox. If God seals a person's heart because He knows they will never believe, it raises the question of whether that individual ever truly had the freedom to choose belief. It is akin to shutting a door on someone and then blaming them for not walking through it—an act that undermines genuine autonomy and moral responsibility. This tension challenges conventional understandings of divine justice, especially if Allah's foreknowledge results in active obstruction of spiritual perception. Some theologians interpret the sealing metaphorically, viewing it as a reflection of spiritual decay resulting from human choices and actions. Others suggest that divine justice operates on a level beyond human logic. Yet the discomfort remains: if Allah intervenes in a way that prevents belief, can the individual be fairly held accountable? The believer's reassurance—that God only seals hearts He knows will reject Him—may offer spiritual comfort. Still, it risks sounding like a retrospective justification rather than an ethically coherent answer.

Ultimately, the issue highlights a fundamental conundrum in Islamic theology: the delicate balance between divine will and human freedom, and whether genuine moral choice can exist if God already predetermines the path to truth.

- **The Pharaoh's Hardened Heart**

In Islamic and Biblical narratives, Pharaoh is portrayed as defying Moses, despite witnessing miracles. His rebellion appears to be orchestrated to fulfill a divine prophecy. If God purposefully hardened his heart, can Pharaoh truly be blamed for his obstinacy?

- **Disabled Children and Accountability**

A child born with severe cognitive impairments may never develop the ability to reason morally. While Islamic tradition often exempts such individuals from punishment, it raises the broader question: if divine justice takes into account circumstances beyond our control, why aren't similar allowances made for people shaped by poverty, trauma, or abusive upbringings?

- **Inherited Dispositions**

Some people are naturally more empathetic, while others struggle with aggression or addiction. These traits stem from genetics and environment—factors one doesn't choose. If our capacity to choose "good" is unevenly distributed, how can judgment be fair across individuals?

The idea that moral capacity is unevenly distributed due to genetics and environment raises a compelling challenge to the notion of fair judgment—especially in religious or ethical systems that emphasize personal accountability. Suppose some individuals are born with a greater predisposition toward empathy, patience, or self-control, while others wrestle with impulsivity, aggression, or addiction. In that case, the playing field of moral choice is inherently unequal. These traits are shaped by factors beyond one's control: neurobiology, early childhood experiences, trauma, socioeconomic status, and even prenatal conditions. In such a landscape, the ability to consistently choose "good" is not merely a matter of willpower—it's a function of one's psychological architecture.

From a theological perspective, particularly within Islam, this tension is addressed through the concept of divine justice (Adl). The Quran emphasizes that Allah does not burden a soul beyond its capacity (Surah Al-Baqarah 2:286), suggesting that judgment is calibrated to individual circumstances. In other words, a person is not judged by the same standard as someone with vastly different internal and external challenges. This implies a form of **contextual justice**, where the sincerity of effort and struggle matters more than the outcome alone. Still, the question remains: if someone's capacity for moral reasoning is impaired, can they honestly be held accountable in the same way as someone with greater faculties?

Philosophically, this touches on the debate between **moral luck** and **free will**. Moral luck refers to the idea that people can be morally judged for actions influenced by factors outside their control. If someone is born into a nurturing environment, they're more likely to develop virtues that make moral choices easier. Conversely, someone raised in chaos may struggle even to recognize those choices. Yet society—and many religious doctrines—often judge both individuals by similar standards, creating a tension between fairness and uniformity.

Objective Analysis of God

Islamic scholars argue that in some verses of the Quran, Allah appears to have vaguely indicated a Graded system of accountability. The following are the two most frequently cited:
- 46:19: "And for all are degrees according to what they did, and that He may pay them back fully their deeds, and they shall not be wronged."
- 6:132: "…For all are degrees according to what they have done…"

Here, it is evident that the word of Allah encompasses no circumstances or expected experiences, nor does it indicate that Human inherent traits will be considered. Here Allah is simply saying what they have "done" – Human direct action – like if a person kills one person or many.

> *Understanding human experience and inherent traits is fundamental to the concept of divine justice. However, the Quran does not explicitly address this complexity in its discussion of judgment. Instead, religious scholars and clerics have stepped in to elaborate, offering interpretive narratives and supplementary explanations to bridge the gaps—often constructing theological sidetracks that aim to reassure followers about what they believe Allah intended to convey.*

- **Repentance in the Face of Fatalism**

The notion that Allah already knows whether an individual will sincerely repent—and whether that repentance will be accepted—raises a profound tension between divine omniscience and human agency. In Islamic theology, repentance (tawbah) is a deeply personal and transformative act, one that is encouraged repeatedly in the Quran and Hadith. Yet, when viewed through a deterministic lens, the act of urging people to seek forgiveness can appear more symbolic than substantive. Suppose the outcome is already predetermined and recorded in the divine plan. In that case, the emotional and spiritual labor of repentance may seem like a ritual destined to succeed or fail, regardless of human effort. This perspective can lead to existential unease: why strive for forgiveness if the result is predetermined?

However, Islamic scholars often argue that divine foreknowledge does not negate human responsibility. Allah's knowledge of future events is not causative—it does not force a person to act in a certain way. Instead, it reflects His perfect awareness of how each soul will freely choose to act. In this view, repentance remains meaningful because it is the individual's conscious response to divine mercy, not a hollow performance. Still, the discomfort persists: if Allah knows that someone will never truly repent, then encouraging that person to seek forgiveness might feel like urging them toward a door that's already locked. This paradox challenges believers to reconcile the sincerity of spiritual striving with the mystery of divine decree.

Ultimately, the tension between determinism and moral agency invites more profound reflection on the nature of divine mercy, human accountability, and the purpose of religious exhortation. Is repentance a test, a gift, or a formality? And if Allah's mercy is infinite, does foreknowledge truly limit its reach—or does it simply affirm the choices we were always free to make? In conclusion, these examples reveal significant inconsistencies in the narrative presented by believers. While the theology strives to balance divine justice with human agency, the explanations often amount to a sophisticated deflection—meant more to protect doctrine than clarify it. The more one interrogates the logic, the clearer it becomes: many of the popular answers serve as intellectual band-aids over wounds that remain unhealed. In this light, the faithful arguments sound less like revelations and more like justifications, leaving the original tension unresolved.

Objective Analysis of God

Analysis of the Quran:

The Quran (also spelled Koran), the central religious text of Islam, is believed by Muslims to be the literal word of God (Allah) revealed to the Prophet Muhammad through the Angel Gabriel over a period of 23 years (610–632 CE).

Quran - History:

The Quran's history combines divine claims with meticulous oral and written preservation. While academic debates persist, early manuscripts and cross-cultural references corroborate its 7th-century origins. Its historical development is rooted in early Islamic tradition and corroborated by external sources, though debates exist in academia. Here's a detailed overview:

1. **Origins & Revelation (610–632 CE)**

Pre-Islamic Arabia: The Quran emerged in a polytheistic, tribal Arabian society with a rich oral poetic tradition. Mecca, a hub for trade and pilgrimage, housed the Kaaba, a shrine to pagan deities. Revelation to Muhammad: Muslims believe the Quran was revealed in Arabic to Muhammad, an illiterate merchant in Mecca, starting in 610 CE. The revelations addressed monotheism, social justice, and eschatology, challenging Meccan paganism.

- **Phases of Revelation:**
    - Meccan Period (610–622 CE): Focused on theology, morality, and the afterlife. Poetic, shorter surahs (chapters).
    - Medinan Period (622–632 CE): After Muhammad's migration (Hijra) to Medina, verses addressed community laws, governance, and interfaith relations (e.g., with Jews and Christians).

2. **Compilation & Standardization**

   a. Oral Preservation: During Muhammad's life, the Quran was primarily memorized (hifz) by companions (sahaba) and recorded on materials like palm leaves, parchment, and bones.
   b. First Written Compilation (c. 650 CE): After Muhammad's death (632 CE), divergent recitations emerged. Caliph Abu

Bakr (r. 632–634 CE) commissioned a written compilation under Zayd ibn Thabit, Muhammad's scribe. This codex was kept with Hafsa, Muhammad's widow.

c. Usmanic Codex (c. 650–656 CE): To resolve disputes, Caliph Uthman (r. 644–656 CE) standardized the Quran into a single text (rasm) based on the Quraysh dialect, destroying variant copies. This became the authoritative Mushaf Uthmani (Uthman's codex), which remains in use today.

3. Preservation & Manuscript Evidence

Early Manuscripts:
- Sana'a Manuscript (c. 7th–8th century): Discovered in Yemen in 1972, it shows minor textual variants but aligns with the Usmanic text.
- Birmingham Quran (c. 568–645 CE): Carbon-dated to Muhammad's lifetime, its text matches modern Qurans.

- **Birmingham Qurans' carbon dating:**

The Birmingham Quran manuscript (dated 568–645 CE via carbon testing of the parchment) presents a nuanced case regarding its potential connection to the Usmanic period (standardization c. 650–656 CE):

a. **Parchment vs. Writing Date:**
The carbon dating (568–645 CE) reflects the age of the animal skin, not the ink. Parchment could be stored for years before use, meaning the text might have been written later, even after 645 CE. However, the 95.4% probability range ends at 645 CE, making the Uthmanic era (post-650 CE) technically outside this window.

b. **Script Analysis:**
The manuscript uses early Hijazi script, a style consistent with mid-7th-century Quranic codices. Some scholars argue this script aligns with the Usmanic standardization effort, suggesting the text was inscribed close to or during that period, even if the parchment predates it.

c. **Textual Consistency:**
The Birmingham Quran's text matches the Usmanic recension, implying it was part of the standardized version. This supports the idea that the manuscript could reflect early Usmanic copies, even if the parchment were slightly older.

Conclusion:
While the parchment's carbon date does not directly overlap with the Umayyad period (650–656 CE), the writing could still belong to that era if the parchment was stored and used later. Scholarly debates hinge on script style, textual fidelity, and the possibility of older materials being reused. Thus, while not definitively written during Usman's rule, the manuscript is closely linked to the standardization process and reflects the Quran's early preservation.

Canonical Status: Unchanged since Usman's standardization, it remains central to worship, law (Sharia), and culture.

Quran – Content

The Quran is a comprehensive guide that encompasses various aspects of faith, law, and morality, guiding life. Below is a broad breakdown of the main topics in the Quran, including **Ethics and Morals** as one of the key themes, along with approximate percentages:

1. Tawhid (Oneness of God – Self Praise) - 25-30%
- The central theme of the Quran is the belief in the absolute oneness of God (Allah).
- This concept encompasses:
    - Allah's sovereignty, power, and uniqueness.
    - The rejection of any form of polytheism (shirk).
    - God's attributes and names.
    - Emphasis on worshiping God alone.

2. Prophethood (Risalah) - 15-20%
- The Quran narrates the stories of various prophets sent by Allah to guide humanity, such as Adam, Noah, Abraham, Moses, Jesus, and Muhammad (peace be upon them all).
- Key themes:
    - The role of prophets in conveying Allah's messages.
    - The importance of following the guidance of prophets.
    - The finality of the Prophet Muhammad as the last prophet.

Section 5 – Islam
Analysis of the Quran:

3. Revelation (Wahy) - 10-15%
- The Quran itself is considered the revealed word of Allah to the Prophet Muhammad through the Angel Jibreel (Gabriel).
- Key themes:
    - The Quran is divine guidance for all aspects of life.
    - Emphasis on the authenticity and preservation of the message.
    - The importance of recitation and reflection on the Quran's verses.

4. Law (Shariah) - 10-15%
- The Quran lays down laws that guide life's personal, social, and legal aspects.
- Key themes:
    - Rules related to marriage, family, inheritance, criminal justice, and contracts.
    - Ethical principles related to honesty, fairness, and social responsibility.
    - The legal framework for worship and ritual practices.

5. Ethics and Morality - 15-20%
- The Quran emphasizes high moral and ethical standards for individuals and society.
- Key themes:
    - Justice, kindness, charity (zakat), patience, humility, and gratitude.
    - Prohibition of immoral acts, such as lying, stealing, backbiting, and oppression.
    - Encouragement of forgiveness, truthfulness, and compassion.

6. Afterlife (Akhirah) - 10-12%
- The Quran teaches about life after death, the Day of Judgment, and the consequences of one's deeds.
- Key themes:
    - Resurrection and accountability for one's actions.
    - Reward and punishment in Paradise (Jannah) and Hell (Jahannam).
    - The importance of faith and good deeds for salvation.

Objective Analysis of God

7. Guidance for Personal Conduct - 5-10%
- The Quran provides guidance for personal character and behaviour.
- Key themes:
    - Maintaining a good relationship with family, neighbours, and society.
    - Guidance on dealing with hardship, trials, and personal development.
    - Emphasis on gratitude, sincerity, and reliance on Allah.

8. Social Justice and Equality - 5-10%
- The Quran promotes the welfare of society and justice for all people.
- Key themes:
    - Fairness in dealings with others, regardless of race, class, or gender.
    - Protection of the weak, orphans, and the poor.
    - The importance of collective responsibility for justice and peace.

9. Creation and the Natural World - 5-8%
- The Quran invites reflection on the creation of the universe, nature, and the signs of Allah in the world.
- Key themes:
    - The creation of the heavens, earth, and all living beings as signs of Allah's power.
    - The relationship between humans and the natural world, including stewardship and gratitude.
    - Scientific and natural phenomena as signs of Allah's existence and wisdom.

Summary Table of the Main Topics in the Quran

Topic	Percentage	Description
Tawhid (Oneness of God)	25-30%	The absolute oneness of Allah, rejecting polytheism, and emphasizing God's attributes.
Prophethood	15-20%	Stories of prophets, prophecy's

Section 5 – Islam
Analysis of the Quran:

Topic	Percentage	Description
(Risalah)		role, and the Prophet Muhammad's finality.
Revelation (Wahy)	10-15%	The Quran is a divine revelation, and it is important to follow its guidance.
Law (Shariah)	10-15%	The legal and moral framework for individual and social conduct, worship, and justice.
Ethics and Morality	15-20%	Emphasis on justice, kindness, truthfulness, charity, and the prohibition of immorality.
Afterlife (Akhirah)	10-12%	Teachings on resurrection, judgment, and the consequences of actions in the afterlife.
Guidance for Personal Conduct	5-10%	Advice on personal behaviour, family relations, and maintaining faith in everyday life.
Social Justice and Equality	5-10%	Advocacy for fairness, protection of the weak, and responsibility for justice.
Creation and the Natural World	5-8%	Reflection on the signs of Allah in nature and the universe.

These percentages are approximate and may overlap, as the Quran often addresses multiple themes simultaneously within the same verses. However, this breakdown gives an overview of the key topics in the Quran and their relative importance in guiding Muslims' lives.

Objective Analysis of God

Quran in the Arabic Language

The Arabic Quran is considered the literal word of God (Allah) in Islam, but it has given rise to multiple interpretations due to several linguistic, historical, and theological factors. Here are the key reasons why interpretations vary so widely:

1. Linguistic Complexity of Classical Arabic
- **Rich Vocabulary & Multiple Meanings**: Many Arabic words have **multiple meanings**, resulting in varied interpretations.
  - Example: "يَأْتِي الرِّجَالَ" (Surah 4:128) – Does it mean "men come (to women)" or "men turn away (from women)"?
  - **Grammatical Ambiguity**: Arabic syntax permits flexible word order, which can influence the meaning.

> Example: " يَتَرَبَّصْنَ" "يَتَرَبَّصْنَ" (Surah 2:228) – " the women themselves are expected to observe this period (rather than being forced) and some interpretation like of Ibn-Khatir says that it carries both legal and spiritual aspects ---- resulting in the famous Imran Khan's AIDAT case in Pakistan – where as Quran linguistic meaning only women to **observe the period themselves, no legal issues**

- **Idiomatic Expressions**: Some phrases are metaphorical but taken literally (or vice versa).
  - Example: "ضَرَبَ اللَّهُ مَثَلًا" (Surah 14:24) – "Allah sets forth a parable"—is it literal or symbolic?

  2. Lack of Diacritical Marks in Early Quranic Script
  - The **original Usmanic Quran (7th century)** had no dots (إعجام) or short vowels (حركات), leading to **variant readings (Qira'at)**.
  - Surah Al-Isra 17:102 - لَقَدْ عَلِمْتَ مَا أَنزَلَ هَـٰؤُلَاءِ إِلَّا رَبُّ ٱلسَّمَٰوَٰتِ وَٱلْأَرْضِ
    - Spoken by Pharaoh to Moses, but some readings render it:

- "You (Moses) know..."
- Others (like Hamza and al-Kisā'ī): "I (Pharaoh) know..."
  - Different subjects reverse entirely the speaker's recognition of truth.
  - Impact: Has theological significance—did Pharaoh admit the truth, or accuse Moses?
- (9:128) سورة التوبة, Unpointed root letters for a phrase:
  - إِنَّكَ لَعَلَىٰ خُلُقٍ عَظِيمٍ
  - خُلُق (khuluq) = character, morals
  - Without dots, خلق could also be read as خَلَق (khalaq) = created
  - So, without vowels/dots, it might be read as:
    - "You are indeed upon a great creation" or
    - "You are indeed upon a great character."
- The word كتب could mean:
  - kataba (he wrote)
  - Kutiba (it was written)
  - kitab (book)
- This complexity was removed with the Usmanic Quran. Still, it means that the present Quran has a human element in its interpretation, during the decision-making process of placing these dots (إعجام) or short vowels (حركات). This opens up a significant possibility of change in the verses' meaning/interpretation

3. Historical Context (Asbab al-Nuzul)
- Many verses were revealed in **specific historical situations**, but without knowing the context, interpretations differ. A few examples that are quoted frequently are :
  - 9:29 – read in context of 9:25-29
  - 9:5 – Read in the context that the Treaty of Hudaybiyyah was broken

4. Abrogation (Naskh) – Some Verses Override Others
- The Quran mentions **abrogation (Surah 2:106)**, where later verses cancel earlier ones. But **which verses are abrogated?**
  - Example: **Alcohol prohibition**:
    - First: "Some benefit, but sin is greater" (Surah 2:219).
    - Then: "Do not pray drunk" (Surah 4:43).

Objective Analysis of God

- Finally: **Total ban (Surah 5:90).**
  o **Jihad verses**: Peaceful (Surah 2:256) vs. militant (Surah 9:5) interpretations.

5. Sectarian Differences (Sunni, Shia, Sufi, etc.)
- **Sunni Islam**: Relies on consensus (Ijma) and analogy (Qiyas).
- **Shia Islam**: Prioritizes interpretations from Imams.
- **Sufi Islam**: Focuses on esoteric (Batin) meanings.
  o Example: "الرَّحْمَٰنُ عَلَى الْعَرْشِ اسْتَوَىٰ" **(Surah 20:5)** – Does Allah "sit" on the Throne?
    - **Literalists (Athari)**: Yes, but "how" is unknown.
    - **Rationalists (Mu'tazila)**: Metaphorical.

6. Modern vs. Traditional Interpretations
1. **Traditionalists**: Follow classical scholars (Ibn Kathir, Tabari).
2. **Modernists/Reformists**: Reinterpret for today's context (e.g., gender equality, science).
   o Example: "وَاضْرِبُوهُنَّ" **(Surah 4:34)** – "Strike" disobedient wives:
     - **Traditional**: Light physical discipline allowed.
     - **Modernist**: Means "separate from them."

Conclusion: Why So Many Interpretations?
1. **Arabic is inherently ambiguous** in places.
2. **The early Quranic script lacked clarity (no dots or vowels).**
3. **Context is sometimes missing** (requiring Hadith).
4. **Abrogation causes contradictions.**
5. **Sectarian biases influence readings.**
6. **Modern debates** (human rights, science) force new views.

This is why **Tafsir (exegesis)** is crucial in Islam—scholars spend lifetimes debating meanings.

We will further explain these issues in detail, as we argue that selecting Arabic for the final revelation may not have been a wise decision by Allah. Arabic, one of the world's oldest and most widely spoken languages, is celebrated for its rich literary heritage, poetic

Section 5 – Islam
Analysis of the Quran:

depth, and cultural significance. Yet, it is also notorious for its formidable complexity, particularly its intricate grammar, unique script, and the polysemy—multiple meanings—of its words. For learners and even native speakers, Arabic presents challenges that stem from its historical evolution, linguistic structure, and cultural nuances. This essay examines why Arabic is often perceived as a complex language and how its words frequently convey multiple layers of meaning.

1. Root-Based Morphology: Adding Complexity

At the core of Arabic's complexity is its root system. Most Arabic words derive from trilateral (three-letter) roots that convey a core concept. For example, the root *k-t-b* (ك-ت-ب) relates to writing, generating words like *kitāb* (book), *maktab* (office), and *kataba* (he wrote). While this system creates logical patterns, it demands memorization of roots and their derivations. A single root can produce dozens of words with subtle shifts in meaning, depending on vowel patterns and affixes. For learners, deciphering these patterns requires both analytical skill and contextual awareness.

2. Diglossia: Two Forms of One Language

Like many other languages, Arabic exists in a state of diglossia, meaning it has two distinct forms: Classical Arabic, also known as Modern Standard Arabic (MSA), and regional dialects. MSA, used in formal writing, media, and religious texts, differs significantly from spoken dialects, which vary by country (e.g., Egyptian Arabic, Levantine Arabic, Gulf Arabic). This duality forces learners to master two linguistic systems. Even native speakers often struggle with MSA's archaic grammar and vocabulary, which are seldom used in daily conversation. The gap between formal and colloquial Arabic complicates comprehension and adds ambiguous word meanings across contexts. Just like local French Quebecers face communication challenges while visiting France.

3. Script and Pronunciation Challenges

The Arabic script, written from right to left, poses multiple challenges. Letters change shape depending on their position in a word (initial, medial, final, or isolated), and many characters resemble one another, differing only by dots (e.g., ب bā', ت tā', ث thā'). Vowel markings (harakat) are often omitted in written texts,

Objective Analysis of God

leaving learners to infer pronunciation and meaning from the context. When referring to the short vowel marks (ؗ , ؚ , ؞) in Arabic, the correct and universally understood term is حَرَكَات (ḥarakāt). They are the essential "movements" that bring written Arabic words to life and determine their meaning, as illustrated in the previous examples. This ambiguity exacerbates the challenge of accurately interpreting text.

The Arabic term we are referring to here is حَرَكَات (Harakat), which are the diacritical marks (vowels) added to Arabic letters to indicate pronunciation and grammatical function. The examples كُتِبَ (kutiba), كُتُب (kutub), and كَتَبَ (kataba) demonstrate how the absence of Harakat in standard Arabic script creates ambiguity, requiring context or additional diacritics to clarify meaning.

Key Terms:
حَرَكَات (Harakat): The diacritical marks (e.g., ؚ fatha, ؚ kasra, ؚ damma) that represent short vowels and grammatical case endings.
Example: كَتَبَ (kataba) vs. كُتِبَ (kutiba).
رَسْم (Rasm): The "skeleton" or consonantal base of a word (e.g., كتب without vowels).
Without Harakat, the same Rasm can represent multiple words.
إِعْرَاب (I'rab): The system of grammatical inflection (case endings) marked by Harakat.
Example: In كِتَابٌ (kitābun, "a book"), the ؚ (damma) indicates nominative case.

Why This Matters:
Arabic is an abjad script, meaning it primarily writes consonants, with vowels implied or optionally marked.
The same Rasm (e.g., كتب) can represent multiple words depending on context and added Harakat:
كَتَبَ (kataba): "He wrote" (past tense).
كُتُب (kutub): "Books" (plural).
كُتِبَ (kutiba): "It was written" (passive voice).

Example Breakdown:

Rasm (Consonants)	With Harakat	Meaning
كتب	كَتَبَ	"He wrote" (verb, past tense)
كتب	كُتُب	"Books" (plural noun)
كتب	كُتِبَ	"It was written" (passive voice)

Also, remember that the initial Quran was revealed, written down, and memorized without Vowels, so there is the added complexity of losing the true meaning of verses during those 17 years.

4. Grammatical Nuances and Flexibility

Arabic grammar is notoriously intricate. Nouns and verbs are inflected for gender, number, case, and mood. The language features a dual form (for pairs of objects), which is rare in most modern languages, adding another layer of complexity. Arabic has a dedicated form for exactly two items:
- ❖ Singular: كِتَابٌ (kitābun) - "a book"
- ❖ Dual: كِتَابَانِ (kitābāni) - "two books"
- ❖ Plural: كُتُبٌ (kutubun) - "books" (3 or more).

Verbs conjugate into multiple tenses and voices, while sentence structure relies heavily on case endings (iʿrāb). Misplacing a diacritic or misapplying a grammatical rule can alter a sentence's meaning entirely. For example, the word عَلِمَ (ʿalima) means "he knew," while عُلِّمَ (ʿullima) means "he was taught"—a distinction marked by a single vowel change.

The distinction between عَلِمَ (ʿalima = "he knew") and عُلِّمَ (ʿullima = "he was taught") in Arabic hinges on two key linguistic features:
1. Verb form (وزن wazn)
2. Vowel patterns and diacritics (حَرَكَات harakāt)

Here's the breakdown:

1. Root and Basic Meaning

Both words derive from the triliteral root ع-ل-م (*ʿ-l-m*), which relates to knowledge.

2. Verb Forms and Grammatical Voice

Word	Verb Form (وزن)	Voice	Meaning
عَلِمَ	Form I (فَعَلَ)	Active	"He knew"
عُلِّمَ	Form II (فَعَّلَ)	Passive	"He was taught/instructed"

Form I (فَعَلَ): The base form, indicating simple action.
ʿalima = "he knew" (active voice).

Form II (فَعَّلَ): A "causative" form, often implying teaching, training, or making someone know.
Active: عَلَّمَ (ʿallama) = "he taught."

Passive: عُلِّمَ (ʿullima) = "he was taught."

3. Vowel and Diacritic Changes

Objective Analysis of God

The difference between ʿalima and ʿullima involves both vowel and consonant emphasis: عَلِمَ (ʿalima): فَعَلَ pattern: فَتْحَة (َ fatḥa) on the first root letter (ع), سُكُون (ْ sukūn) on the second (ل).
Pronounced: ʿa-li-ma (he knew).
عُلِّمَ (ʿullima): Form II passive pattern: ضَمَّة (ُ ḍamma) on the first root letter (ع), شَدَّة (shadda) + كَسْرَة (ِ kasra) on the second (ل).
Pronounced: ʿul-li-ma (he was taught).

4. Critical Role of Diacritics (حَرَكَات)
In written Arabic, the distinction between these words relies on diacritics:
Without diacritics, both words would appear as علم, requiring context or added marks to clarify.
Example: عَلِمَ vs. عُلِّمَ
The ḍamma (ُ) and shadda () in ʿullima signal the passive voice and Form II structure.

5. Why This Matters
Arabic employs verb forms (أوزان) and diacritics to encode grammatical nuances, such as voice (active or passive) and causation.

A single vowel or diacritic shift can radically alter meaning:
ʿalima (he knew) → ʿullima (he was taught) involves:
Changing the verb form (I → II).
Adding a shadda (consonant doubling).
Shifting vowels (َ → ُ).

Analogy in English
Think of it like the difference between "break" (active) and "is broken" (passive). In Arabic, such distinctions are baked into the verb's structure via vowel/diacritic rules.
Key Takeaway
Arabic's reliance on root patterns and diacritics allows a single root (ع-ل-م) to generate a family of related meanings. The shift from ʿalima to ʿullima isn't just a "single vowel change"—it's a systematic grammatical transformation that reflects voice, causation, and emphasis.

5. Polysemy: Words with Multiple Meanings

The phenomenon of polysemy (a single word has multiple meanings) is pervasive in Arabic. This arises from the language's

historical depth, poetic traditions, and the adaptability of its root system. For example:
- عين ('ayn) can mean "eye," "spring," "spy," or "essence," depending on context.
- قلب (qalb) translates to "heart," "core," or "to flip/turn something over."
- سلم (salam) means "peace," "surrender," or "to greet."

Such multiplicity stems from Arabic's capacity to stretch semantic boundaries, allowing poets and scholars to infuse words with metaphorical or abstract connotations. However, this richness becomes a stumbling block for learners and translators, who must navigate context clues and cultural knowledge to grasp intended meanings.

Here are some more **examples of polysemy in Arabic for reference only**, where single words carry multiple related meanings, often derived from the same root or shaped by cultural context:

- ❖ جَمَل (*jamal*)
  - ➢ Root: ج-م-ل (J-M-L)
  - ➢ Meanings: "Camel" (الجَمَل), "beauty" (الجَمَال).
- ❖ قَرَأ (*qara'a*)
  - ➢ Root: ق-ر-أ (Q-R-A)
  - ➢ Meanings: "To read," "to recite" (e.g., the Quran).
- ❖ لِسَان (*lisān*)
  - ➢ Root: ل-س-ن (L-S-N)
  - ➢ Meanings: "Tongue," "language" (e.g., لِسَان عَرَبِي = "Arabic language").
- ❖ دَرَسَ (*darasa*)
  - ➢ Root: د-ر-س (D-R-S)
  - ➢ Meanings: "To study," "to erase" (e.g., دَرَسَ الأَثَر = "he erased the trace").
- ❖ وَرَق (*waraq*)
  - ➢ Root: و-ر-ق (W-R-Q)
  - ➢ Meanings: "Paper," "leaves" (of a tree), "sheets."
- ❖ يَد (*yad*)
  - ➢ Root: ي-د (Y-D)
  - ➢ Meanings: "Hand," "power/control" (e.g., بِيَدِهِ = "in his possession"), "help" (e.g., يَدُ العَوْن = "a helping hand").
- ❖ صَلَحَ (*ṣalaḥa*)
  - ➢ Root: ص-ل-ح (Ṣ-L-Ḥ)

Objective Analysis of God

- ➤ Meanings: "To fix/repair," "to be righteous," "to reconcile."
- ❖ خَلَقَ (khalaqa)
  - ➤ Root: خ-ل-ق (KH-L-Q)
  - ➤ Meanings: "To create," "to behave" (e.g., خُلُق = "character/morals").
- ❖ بَاب (bāb)
  - ➤ Root: ب-و-ب (B-W-B)
  - ➤ Meanings: "Door," "chapter" (in a book), "method/means."
- ❖ مَادَة (mādda)
  - ➤ Root: م-د-د (M-D-D)
  - ➤ Meanings: "Substance/material," "subject" (academic), "clause" (in a contract).
- ❖ حُكْم (ḥukm)
  - ➤ Root: ح-ك-م (Ḥ-K-M)
  - ➤ Meanings: "Judgment," "wisdom," "ruling/governance."
- ❖ شَعْر (shaʻr)
  - ➤ Root: ش-ع-ر (SH-ʻ-R)
  - ➤ Meanings: "Hair," "poetry" (e.g., شِعْر = "poetry").
- ❖ عَقْل (ʻaql)
  - ➤ Root: ع-ق-ل (ʻ-Q-L)
  - ➤ Meanings: "Mind/intellect," "restraint" (e.g., عَقَلَ الجَمَل = "he tied the camel").
- ❖ رَأْس (ra's)
  - ➤ Root: ر-أ-س (R-'-S)
  - ➤ Meanings: "Head," "leader," "summit" (e.g., رَأْس الجَبَل = "mountain peak").
- ❖ وَجْه (wajh)
  - ➤ Root: و-ج-ه (W-J-H)
  - ➤ Meanings: "Face," "direction" (e.g., وَجْهَة = "destination"), "essence" (metaphorical).
- ❖ جِسْم (jism)
  - ➤ Root: ج-س-م (J-S-M)
  - ➤ Meanings: "Body," "mass/physical object," "substance."
- ❖ سَاق (sāq)
  - ➤ Root: س-و-ق (S-W-Q)
  - ➤ Meanings: "Leg," "stalk" (of a plant), "to drive/move forward."
- ❖ رَسْم (rasm)
  - ➤ Root: ر-س-م (R-S-M)
  - ➤ Meanings: "Drawing," "tradition/custom," "official decree."
- ❖ حَرْف (ḥarf)
  - ➤ Root: ح-ر-ف (Ḥ-R-F)

- Meanings: "Letter" (of the alphabet), "edge" (e.g., حَرْف السَّيْف = "edge of a sword").
❖ سَاعَة (sā'a)
  - Root: س-و-ع (S-W-')
  - Meanings: "Hour," "clock/watch," "moment" (e.g., فِي أَيِّ سَاعَةٍ = "at what time?").

Why Polysemy Abounds in Arabic
These examples illustrate how Arabic's root system and cultural evolution enable words to expand semantically. A single root can generate nouns, verbs, and adjectives with interconnected meanings, while metaphors and historical usage add layers (e.g., وَجْه for both "face" and "essence" and …). For learners, this demands not just vocabulary memorization but also sensitivity to context, idiom, and Arab thought patterns. Yet, this complexity makes Arabic a treasure trove for poetry, philosophy, and nuanced expression, but not an option for conveying the most essential message that needs to be translated into all languages of the world with extreme accuracy, meaning, and context.

The Quran's linguistic richness often hinges on polysemous words (words with multiple meanings), which can lead to diverse interpretations of verses. Classical exegetes (mufassirūn) have debated these nuances for centuries, as subtle shifts in meaning can alter theological, legal, or ethical understandings. Below are six examples of Quranic verses where polysemy plays a pivotal role:

✓ **Surah Al-Waqi'ah (56:89): Hospitality or Descending?**
Verse: فَرَوْحٌ وَرَيْحَانٌ وَجَنَّتُ نَعِيمٍ
Translation: "Then [he will have] rest, fragrance, and a Garden of Bliss."
Polysemous Word: رَوْحٌ (rawḥun)
Meanings: Derived from the root ر-و-ح (R-W-Ḥ), it can mean "rest/comfort" or "a breeze/spirit."
Interpretive Impact: Some scholars interpret rawḥun as "spiritual relief," while others link it to a literal "cool breeze" in Paradise. This affects how believers conceptualize divine reward.

✓ **Surah Al-Baqarah (2:228): Menstruation or Purity?**
Verse: وَالْمُطَلَّقَاتُ يَتَرَبَّصْنَ بِأَنْفُسِهِنَّ ثَلَاثَةَ قُرُوءٍ
Translation: "Divorced women shall wait for three periods (qurū')."
Polysemous Word: قُرُوءٍ (qurū')

Objective Analysis of God

Root: ق-ر-ء (Q-R-'), meaning "to read" or "to collect."
Meanings: Menstruation (the waiting period after divorce is tied to menstrual cycles). Purity periods (the intervals between menstruation).
Legal Impact: Jurists debate whether the waiting period ('iddah) is counted during menstruation or the clean days between cycles, which could affect divorce rulings in Islamic law.

✓ **Surah Al-Ma'idah (5:6): Hand or Power?**
Verse: يَا أَيُّهَا الَّذِينَ آمَنُوا إِذَا قُمْتُمْ إِلَى الصَّلَاةِ فَاغْسِلُوا وُجُوهَكُمْ وَأَيْدِيَكُمْ إِلَى الْمَرَافِقِ
Translation: "O believers! When you rise for prayer, wash your faces and your hands (aydiyakum) up to the elbows."
Polysemous Word: أَيْدِيَكُمْ (aydiyakum)
Root: ي-د (Y-D), meaning "hand" or "power."
Interpretive Impact: While the verse is commonly understood to mean washing the physical hands up to the elbows (for ablution), some Sufi scholars metaphorically interpret yad as "power," suggesting spiritual purification of one's actions.

✓ **4. Surah An-Nisa (4:43): Intoxication or Overindulgence?**
Verse: يَا أَيُّهَا الَّذِينَ آمَنُوا لَا تَقْرَبُوا الصَّلَاةَ وَأَنْتُمْ سُكَارَىٰ
Translation: "O believers! Do not approach prayer while you are intoxicated (sukārā)."
Polysemous Word: سُكَارَىٰ (sukārā)
Root: س-ك-ر (S-K-R), meaning "to intoxicate" or "to overwhelm."
Meanings: Literal drunkenness (from alcohol).
Metaphorical distraction/overindulgence (e.g., excessive worldly attachments).
Ethical Impact: Some scholars argue that the verse condemns all forms of spiritual heedlessness, not just the consumption of alcohol.

✓ **Surah An-Nisa (4:34): Discipline or Separation?**
Verse : وَاضْرِبُوهُنَّ
Translation: "And strike them [lightly]."
Polysemous Word: اضْرِبُوهُنَّ (waḍribūhunna)
Root: ض-ر-ب (Ḍ-R-B), with over 20 meanings, including "to strike," "to travel," "to set an example," or "to separate."
Interpretive Impact: This controversial verse about marital discord is often interpreted as permitting physical discipline. However, some modern scholars argue that ḍaraba here means "to separate" or "to leave," radically shifting the verse's ethical implication.

Section 5 – Islam
Analysis of the Quran:

✓ **Surah Al-Kahf (18:86): Setting or Source?**
Verse: حَتَّىٰ إِذَا بَلَغَ مَغْرِبَ الشَّمْسِ وَجَدَهَا تَغْرُبُ فِي عَيْنٍ حَمِئَةٍ
Translation: "Until he reached the setting of the sun (maghrib al-shams), he found it setting in a murky spring."
Polysemous Word: مَغْرِبَ (maghriba)
Root: غ-ر-ب (GH-R-B), meaning "to set" (sun) or "the west."
Meanings:
Literal: The sun's setting point (geographical location).
Figurative: The western horizon (direction).
Theological Impact: Early debates arose over whether this verse describes a physical location (e.g., a literal spring where the sun sets) or a metaphorical vision, challenging literalist interpretations of Quranic cosmology.

Why Polysemy Matters in Quranic Exegesis

These examples illustrate how polysemy enriches Quranic interpretation (tafsīr) and sparks theological and legal debates. Classical scholars, such as Al-Tabari, Ibn Kathir, and Al-Razi, meticulously analyzed context (siyāq), historical usage, and parallel verses to resolve ambiguities. Modern linguists and reformers also use polysemy to reconcile ancient texts with contemporary values. Ultimately, the Quran's layered meanings reflect its divine designation as a "clear book" ---- > whose depths remain inexhaustible, just as the following verse:
12:1 -- Alif, Lām, Rā. These are the verses of the clear Book?

6. Cultural and Historical Influences

Arabic's lexicon has absorbed influences from Aramaic, Persian, Turkish, and French, further diversifying word meanings. Additionally, classical texts such as the Quran and pre-Islamic poetry employ archaic vocabulary and figurative expressions that remain in use but are often opaque to modern speakers. For instance, the Quranic term تقوى (taqwā) is often simplistically translated as "piety" but encompasses a broader concept of "consciousness of God." Such terms require a cultural and theological understanding to be interpreted accurately.

7. Context-Dependent Interpretations

Unlike languages with rigid syntactic rules, Arabic often relies on context to resolve ambiguities. A word's meaning might shift

Objective Analysis of God

dramatically based on its position in a sentence or the speaker's intent. For example, the phrase وجه الله (wajh Allāh) means "the face of God" but is metaphorically interpreted as "the essence of God" in religious contexts. This fluidity demands linguistic proficiency and familiarity with Arab customs, history, and rhetorical traditions.

8. Idioms and Figurative Language

Arabic is replete with idioms, proverbs, and metaphors that defy literal translation. Phrases like ضرب عصفورين بحجر (ḍaraba ʿuṣfūrayn bi-ḥajar, "to hit two birds with one stone") are straightforward, but others, like طلعله البخت (ṭalaʿlu al-bakht, "his luck came out"), rely on cultural knowledge. Such expressions deepen the language's beauty but confound learners and translators who approach them without contextual guidance.

Use of Idioms:

The use of idioms is an essential aspect of the Quran, which has led me to question whether it is the words of God/Allah, given that the sole purpose of this text is to convey His divine message to humanity for centuries to come.

> *Idioms are peculiar to a language and culture and change meaning when used in another culture. So, either Allah does not want humans to understand his message truly, or He is very shortsighted. He struggled to grasp the complexities of using idioms in Arabic for the Quran. In either case, it raises a question about Allah being "Allah."*

These phrases may be linguistic miracles (iʿjāz) of the Quran, but their depth collapses in translation. For example:

صِبْغَةَ اللَّهِ (Q2:138) requires understanding of:
- Pre-Islamic ritual dyes (ṣibghah).
- Abrahamic contrast with baptism.
- Concept of fiṭrah (innate monotheism).

Without this, it becomes "God's paint, "a total distortion!

Section 5 – Islam
Analysis of the Quran:

Here are a few other examples of how these idioms, when translated into other languages, will distort the message and might destroy the purpose of the Quran as a divine message:

- 26:89 قَلْبٌ سَلِيمٌ (A Sound Heart) → إِلَّا مَنْ أَتَى اللَّهَ بِقَلْبٍ سَلِيمٍ
    - "Except one who comes to God with a sound heart."
    - Meaning Shift in non-Arabic languages:
    - English: "Sound heart" → implies physical cardiac health.
    - Chinese: 健全的心 (jiànquán de xīn) → "intact heart" (loses spiritual purity).
    - Loss: Moral/spiritual integrity (free from shirk or hypocrisy).

- 2:25. جَنَّاتٍ تَجْرِي مِن تَحْتِهَا الْأَنْهَارُ (Gardens Beneath Which Rivers Flow) -- أَنَّ لَهُمْ جَنَّاتٍ تَجْرِي مِن تَحْتِهَا الْأَنْهَارُ
    - "For them are Gardens beneath which rivers flow."
    - Meaning Shift in other languages:
    - German: "Gärten, unter denen Flüsse fließen" → suggests illogical hydrology.
    - Swedish: "floder under trädgårdar" → evokes landscaping, not divine reward.
    - Loss: Desert-culture symbolism of Paradise as eternal relief from aridity.

- 29:34 - رِجْزٌ مِّنَ السَّمَاءِ (Torment from the Sky) -- إِنَّا مُنزِلُونَ عَلَىٰ أَهْلِ هَٰذِهِ الْقَرْيَةِ رِجْزًا مِّنَ السَّمَاءِ
    - "We will bring down upon this city punishment from the sky."
    - Meaning Shift in translation:
    - French: "un châtiment venu du ciel" → implies natural disasters.
    - Japanese: 天からの罰 (ten kara no batsu) → "heavenly punishment" (ambiguous moral cause).
    - Loss: Nuance of divine retribution for human corruption (e.g., Sodom's destruction).

- 45:23 - غِشَاوَةٌ عَلَىٰ بَصَرِهِ (A Covering Over His Sight) -- وَجَعَلَ عَلَىٰ بَصَرِهِ غِشَاوَةً
    - "And placed a cover over his sight."
    - Meaning Shift in other languages:

Objective Analysis of God

- Spanish: "un velo sobre su vista" → suggests temporary obstruction (e.g., fog).
- Russian: "покрывало на его зрении" → implies curable blindness.
- Loss: Concept of willful spiritual blindness due to arrogance (istikbar).

- 2:138 صِبْغَةَ اللَّهِ (The Dye of God) -- صِبْغَةَ اللَّهِ ۖ وَمَنْ أَحْسَنُ مِنَ اللَّهِ صِبْغَةً
  - "[Adopt] the dye of God, and who is better than God at dyeing?"
  - Meaning Shift in translation:
  - Italian: "tintura di Dio" → sounds like fabric dye.
  - Korean: 신의 염색 (sin-ui yeomsaek) → "God's colouring" (trivializes ritual metaphor).
  - Loss: Critique of baptismal rites and affirmation of innate tawḥīd (monotheism).

- 40:36–37 حَبْلٌ مِنَ السَّمَاءِ (A Rope from the Sky) - ابْنِ لِي صَرْحًا لَعَلِّي أَبْلُغُ الْأَسْبَابَ ۚ أَسْبَابَ السَّمَاوَاتِ
  - "Build me a tower that I may reach the ways—the ways of the heavens."
  - Meaning Shift in other languages:
  - Portuguese: "uma corda do céu" → implies rescue line (e.g., helicopter).
  - Hindi: आकाश से रस्सी (ākāś se rassī) → "rope from sky" (loses irony).
  - Loss: Arrogance of challenging divine authority (Pharaoh's fu demand).

- 4:57 ظِلٌّ ظَلِيلٌ (Extended Shade) فِي ظِلَالٍ ظَلِيلٍ –
  - "In [cool] extended shade."
  - Meaning Shift in translation:
  - Dutch: "uitgebreide schaduw" → suggests a large shadow (neutral).
  - Indonesian: "naungan yang luas" → "wide shade" (loses eschatological weight).
  - Loss: Symbolism of God's protection on Judgment Day (contrasted with Hell's scorching void).

Section 5 – Islam
Analysis of the Quran:

Similar examples are used in the Quran, but not in idioms, as a means of communicating the pitfalls of using Idioms in a text that is intended to be translated into all languages worldwide.

- Arabic Idiom: "يأكل هوا" (Yaakul hawa | "He eats air")
    - Meaning in Arabic: Someone is unemployed/idle.
    - Same Literal Translation in Indonesian: "Makan angin" ("Eat air/wind").
    - In Indonesian, it means "To go for a stroll" or "to wander around."
    - Contrast: In Arabic, it's about unemployment; in Indonesian, it's about relaxing outdoors!

- Arabic Idiom: "القرد في عين أمه غزال" (Al-qird fi ain ommo ghazal | "A monkey is a gazelle in his mother's eyes")
    - Meaning in Arabic: A parent's biased love for their child.
    - Same Literal Translation in French: "Un singe est une gazelle aux yeux de sa mère." - A monkey is a gazelle in the eyes of its mother
    - Meaning in French: A nonsensical statement (no idiom). The French might interpret it as a literal joke about animal hybrids!
    - Contrast: Arabic uses it metaphorically for parental bias; French sees it as absurdity.

- Arabic Idiom: "إللي إيده في المي إللي إيده في النار" (Illi ido fi al-mayya... | "The one whose hand is in water vs. the one in fire")
    - Meaning in Arabic: People in different circumstances can't understand each other.
    - Same Literal Translation in German: "Der eine hat die Hand im Wasser, der andere im Feuer."
    - Meaning in German: The phrase "Hand im Feuer haben" ("to have a hand in fire") means to vouch for someone (e.g., "I'd put my hand in fire for him").
    - Contrast: Arabic focuses on empathy gaps; German ties "fire" to trust/guaranteeing someone's reliability.

- Arabic Idiom: "طلعله القمر" (Tala'lu al-qamar | "The moon rose for him")
    - Meaning in Arabic: Someone had extraordinary luck/success.

Objective Analysis of God

- Same Literal Translation in Turkish: "Ay onun için doğdu" ("The moon rose for him").
- Meaning in Turkish: A poetic way to say someone is romantically special (e.g., "The moon rises only for you").
- Contrast: Arabic ties the moon to luck; Turkish links it to romantic idealization.

- Arabic Idiom: "بعد ما طقعت القلة راحت تلف" (Ba'd ma taga'at al-qullah... | "After the jug broke, it started to roll")
  - Meaning in Arabic: Acting too late to fix a problem.
  - Same Literal Translation in Spanish: "Después de romperse la jarra, empezó a rodar."
  - Meaning in Spanish: A literal description of a jug rolling (no deeper meaning). Spanish uses "A buenas horas, mangas verdes" ("Good timing, green sleeves") to mock delayed action.
  - Contrast: Arabic critiques procrastination; Spanish ignores the imagery entirely.

Why This Matters:
These examples show how identical phrases can misfire across languages. The Arabic idioms are rooted in cultural metaphors (e.g., the moon as a symbol of luck, monkeys versus gazelles as a metaphor for bias), while other languages either repurpose the imagery (e.g., German's "fire hand") or strip it of its symbolic meaning (e.g., Spanish's rolling jug). So, using Arabic idioms to communicate across all languages is something we cannot expect from the All-Knowing, All Wise God/Allah, and this is not a one-off thing but a very regular feature, like Allah is only meant to address Arabic people of that time, which is not aligned with the religious concept of Allah as God. Please see the following examples:

✓ **Stubbornness & Ignorance**
   2:7 – *"Allah has set a seal upon their hearts and hearing."*
   2:18 – *"Deaf, dumb, and blind—they will not return (to the right path)."*
   2:74 – *"Then your hearts hardened like stone or even harder."*
   5:13 – *"They disregarded their covenant, so We hardened their hearts."*
   6:25 – *"We have placed coverings over their hearts,*

preventing them from understanding it."
7:179 – *"They have hearts but do not understand; they have eyes but do not see."*
17:97 – *"We will resurrect them on Judgment Day, dragged on their faces—blind, dumb, and deaf."*
18:57 – *"Who does more wrong than one who is reminded of Allah's signs but turns away?"*
45:23 – *"Allah has left him astray, sealing his hearing and heart."*

✓ **Arrogance & Pride**
17:37 – *"Do not walk on the earth arrogantly. You cannot tear the earth apart."*
31:18 – *"Do not turn your cheek in scorn toward people, nor walk proudly."*
31:19 – *"Lower your voice, for the ugliest of voices is the braying of donkeys."*
44:31 – *"Pharaoh was a tyrant who exceeded all bounds."*
79:21-24 – *"Pharaoh said, 'I am your supreme lord!'"*

✓ **Hypocrisy & Deception**
4:142 – *"The hypocrites try to deceive Allah, but He is deceiving them."*
24:39 – *"The deeds of disbelievers are like a mirage in the desert."*
29:41 – *"The example of those who take protectors besides Allah is like a spider's web."*
63:4 – *"When you see them, their appearance pleases you; but when they speak, you listen to their words as if they were stacked logs."*

✓ **Greed & Miserliness**
2:188 – *"Do not consume one another's wealth unjustly."*
4:29 – *"Do not devour each other's wealth unlawfully."*
17:29 – *"Do not be so tight-fisted that you are blamed."*
68:17-33 – *"We tested the garden owner who swore he would harvest it all."*

✓ **Weakness & Futility**
7:176 – *"His example is like a dog: whether you chase it or leave it, it pants."*
14:18 – *"The deeds of disbelievers are like ashes blown away by wind."*
22:31 – *"Be upright for Allah, not associating partners with Him. Whoever associates partners with Allah is like one falling from the sky, snatched by birds."*

Objective Analysis of God

25:44 – *"Do you think most of them hear or understand? They are like cattle—no, even more misguided."*

✓ **Divine Power & Judgment**
21:104 – *"On that Day, We will roll up the sky like a scroll."*
39:67 – *"They have not shown Allah His true measure. The whole earth will be in His grip on Judgment Day."*
48:10 – *"Allah's Hand is over their hands."*
50:22 – *"You were heedless of this, but now We have removed your veil, so your sight is sharp today."*
54:7 – *"Their eyes humbled, they will emerge from graves like scattered locusts."*

✓ **War & Conflict**
8:16 – *"Whoever turns his back on them on that day has incurred Allah's wrath."*
33:61 – *"They are cursed wherever found, seized and slaughtered mercilessly."*

✓ **False Security**
10:24 – *"The life of this world is like rain We send down; the plants flourish but then turn to chaff scattered by wind."*
18:45 – *"The life of this world is like water. We send from the sky—it nourishes plants, but they later crumble to dust."*

✓ **Spiritual Blindness**
36:9 – *"We have put barriers before them and behind them, covering them so they cannot see."*
41:5 – *"They say, 'Our hearts are veiled from what you call us to.'"*

✓ **Mockery & Ridicule**
83:29-30 – *"The wicked used to laugh at the believers, winking at one another when they passed by."*

✓ **Divine Decree**
57:22 – *"No disaster strikes except by Allah's permission."*

✓ **Human Nature**
70:19 – *"Indeed, mankind was created anxious."*

✓ **Justice & Retribution**
5:38 – *"As for the thief, cut off his hand as a penalty."*

✓ **False Worship**
46:5 – *"Who is more astray than one who calls upon others besides Allah—those who cannot respond?"*

✓ **Death & Resurrection**
50:20 – *"The Trumpet will be blown: 'This is the Day of Warning.'"*

Conclusion: A Language of Depth and Demands – made even more dubious

Arabic's difficulty lies in its layered structure, historical depth, and cultural specificity. Its words are not mere vessels of meaning but portals to a rich intellectual and artistic legacy. While the language's polysemy and grammatical complexity present formidable challenges, they also make it a tool of unparalleled expressive power. For those who persevere, mastering Arabic offers not only linguistic proficiency but also a profound connection to the Arab world's heritage, literature, and worldview.

> *With all the above examples, it is irrational and in fact wildly misleading for Allah to choose Arabic—a language native to a specific region—as the medium for a universal divine message intended for all of humanity.*

Objective Analysis of God Leading to Sectarianism:

The inherent complexity of the Quranic/Arabic language and the Quran's writing approach, which makes it even more difficult to understand when translated into other languages, has created grassroots issues within Islam. The following are a few examples of how polysemous words and verses have historically contributed to theological and sectarian divisions in Islam, as differing interpretations of key passages shaped competing doctrines. Below are five significant examples where divergent readings of Quranic verses led to the formation of distinct sects or schools of thought:

1. Free Will vs. Predestination: Qadariyya vs. Jabriyya
Verse (Surah Al-An'am 6:125):

فَمَنْ يُرِدِ اللَّهُ أَنْ يَهْدِيَهُ يَشْرَحْ صَدْرَهُ لِلْإِسْلَامِ وَمَنْ يُرِدْ أَنْ يُضِلَّهُ يَجْعَلْ صَدْرَهُ ضَيِّقًا حَرَجًا

"So whoever Allah wills to guide, He opens their heart to Islam. And whoever He wills to leave astray, He makes their chest tight and constricted."
Interpretive Divide: Jabriyya (Predestinarians): Emphasized "Allah wills" to argue humans have no free will (jabr = compulsion). Whereas, Qadariyya/Mu'tazila (Free Will Advocates): Interpreted "Allah wills" as His foreknowledge, not direct causation, preserving human moral agency.
Outcome: The Mu'tazila became a rationalist school opposing the fatalist Jabriyya, influencing early Abbasid theology.

2. Leadership (Imamate): Sunni vs. Shia
Verse (Surah Al-Ma'idah 5:55): إِنَّمَا وَلِيُّكُمُ اللَّهُ وَرَسُولُهُ وَالَّذِينَ آمَنُوا الَّذِينَ يُقِيمُونَ الصَّلَاةَ وَيُؤْتُونَ الزَّكَاةَ وَهُمْ رَاكِعُونَ

"Your allies are Allah, His Messenger, and the believers who establish prayer, give zakah, and bow down [in worship]."
Interpretive Divide:
Shia: They argue that "those who bow down" refer exclusively to Ali ibn Abi Talib, who (they claim) gave charity while bowing in prayer. This supports their doctrine of divinely appointed Imams.
Sunni: Interpret the verse as general praise for righteous believers, rejecting exclusive leadership claims.
Outcome: This verse became a cornerstone of Shia-Sunni debates over succession after the Prophet, solidifying the Sunni-Shia split.

3. Grave Sinners: Kharijites vs. Murji'a

Section 5 – Islam
Analysis of the Quran:

Verse (Surah Al-Nisa 4:48): إِنَّ اللَّهَ لَا يَغْفِرُ أَنْ يُشْرَكَ بِهِ وَيَغْفِرُ مَا دُونَ ذَٰلِكَ لِمَنْ يَشَاءُ

"Allah does not forgive association with Him [shirk], but forgives what is less than that for whom He wills."
Interpretive Divide: Kharijites: Insisted that major sins (e.g., murder, adultery) equate to kufr (disbelief), rendering the sinner an apostate deserving death. Murji'a: Argued faith alone (not deeds) defines a Muslim; judgment on sins is deferred (irjā') to Allah.
Outcome: The Kharijites split from mainstream Muslims, declaring rulers and sinners apostates, while the Murji'a's leniency influenced early Sunni orthodoxy.

4. Divine Attributes: Ash'ari vs. Mu'tazila

Verse (Surah Taha 20:5): الرَّحْمَٰنُ عَلَى الْعَرْشِ اسْتَوَىٰ
"The Most Merciful [Allah] ascended the Throne."
Interpretive Divide: Mu'tazila: Rejected the literal "ascended" (استوى), arguing Allah is beyond physicality. They interpreted it metaphorically (e.g., "established authority"). Again, Ash'ari affirmed Allah's "ascension" without questioning how (bi-la kayf), accepting the text literally but rejecting anthropomorphism.
Outcome: The Mu'tazila's rationalism clashed with Ash'ari literalism, shaping Sunni theology's balance between scripture and reason.

5. The Createdness of the Quran: Mihna Controversy

Verse (Surah Al-Zukhruf 43:3): إِنَّا جَعَلْنَاهُ قُرْآنًا عَرَبِيًّا لَعَلَّكُمْ تَعْقِلُونَ
"We have made it an Arabic Quran so you may understand."
Interpretive Divide:
Mu'tazila: Argued "We have made it" (جعلناه) implies the Quran is created (makhluq), not eternal. Traditionalists (Ahl al-Hadith): Insisted the Quran is Allah's uncreated speech, eternal like His attributes.
Outcome: The Abbasid Caliph al-Ma'mun enforced the Mu'tazili view during the Mihna (inquisition), persecuting dissenters like Imam Ahmad ibn Hanbal. The controversy entrenched Sunni rejection of the "created Quran" doctrine.

Why These Divisions Matter

These examples show how polysemy and interpretive flexibility in the Quran fueled theological disputes that hardened into sectarian identities. While Sunni orthodoxy eventually coalesced around frameworks like Ash'ari theology, minority sects like the Shia,

Objective Analysis of God

Mu'tazila, and Kharijites preserved distinct readings. Even today, debates over Quranic meaning—such as whether jihad denotes spiritual struggle or warfare—continue to shape intra-Muslim dynamics. The Quran itself acknowledges this potential for divergence:
"*He sent down the Book, in which there are verses clear in meaning—they are the foundation of the Book—and others ambiguous.*" (Quran 3:7).

The last phrase kills the purpose of the Quran in every sense.

> *One argument that many thoughtful individuals might raise is that selecting Arabic as the final and exclusive language of divine revelation appears problematic. This concern is compounded by the fact that Arabic is used in the Quran—rich in nuance, idiom, and structure that often defies straightforward translation. It raises the question: Was God unaware of the long-term implications of choosing a language inaccessible to the vast majority of humanity without years of study and effort?*
> *If God is truly all-wise and intends to communicate a universal message to all people, expecting billions to either master classical Arabic or rely on potentially flawed translations seems deeply impractical, perhaps even unjust. Such an approach appears inconsistent with the notion of a God who desires clear, direct, and universal communication. This leads to a difficult conclusion: either God is not all-wise and all-knowing, or He did not intend for His message to be equally accessible to all. Both possibilities challenge traditional theological claims about divine justice and wisdom.*

Section 5 – Islam
Analysis of the Quran:

The basis of Prophet Mohammed's knowledge

Before proceeding, we will examine the first 40 years of Muhammad's life, as well as the possible sources and avenues of his knowledge. Upon closer examination of his life, we learn that he was exposed to diverse cultures and various religions from a very early age. This learning process has continued for over 28 years. It is essential to explain this concept here, as later questions and sections will argue that the concepts presented in the Quran were already existing in pre-Islamic civilization, and the Prophet had an in-depth exposure to this information, providing proof that these ideas can be found in the Quran.

> *Now we turn to the question of where Prophet Muhammad obtained his knowledge. He began his practical life around the age of 12, accompanying his uncle on trade missions that exposed him to centers of Judaism and Christianity. He is also said to have spent years learning from a monk well-versed in Hinduism and Buddhism. This suggests that he had significant exposure to diverse religious ideas, and the content of the Quran reflects this influence—presenting these narratives as revealed truth, even though we now recognize them as stories rather than historical facts.*

The question of how Prophet Muhammad (peace be upon him) might have come into contact with Greek and Hindu religious scriptures is intriguing, especially considering the historical context of 7th-century Arabia. While there is no direct evidence that he read these texts, several avenues could have facilitated indirect exposure.

1. Trade Routes and Cultural Exchange

Mecca, where Prophet Muhammad was born, was a significant hub for trade routes connecting the Arabian Peninsula with regions like the Byzantine Empire and the Indian subcontinent. Merchants and travellers from these areas often passed through Mecca, bringing with them not only goods but also cultural and religious ideas. It is plausible that through interactions with these traders, the Prophet

Objective Analysis of God

could have been exposed to concepts from Greek and Hindu philosophies.

2. Interaction with Christian and Jewish Communities

During his lifetime, Prophet Muhammad had interactions with Christian and Jewish communities in the Arabian Peninsula. These communities had their interpretations and stories, some of which were influenced by Greek philosophical thought. For instance, the Nestorian Christians, who were prevalent in the region, had translated Greek philosophical works into Syriac and Arabic. Through dialogues with these communities, the Prophet may have encountered ideas with roots in Greek philosophy.

3. Oral Traditions and Storytelling

Arabia had a rich tradition of oral storytelling, where tales from various cultures were passed down through generations. Some of these stories could have contained elements influenced by Greek and Hindu narratives. Given the Prophet's engagement with various tribes and communities, he might have heard such stories, which could have shaped his understanding of certain concepts.

4. Divine Revelation

From an Islamic perspective, Muslims believe that the Quran was revealed to the Prophet Muhammad by Allah. The Quran acknowledges the existence of previous scriptures and prophets, some of whom might have had interactions with Greek and Hindu cultures. The Prophet's knowledge of these cultures could, therefore, be seen as part of the divine wisdom imparted to him.

The early life, travels, and interactions of the Prophet Muhammad with other civilizations.

The Quran is deeply interwoven with the lived experiences of the Prophet Muhammad, whom he acquired during his early career as a merchant. Long before receiving divine revelations, Muhammad's extensive travels and interactions with diverse cultures shaped his understanding of ethics, spirituality, and societal dynamics. These formative experiences provided a practical and intellectual foundation that later resonated in the Quran's teachings, stories, and principles. By examining Prophet Muhammad's exposure to trade networks, foreign civilizations, and interfaith dialogues, we can trace how his worldly knowledge contributed to the Quran's emphasis on monotheism, social justice, and universal morality.

Ethical Commerce: From Trade Practices to Divine Mandates

Prophet Muhammad's reputation as Al-Amin ("the Trustworthy") during his trading career laid the groundwork for the Quran's stringent ethical guidelines on commerce. As a merchant, he witnessed the exploitation inherent in pre-Islamic Arabian trade, where usury (interest or riba), fraud, and tribal monopolies were rampant. His commitment to fairness and transparency in dealings with Bedouin tribes, Syrian Christians, and Yemeni Jews informed his later condemnation of economic injustice.

The Quran's explicit directives on trade reflect this lived experience. Verses such as "Do not consume one another's wealth unjustly, but only through lawful trade by mutual consent" (Quran 4:29) and the prohibition of usury ("God has permitted trade and forbidden interest," Quran 2:275) mirror Prophet Muhammad's merchant ethos. Similarly, the Quran's metaphor of life as a transaction with God (e.g., *"God has purchased from the believers their lives and wealth in exchange for Paradise,"* Quran 9:111) draws on commercial terminology familiar to the Prophet Muhammad and his audience. His firsthand understanding of trade's moral pitfalls and possibilities allowed the Quran to articulate economic ethics in relatable, actionable terms.

Monotheism and Interfaith Encounters

Muhammad's travels exposed him to the monotheistic traditions of Judaism, Christianity, and Zoroastrianism, which profoundly influenced the development of the Quran's theological framework. During his adolescent journey to Syria with his uncle at the age of 12, he reported an encounter with Bahira. This Christian monk introduced him to messianic prophecies and scriptural narratives. Later, as Khadijah's agent, he engaged with Jewish merchants in Yemen and Christian communities in Byzantine Syria, absorbing their beliefs about prophets, divine law, and the afterlife.

These interactions are echoed in the Quran's frequent references to biblical figures—such as Abraham, Moses, and Jesus—and its assertion of Islam as a continuation of the Abrahamic faiths ("*He*

Objective Analysis of God

has ordained for you the religion He enjoined upon Noah, and what We revealed to you, and what We enjoined upon Abraham, Moses, and Jesus," Quran 42:13). The Quran's insistence on tawhid (the oneness of God) and its rejection of Meccan idolatry may also reflect Prophet Muhammad's critique of polytheism in contrast to the cohesive monotheism he observed abroad. However, the Quran distinguishes itself by presenting Islam as a correction of earlier traditions, rejecting the Trinity (Quran 4:171) and affirming Prophet Muhammad as the *"Seal of the Prophets"* (Quran 33:40). This nuanced engagement with foreign faiths suggests that Muhammad's cross-cultural exposure informed the Quran's universalist yet distinct theology.

Social Justice and Critique of Materialism

The stark economic disparities Muhammad witnessed during his travels—between Mecca's wealthy elite and the impoverished Bedouins, or the asceticism of Syrian monks and the excesses of caravan traders—shaped the Quran's emphasis on equity and charity. His journeys through Arabia's harsh deserts, where survival depended on communal cooperation, likely reinforced his disdain for hoarding wealth and neglecting the vulnerable.
Quranic mandates such as zakat (obligatory alms, Quran 9:60) and the condemnation of greed ("Woe to every slanderer and backbiter who amasses wealth, counting it over," Quran 104:1–2) reflect this ethos. The Quran's portrayal of the Day of Judgment as a reckoning for societal exploitation (*"And do not consume the orphan's property except in a way that is best,"* Quran 17:34) parallels Prophet Muhammad's early observations of Meccan elites preying on the weak. His merchant career, which required balancing profit with integrity, translated into a Quranic vision of wealth as a trust from God to be managed responsibly.

Universal Morality and Cross-Cultural Diplomacy

Prophet Muhammad's interactions with foreign civilizations instilled a universalist perspective that transcended tribal loyalties. The Quran's address to "mankind" (e.g., Quran 49:13) and its recognition of cultural diversity ("We created you from male and female and made you peoples and tribes that you may know one another," Quran 49:13) reflect his exposure to Arabia's multicultural trade networks. The Quran's stories of ancient civilizations—such as the prosperous but doomed people of ʿĀd and Thamūd (Quran 7:65–79)—may also draw on oral histories Muhammad encountered during his travels, serving as moral parables about arrogance and divine justice.

Furthermore, the Quran's diplomatic tone toward People of the Book (ahl al-kitab)—encouraging debate "in the best manner" (Quran 29:46)—mirrors Prophet Muhammad's pragmatic engagement with Jews and Christians as a trader. His later alliances with Medinan tribes and correspondence with foreign rulers, such as the Negus of Abyssinia, reflect the intercultural negotiation skills he honed on caravan routes.

Narrative Resonance: Trade Journeys and Quranic Analogies

The Quran frequently employs metaphors rooted in trade and travel, resonating with Muhammad's lived experiences. The concept of life as a journey (sabil) toward God (Quran 29:69), the comparison of hypocrites to a mirage in the desert (Quran 24:39), and the depiction of divine guidance as a "straight path" (sirat al-mustaqim, Quran 1:6) all evoke the imagery of desert caravans. Even the Quran's description of revelation as a "light" (Quran 5:15–16) may parallel the guidance of stars used by Bedouin navigators.

These analogies not only made Quranic teachings accessible to a merchant society but also anchored its spiritual messages in the physical realities of the Prophet Muhammad's world. His firsthand knowledge of the risks and rewards of travel—sandstorms, bandits, and the joy of reaching an oasis—infused the Quran's parables with vivid authenticity.

Knowledge of South Asian civilizations

While historical records of Prophet Muhammad's life focus primarily on his interactions with Jewish, Christian, and Zoroastrian communities, the question of whether he encountered ideas from Vedic, Hindu, or Buddhist traditions remains speculative. However, Arabia's position as a crossroads of ancient trade routes invites inquiry into potential cultural and religious exchanges between the Hijaz and South Asia. Though direct evidence is scarce, indirect connections through trade networks, oral traditions, and shared philosophical themes suggest intriguing possibilities.

Objective Analysis of God

Trade Routes Linking Arabia and South Asia

By the 6th century CE, Arabia was part of a vast land and maritime trade network connecting the Mediterranean, Persia, India, and beyond. The **Incense Route** and the **Indian Ocean trade** facilitated exchanges between Arabian merchants and South Asian civilizations:

- ✓ **Yemen and the Indian Ocean**: Southern Arabian ports, such as Aden and Hadhramaut, were hubs for ships travelling to India's Malabar Coast and Sri Lanka. Indian spices, textiles, and gemstones reached Mecca via overland caravans.
- ✓ **Persian Gulf Connections**: The Sassanian Empire (modern Iran) controlled trade with India, and Arab merchants likely encountered Indian goods and ideas through Persian intermediaries.
- ✓ **Overland Caravans**: The **Hijaz route** to Syria intersected with Silk Road networks, which transmitted Buddhist ideas from Central Asia to the Mediterranean.

While Prophet Muhammad's documented travels were limited to Syria, Yemen, and the surrounding regions, the cosmopolitan nature of these routes suggests that he may have interacted with merchants or travelers familiar with South Asian religions.

> *While there is no concrete evidence that Prophet Muhammad directly accessed Greek and Hindu religious texts, various indirect avenues could have facilitated his exposure to ideas from these traditions. Whether through trade, interactions with other communities, oral traditions, or divine revelation, the Prophet's understanding of diverse cultures and philosophies was multifaceted and nuanced.*

Indirect Cultural Exchanges

1. Shared Ethical and Philosophical Themes
The Quran's emphasis on **monotheism**, **compassion**, and **social justice** bears resemblance to certain Vedic, Hindu, and Buddhist principles. However, these parallels likely stem from universal human concerns rather than direct borrowing. For example:

- **Non-Attachment (Buddhism)**: The Quran's critique of materialism (*"The life of this world is but amusement and diversion,"* Quran 57:20) echoes Buddhist teachings on detachment.
- **Charity and Dharma (Hinduism)**: The concept of *zakat* (obligatory alms) parallels *dāna* (charity) in Hindu and Buddhist traditions.
- **Oneness of God (Vedic Influences)**: The Rigveda's *"Ekam Sat"* (Truth is One) and the Quranic *tawhid* (oneness of God) both emphasize a singular divine reality.

These similarities could reflect convergent spiritual insights rather than direct influence.

2. Oral Traditions and Travellers' Tales
Merchants and travellers often shared stories of distant lands. Prophet Muhammad may have heard accounts of Indian ascetics, Buddhist monks, or Hindu temples from traders who ventured to Sindh (modern Pakistan) or Gujarat (modern India). The Quran's references to **universal prophethood** (*"For every community, there is a messenger,"* Quran 10:47) and its acknowledgment of diverse civilizations (*"We sent messengers before you, [some] of whom We have told you about and others We have not,"* Quran 40:78) leave room for interpretation about non-Abrahamic traditions.

3. The Case of Bahira and Interfaith Dialogue
Early biographies mention Prophet Muhammad's childhood encounter with Bahira, a Christian monk in Syria. If monks in regions like Syria or Yemen were aware of Buddhist or Hindu thought—transmitted via Silk Road exchanges—such ideas might have entered broader theological discussions.

Objective Analysis of God

The Pre-Islamic era was not that backward.

Some examples of the knowledge pre-Islamic cultures had.
Most of us are not fully aware of the significant development that occurred during the pre-Islamic period among ancient civilizations. We, especially Muslims, are informed that the prehistoric Arabs were very backwards and isolated, which is not correct at all. The following are a few examples of practices developed before Islam, in fact, many centuries before the advent of Islam, which we continue to follow and practice.

1. Seven-Day Week
- Origin: Babylonian astronomy (circa 7th–6th century BCE).
- Practice: The Babylonians divided the month into 7-day cycles, associating each day with a specific celestial body (such as the Sun, Moon, Mars, etc.).
- Modern Use: The seven-day week remains a global standard, deeply ingrained in calendars and various religious traditions (e.g., the Sabbath in Judaism and Christianity, Friday in Islam).

2. Solar Calendar
- Origin: Ancient Egypt (circa 3000 BCE) and later refined by the Romans (Julian calendar, 45 BCE).
- Practice: The 365-day solar calendar with leap-year adjustments.
- Modern Use: The Gregorian calendar, used worldwide, is a direct descendant of the Julian calendar.

3. Earth's Circumference
- Origin: Calculated by Eratosthenes (3rd century BCE, Hellenistic Egypt).
- Practice: Using geometry and shadows during the summer solstice, he estimated Earth's radius with 99% accuracy.
- Modern Use: His method laid the foundation for geodesy and global mapping.

4. Herbal Medicine
- Origin: Ancient Egypt, China (Traditional Chinese Medicine), India (Ayurveda), and Greece.
- Practice: Use aloe vera, turmeric, garlic, and ginger for their healing properties.
- Modern Use: Herbal remedies remain popular in holistic medicine (e.g., echinacea for immunity, chamomile for

relaxation). Many modern pharmaceuticals (e.g., aspirin from willow bark) are derived from plants.

5. Surgical Sutures
- Origin: Ancient Egypt (Edwin Smith Papyrus, 1600 BCE).
- Practice: Stitching wounds with linen thread and needles.
- Modern Use: Absorbable and non-absorbable sutures are standard in surgery.

6. Hippocratic Oath
- Origin: Ancient Greece (Hippocrates, 5th–4th century BCE).
- Practice: Ethical guidelines for physicians, emphasizing patient care and confidentiality.
- Modern Use: The oath (revised) is still sworn by graduating doctors globally.

7. Bone Setting
- Origin: Ancient Egypt and Greece (Hippocrates described techniques).
- Practice: Realigning fractures and dislocations manually.
- Modern Use: Still taught in emergency medicine and orthopedics.

8. Cupping Therapy
- Origin: Ancient Egypt, China, and Greece.
- Practice: Applying heated cups to the skin to stimulate blood flow.
- Modern Use: Popular in alternative medicine for muscle pain and detoxification.

9. Zodiac Signs
- Origin: Babylonian astronomy (circa 5th century BCE).
- Historical Practice: Divided the sky into 12 constellations linked to seasonal cycles, influencing personality and fate.
- Modern Use: Basis for horoscopes, cultural symbolism, and pop psychology.

10. Planetary Influence
- Origin: Hellenistic Greece (2nd century BCE, merging Babylonian and Egyptian astrology).
- Historical Practice: Associating planets with gods and human traits (e.g., Mars for war, Venus for love).
- Modern Use: Foundational to Western astrological charts and "planetary retrogrades" in contemporary spirituality

11. Decimal Numeral System

Objective Analysis of God

- Origin: Ancient India (circa 3rd century BCE, formalized by Aryabhata in 5th century CE).
- Historical Practice: Use place-value notation with digits 0–9 for calculations.
- Modern Use: Universal arithmetic, finance, and digital computing standard.

12. Pythagorean Theorem
- Origin: Ancient Mesopotamia (1800 BCE) and later Pythagoras (6th century BCE Greece).
- Historical Practice: Calculating distances in land surveys and architecture.
- Modern Use: Essential in geometry, engineering, and physics (e.g., construction, GPS triangulation).

13. Archimedes' Principle
- Origin: Archimedes (3rd century BCE Greece).
- Historical Practice: Determining buoyancy and density of objects in water.
- Modern Use: In aerospace engineering, shipbuilding, submarines, and fluid dynamics.

14. Water Mill Technology
- Origin: Ancient Greece (3rd century BCE) and Han Dynasty China.
- Historical Practice: Harnessing hydropower for grinding grain and irrigation.
- Modern Use: Basis for hydroelectric dams and renewable energy systems.

15. Celestial Navigation
- Origin: Polynesian voyagers (circa 2000 BCE) and Phoenician sailors.
- Historical Practice: Using stars, the sun, and ocean currents to navigate oceans.
- Modern Use: Backup for GPS systems in aviation and maritime travel.

16. Caravanserais
- Origin: Persian Empire (circa 500 BCE) along Silk Road routes.
- Historical Practice: Rest stops for traders offering lodging, food, and security.
- Modern Use: Inspiration for modern motels, truck stops, and hospitality hubs along highways.

17. **Crop Rotation**
    - Origin: Ancient Mesopotamia and Rome (circa 6000 BCE).
    - Historical Practice: Alternating crops (e.g., legumes with grains) to preserve soil fertility.
    - Modern Use: Core practice in sustainable farming to prevent soil depletion.
18. **Qanat Irrigation**
    - Origin: Ancient Persia (circa 1000 BCE).
    - Historical Practice: Underground channels transporting water from aquifers to arid fields.
    - Modern Use: Model for sustainable water management in dry regions (e.g., Iran, Oman).
19. **Iron Smelting and Steel Production**
    - Origin: Ancient Hittites (Anatolia, c. 1500 BCE): The Hittites pioneered early iron smelting techniques, producing wrought iron for tools and weapons. Wootz Steel (India/Sri Lanka, circa 300 BCE): South Asian blacksmiths developed wootz steel, a high-carbon alloy renowned for its exceptional durability, which was used in the legendary Damascus swords.
    - Historical Practice: To remove impurities, iron ore was heated with charcoal in furnaces. Wootz steel involved crucible smelting, where iron and carbon-rich materials were melted in sealed clay pots.
    - Modern Use: Blast furnaces and electric arc furnaces still rely on the principles of reducing iron ore with carbon. Wootz steel's microstructure inspired modern alloy research and the development of high-performance steels for aerospace and cutting tools.

20. **Lost-Wax Casting (Cire Perdue)**
    - Origin: Ancient Mesopotamia and Egypt (c. 3000 BCE): Used to create intricate jewelry, statues, and tools. Indus Valley Civilization (c. 2500 BCE): Produced bronze figurines and ornaments.
    - Historical Practice: A wax model was coated in clay, then melted away, and replaced with molten metal (typically bronze, gold, or silver).
    - Modern Use: Still employed in artisanal jewelry, dental implants, and aerospace engineering (e.g., turbine

blades). 3D printing now combines with lost-wax techniques for precision casting.

Conclusion
Prophet Muhammad's life is often reductively framed as emerging from a "backward" Arabian culture, implying intellectual and cultural isolation. This narrative starkly contradicts his lived reality. Born in Mecca, a bustling crossroads of global trade and pilgrimage, Prophet Muhammad was immersed in a cosmopolitan environment from childhood. By the age of 12, he had journeyed to Syria, where he engaged with Christian monks, Byzantine traders, and diverse spiritual traditions. As a merchant, he traversed routes linking Yemen, the Levant, and Persia, interacting with Jewish, Zoroastrian, and Nestorian Christian communities. These experiences cultivated a nuanced worldview far removed from insularity. His exposure to monotheistic faiths, ethical commerce, and intertribal diplomacy informed his later critiques of Meccan materialism and idolatry, shaping the Quran's universalist ethos. Far from being culturally "basic," Prophet Muhammad's upbringing was marked by cross-cultural fluency, enabling him to synthesize diverse ideas into a transformative vision. His life exemplifies how Arabia's "periphery" was, in fact, a nexus of civilizational exchange.

> *As explained with multiple examples, Quranic verses primarily recount the stories prevalent at that time, introducing new and accurate events and ideas that are expected from the creator of the universe.*

In this light, the Quran is not merely a spiritual text, but can also be seen as a reflection of the Prophet Muhammad's journey through the material and moral landscapes of his time. His experiences as a traveller and trader equipped him to articulate a message that resonated across tribal, cultural, and religious boundaries, transforming local insights into universal truths. The Quran's enduring relevance owes much to the fact that its Messenger was, first and foremost, a student of the world.

The Making of a Prophet Shaped by the World, Framed as Divine

Objective Analysis of God
Questions from Muslims

Section 5 – Islam
Questions from Muslims

Question:
Split in Islam within 4-6 hours

M1

Analysis and background:
According to Islamic belief, Allah bestowed upon the Prophet Muhammad complete and perfect knowledge of the religion, which he faithfully transmitted to his followers. The Quran itself affirms that Islam was finalized and perfected during the Prophet's lifetime, intended to serve as a timeless guide for humanity. His companions—those closest to him—were known for their unwavering loyalty and devotion. Yet, strikingly, within mere hours of his death, a deep division emerged over the question of leadership. This schism fractured the unity of the very religion that had just been declared complete.

Such an immediate and fundamental disagreement raises profound questions. If the message of Islam was obvious, comprehensive, and divinely protected, how could confusion arise among those most intimately familiar with it? Whether the fault lies in the clarity of the message or in the human transmission of it, both ultimately reflect on divine responsibility. If Allah is all-knowing and all-wise, why was the succession—a matter so critical to communal stability—not addressed in a way that would prevent discord?

This dilemma challenges the notion of religious perfection. If the earliest and most trusted followers of the Prophet could not agree on a foundational issue, how can later generations be expected to confidently grasp the true essence of Islam? The rapid fragmentation of the community suggests that either the message was not as complete as claimed or that divine wisdom allowed for ambiguity, raising difficult theological questions about the nature of guidance, unity, and divine intent.

Conclusion:
All-perfect Allah could not have communicated His final message, which is supposed to last for centuries, in such an ill-mannered way.

Please rate this Conclusion:

Objective Analysis of God

| **Question:** Allah and Shaitan/ Satan / Devil | **M2** |

Analysis and background:
In all Abrahamic faiths, Allah is revered as the supreme Creator and Sustainer of the universe—the architect of galaxies, stars, angels, jinn, and humanity itself. The cosmos, with its intricate laws and vast complexity, is seen as a reflection of divine intelligence and power. Yet, despite this overwhelming superiority, Allah remains in a prolonged, indirect confrontation with Satan—a rebellious being He Himself created.

This tension becomes even more puzzling when we consider Quran 32:13, which states that Hell will be filled with both jinn and humans. This implies that Satan's influence continues to succeed, leading many astray despite the presence of divine guidance. The paradox deepens: Satan acknowledges Allah as his Creator and once worshipped Him, yet the conflict endures. If Allah is omnipotent and all-knowing, why does this adversarial dynamic persist? Why allow a created being to derail the spiritual path of so many?
Even before engaging in worship, believers are instructed to seek protection from Satan:
أَعُوذُ بِٱللَّهِ مِنَ ٱلشَّيْطَانِ ٱلرَّجِيمِ بِسْمِ ٱللَّهِ ٱلرَّحْمَٰنِ ٱلرَّحِيمِ "I seek refuge in Allah from the outcast Satan. In the name of Allah, the Most Gracious, the Most Merciful."

This ritual acknowledgment of Satan's threat, despite Allah's supreme authority, raises profound theological questions. Why must humans plead for protection from a being whose power pales in comparison to God's? The ongoing struggle between Creator and creation—between divine will and satanic influence—challenges our understanding of justice, free will, and the nature of sacred sovereignty."

| **Conclusion:** Even a trillion Satans with all their capabilities cannot even come remotely close to confronting the all-mighty Allah. Which proves it is just a story | Please rate this Conclusion: |

Section 5 – Islam
Questions from Muslims

| **Question title:** Allah – the name | **M3** |

Analysis and background:
The Quran consistently refers to "Allah" as the one true God—the Creator, Sustainer, and sole being worthy of worship. In earlier Abrahamic tradition, particularly in the time of Moses, the divine name was rendered as YHWH.

Historical inscriptions provide insight into the evolution of the name. Around 328 CE, a Nabataean inscription (in modern-day Syria) mentions the Lakhmid king Imru al-Qays and his devotion to Allah. By 512 CE, the name appears in the Zabad inscriptions, reflecting its integration into Christian contexts. Over time, "Allah" became prominent among pre-Islamic Arab deities, ultimately regarded as the supreme deity in the Kaaba during the pre-Islamic era.

This is evident from key examples:
The Prophet Muhammad's father was named Abdullah—meaning "servant of Allah"—conveying his role as a custodian of the Kaaba's idols.
The Quran (31:25 and 29:61) states: "*If you ask them who created the heavens and the earth, they will surely say, 'Allah.'*"

These verses indicate that pre-Islamic Arabs were already familiar with and worshipped a deity known as Allah. Islam did not invent a new divine name; instead, it reinterpreted and elevated an existing concept. By affirming strict monotheism, Islam preserved the term "Allah" while transforming its theological meaning—shifting from a general or tribal deity to the singular, all-encompassing Creator of the universe. This approach allowed the faith to resonate with Arab cultural identity while introducing a profound redefinition of divine unity.

| **Conclusion:** Allah is not a new name; it has been used and practiced as a significant deity in the pre-Islamic era. Islam only changed its characteristics. | Please rate this Conclusion: |

Objective Analysis of God

| **Question:** Satan is part of Allah's big Plan | **M4** |

Analysis and background:
When examining the broader theological narrative involving Allah, Adam, and Satan, a striking structure emerges: Allah sends Adam and his descendants to Earth as a consequence of disobedience—an act triggered by Satan's deception. From this moment, the entire cosmic framework is set in motion. Heaven and hell are established, the universe is shaped, and human life becomes a test. The criteria for success or failure? Whether individuals resist or fall prey to Satan's influence.

This places Satan in a pivotal role. Without his presence, the entire system of divine testing collapses. The drama of human free will, moral struggle, and eternal judgment depends on the existence of a tempter. In this light, Satan doesn't merely oppose divine will—he enables it. His actions, though rebellious, become essential to the unfolding of Allah's plan. One could reasonably argue that Satan functions as an instrument of divine purpose, even if indirectly.

This leads to a philosophical tension. If Satan is fulfilling a role that sustains the divine framework, is he truly in opposition—or is he part of a larger design? And if Allah is all-wise and rational, why construct a system where the very foundation of human existence hinges on deception and punishment?

The logic appears paradoxical. A God of infinite wisdom creates a being whose rebellion becomes necessary for the moral testing of humanity. This raises profound questions about divine intent, justice, and the coherence of a system where the antagonist is indispensable to the plan.
The matter of free will remains, and we'll explore that in future discussions.

| **Conclusion:** Considering the above, there exists a possibility that Satan will go to Heaven. | Please rate this Conclusion: |

Section 5 – Islam
Questions from Muslims

Question title: Faith = "Iman" in the Bible	**M5**

Analysis and background:

Belief in four divinely revealed scriptures—the Torah, the Psalms, the Gospel (Injil), and the Quran—is a foundational tenet of Islam. These texts are considered revelations from Allah to various prophets, intended to guide humanity across different eras.

However, when examining the New Testament, which is commonly associated with the Gospel in Islamic discourse, a significant theological and historical dilemma arises.

Unlike the Quran, which explicitly claims to be the direct word of God, and the Torah, which is similarly affirmed in both Jewish and Islamic traditions as divinely revealed, the New Testament does not present itself as a direct revelation from God. It contains no explicit internal declaration of divine authorship. Instead, it is composed mainly of letters, narratives, and theological reflections attributed to early followers of Jesus—such as Paul, Matthew, Luke, and John. These writings were compiled over time and canonized centuries after Jesus's death, with the final form of the Bible emerging around the 4th century CE. There is no verifiable historical evidence linking its contents directly to divine revelation or to Jesus himself.

This raises a theological tension: if Allah commands belief in four revealed books, but why is one of them, The Gospel, neither a book from Allah nor one authored by Jesus? It mainly comprises letters attributed to disciples such as Paul, Matthew, Luke, and John, alongside religious practices—facts acknowledged in the text. So, what Allah is asking Muslims to believe only exists as the common understanding of the time, but it is also a historically provable fact.

The Quran affirms belief in the Torah and the Gospel. At the time of the Prophet Muhammad, the prevailing Christian narrative was widely accepted, and he likely continued to promote it primarily to attract Christians into the Islamic fold.

Conclusion: An all-knowing Allah would not ask Muslims to believe in a book that never existed—one neither claimed to be from God nor written or dictated by His prophet.	Please rate this Conclusion:

Objective Analysis of God

Question: "Syed" is a caste system	**M6**

Analysis and background:
While Islam strongly advocates for human equality—emphasizing that all individuals are equal before God regardless of race, wealth, or lineage—it has, over time, developed a social distinction that resembles a caste-system, every definition of Caste: the divide between Syeds and non-Syeds.

Syeds are those who trace their lineage directly to the Prophet Muhammad, and this ancestry is often associated with elevated social and religious status. In many communities, Syeds are afforded special recognition, sometimes even financial privileges, and are considered spiritually superior. This reverence extends across generations and, in some interpretations, is believed to last until the Day of Judgment.

Such a distinction bears the hallmarks of a caste system, where birthright determines one's societal standing and access to certain privileges. The concept of caste is typically defined by inherited status, offering lifelong advantage based solely on lineage. In this context, the Syed identity functions similarly, granting honor and influence not through personal merit or piety, but through ancestral connection.

This structure appears to have been institutionalized to preserve the dignity and legacy of the Prophet's family. However, it raises a critical contradiction: if Islam truly upholds the principle of universal equality, how can it simultaneously endorse a hierarchy rooted in birth? The elevation of Syeds over others based on lineage undermines the egalitarian ethos that Islam professes—suggesting that, in practice, inherited privilege can override the ideal of spiritual and social parity.

Conclusion: By introducing Syed's privileges, Islam has introduced a caste system in its religion.	Please rate this Conclusion:

Section 5 – Islam
Questions from Muslims

Question:
Topics of the Quran

M7

Analysis and background:
As mentioned earlier, the majority of the Quran has self-praise for Allah, and only about 10% is related to how man should lead life on earth

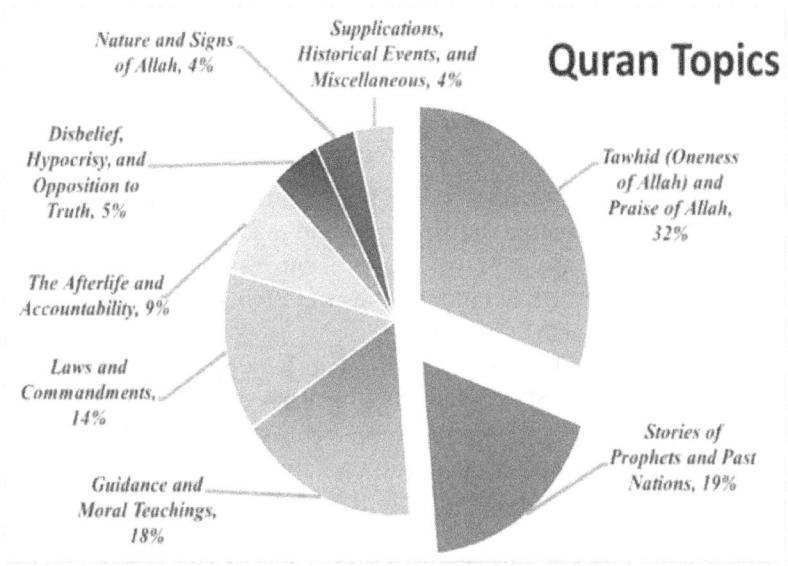

Conclusion:
Given Quarn's position, the distribution of topics does not logically support the idea that Allah created it as a divine and everlasting book of guidance.

Please rate this Conclusion:

Objective Analysis of God

Question: Quran after 17 years	M8

Analysis and background:
Much like the Bible, the transmission of divine revelation in Islam did not begin with a finalized written document. The Quran, regarded by Muslims as the literal word of God, was compiled into its complete written form approximately 17 years after the death of the Prophet Muhammad. This delay in documentation raises several important questions and concerns.

Absence of a finalized scripture at the Prophet's death: Despite being the central figure of Islam, Prophet Muhammad did not leave behind a fully compiled and written version of the Quran. This absence is striking, given the significance of the message and its role in guiding humanity.

Reliance on human memory: The preservation of the Quran initially depended on oral transmission and memorization. While oral tradition was strong in Arab culture, entrusting a timeless divine message to human memory—especially when writing tools were available—seems precarious.

Loss of key persons: Many of the Prophet's companions who had memorized portions of the Quran died in early battles, like the Battle of Yamama. Their deaths prompted an urgent need to compile the Quran, but also meant that some firsthand sources were lost.

Challenges of accurate compilation: With over 6,000 verses scattered across various memories and written fragments, expecting perfect reconstruction is difficult. The analogy of the childhood game "Telephone" illustrates how easily messages can distort—even over minutes, let alone years.

This raises a fundamental concern: if God is all-knowing and intends the Quran to be the ultimate guide for humanity, why allow such a vulnerable process for its preservation? The reliance on human recollection and posthumous compilation introduces uncertainty into a message meant to define the very purpose of existence.

Conclusion: Allah will never make a mistake with His most important message to Humans, if He truly wants His message to be passed on to generations.	Please rate this Conclusion:

Section 5 – Islam
Questions from Muslims

Question: Indication that writers manipulated the Quran verses	**M9**

Analysis and background:

30:2–4: *"The Romans have been defeated in a nearby land. Yet, following their defeat, they will triumph within a few years. The decision of the matter, before and after, is with Allah. And on that day the believers will rejoice."*

This passage is traditionally understood to refer to the Byzantine Empire's loss to the Sasanian Persians between 615 and 620 CE, a period marked by the fall of Jerusalem and other major setbacks for the Romans. For early Muslims, this defeat was disheartening, as the Byzantines were seen as "People of the Book," while the Quraysh—opponents of Islam—aligned themselves with the Zoroastrian Persians. The verse predicts a Roman comeback within a few years, which did occur around 627–628 CE. However, the Quran was not compiled into its final written form until nearly two decades later, during the caliphate of Uthman (~650 CE), long after these events had unfolded. This verse is promoted as divine prophecy; - indicates human authorship:

Why predict a short-term event? If Allah intended to demonstrate divine foresight, why not offer a prediction spanning centuries—something **beyond the reach of human anticipation?**

Is the Quran truly the unaltered word of an all-knowing deity? The timing of its compilation raises questions about whether verses were shaped or selected to align with known historical outcomes.

Could the text have been retroactively adjusted? The possibility that this verse was refined or inserted during the formalization process cannot be dismissed, especially given the oral nature of early transmission.

In this light, the verse may reflect more than prophecy—it may reveal how religious texts evolve in response to historical context, raising deeper questions about divine authorship, or Human efforts to make it Divine.

Conclusion: If Allah intended to offer a prophecy, He could have chosen one far in the future—verifiable and beyond dispute. Instead, selecting a prophecy tied to the Quran's documentation timeline seems flawed.	Please rate this Conclusion:

Objective Analysis of God

Question: Allah has given favors to greater sinners	M10

Analysis and background:
In both Islam and Christianity, the gravest theological offense is the act of associating partners with God—known in Islam as Shirk. The Quran is unequivocal on this matter. In Surah An-Nisa (4:48), it states:
"Indeed, Allah does not forgive associating others with Him in worship, but He forgives anything else for whomever He wills..."
This verse establishes Shirk as an unforgivable sin if one dies without repentance, placing it above all other transgressions. From an Islamic standpoint, the Christian belief in the Trinity—which includes the concept of the divinity of Jesus—is considered a direct form of Shirk, as it attributes divine status to more than one being. Yet, paradoxically, the Quran also extends a degree of respect and leniency toward Christians, referred to as "People of the Book." Verses such as 29:46, 5:82, and 5:69 encourage peaceful dialogue, acknowledge shared values, and even permit Muslim men to marry Christian women. This favorable treatment stands in contrast to the theological severity of Shirk.

This raises a compelling contradiction. Followers of Buddhism, Confucianism, or Taoism, who generally do not associate partners with a singular deity—or may not even worship a personal god—would, by strict theological logic, seem less guilty of Shirk. Yet they are not granted the same scriptural concessions or recognition as Christians.

The result is a theological tension: Islam condemns Shirk as the most serious sin, yet offers spiritual proximity and social integration to those who, by its own definition, commit it. This inconsistency suggests a kind of doctrinal double standard, where theological severity does not always align with scriptural treatment—raising broader questions about divine justice, inclusivity, and the interpretive flexibility within religious texts.

Conclusion: While saying SHIRK is the worst sin and He will not forgive such a person, Allah is contradicting Himself by giving favors to Christians and asking Muslims to be close to them.	Please rate this Conclusion:

Section 5 – Islam
Questions from Muslims

Question:
Abrahim is asking for proof

M11

Analysis and background:
2:260:- *"And [mention] when Abraham said, 'My Lord, show me how You give life to the dead.' [Allah] said, 'Have you not believed?' He said, 'Yes, but [I ask] only that my heart may be satisfied.' [Allah] said, 'Take four birds and commit them to yourself. Then [after slaughtering them] put on each hill a portion of them; then call them - they will come [flying] to you in haste. And know that Allah is Exalted in Might and Wise."*

This passage is often interpreted as a testament to Abraham's deep faith, yet it also reveals his desire for experiential confirmation—a tangible sign to satisfy his heart. Despite being a prophet with direct access to divine communication, Abraham still sought reassurance through a miracle.

Firstly, suppose a prophet needed a sign to reinforce his belief. How can ordinary individuals—who lack prophetic experiences or direct dialogue with the divine—be expected to maintain unwavering faith? The human condition is marked by doubt, curiosity, and the need for evidence. If even the most spiritually elevated figures required confirmation, it seems unreasonable to expect absolute certainty from those with far less access to divine insight.

Secondly, why are miracles selectively granted? If Allah responded to Abraham's request with a supernatural demonstration, why are similar reassurances withheld from others? Expecting belief without revelation or signs introduces a tension between divine justice and human limitation. If humans are created with finite understanding and are denied the very signs that could strengthen their faith, is disbelief truly a fair basis for punishment?

This verse, while often celebrated for its spiritual depth, also invites reflection on the nature of belief, the fairness of divine expectations, and the accessibility of truth for all people—not just prophets.

Conclusion:
Even prophets sought confirmation from God, so my doubts feel natural. They were given signs, yet I am given only silence—and that silence feels unfair.

Please rate this Conclusion:

Objective Analysis of God

Question: Monothelitism before Islam	M12

Analysis and background:
The widespread assumption that all pre-Islamic Arabs were idol worshippers oversimplifies the religious landscape of the time. In reality, a group known as the Hanifs stood apart from the dominant polytheistic culture. These individuals were monotheists who consciously rejected idol worship and sought to revive the original, uncorrupted faith of Ibrahim (Abraham). Notably, the Hanifs were not a unified tribe or sect; they were scattered individuals bound by a shared spiritual conviction in the oneness of God.

Prominent figures such as Zayd ibn Amr and Ummayyah ibn Abi al-Salt—both of whom had connections to the Prophet Muhammad (PBUH)—are often cited as examples of Hanifs. Their rejection of pagan practices and their pursuit of ethical monotheism suggest that many of the core theological principles later embraced by Islam were already present in Arabian society. These beliefs, while not yet codified into a formal religion, laid the groundwork for what would become Islamic doctrine.

This historical context implies that Islam did not emerge in a vacuum, nor did it introduce an entirely novel spiritual paradigm. Instead, it refined, organized, and institutionalized existing monotheistic ideas into a comprehensive religious system. The Quran and the teachings of the Prophet provided structure, law, and community to beliefs that had previously lived in fragmented and informal forms.

In essence, Islam can be seen as both a continuation and a transformation—preserving ancient truths while giving them new packaging.

Conclusion: Just like many other practices and names introduced by Islam, Monotheism was also practiced by the Arabs at the time of the revelation of Islam. Islam did not make significant changes.	**Please rate this Conclusion:**

Section 5 – Islam
Questions from Muslims

Question:
Rituals such as Namaz, Roza & Hajj, were present before Islam.

M13

Analysis and background:
Building on the previous question, many core rituals in Islam can be traced back to religious customs observed in pre-Islamic Arabia and neighboring faith traditions. Rather than emerging in isolation, Islamic practices often evolved from existing cultural and spiritual expressions, which were then reinterpreted and codified within a monotheistic framework. Here's how:

Fasting: Long before the advent of Islam, various Arab tribes observed fasting for purposes such as repentance, fulfilling vows, or spiritual purification. The Hanifs, a group of pre-Islamic monotheists, are known to have practiced fasting in ways that closely resemble the observance of Ramadan. Islam preserved this tradition but gave it a structured theological foundation and communal significance. Some examples are:

Pilgrimage (Ḥajj): The Kaaba was a revered site even before the advent of Islam. Rituals such as ṭawāf (circumambulation), animal sacrifices, and devotional chants were already part of the pilgrimage experience. Islam retained these elements but reoriented them toward the worship of one God, stripping away polytheistic associations.

Eid Celebrations: Annual festivals marked by communal joy and feasting were a common feature of Arabian culture. Islam institutionalized these festivities as Eid al-Fitr & Eid al-Adha, aligning them with specific religious milestones & spiritual themes.

Wudu (Ablution): Ritual purification was deeply embedded in Semitic traditions. Jewish practices included full-body immersion in a mikveh, while Christians often washed their hands and feet before prayer or reading scripture.

Islam did not invent spiritual practice from scratch; instead, it just redefined existing rituals. This approach allowed Islam to resonate with familiar traditions while offering a renewed spiritual vision.

Conclusion:
So, the religious rituals of fasting (Ramazan) and Hajj are old practices of pre-Islamic idol-worshipping Arabs. Islam is just a continuation in a different form.

Please rate this Conclusion:

Objective Analysis of God

Question: Treatment of women	M14

Analysis and background:
I am repeating myself here. It is my deeply held conviction that when women engage in a thorough and reflective reading of the Quran, many may conclude that they occupy a secondary position. This perception is not exclusive to Islam—it reflects a broader historical pattern of patriarchal dominance that long predates organized religion. From the ancient Code of Hammurabi, which codified unequal treatment of women, to the structures of modern religious institutions, male authority has often been reinforced through physical power and societal control.

This systemic imbalance is evident across virtually all major faith traditions and historical eras; the present #MeToo movement is a testament to this. Critics frequently point out that the Quran predominantly addresses men in its language and directives. At the same time, women are often mentioned in relation to men—whether as wives, daughters, or mothers, rather than as autonomous individuals. Even Surah An-Nisa (Chapter of Women), which is often cited as a progressive chapter on women's rights, focuses heavily on inheritance laws & familial roles, rather than articulating a vision of gender equality in broader social or spiritual terms.

Islam did introduce rights for women that were revolutionary in the 7th-century Arabian context—such as property ownership, consent in marriage, and legal recognition. However, these reforms, while progressive for their time, fall short of providing gender justice. Raising a question, how can a religion that is meant to last till the end of the universe by an all-knowing, all-just God contain structures that perpetuate inequality?

The tension between divine perfection and historical patriarchy invites ongoing reflection and consideration. Is the inequality a reflection of divine will, or of human interpretation shaped by the norms of its time? And if the latter, how should believers reconcile timeless scripture with evolving understandings of justice and dignity?

Conclusion: Allah, the "manifestation of Justice", cannot have such a biased attitude towards half of Humanity.	Please rate this Conclusion:

Section 5 – Islam
Questions from Muslims

Question:
Treatment of slaves

M15

Analysis and background:
Islam teaches that Allah created all human beings with equal spiritual worth and judges them by their deeds, not their status, lineage, or wealth. This principle of moral equality is foundational to Islamic theology. Yet, a troubling contradiction arises when we consider that Islam, while regulating and softening the conditions of slavery, nonetheless permits its existence.

This allowance stands in stark contrast to the divine attributes of Al-'Adl (The Just) and Al-Rahman (The Most Merciful). The Quran encourages humane treatment of slaves, promotes their emancipation as a virtuous act, and offers pathways for their freedom. However, it does not explicitly abolish slavery, nor does it declare the ownership of human beings as fundamentally unjust. Instead, it integrates slavery into its legal and social framework, offering guidelines for its regulation rather than its elimination.

This raises a question. If justice and mercy are central to divine nature, how can the ownership and commodification of human lives be sanctioned under divine law? The preservation of slavery within religious doctrine suggests a tension between timeless moral ideals and the socio-political realities of 7th-century Arabia.

Some scholars argue that Islam's approach to slavery was pragmatic—aimed at gradual reform rather than immediate abolition. Yet this incrementalism may have served to protect entrenched interests, particularly among the powerful and elite who benefited from the institution, "till the end of times". The result is a theological dilemma: how can a religion believed to be revealed by an all-knowing, all-just God accommodate a system so fundamentally at odds with modern conceptions of human dignity and freedom?

Conclusion:
Here again, Allah is endorsing the difference in treatment among His human creatures.

Please rate this Conclusion:

Objective Analysis of God

Question: Why only Muslims will enter Jinnat / Heaven	**M16**

Analysis and background:
The Quran presents a clear stance on salvation, emphasizing Islam as the only, final, and complete path.
3:85: *"Whoever seeks a religion other than Islam, it will not be accepted from him, and in the Hereafter, he will be among the losers."*
This directly challenges interpretations suggesting that righteous deeds alone ensure salvation.
3:19: *"Indeed, the religion in the sight of Allah is Islam."*
4:115: *"But whoever opposes the Messenger, after guidance has been made clear to him, and follows a way other than that of the believers... We shall cause him to burn in Hell."*
These verses collectively affirm the core Islamic doctrine that Islam is the divinely ordained path to eternal salvation. While some modern scholars advocate for a more inclusive interpretation, suggesting that individuals like Mother Teresa might attain paradise based on their righteous deeds, such views lack direct support from the Quranic text.
Traditional scholars, particularly mullahs, interpret these verses as applying to those who convert to Islam and later abandon it. But this is flawed, as someone who leaves due to doubt or inquiry is exercising free thought—something the Quran claims to encourage. Here, Allah favors free thinking only when it serves His goal. Ultimately, this tension highlights a deeper theological challenge: if Islam is meant to be a universal and rational path, then its approach to doubt, inquiry, and spiritual return must reflect the mercy and wisdom attributed to Allah. Otherwise, the framework risks alienating those who seek truth through honest questioning— ironically, the very process the Quran encourages.

Conclusion: Allah's decision seems unjust, given that He only approached a small fraction of humanity. All known prophets appeared within a limited 5,000 km region—less than 5% of the Earth's surface.	Please rate this Conclusion:

Section 5 – Islam
Questions from Muslims

Question:
No place for Good Non-Muslims in Jinnah/ Heaven

M17

Analysis and background:
In continuation from the previous question, the Quran addresses the fate of non-Muslims and the acceptance of their deeds in several verses, emphasizing that belief in Islam is critical for salvation.

3:85: - *"And whoever desires a religion other than Islam—never will it be accepted from him, and he, in the Hereafter, will be among the losers."*

This verse underscores Mulla's interpretation and adjustments that a good deed done without faith will be treated fairly. Perhaps 'fairly' means lower ranks in Hell. At the same time, Allah says that only Islam is accepted as the true path to salvation.

25:23: *"And We shall turn to whatever deeds they did and make such deeds as scattered floating particles of dust."*

This indicates that the good deeds of disbelievers are rendered ineffective due to their lack of faith.

39:65: *"And it was already revealed to you and those before you that if you should associate [anything] with Allah, your work would surely become worthless, and you would surely be among the losers."*

This highlights the importance of monotheism and the rejection of shirk (associating partners with Allah) for the acceptance of deeds. These verses collectively convey that without embracing Islam, even the most virtuous deeds of non-Muslims are not accepted, and they face the consequences of their disbelief in the Hereafter.

Conclusion:
Just like Christianity, all merciful Allah is not flexible enough to allow good deeds to come in the way of punishing you. The only way to heaven is through Islam.

Please rate this Conclusion:

Objective Analysis of God

Question: The whole feeble foundation of Islam	**M18**

Analysis and background:
No matter how Mullas try to twist Islam and sugarcoat it, going by what is in the Quran, one gets the clear picture of what the whole religion of Islam is saying:
- Allah created humans to test them about their deeds in their lives, which is the whole reason this whole universe was created
- Allah will reward humans' deeds with everlasting life in heaven and punish them for evil deeds
- But Deeds aside, Allah will give heaven only to people who recognize him as the only creator and worthy of worship
- But Allah does not need Humans' worship and already has trillions and trillions of angels worshiping him at all times for ages
- So, deeds were surpassed by "not doing SHIRK", worshiping other gods, and making any other His equivalent
- But Allah only revealed it to a radius of 2000 km, which is less than 10% of the earth and less than 0.1% of the population, and for less than 0.001% of the total period of Human history
- And this message was delivered in perhaps the most concealed way in the most ambiguous form for as long as humans will live --- but could not survive 3-4 hours
- Yet, if someone does not worship Him, that person will rot in Hell for eternity, as decided by the All merciful and all-loving Allah

Above is the contradiction of what will be the savour, one's deeds or blind faith in Islam

Conclusion: This statement from Allah that only Muslims will be allowed in Heaven, while He communicated His message only to a tiny fraction of Humans, is very unjust.	Please rate this Conclusion:

Section 5 – Islam
Questions from Muslims

Question:
Allowing Polygamy – knowing that men cannot do justice

M19

Analysis and background:

Quran 4:3: "*Then marry those that please you of [other] women, two or three or four. But if you fear that you will not be just, then [marry only] one...*"

Quran 4:129: - "*You will never be able to be equal between wives, even if you should strive [to do so]. So do not incline completely [toward one] and leave another hanging.*"

The Quran permits a man to marry up to four wives. Still, this allowance comes with a critical condition: he must treat each wife with fairness and justice, as above 4:3. Yet in the same chapter, the Quran acknowledges the inherent difficulty of fulfilling this condition 4:129

On one hand, polygamy is permitted; on the other, the Quran itself concedes that true equality—especially emotional and relational—is virtually unattainable. If Allah, as the all-knowing Creator, understands human limitations, why allow a practice that so easily leads to injustice?

It echoes the irony in Henry Ford's famous quote: "Any customer can have a car painted in any color that he wants so long as it is black." In other words, permission is granted in theory, but the conditions make it nearly impossible in practice.

This contradiction invites reflection on the purpose and wisdom behind divine legislation.

Conclusion:
The above two verses negate each other and cannot come from the same all-knowing source of Allah.

Please rate this Conclusion:

Objective Analysis of God

Question: Critical Analysis of the Quran's contents	M20

Analysis and background:
The Quran is regarded by Muslims as the final and eternal word of God, serving as a spiritual and moral guide for over fifteen centuries. Yet, this claim invites scrutiny when examined through a practical and philosophical lens. Several concerns arise:
- A significant portion of the text—estimated around 30%—is devoted to self-praise of Allah, emphasizing His attributes, power, and authority.
- Concrete guidance on daily life, governance, and comprehensive moral or ethical systems is limited or ambiguous, leaving much to interpretation or reliance on supplementary texts like Hadith.
- The Quran offers no detailed predictions or insights into future global developments, nor does it provide strategies for navigating the evolving challenges of modern civilization.
- Instructions for foundational practices, such as the method of performing Namaz (prayer), are not clearly outlined, requiring reliance on later traditions for clarity.
- Many ethical principles found in the Quran mirror ancient legal systems, such as the Code of Hammurabi, suggesting continuity rather than originality in moral legislation.
- The challenge of engaging with a divine figure who remains unseen, unknown, and frequently self-referential creates a philosophical barrier, especially when that figure demands unquestioning belief.
- Claims of divine mercy, such as "Allah is Most Merciful," can only be evaluated through the observable realities of the world He governs, including suffering, inequality, and natural disasters.

If the Quran is meant to be a timeless manual for humanity, one might expect more emphasis on actionable guidance rather than repeated affirmations of divine greatness.

Conclusion: All-knowing Allah did not write the Quran in the correct proportion of its message intentions and requirements.	Please rate this Conclusion:

Section 5 – Islam
Questions from Muslims

Question: Mostly vague messages, goals, and expectations	**M21**

Analysis and background:
The Quran was revealed in Arabic, a language revered for its poetic depth & expressive richness. However, this stylistic complexity leads to ambiguity, particularly in the specificity of its directives. Many verses offer broad guidance rather than detailed instructions, leaving room for varied interpretations across cultures, schools of thought, & historical periods.

In contrast, modern human communication—especially in fields like education, management, and policy—has evolved to prioritize clarity and precision. Frameworks such as the SMART model (Specific, Measurable, Achievable, Relevant, Time-bound) are designed to eliminate vagueness and ensure actionable outcomes. When compared to this standard, many Quranic commands can feel open-ended. For instance, a directive akin to "go north" could mean anything from a short walk to a lifelong journey, depending on the interpreter's perspective.

The Arabic language itself contributes to this interpretive fluidity. It is built on root-based morphology, where a single root—like ج-ل-س—can produce multiple meanings:

"Jalasa" (he sat) – an action
"Majlis" (assembly) – a noun
"Tajallus" (formal sitting posture) – a derived verb form

It multiplies the complexity when multiple similar words are in a verse. This linguistic flexibility complicates the task of extracting consistent meaning from scripture. This clearly is not the most effective language for delivering timeless, globally binding guidance. The challenge lies not in the sincerity of the message, but in the clarity of its transmission, mainly when it is meant to be translated into all languages.

Conclusion: The Quran lacks specific instructions and entirely relies upon human-dependent sources, like Hadith, to interpret Allah's wishes. The Hadith is not the words of Allah, so Allah allows humans to lead and interpret Islam.	Please rate this Conclusion:

Objective Analysis of God

Question: Lacks basic guidance, like "System of governance"	M22

Analysis and background:
The Quran presents itself as a comprehensive and sufficient guide for human life, a claim most clearly articulated in 5:3: *"Today I have perfected your religion for you and completed My favor upon you and have approved Islam as your religion."*

This verse is often cited to affirm the finality and completeness of Islamic guidance. However, when examined through the lens of practical governance and societal organization, a notable gap emerges. The Quran does not offer a detailed blueprint for administrative structures or political systems following the death of the Prophet Muhammad. There is no explicit verse outlining how leadership should be selected, how justice should be administered, or how a Muslim society should be governed in the absence of prophetic authority.

This reliance on secondary sources and post-prophetic interpretation raises critical questions about the Quran's claim to completeness. Compounding this issue is the fact that the Quran was not fully compiled in written form during the Prophet's lifetime. Much of it was preserved orally, and its final arrangement occurred years later under the third Caliph, Uthman ibn Affan.

Given these historical realities, the assertion that "everything" was provided in one book becomes difficult to reconcile. The need for oral transmission, later compilation, and supplementary texts suggests that the Quran functions more as a spiritual and moral foundation than as a fully self-contained manual for all aspects of human civilization. This raises questions on the nature of divine guidance and His foresight.

Conclusion: It is irrational to believe that an all-knowing Allah would establish a system meant to guide followers for centuries, yet leave its core foundations and enforcement dependent on human effort.	Please rate this Conclusion:

Section 5 – Islam
Questions from Muslims

Question: How Allah handed Islam over to humans	M23

Analysis and background:
Continuing on a similar topic, if Allah is truly all-knowing and all-wise, one would expect the final revelation to offer clear, timeless guidance on all essential aspects of life—spiritual, moral, social, and political. However, the Quran leaves many foundational matters undefined and provides little guidance in these respects. All subsequent developments were generated by human and Muslim scholars, which is contradictory and non-authentic.

There is no explicit framework for governance after the Prophet's death, no detailed instructions for performing core rituals like prayer (Salat), and no comprehensive blueprint for navigating future societal transformations. Instead, Muslims have historically relied on the Hadith, scholarly interpretation, and human institutions to fill these gaps.

Moreover, the Quran was not compiled into a single written volume during the Prophet's lifetime. Its preservation depended on oral transmission and later codification, raising questions about the vulnerability of such a process for a supposedly complete and eternal message.

If Allah intended Islam to be a living tradition, then perhaps its "completion" refers not to exhaustive instruction, but to a foundational framework meant to evolve through human engagement and interpretation.

Islam that Muslims follow now (apart from foundation concepts) is all made by Humans.

Conclusion: Such a perfect God cannot say that He has completed religion and left it in such a disarray.	**Please rate this Conclusion:**

My-OAG.com

Objective Analysis of God

Question: Issues with the Arabic language

M24

Analysis and background:
Arabic is undeniably a remarkable and intricate language, celebrated for its depth, poetic beauty, and linguistic flexibility. Central to its structure is the system of root words, typically composed of three consonants, though some roots contain two or four. These roots serve as the foundation for a vast array of derived words, each shaped by context, grammatical form, and usage. A single root can generate dozens of meanings—ranging from verbs and nouns to abstract concepts—making Arabic both expressive and rich in interpretation.

This linguistic complexity has proven advantageous for religious scholars, such as Mullahs and Maulvis, who often draw multiple interpretations from a single Quranic verse. The fluidity of meaning subjective readings, which can vary widely depending on the interpreter's perspective and intent. In this background, its choice for what is claimed to be God's final and universal revelation is beyond my logic.

This historical context raises essential questions about clarity and accessibility. If the Quran is meant to guide all of humanity for all time, delivering it in a linguistically evolving medium—one that was still in its formative stages—may complicate its interpretation and universal applicability.

We have addressed this topic in detail elsewhere.

Conclusion:
The selection of the Arabic language, which has so many ambiguities and misinterpretations, is itself a poor selection for a book of divine guidance.

Please rate this Conclusion:

Section 5 – Islam
Questions from Muslims

Question: M25
Simple mathematical errors
Only at one place, even that is wrong

Analysis and background:
Surah An-Nisa (Chapter 4 of the Quran) is the only place in the entire scripture where Allah provides explicit numerical instructions—fixed fractional shares—for the distribution of inheritance. Unlike other verses that rely on metaphor, moral guidance, or general principles, these inheritance laws are mathematically quantifiable and can be directly added up. Yet, paradoxically, these are also the verses that reveal an apparent mathematical inconsistency.

For example, if a deceased individual leaves behind two daughters (2/3 of the estate), both parents (1/6 each), and a wife (1/8), the total allocation becomes 1 1/8, or 112.5% of the estate—exceeding the whole. This over-allocation is not a rare anomaly but a recurring issue in multiple inheritance scenarios outlined in the Quran.

This contradiction was recognized early in Islamic history. Caliph Abu Bakr, faced with such a case, introduced the principle of 'AWL—a method of proportionally reducing each heir's share so that the total fits within 100%. Later, Caliph Umar ibn al-Khattab institutionalized this approach, making it a standard practice in Islamic Jurisprudence, but negating the Quran. What's striking is that this is the only instance in the Quran where divine instruction can be mathematically tested, and yet it fails to hold up under basic arithmetic.

If Allah is all-knowing and all-wise, why would the only mathematically verifiable command in the Quran contain an error that humans had to resolve?

Conclusion:
Allah cannot make a mistake; his calculations and distribution do not add up to 100% and Mullas come to Allah's rescue.

Please rate this Conclusion:

Objective Analysis of God

Question: Quranic Law taken from Hammurabi Code (HC)	M26

Analysis and background:
Like previous religions, notable parallels exist between the legal and ethical principles found in the Quran and those outlined in the Code of Hammurabi, particularly in areas concerning criminal justice, family law, and social conduct. While Muslims consider the Quran to be a divine revelation, Hammurabi's Code—written nearly 2,700 years earlier—was a human-crafted legal system designed to maintain order and justice in ancient Mesopotamia.

What stands out is the practical and action-oriented nature of Hammurabi's laws. They are direct, prescriptive, and often harsh, reflecting the realities of a society governed by strict accountability and transparency. In contrast, Quranic laws tend to be vague and usually require interpretation and supplementation through Hadith and jurisprudence.

Here are some striking examples of overlap: This subject has been developed in detail in this book:
1. Punishment for Theft – HC #6 and Quran 5:38
2. Punishment for Adultery – HC 128-130 and Quran 24:2
3. Laws Regarding Marriage and Family – HC # 144-146) and Quran 4:19-21
4. Retaliation for Injury (Qisas) – HC 196) and 2:178
5. Rights of Inheritance- HC # 170-171) and Quran 4:7-13
6. Slavery and Treatment of Slaves - Hammurabi Code (Law # 117-118) and Quran 4:36
7. Laws Regarding False Accusations (Qadhf – HC # 129) and 24:4

These similarities suggest that divine law often builds upon human experience, and Allah could not devise effective and authentic laws.

Conclusion: It appears that Allah is copying from Laws developed by Humans, such a God cannot be the all-knowing and all-perfect one.	Please rate this Conclusion:

Section 5 – Islam
Questions from Muslims

Question:
Qisas Laws taken from Hammurabi

M27

Analysis and background:

The laws of **Qisas** (retaliation or retribution) are mentioned in the Quran.

2:178 - "O you who have believed, prescribed for you is legal retribution (Qisas) in the case of murder: the free for the free, the slave for the slave, and the female for the female. But if anyone is granted pardon by his brother, then pursuit of what is reasonable and payment of compensation to him in good conduct should be made. This is a mercy from your Lord. So, whoever transgresses after that will have a painful punishment."

This verse outlines a system of justice based on equivalence—life for life, injury for injury—but also introduces the possibility of forgiveness and financial compensation, framing mercy as a divine virtue. It reflects a balance between justice and compassion, allowing for resolution beyond strict retaliation.

Interestingly, this principle of proportional justice was already codified centuries earlier in the Code of Hammurabi, written around 1750 BCE. For example:

HC 196: "If a man puts out the eye of a nobleman, his eye shall be put out." This is the origin of the phrase "an eye for an eye," a foundational concept in ancient legal systems.

The Quran also prescribes corporal punishment for theft 5:38: *"As for the thief, male or female, cut off their hands…"*

This mirrors Hammurabi's Law #218: If a physician causes harm during surgery, their hands are to be cut off.

Law 195: If a son strikes his father, his hands should be cut off.

These parallels suggest that, in Islamic belief, the Quran, while divinely revealed, follows long-standing legal traditions that predate it. The resemblance to Hammurabi's Code—one of the earliest known legal systems—indicates that Islamic law may have refined and recontextualized existing norms, a trait not expected from all-knowing Allah.

Conclusion:
Hammurabi was Human and developed this barbaric code, but we expect better laws from all merciful Allah.

Please rate this Conclusion:

Objective Analysis of God

Question:
Birth stages - old information

M28

Analysis and background:
Muslims often take pride in the Quran's references to fetal development, viewing them as signs of divine knowledge and miraculous insight. Verses such as "We made the sperm-drop into a clinging clot, and We made the clot into a lump, and We made the lump into bones, then We clothed the bones with flesh..." (Quran 23:14) are frequently cited as evidence of the Quran's scientific foresight. However, it's essential to recognize that detailed descriptions of embryology existed long before the 7th century.
In Hindu theology, ancient scriptures such as the Garbha Upanishad, the Mahabharata, and various Puranas offer remarkably intricate accounts of human development in the womb. These texts explore:
- The five elements (Pancha Mahabhutas) and three Gunas (qualities) that shape the physical and mental constitution of the fetus.
- A month-by-month breakdown of fetal growth over the nine-month gestation period.
- The impact of karma on the soul's journey and its embodiment in the womb.
- The womb, as a sacred space, symbolizes transformation, purification, and preparation for earthly life.

From a scientific standpoint, modern embryology reveals that bones and muscles develop simultaneously, rather than sequentially. The Quranic phrasing—"then clothed the bones with flesh"—has been interpreted as implying a developmental order that doesn't align with biological evidence.
While the description may have been impressive for its time, the theological claim is that the Quran is the literal word of an all-knowing Creator, not merely a 7th-century document. If that is the case, then its descriptions should reflect absolute precision.

Conclusion:
The Quran is just rephrasing the wrong known facts about the development of the fetus, and it is not a miracle of the Quran. It proves that these words are not the creator.

Please rate this Conclusion:

Section 5 – Islam
Questions from Muslims

Question:
Why does Allah need reinforcement

M29

Analysis and background:
51:56 - *"And I did not create the jinn and mankind except to worship Me."*
Allah created Angels who worship him, then He created jinn and Humans for the same purpose.
This declaration establishes worship as the central purpose of human and jinn existence. Before this, Allah had already created angels, beings who worship Him without question or deviation. The creation of jinn and humans—endowed with free will—introduces a dynamic where worship is not automatic but chosen, making obedience a conscious act of devotion.
Here, the question is: Why does an all-powerful, all-knowing deity repeatedly emphasize His worthiness of worship and demand recognition from His creation? From a human psychological perspective, such insistence on praise and exclusive devotion can resemble traits associated with ego or self-centeredness. The Quran consistently reinforces Allah's supremacy, authority, and the necessity of glorifying Him. Disobedience is met with punishment, while submission is rewarded—creating a framework where divine affirmation appears to be the ultimate goal. This is a reflection of a deity who seeks validation, especially given the repeated declarations such as "Allah is the best of creators" or "To Him belongs all praise.".
However, within Islamic theology, this emphasis is not seen as self-serving but as a reflection of ultimate truth and justice. Worship is not for Allah's benefit, but for the spiritual elevation of the worshipper. Still, the recurring theme of divine centrality reflects on the nature of God's relationship with creation—and whether the demand for worship is a test of humility, a path to transcendence, or a projection of divine ego.

Conclusion:
Creating all things in the universe, including angels, Jinn, and Humans, solely for worship and praise, seems to be a demand from a very self-centered entity, rather than the completely independent and self-sufficient Allah.

Please rate this Conclusion:

Objective Analysis of God

Question: Heaven, hell, and all materialistic	**M30**

Analysis and background:
The Quranic descriptions of Paradise are rich with imagery that emphasizes material pleasures—gardens with flowing rivers, abundant fruits, lakes of milk and honey, luxurious garments of silk and brocade, ornate jewelry, and even wine served in crystal goblets. These depictions suggest a Heaven where enjoyment is deeply tied to physical sensation, implying the presence of a corporeal body to experience taste, touch, and pleasure.

Rewards such as meat from birds, dried fruits, and a perfect climate would have held immense appeal to the desert-dwelling Arabs of the 7th century, who lived in harsh environments with limited access to such luxuries. In that context, Paradise was envisioned as the ultimate reversal of worldly deprivation—a place of comfort, abundance, and sensual delight.

However, if Heaven is a spiritual realm, why are its rewards so materially grounded? There appears to be little emphasis on non-physical or transcendent experiences—such as intellectual fulfillment, emotional peace, or metaphysical union with the divine—that might be more fitting for a soul without a body. The Quran's portrayal of wine without intoxication seems paradoxical. If the defining feature of wine is its effect, removing it leaves a beverage that may not hold the same allure. The emphasis on sexual rewards, often framed in terms of male pleasure, further complicates the vision of Paradise. It prompts reflection on whether these depictions are culturally influenced projections rather than universal ideals.

Given that Allah is described as all-powerful and infinitely creative, one might expect Heaven to transcend earthly desires and offer entirely new dimensions of joy—beyond food, drink, and sensuality.

Conclusion: Heaven's rewards appear to be the wishes of men at that time. It seems irrational that whatever He is restricting in the world, He is allowing in heaven, no moral consistency.	Please rate this Conclusion:

Question:
Quran and Aristotle's view on Human Embryology

M31

Section 5 – Islam
Questions from Muslims

Analysis and background:
9:62: - *"Created man from a clinging clot."*
The Quranic view of human origin, particularly in Surah Al-'Alaq (96:2), describes man as being created from 'alaq—a term often translated as "clot of blood," "clinging substance," or "leech-like clot."

In contrast, Aristotle's theory of reproduction, rooted in ancient Greek philosophy, suggests that the male semen carries the "form" or essence of life. At the same time, the female contributes the "matter"—specifically, menstrual blood. According to Aristotle (about 335 BCE), this blood serves as the raw material that the male principal shapes into a human being. However, he did not view this blood as a clot or a viable origin of life on its own; instead, it was inert and required the active force of semen to animate it.

Both views share a symbolic reliance on blood-related imagery to describe the beginning of life. They reflect the observational limitations of their time, where women's menstrual blood was assumed to be related to the birth of a child, for various logical and observational reasons. Yet, the Quran's 'alaq is portrayed as a living, developing substance, while Aristotle's menstrual blood is seen as passive and lifeless, incapable of producing life without male input.

Modern embryology, however, shows that neither a literal blood clot nor menstrual blood plays a direct role in the formation of a human embryo. The process involves the fusion of sperm and egg, followed by cellular differentiation—an understanding that renders both ancient views totally incorrect.

However, it also highlights the fact that Prophet Muhammad received his knowledge (which he translated into the Quran) from the sources available at that time.

Conclusion:
The creator does not know how humans are formed and is narrating incorrect knowledge of the times.

Please rate this Conclusion:

Objective Analysis of God

Question: Noah's flood – an old cultural story	M32

Analysis and background:
The story of Noah's flood, as described in the Quran, appears to echo a broader historical memory of catastrophic flooding events that occurred across various ancient civilizations. These flood narratives likely trace their origins to the post-Ice Age period, when melting glaciers caused widespread inundation of land, reshaping coastlines and displacing populations. As a result, many cultures developed their own interpretations of these events, embedding them into mythologies and religious texts.

In Indian literature, for instance, the Satapatha Brahmana and the Puranas recount a strikingly similar tale: the Matsya Avatar of Vishnu warns Manu, the progenitor of humanity, about an impending deluge and instructs him to build a boat to preserve life. This mirrors the biblical account of Noah and his ark, suggesting a shared archetype of divine intervention during a global flood.

Meanwhile, Chinese civilization, though geographically isolated by the Himalayas, also preserved flood legends. Rather than mythologizing the event, the Chinese responded with practical innovation—developing vast irrigation systems to manage water flow. These advancements played a pivotal role in the rise of organized states, including the Qin Dynasty, which laid the foundation for imperial China.

Perhaps the most ancient and influential flood narrative comes from Mesopotamia: the Epic of Gilgamesh. Written around 2100 BCE, it tells of Utnapishtim, who is warned by the god Ea to build an ark and save his family and animals from a divine flood. This account predates the biblical story by centuries, and many scholars believe it may have had a direct influence on the Genesis narrative.

This fact shows how the Flood story got into Torah, then the Bible, and then into the Quran, not as divine information but as the cultural story of times

Conclusion: It's more likely that Great floods are a fact after the ice age, but these were limited to local geographies and local religions. Allah's narrative does not hold.	Please rate this Conclusion:

Section 5 – Islam
Questions from Muslims

Question:
How Angels can argue with God

M33

Analysis and background:

2:102 - *They followed what the evil ones gave out (falsely) against the power of Solomon: the blasphemers were not Solomon but the evil ones, teaching men magic and such things as came down at Babylon to the angels Harut and Marut. But neither taught anyone (such things) without saying: 'We are only for trial; so, do not blaspheme.' They learned from them the means to sow discord between man and wife. But they could not thus harm anyone except by Allah's permission. And they learned what harmed them, not what profited them. And they knew that the buyers of (magic) would have no share in the happiness of the Hereafter. And vile was the price for which they did sell their souls, if they but knew!*

The verse referring to Haroot and Maroot presents a theological puzzle. According to the Quran, these two were angels sent to Babylon. Yet, the core Islamic understanding of angels is that they are incapable of disobedience, lacking free will, and acting solely in accordance with Allah's commands. This raises a critical question: how could beings designed to be perfectly obedient engage in actions that suggest independent thought or even rebellion?

While traditional Tafaseers attempt to reconcile this by offering elaborate narratives—such as the angels being tested or temporarily given human traits—these explanations often feel like post hoc rationalizations. Scholars and clerics, including Mullahs and Maulvis, have constructed layers of interpretation to resolve what appears to be a theological inconsistency.

If angels are truly without agency, then the story of Haroot and Maroot challenges the internal logic of divine creation.

Conclusion:
It appears that Allah cited this story in the Quran, which does not align with the rest of His narration and does not add up.

Please rate this Conclusion:

Objective Analysis of God

Question: Angels on shoulders	**M34**

Analysis and background:

50:16: *"Indeed, it is We Who created humankind and fully know what their souls whisper to them, and We are closer to them than their jugular vein."*

50:17: *"As the two recording angels—one sitting to the right, and the other to the left—note everything."*

50:18: *"Not a word does a person utter without having a vigilant observer ready to write it down."*

At first glance, these verses seem to present a contradiction. If Allah is omniscient, intimately aware of every thought and whisper within the human soul, and closer than one's own jugular vein, then the presence of recording angels appears redundant. Why would an all-knowing deity require documentation of human speech and actions?

Is Allah dependent on these records to judge humanity, or are they symbolic tools for human understanding? If the angels are tasked with recording every word and deed, does that imply a need for external validation of divine knowledge?

Traditional interpretations often suggest that the angels serve not to inform Allah, but to provide a transparent record for humans themselves—evidence to be presented on the Day of Judgment. Yet this explanation still invites scrutiny. If Allah's knowledge is perfect and immediate, why the need for intermediaries and validation?

From a critical lens, this system may reflect a humanized framework of justice, and also challenge the notion of absolute divine self-sufficiency.

Conclusion: It is very irrational for Allah to have angels write the deeds of Humans, and on the day of judgment, Allah verifies that if He wants, he could have and should have done without the angels.	Please rate this Conclusion:

Section 5 – Islam
Questions from Muslims

Question:
God guides whoever He wishes

M35

Analysis and background:
22:16 - *And so, We revealed this Quran as clear verses. And Allah indeed guides whoever He wills.*

This verse emphasizes the clarity of divine revelation while simultaneously asserting that guidance is entirely at Allah's discretion. It's not earned through merit alone, nor guaranteed by human effort—it is granted to whomever Allah chooses. The broader Quranic theme reinforces this notion: "He does what He pleases." Such phrasing suggests that divine will operates independently of human actions or expectations.

This theological stance mirrors concepts found in the Torah and the Bible, where God's sovereignty is portrayed as absolute. In both traditions, divine favor or punishment is often attributed to God's will rather than strictly to human behavior. The implication is that the cosmos and salvation are governed by divine prerogative, not transactional justice.

This raises fundamental questions about free will, moral responsibility, and divine justice. If Allah rewards or withholds guidance based solely on His will, then human deeds—while encouraged—may not be the ultimate determinant of spiritual outcome. This portrayal can be interpreted as depicting God as unbound by human logic or fairness, operating from a position of supreme autonomy and independence.

To believers, this reflects divine majesty and mystery. To skeptics, it may suggest a system where human effort is secondary, and divine favor appears arbitrary. Either way, it shakes the very foundation of Islamic reasoning and the creation of the Universe and Humans.

Conclusion: These lines undermine the entire purpose of heaven and hell, which is to reward deeds, and the reason for creating this universe.	Please rate this Conclusion:

Objective Analysis of God

Question: Satan changes verses	**M36**

Analysis and background:

22:52 – *"Whenever We sent a messenger or a prophet before you, O Prophet, and he recited Our revelations, Satan would influence people's understanding of his recitation. But eventually Allah would eliminate Satan's influence. Then Allah would firmly establish His revelations. And Allah is All-Knowing, All-Wise.*

This verse introduces a striking theological tension. It acknowledges that Satan has historically interfered with the delivery or reception of divine messages, influencing how revelations were understood. Yet it also promises that Allah will eventually remove Satan's distortions and firmly establish the true message. The use of future tense—"will eliminate," "will establish"—suggests that this purification is not immediate, but deferred. This implies that during the time of revelation, Satan's influence may still be active, even as the Quran is being revealed.

This raises a contradiction when considered alongside other Quranic verses that assert previous scriptures—such as the Torah and the Bible—were altered or corrupted:

- 2:79: Accuses some of writing scripture with their own hands and claiming it is from God.
- 5:13, 5:41: Mentions distortion and concealment of divine words.
- 3:78 and 4:46: Refer to twisting words out of context and misrepresentation.

The implication is that Satan's interference was not fully neutralized, even in earlier revelations by all-powerful and dominant Allah, which means that Allah wanted these messages to be distorted and misguided. This undermines the claim of divine apparachor sincerity to judge Humans.

Conclusion: All-knowing Allah does not have control over His communication channels and let a small thing like Satan change it.	Please rate this Conclusion:

Section 5 – Islam
Questions from Muslims

Question: Killing is allowed - why do it through Muslims	**M37**

Analysis and background:

9:5 I - *But once the Sacred Months have passed, kill the polytheists who violated their treaties wherever you find them, capture them, besiege them, and lie in wait for them on every way. But if they repent, perform prayers, and pay alms-tax, then set them free. Indeed, Allah is All-Forgiving, Most Merciful.*

This verse is one of the most debated in the Quran due to its stark language and the implications it carries. It outlines a directive to pursue and eliminate polytheists who have broken their treaties, but also offers a path to safety through repentance, prayer, and payment of zakat (alms tax). The conditional mercy here hinges not on universal compassion, but on religious conformity and financial contribution.

For me, it reflects a troubling aspect of Islam - the sanctioning of violence against non-believers unless they convert and contribute economically. The fact that Allah, described as All-Forgiving and Most Merciful, delegates this task to humans—through warfare, siege, and surveillance—raises theological concerns. If God is omnipotent, why rely on human agents to enact such harsh measures? Why not resolve disbelief through divine wisdom rather than human bloodshed?

Furthermore, the emphasis on tax payment as a condition for mercy introduces a transactional element to the concept of salvation. It suggests that material compliance can override spiritual dissent, which some interpret as undermining the moral purity of divine justice.

This verse institutionalized violence and coercion, casting doubt on the notion of a benevolent deity.

Conclusion: A true all-powerful God cannot ask humans to go and kill non-believers through humans. It is entirely irrational to enforce one's will or desire using one's subjects. This appears more like the attitude of a tyrannical ruler than that of Allah, as defined by Islam..	Please rate this Conclusion:

Objective Analysis of God

Question: Allah is cursing Abu Lahab and his wife???	**M38**

Analysis and background:
111:1-5. *May the hands of Abu Lahab be ruined, and ruined is he. His wealth will not avail him or that which he gained. He will (enter to) burn in a Fire of (blazing) flame. And his wife (as well)— the carrier of firewood. Around her neck is a rope of twisted fibre."*

This passage delivers a direct condemnation of Abu Lahab, a staunch opponent of Prophet Muhammad, and his wife Umm Jamil, portraying their fate as one of divine punishment. The language used raises a question: Why would an all-powerful, all-knowing Creator use such specific and emotionally charged language to curse two individuals?

From a divine standpoint, one might expect a tone of transcendent justice, not personal vengeance. The curse appears unusually targeted, especially considering the Quran's broader emphasis on mercy, wisdom, and universal guidance. Moreover, while Abu Lahab's opposition to Islam is well-documented, the historical record does not clearly confirm the fulfillment of the curse upon Umm Jamil. Her death is not prominently recorded in Islamic sources. I am sure if she had died in a similar way as cursed by Allah, Muslim Mullahs would have been blowing their trumpets.

Secondly, if Allah chose to curse a specific human and his wife, why did it not happen, as mentioned in the Quran, which contains several verses that affirm Allah's absolute will and power, declaring that **whatever He wills, happens**

Conclusion: It conveys an angry "human" who is helpless, and the only way to relieve himself of the anger is to curse.	Please rate this Conclusion:

Section 5 – Islam
Questions from Muslims

Question: No guidance for 98% of Humanity Considering the Islamic perspective	**M39**

Analysis and background:
According to Islam, the last prophet and divine message ended with the Prophet Muhammad. If we consider the Islamic scholars' (and Christian) timelines of prophets and their said ages, and try to calculate the number of people coming before Prophet Muhammad. After him, the percentages come to about 7%, mainly considering the religious timeline from Adam to Muhammad. Here, we are taking a religious approach rather than relying on scientific estimates. With scientific estimates of Homo sapiens living for about 200,000 plus years, this percentage reduces to less than 1%. So, Allah provided guidance based on the accounts of religion and Islam, until 7% of the total population was born, and after that, He allowed everyone to find their true path.

According to religious estimates, approximately 100 billion humans have lived since the beginning of humanity. The number of people alive today is roughly equal to the total population from the time of Prophet Adam to the time of Prophet Muhammad, spanning thousands of years. Yet, according to the Quran, only around 20 named prophets were sent during that entire period. This means divine guidance—at least in documented form—reached perhaps 7% of humanity, leaving the remaining 93% without direct prophetic instruction. Moreover, the reach of these prophets was inherently limited. In a world without modern communication, transportation, or global infrastructure, their messages could only extend to small, localized communities.

These events occurred in eras without recorded history, archaeological verification, or independent documentation. For contemporary observers, these accounts remain unverifiable narratives, passed down through oral tradition and religious texts.

Conclusion: With the above facts, it appears that Allah has given up on Humans or He was very biased in His efforts to communicate His message.	Please rate this Conclusion:

Objective Analysis of God

Question: Internal contradiction: Messengers' Language	M40

Analysis and background:

Quran 14:4: *"And We did not send any messenger except in the language of his people to make [the message] clear for them. Then Allah leaves whom He wills astray and guides whom He wills, and He is the Exalted in Might, the Wise."* - Examples: Moses (to Pharaoh, not his people), Muhammad (to all mankind, not just Arabs).

Prophet	Originally From	Sent To	Prophet Native Language	Language of the People
Yunus (Jonah)	Children of Israel	Nineveh (Mesopotamia/Iraq)	Hebrew/Aramaic	Akkadian/Aramaic
Lut (Lot)	Ur (Mesopotamia/Iraq)	Sodom (Near the Dead Sea)	Akkadian/Sumerian	Canaanite/Amorite
Ibrahim (Abraham)	Ur (Mesopotamia/Iraq)	Canaan (Palestine/Israel)	Akkadian/Sumerian	Canaanite

Here, we are not considering Moses, as he was Bilingual, but his Native language was Hebrew, not Egyptian. The Quran describes the history of 25 Prophets, excluding the First and last prophets in this context. Therefore, out of 23, at least 3 Prophets were sent to different regions of the world. This comes to about 13%, which is not a large number but still a significant one, going against the verse said by Allah. (With Moses, it comes to about 18%)

Here, Allah is not only stating something that is not true, but also creating an issue with the basic ability of prophets to communicate effectively, which is their sole job and purpose.

Conclusion: These prophets were sent to regions where the local language differed from their native tongue, contradicting Allah's claim.	Please rate this Conclusion:

Section 5 – Islam
Questions from Muslims

Question:
Noah's Ark has all the animals in pairs

M41

Analysis and background:
(11:40): *"And when Our command came and the oven burst [with water], We said [to Noah], 'Carry into the Ark a pair from every species, along with your family—except those against whom the decree [of destruction] has already been passed—and those who believe.' But none believed with him except a few."*

In biological terms, a species is defined as a group of organisms capable of interbreeding and producing fertile offspring. Today, scientists estimate there are 1.5 to 2 million land animal species, spanning mammals, birds, reptiles, amphibians, and insects. If Noah were to carry a pair of each, the Ark would need to accommodate 3 to 4 million individual animals, which exceeds the capacity of even the largest ships ever constructed.

How could Noah have had access to every known species - physically implausible? In addition, all animals and plants are interdependent for survival; maintaining all animals on a ship for days without hunger is impossible by any means. Furthermore, if Noah had accomplished all this, what would have happened after the flood? What herbivores would have eaten, and how long would carnivores have to wait for their food to produce enough offspring to continue their life cycle?

Furthermore, if the flood truly wiped out all humans and land animals, then the current human population would have originated entirely after the flood, implying a complete reset of human history. This contradicts archaeological and genetic evidence showing continuous human presence across the globe for tens of thousands of years.

Conclusion: The story of Noah's boat carrying all species of land animals does not add up in any physical or rational sense. It will be better and more logical for God to create all species again than to go through this much trouble.	Please rate this Conclusion:

Objective Analysis of God

Question: Creation of Man – Nothing or Clay	M42

Analysis and background:
Surah 19:67: *"Does man not remember that We created him before, when he was nothing?" (Suggests creation from nothing.)* – **Surah 15:26**: *"And We created man from sounding clay, from mud moulded into shape." (Suggests creation from clay also 38:71-72.)* These verses present two seemingly incompatible accounts of human origin: one from "nothing" and another from "clay." The contradiction is apparent—nothing implies a lack of substance, while clay is a tangible material. Traditional tafseers attempt to reconcile this by suggesting that "nothing" refers to non-existence, while "clay" describes the physical medium used in the act of creation. But this interpretive layering often feels like a theological patchwork, designed to resolve what appears to be a textual inconsistency.

If Allah is all-knowing and aware of how His words will be interpreted across cultures and centuries, why use language that invites confusion or contradiction? A more explicit articulation could have prevented the need for scholars and clerics to reinterpret or defend the text continually.

Moreover, the Quran's account of human creation does not address the scientific reality of multiple hominin species—such as Homo habilis, Homo erectus, Neanderthals, and others—whose fossils have been found across Africa, Europe, and Asia. These species predate Homo sapiens, suggesting a gradual evolutionary process rather than a single moment of divine creation.

If Allah created humans uniquely, what is the rationale behind the existence of these other human-like beings? Were they part of a divine experiment, or do they challenge the notion of a singular, special creation?

Conclusion: For a human writer, yes, this is acceptable, but coming from God in His last communication to humans, it is not perfect.	Please rate this Conclusion:

Section 5 – Islam
Questions from Muslims

Question:
The old concept of creating Humans from Clay

M43

Analysis and background:
We will address it from two aspects – scientific and historical. Allah mentions that He created humans from clay:

37:11 - *"Ask them: Are they more difficult to create, or those We created? Indeed, we created them from sticky clay."*

15:26 - "And We did certainly create man out of clay from an altered black mud."

55:14 - *"He created man from clay like [that of] pottery."* Explore further.

6:2 - *"He it is Who has created you from clay, and then has decreed a [stated] term [for you to die]."*

-- and 23:12, 55:14 etc.

Scientifically, humans cannot be created directly from clay due to several fundamental reasons:

1. **Chemical Composition** – The human body is primarily composed of carbon-based organic molecules. At the same time, Clay consists mainly of silicates, aluminum, & minerals, which do not naturally form the complex biological structures needed for life.
2. **Cellular Complexity** – Life requires **cells**, which are highly organized structures and genetic material. Clay cannot self-organize into living cells or replicate biological functions.
3. **DNA and Genetic Information**—DNA is the foundation of life, carrying genetic instructions for growth and reproduction. Clay does not contain or generate DNA.
4. **Biochemical Processes**—Living organisms rely on metabolism, enzymatic reactions, and energy conversion. Clay does not possess the ability to sustain the biochemical reactions necessary for life.
5. **Evolutionary Evidence** – Fossil records and genetic studies show that humans evolved from **single-celled organisms** over billions of years, rather than being formed instantly from clay.

Historically, where did this idea come from?

Origins of the Clay Myth
Clay creation myths emerged in early civilizations due to:

Objective Analysis of God

- Cultural symbolism: Pottery and fire soil are associated with life and formation.
- Lack of scientific understanding: Myths filled explanatory gaps before biology or chemistry existed.

The idea that humans were created from clay appears in ancient religious texts and mythologies across various civilizations:
- Mesopotamia (Sumerians, circa 4500–1900 BCE): Gods such as Enki and Ninhursag formed humans from clay.
- Greek Mythology (~800 BCE onward): Prometheus moulded humans from clay.
- Chinese Mythology (~1500 BCE onward): Goddess Nuwa shaped people from yellow clay.
- Abrahamic Traditions (e.g., Genesis 2:7 and the Quran): God/Allah created Adam from dust or clay (~1400 BCE in Jewish tradition; until the 7th century CE in Islam).

Therefore, we can say that, in both a literal and scientific sense, the notion of human creation from clay is incorrect and has been effectively refuted by evolutionary biology, genetics, and paleontology. The use of clay as a symbol of human origins is mentioned in the Quran, reflecting the beliefs prevalent during the pre-Islamic era. It is a metaphor found across numerous ancient civilizations.

Conclusion: Chemically, clay can't transform into components that the Human body is made up of, and this seems to originate from the information of that time, not from the actual creator.	Please rate this Conclusion:

Section 5 – Islam
Questions from Muslims

Question:
Order of Creation (Earth vs. Heavens)

M44

Analysis and background:
Surah 2:29: *"It is He who created all that is on the earth for you, then He directed Himself to heaven and made them seven heavens..."*
(Earth first, then heavens.)

Surah 79:27-30: *"Are you a more difficult creation or is the heaven that He built? ... And after that He spread the earth."*
(Heaven first, then Earth.)

This discrepancy has led to centuries of scholarly debate. Traditional commentators (including classical tafsir scholars) have offered various reconciliations:

Sequential vs. Functional Creation: Some argue that Surah 2:29 refers to the creation of materials or the contents of the Earth (e.g., vegetation, minerals), while Surah 79:27–30 refers to the spreading and shaping of the Earth after the heavens were formed.

Perspective-Based Language: Others suggest that the Quran uses non-linear narrative structures, where the order of mention does not necessarily reflect chronological sequence.

Metaphorical Interpretation: A few scholars propose that these verses are metaphorical, emphasizing divine power rather than literal chronology.

However, these explanations often rely on interpretive flexibility rather than textual clarity. From a critical standpoint, the contradiction remains unresolved if one reads the verses literally and sequentially.

Modern cosmology suggests that the universe (heavens) came into existence long before Earth formed—roughly 13.8 billion years ago for the universe, and 4.5 billion years ago for Earth.

If Allah is all-knowing and aware of how His words will be interpreted across generations, one might expect consistency and clarity in describing such foundational events. The need for Mullahs and scholars to reinterpret or reconcile these verses suggests that the text leaves room for ambiguity—whether intentional or not.

Conclusion:
Such remarks can come from a human trying to create a story, but not from all-knowing and all-wise Allah.

Please rate this Conclusion:

Objective Analysis of God

| Question: Number of Days of Creation | M45 |

Analysis and background:
7:54, 10:3, 11:7, 25:59: Heavens and Earth created in "six days." –
41:9-12: *"Say, 'Do you indeed disbelieve in He who created the earth in two days ... and He placed on its firm mountains ... in four days ... Then He directed Himself to the heaven ... and made them seven heavens in two days...'"* (2 + 4 + 2 = 8 days.)

To resolve this, many scholars argue that the four days of provisioning include the initial two days of Earth's creation, meaning the total remains six. But this explanation hinges on overlapping durations, which the text does not explicitly clarify. The Quran assigns distinct timeframes to each stage. If overlap were intended, one would expect more precise language—such as "within four days, including the first two"—especially given the Quran's claim to be a clear and detailed revelation.

This inconsistency becomes more striking when considering the Quran's emphasis on divine precision. Allah is described as the designer of atoms, cells, and the balance of the cosmos—so why would the timeline of creation, arguably one of the most magnificent acts, be presented in a way that invites confusion?

In addition, we have already seen the vastness of the universe and its complexity. If we consider linear efforts to create the earth and the heaven, the time mentioned by Allah does not add up.

It may reflect the understanding and observational limitations of people from that era, who perceived stars as tiny glowing lights—like small bulbs scattered across the sky. But a creator should know much better.

| **Conclusion:** Indeed, I do not expect these inconsistencies from God, who created such an intricate and precise functioning universe. | Please rate this Conclusion: |

Section 5 – Islam
Questions from Muslims

Question:
Intercession on Judgment

M46

Analysis and background:
2:48, 6:51, 82:19: *No intercession is allowed on the Day of Judgment.*
34:23, 53:26: *Intercession is permitted with Allah's approval.*
34:23: *"And intercession does not benefit with Him except for one whom He permits. Until fear is banished from their hearts, they will say, 'What has your Lord said?' They will say, 'The truth.' And He is the Highest, the Most Great."*

53:26: *"And how many angels there are in the heavens whose intercession will not avail except only after Allah has permitted it and has accepted."*

Intercession is both denied and affirmed in the Quran. Mullahs explain that it's only permitted with Allah's explicit permission—yet this seems redundant, considering Allah is all-knowing. Would He initially make an incorrect judgment that someone else's intercession would later correct? That would contradict the concept of Allah's perfect knowledge and fairness.

This inconsistency prompts further questions: Why would Allah need intercession at all? Is his judgment not complete without input from others? Furthermore, in **Surah 53:26**, the idea that angels can intercede seems problematic—how can beings who only act by God's command have the power to influence His decisions? This appears to contradict the nature of angels and challenges the coherence of the concept of intercession itself.

Conclusion:
The Quran's validity of this intercession totally negates the general stance of Islam, shakes its foundation, and also creates doubt on Allah's objective and being just.

Please rate this Conclusion:

Pg. 381
My-OAG.com

Objective Analysis of God

Question: Compulsion in Religion	M47

Analysis and background:
2:256: "*There is no compulsion in religion...*"
9:5 - "*And when the sacred months have passed, then kill the polytheists wherever you find them and capture them and besiege them and sit in wait for them at every place of ambush. But if they repent, establish prayer, and pay the zakah, let them go on their way. Indeed, Allah is Forgiving and Merciful....*" (Verse of the Sword.)

Freedom of belief contradicts commands to fight unbelievers. Again, Mullas explain that the 9:5 is only applied when and if a polytheist has broken the treaty –Three arguments against it:

First - What is a bigger sin, worshipping Idols or breaking a one-time treaty? For worshipping an Idol, Allah allows them to continue to live as if nothing had happened, no force, no harsh punishment, etc, etc. But for breaking one treaty, their punishment is death, and not only death, but Allah is commanding Muslims to follow them, besiege them, ambush them, and kill them.

Second - Prior verse 9.4 says to wait and fulfill the treaty, and then comes 9:5 which implies that even if they satisfy the treaty and the terms have ended, Muslims can kill them.

Thirdly, why so much emphasis on Zakah (Zakat)? Zakat is only applicable to Muslims, so Allah is indirectly saying to let them go if they accept Islam. In other words, if they broke the treaty, they had no other choice but to accept Islam or be killed.

Conclusion: Here, effectively, Allah is instructing to kill the polytheists after the end of the treaty, unless they accept Islam.	Please rate this Conclusion:

Section 5 – Islam
Questions from Muslims

Question:
Source of Evil: Allah or you

M48

Analysis and background:

4:78: "*Wherever you may be, death will overtake you—even if you are in fortified towers. And when good befalls them, they say, 'This is from Allah,' but when evil befalls them, they say, 'This is from you [O Muhammad].' Say, 'All things are from Allah.' So what is the matter with these people that they hardly understand any statement?*" This verse suggests that everything—both good and bad—comes from Allah.

4:79: "*Whatever good happens to you is from Allah, but whatever evil befalls you is from yourself. And We have sent you, 'O Prophet', as a messenger to humanity. And Allah is sufficient as a Witness.*" This verse, however, implies that good comes from Allah, but evil results from **human action**. Mulla explains that Allah allows Evil to come to you. Still, action is the cause; for instance, if someone gets sick, it is ultimately by Allah's will (4:78), but it might also be due to their neglect of health or poor lifestyle choices (4:79).

My submission to that is, if I do not take care of my health and get sick, it is due to my negligence, but if I take good care of my health and remain healthy, it is from Allah -- readers, please evaluate in your logic ....

Secondly, if Allah can intervene and save me from sickness even though I have not neglected my health, then why can't He do it consistently? He has the power. And if He does not, then that sickness is also due to Allah's action (of not taking action)

The first part of 4:79 is also very arrogant, questioning the reason and expectations of Allah – Allah sends only good things.

Conclusion:
Both verses contradict each other and cannot be true at the same time

Please rate this Conclusion:

Objective Analysis of God

| **Question:** Who misguides Humans – Allah, Satan, or do they do it to themselves | **M49** |

Analysis and background:
Allah misguide Humans – in 6:25, 10:100 and 35:8 Satan Misguide Humans – in 4:119, 5:39 and 114: 5
Humans' deeds – 6:12, 9:70, and 30:9

A complete confusion from Allah, how can this be from the All-Knowing and All-Intelligent Allah, when He was writing His final message to Humans? Mullas give explanations considering scenarios, but if I am misguided, my ultimate result is that I am

My other submission is that if Allah has decided and put veils in Humans' hearts and or minds, then how can a human overcome it? It is impossible to confront the omnipotent Allah and his desire. The Mullahs explain that Allah has done it because he knows the future and who will stray. So Allah's action is due to His knowledge of the Future.

My submission is that if He is making a decision based on His knowledge and is sure what a person will do, then why even go about blocking that person's heart and mind from good deeds? And, why not? \\ have the judgment day just after creating Humans, as He knows the fate and all about the life of a person, and puts him in Heaven or Hell straightaway, as He knows all, why go about creating and maintaining the long and huge universe

| **Conclusion:** These verses contradict each other, and the explanation given by Mullas is even more illogical. | Please rate this Conclusion: |

Section 5 – Islam
Questions from Muslims

Question:
Quran- simple/difficult, open/hidden

M50

Analysis and background:
3:7: - *"It is He who has sent down to you, [O Muhammad], the Book; in it are precise verses – they are the foundation of the Book – and others unspecific. As for those in whose hearts is deviation [from truth], they will follow that of it which is unspecific, seeking discord and seeking an interpretation [suitable to them]. And no one knows its [true] interpretation except Allah. But those firm in knowledge say, "We believe in it. All [of it] is from our Lord." And no one will be reminded except those of understanding."*

This is perhaps the most controversial verse, as it is about Quran and the way it is written. The Quran is the last message for Humans in which Allah wants to open up and provide humans a straight path which they are supposed to follow to have everlasting peace and rewards, or end up in Hell. The most important thing for billions of humans is the all-wise and all-loving Allah. However, Allah still chose to convey this vague message, making it difficult to comprehend. Why does Allah want to play with us, or does He want just blind followers? If this is the case, then why give us Free Will and ask us to seek knowledge?

On the other side, Allah is saying 54:17, 22, 32, 40

Why include these complex verses without identifying and making the whole process more controversial

If Allah has made this situation intentional, then how can His creation—a fallible human—be expected to find the correct path amid such a vast variety of religions?

Conclusion:
Allah, the All-wise, cannot make His only and last message complex to understand.

Please rate this Conclusion:

Objective Analysis of God

Question: Allah's Justice with "Favouritism"	M51

Analysis and background:
2:47 - *"O Children of Israel, remember My favour which I have bestowed upon you and that I preferred you over the worlds."*
2:122 - *"O Children of Israel, remember My favour which I have bestowed upon you and that I preferred you over the worlds."*

These verses clearly affirm that the Children of Israel were given a special status—a divine preference over other nations. The Quran repeats this statement, emphasizing that they were recipients of unique blessings, including prophets, scriptures, and divine guidance. But how can Allah claim to be perfectly just if He openly favors one group over others?

The phrase "preferred you over the worlds" implies special treatment, not just in spiritual opportunity but in historical privilege. Suppose one group is given more access to divine messengers, miracles, and revelation. In that case, their moral and spiritual performance cannot be fairly compared to those who received less or none. This challenges the notion of universal accountability, particularly when salvation and judgment are said to be based on individual actions.

If Allah is all-knowing and timeless, He would foresee how such favoritism could be interpreted across generations. The repetition of this preference in the Quran suggests that it was not merely historical but theologically significant, making it difficult to dismiss as a temporary or symbolic gesture.

In essence, the notion of divine favoritism—especially when explicitly stated—contradicts the true nature of justice, the concept of equality before God, and the distribution of spiritual opportunities fairly across humanity.

Conclusion: These verses are shaking the foundation of Justice, and to execute Justice, without which Allah has no meaning.	Please rate this Conclusion:

Section 5 – Islam
Questions from Muslims

Question:
Story of Adam

M52

Analysis and background:
The story of Adam is narrated in many verses, each having a slightly different version:
2:36-39, 7:22-25 and 20:121-124
These verses recount the same foundational event—Adam and his wife's fall from Paradise—but they differ in sequence, emphasis, and theological tone. Here's a structured comparison

Theme	Surah-e-Baqarah (2:36-39)	Surah-e-Al-A'raf (7:22-25)	Surah-e-Taha (20:121-124)
Cause of fault	Satan causes them to slip	Satan deceives the; the eat from tree	Adam forgets and disobeys
Emotional response	No mention of shame or nakedness	They become aware of nakedness and cover themselves	No mention of repentance focus on forgetfulness
Tone of Devine	Immediate mention of future guidance and mercy	Emphasis punishment and exile	Emphasis on repentance and divine guidance
Sequence of events	Slip → decent → Guidance	Deception → shame → blame → exile	Disobedience → regret → repentance → guidance
Responsibility	Shared between Adam and his wife	Mutual blame and human weakness	Adam is individually held accountable for forgetting
Satan's role	Causes them to slip	actively deceives them	Not mentioned directly in this passage

These relatively slight but significant variations suggest that a human is narrating the same event at different times and attempting to tailor or phrase it to suit their goal.

Conclusion:
Such a difference only occurs in the case of a made-up story narrated at different times and not in an actual happening in front of you.

Please rate this Conclusion:

Objective Analysis of God

Scientific facts revelation – Debunk

The Quran, the holy book of Islam, is often cited by Muslims as containing scientific facts that were impossible to know at the time of its revelation in the 7th century. These claims are part of the broader argument for the Quran's divine origin, known as "scientific miracles in the Quran." Below is a list of 50 commonly cited scientific facts in the Quran, along with counterarguments. Note that interpretations of these verses can vary. Not all Muslims agree with the scientific claims, including many prominent Quran translators of the past, such as Ibn Kathir and Maududi, as well as Yousuf Ali, who were involved in the initial translations. Their translations are considered the most authentic and accurate translations of the Quran.

> *Here, we will attempt to address the wave of social media posts claiming that the Quran revealed recent scientific findings from 1400 BC, as validation of the Quran as the words of Allah, the all-knowing God. We will document the available knowledge of the time and what previous philosophers (scientists) have explored, as well as the knowledge available in the world at the time — to Prophet Muhammad at the age of 40.*

In many examples, the Quran cites idioms prevalent at that time, which were translated in their literal sense and distorted to align with modern scientific understanding. I am using the word "twisted to align" with science, as there is no further explanation or indication in the Quran beyond those words. After manipulating those idioms and phrases, Allah continued without providing any related scientific facts. We will discuss it in detail once we arrive, giving specific examples.

Secondly, the use of idioms in an instruction book intended for translation into numerous languages is, in itself, a flaw in the Quran. This indicates that Allah is only addressing Arabs and is not expecting others to translate it and understand it.

History:
This aspect of Quran interpretation was initiated by Tantawi Jawhari (1862–1940), an Egyptian scholar who wrote "Al-Jawahir fi Tafsir al-Quran al-Karim" (The Jewels in the Interpretation of the Noble

Quran), in which he linked Quranic verses to scientific phenomena. Later on, he also followed his example,
- Abdul Razzaq Nawfal (Early 20th Century) – Wrote books like "The Quran and Modern Science"
- Sheikh Abdul Majeed al-Zindani (late 20th Century) – Promoted scientific miracles in the Quran, working with figures like Keith Moore (an embryologist).
- But the prominent recognition of this concept was given to Dr. Maurice Bucaille, a medical doctor by profession, when he published his book "The Bible, The Quran and Science" in 1976. In this book, he took the concepts of earlier authors (as described above) but examined & explained them in more detail. In his book, he argued that the Quran contains scientifically accurate statements that were unknown in the 7th century. His work gained widespread attention because:
- He was a Western scientist (a doctor) who embraced Islam.
- His book was translated into multiple languages.
- He focused on embryology, astronomy, and geology, making his arguments appealing to modern audiences.
- Later, with social media, this took off with many strange quotes cited in small clips, and people, especially Muslims, started quoting those without doing any validation

However, the interpretation of these verses in light of modern science is a topic of debate, and there are counterarguments from scholars, scientists, and critics who question the claim that these verses reveal scientific knowledge ahead of their time. Below, I will list 50 commonly cited examples of "scientific miracles" in the Quran and present some counterarguments.

While the Quran contains verses that some Muslims interpret as scientific miracles, in the following lines, I will argue that these interpretations are often retrospective and lack specificity. The debate continues, with believers seeing divine wisdom and skeptics viewing these claims as examples of confirmation bias.

As I will try to show, all belong to the following categories:
- Vagueness: Many Quranic verses are open to interpretation and lack specific scientific details.
- Prior Knowledge: Similar ideas existed in earlier cultures (e.g., Greek, Indian, and Babylonian).

Objective Analysis of God

- Metaphorical Language: Many verses are poetic or metaphorical, not literal scientific statements, or were the idioms used at that time
- Confirmation Bias: Muslims often interpret verses in light of modern science, which may not have been the original intent.
- Lack of Predictive Power: The Quran does not provide new, testable scientific predictions.

Section 5 – Islam
Questions from Muslims

| **Question:** The Big Bang creation of the Universe | **M53** |

Analysis and background:
21:30: "*Do the disbelievers not realize that the heavens and earth were one mass, then We split them apart?*"
Muslims claim that this describes the Big Bang and the expansion of the universe. Still, they only take the part that seems to suit them, like taking the component of how the universe started and not taking into account that it all happened 13.8 billion years ago – because then they have to explain why God waited 13.8 billion years to form humans, who are the reason for creating the universe.
Secondly, the verse is poetic and vague. Similar cosmological ideas existed in earlier civilizations, though they were often framed in mythological or philosophical terms rather than scientific ones. Here's a comparison of ancient cosmological beliefs with the Big Bang concept:

1. Hindu Cosmology (Vedas & Puranas, ~1500 BCE–500 CE) – Cyclic Expansion & Contraction
- Rigveda (10.129) – The Nasadiya Sukta describes a primordial state:
- "*There was neither existence nor non-existence then... That One breathed, windless, by its impulse.*"
    - Suggests a singularity-like void before creation.
- Puranic Cosmology – The universe undergoes cycles of creation (Brahma's day) and destruction (Pralaya), somewhat like a cyclic Big Bang and Big Crunch.
- Modern Parallel: The oscillating universe theory (a variant of the Big Bang) suggests repeated expansions and contractions.

2. Greek Philosophy (Pre-Socratic Thinkers, 6th–5th Century BCE) – Primordial Chaos & Expansion
- Anaxagoras (500–428 BCE) – Proposed that the universe began as a chaotic mix of all elements, then a cosmic mind ("Nous") set it in order.
- Empedocles (490–430 BCE) – Suggested that the universe cycles between unity (Love) and separation (Strife), somewhat like expansion and contraction.
- Modern Parallel: The idea of an initial chaotic state aligns with

the Big Bang's hot, dense early universe.

3. Chinese Cosmology (Taoist & Buddhist Texts) – Cosmic Egg & Emergence from Void
- Pangu Myth (3rd Century CE) – The universe began as a cosmic egg that split, forming heaven (Yang) and earth (Yin).
- Laozi's Tao Te Ching (~6th Century BCE) – Describes the Tao (the Way) as the origin of all things, emerging from a formless void.
- Modern Parallel: The "cosmic egg" resembles the singularity before the Big Bang.

4. Abrahamic Traditions (Judaism, Christianity, Islam) – Creation from Nothing
- Genesis 1:1 (Hebrew Bible, ~6th Century BCE) – *"In the beginning, God created the heavens and the earth."*

Secondly, comparing Heaven and Earth is also misleading, as there is no comparison between the universe and Earth, as explained earlier. Considering the word "heaven" as the representative of all universes, excluding Earth, is completely illogical for someone who knows the different spaces both occupy in the known universe. Therefore, the assertion that this verse refers to a major ban is also entirely absurd.

Conclusion: The concept of the universe existing at the start of time was present in all known ancient civilizations before Islam, albeit in a general form, which is also reflected in the Quran, with nothing new added.	Please rate this Conclusion:

Section 5 – Islam
Questions from Muslims

Question: The Quran's narration of Embryology	**M54**

Analysis and background:

23:12-14: *"We created man from an extract of clay. Then We made him as a drop in a place of settlement, firmly fixed. Then We made the drop into an alaqah (leech-like clot), then We made the alaqah into a mudghah (chewed-like substance) ..."*

This passage outlines a step-by-step transformation from clay to a sperm drop, to a clot, to a chewed-like lump—an account that has often been interpreted as a description of embryonic development. However, there are several inconsistencies:

- Bones and muscles form simultaneously, not in the sequential order implied by the verse.
- The term "clot" (alaqah) does not accurately reflect any stage of embryogenesis. Early embryos are not blood clots nor leech-like entities; the metaphor—while vivid—does not accurately match biological reality.
- Human development is a continuous, integrated process, not a series of discrete transformations as the verse suggests.

While the Quranic language may carry symbolic or metaphorical weight, it does not align with the scientific understanding of embryonic development. Moreover, as discussed earlier, ancient civilizations—including the Greeks, Indians, and Egyptians—had their own rudimentary knowledge of fetal growth, often expressed in metaphorical or observational terms. The Quran's account, though spiritually resonant, appears to reflect a similar level of descriptive insight, rather than a uniquely advanced or scientifically precise revelation.

I consider that if it is coming from the creator and designer of this process, this fell well short of being an accurate depiction.

Conclusion: The Quran's description of fetal development is not accurate, coming from the all-knowing creator . Instead, it reiterates ideas already circulating at that time, showing that the Quran merely echoed existing knowledge, much of which was inaccurate.	Please rate this Conclusion:

Objective Analysis of God

Human Embryonic Development in the Quran: A Comparative and Scientific Analysis

1. Quranic Verses and Claimed Developmental Stages
Surah Al-Mu'minun *(23:12–14)* outlines a step-by-step description of human development:
*"We created man from an extract of clay. Then we placed him as a **sperm-drop (nutfah)** in a firm lodging. Then We made the sperm-drop into a **clinging clot (alaqah)**, and We made the clot into a **chewed-like lump (mudghah)**, and We made from the lump **bones**, then **covered the bones with flesh**; then We developed him into another creation..."*

These stages are:
- **Nutfah** – sperm-drop
- **Alaqah** – clinging clot or leech-like
- **Mudghah** – chewed-like lump
- **Izam** – bones
- **Lahm** – flesh over bones
- Then a transition into a whole human being ("another creation")

2. Ancient Views on Embryology
Hindu (Ayurvedic) – ~1500 BCE–200 CE
- **Key texts**: Rigveda, Atharvaveda, Charaka, Sushruta Samhita.
- Theory: Embryo forms from **Shukra (sperm)** + **Shonita (ovum)** — aligned with fertilization.
- Stages:
    - **Month 1**: Jelly-like (Kalala)
    - **Month 2**: Solid mass (Pinda)
    - **Month 3+**: Organs and limbs form
- It also incorporates soul entry (Atman), which is a blend of biology and spirituality.

Greek & Roman – ~500 BCE–200 CE
- *Aristotle*: Male semen = form, female blood = matter; soul stages: vegetative → sensitive → rational.
- *Galen*: Described the placenta, but misunderstood fetal nourishment and organ sequencing.

3. Modern Embryology – Key Findings
- *Fertilization*: Confirmed in 1876 (sperm + egg fusion).

- **DNA Discovery**: 1953 – both parents contribute equal genetic material.
- **Developmental Milestones**:
  - **Week 1–2**: Zygote implants in the uterus (resembles "alaqah").
  - **Week 3–5**: Somite grooves appear (like chewed "mudghah").
  - **Week 6–8**:
  - **Cartilage (precursor to bones) forms**
  - **Muscles develop simultaneously, not sequentially.**

Comparison of Quranic Terms with Modern Science

Quranic Term	Meaning	Scientific Match?
Nutfah	Sperm-drop	Yes. Matches fertilization & implantation (zygote stage).
Alaqah	Clot/clinging/leech	Maybe. "Clot" is inaccurate; "leech-like" fits the early embryo's appearance and function.
Mudghah	Chewed lump	Yes. Somite development has a grooved, chewed-like appearance.
Bones → Flesh	Sequential development	No. Scientifically inaccurate: bones and flesh develop **together**, not one after the other.
"Another Creation"	Human fetus	Yes. Fetus transitions visibly around week 8+.

Strengths of the Quranic Embryological Description
- Metaphors such as **alaqah (leech-like)** and **mudghah (chewed)** are **visually striking** and resonate with modern microscopy.
- Avoids **Greek errors** (e.g., muscles before bones or fetus feeding directly on blood).
- Describes a **developmental process**, which is rare for texts from the 7th century.
- Aligns partially with **modern timelines** of embryo → fetus transition.

Objective Analysis of God

Scientific Challenges and Limitations

1) **Sequential Order Misalignment**
   a) Bones and muscles develop **simultaneously**, not with bones first.
   b) Quranic sequence oversimplifies the real, overlapping biological timeline.
2) **"Clot" Interpretation of Alaqah**
   a) Early translations defined alaqah as a "clot of blood" — **not scientifically accurate**.
   b) Modern interpretation as "leech-like" is visually closer but raises the question of **retroactive reinterpretation**.
3) **Missing Role of the Female Egg (Ovum)**
   a) Quran mentions only the **male sperm (nutfah)**—not the **ovum**, despite both being necessary.
   b) Reflects **pre-modern male-centric theories** of reproduction.
4) **No Reference to Genetic Material or Heredity**
   a) DNA, chromosomes, or inherited traits—central to modern embryology—are not referenced.
5) **Absence of Placenta and Umbilical Cord**
   a) These essential components for **fetal nutrition, oxygen, and waste removal** are entirely missing.
6) **Soul Insertion Timing Conflict (120 Days)**
   a) Hadith literature (not Quran) mentions the **soul entering at 120 days**, conflicting with biological personhood markers like brain activity (~8 weeks).
7) **Metaphorical Flexibility Can Be a Double-Edged Sword**
   a) While metaphor allows compatibility with later science, it also opens the door to **post hoc rationalization**, not objective prediction.

Comparative Summary Table

Tradition	Key Insight	Scientific Match?
Ayurveda	Shukra + Shonita = embryo	Yes. Fertilization theory matches modern genetics.
Aristotle	Semen + blood → soul development	No. Misunderstood roles of parents and biology
Galen	Describes structures but with errors	No. Incorrect nutrient theory and sequencing
Quran (23:12–14)	Stages of embryo → fetus	Maybe. Mostly metaphorically aligned, but not entirely

Tradition	Key Insight	Scientific Match?
		scientific
Modern Science	Microscopy, DNA, organogenesis	Yes. Based on observation, genetic evidence

Conclusion

The Quran's account in **Surah 23:12–14** *is* **notable** *for its poetic structure, metaphorical vividness, and partial correlation with observable stages of human development. In comparison to ancient sources, it reflects a more organized and arguably* **progressive understanding** *of the human developmental process.*

However, when held to the lens of **modern scientific rigour**, *it:*
- **Omits critical scientific elements** *(genetics, egg, placenta).*
- **Misrepresents some biological sequences** *(bones before flesh).*
- **Relies on metaphors** *that, while compelling, are open to flexible reinterpretation.*

In short, while the Quranic verses demonstrate a **remarkable approximation of biological processes for a 7th-century context**, *they* **do not meet the standard of scientific accuracy** *by today's embryological knowledge. Their significance may lie more in theological and literary influence than in empirical science.*

Objective Analysis of God

Question:	
Water as the Origin of Life	**M55**

Analysis and background:
21:30: *"Do the disbelievers not see that the heavens and the earth were a joined entity, and We separated them and made from water every living thing? Then will they not believe?"*
Additionally, in other verses, such as 24:45 and 25:45.

Few arguments:
- The whole verse seems to indicate that everything was created with water, not just the living things, and just after the origin of life. Which is entirely false and cannot be true., But we will give the benefit of the doubt and consider that in this second part of the verse, the Quran is only referring to living things.
- The idea that water is the source of life was widespread in pre-Islamic cultures

Culture/Text	Time Period	View on Water as a Source of Life	Key Quotes/Concepts
Babylonian (Enuma Elish)	~18th -7th BCE	Primordial waters (Tiamat/Apsu) as the chaotic origin of creation.	"Marduk splits Tiamat's body to form heaven & earth."
Egyptian (Ogdoad/Nun)	~2700 BCE onward	Nun (primordial waters) as the infinite void from which A tum arose.	"All life emerged from Nun's waters."
Vedic (Rigveda 10.129)	~1500-500 BCE	Cosmic waters as the undifferentiated state before creation	"Darkness hidden in darkness; all was water."
Greek (Thales of Miletus)	~624-546 BCE	Water (hydor) as the fundamental substance (arche) of all things.	"All things are from water."
Zoroastrian (Avesta)	~1soo soo BCE	Sacred water (Aban) as a purifying, life giving force	"First creation was water." (Bundahishn 3.10)
Chinese (Dao De Jing)	~6th-4th BCE	Water as a metaphor for the Dao's life nourishing power.	"Highest good is like water; it gives life."

- Yes, the Quran states that all living things are made from water, but it does not specify whether water was the chemical origin (as in a primordial soup) or simply an essential component of life. The purpose of these verses is theological rather than biochemical. They provide a general statement without clarifying whether water is considered the source or the main ingredient. For life to evolve, various environmental, physical, and chemical parameters must come together precisely. Even

- with our current knowledge, we still do not fully understand the vital component known as the soul or consciousness.
- Water was formed billions of years after the Big Bang, so if Mullahs link these verses as proof that the Quran has stated scientifically correct, then they should also admit that the Quran was not accurate when it mentioned that after the creation of the universe, life came into being directly.
- Against the above argument, Mullahs mention that the Quran is not a scientific book, so the details are not mentioned. My submission to that is (Quran is only self-praising and a story book – as shown earlier), if the Quran is not a scientific book, then these metaphors should not be used to provide scientific proof.

Conclusion: Once again, the Quran reflects only the knowledge of its time. Had Allah revealed something that went against the prevailing beliefs, then—but is confirmed by knowledge now—only then could it be seen as truly coming from the Creator	Please rate this Conclusion:

Objective Analysis of God

Water as the Origin of Life in Ancient Civilizations
From the earliest human thought, **water has been universally regarded as the origin and essential foundation of life**. Ancient civilizations across the world, despite geographical separation and differing cultures, shared a profound recognition of water not just as a physical necessity, but as a **cosmic and spiritual source from which all life emerged**.

1. Mesopotamia: Life Begins with Water
In the Sumerian and Babylonian worldview, water existed **before the earth and the heavens**. The Mesopotamian creation myth, the Enuma Elish, begins with **two primordial waters—Apsu (freshwater) and Tiamat (saltwater)**—whose mingling gave rise to the gods and, eventually, the world. This duality of water reflected their belief that **life itself was born from the union and motion of water**.

2. Ancient Egypt: Water as the Primordial Substance
Egyptian cosmology centred on **Nu or Nun**, the boundless primordial waters that existed before creation. The creator god **Atum** emerged from this chaotic watery abyss to form all life. The Nile River, seen as a physical extension of this divine water, reinforced the belief that **water was both the beginning and sustainer of life**, cycling through birth, nourishment, and renewal.

3. Vedic and Hindu Thought: Water as Cosmic Seed
In the ancient Vedic texts, water (Apah) is described as one of the **first elements to exist**, predating the earth and sky. The **Rigveda** says that all things arose from the waters. In the Upanishads, the embryo is said to develop in a moist environment, and **life begins in water within the womb**, connecting macrocosmic water with the microcosm of human life. The concept of **Shukra (semen) and Shonita (ovum)** combining to initiate life highlights the vital biological role of water.

4. Greek Philosophy: Water as the First Principle
The pre-Socratic philosopher **Thales of Miletus (6th century BCE)** famously stated, "Everything is from water." He viewed water not just as a substance but as the **underlying principle (arche) of all** matter and life. His claim was one of the earliest attempts to explain the origin of life **in naturalistic terms**, without resorting to myth, and emphasized the primordial role of water **in existence**.

5. Indigenous and Other Traditions
Across African, Native American, and Oceanic cultures, water is almost always tied to **creation stories**. Many believe the world originated from or emerged from a **primordial ocean**, with divine beings forming land and life from this watery chaos. Water is consistently linked to **fertility, birth, and spiritual energy**, reinforcing the understanding of **life's origin in water**.

Echo in Modern Science
Modern biology confirms that **life began in water**:
- Earth's earliest life forms were **single-celled organisms in oceans** over 3.5 billion years ago.
- Water is essential for **cell structure, metabolism, DNA function, and reproduction**.
- The human embryo still develops in **amniotic fluid**, mirroring the watery origin of life.

In a sense, **ancient intuitions mirrored scientific reality**—water is indeed not only vital for sustaining life, but was also **the medium in which life first emerged**.

Conclusion: Eternal Truths from Ancient Wisdom
Though their languages and symbols varied, ancient civilizations converged on one idea:
Water is the mother of life.
Whether through mythology, spiritual philosophy, or early natural observation, ancient people **recognized water as the essential starting point of life**, a view now supported by modern science. This shared reverence reminds us that the **roots of scientific truth often lie in the soil of ancient wisdom**.

Objective Analysis of God

| Question: Mountains as Stabilizers | M56 |

Analysis and background:
78:6-7 Quranic Verse: "*Have We not made the earth a resting place? And the mountains as stakes?*"

Muslims claim that Mountains have deep roots that stabilize the Earth's crust, as described in the Quran.

The metaphor of mountains as "stakes" is poetic and not unique to the Quran. Ancient cultures also used similar imagery.

A detailed calculation is provided on the next page, explaining that the mountains cannot contribute to stabilizing or balancing the rotational angular momentum or forces, just as balancing tires is performed in auto or mechanical shops.

First, to claim that these mountains provide balance to the Earth's rotation, Allah must have confirmed that the Earth is rotating; however, in the Quran, people are still debating whether the Earth is flat.

Conclusion:
With this calculation, it becomes clear that the claim that mountains contribute to balancing rotational momentum does not have any solid grounds.

Please rate this Conclusion:

Section 5 – Islam
Questions from Muslims

Mountains stopping Earth's shaking – calculations: (16:15)

Introduction
When I first encountered the question, *"Can a mountain on the Earth be compared with a grain of sand on a cricket ball or baseball?"*—my initial reaction was one of curiosity. At face value, it seems like an attempt to draw an analogy between two vastly different scales, but is there a meaningful comparison to be made? To explore this, I decided to break down the problem into manageable parts, examining the sizes involved, the scales at play, and the feasibility of such a comparison.

Here we will make a few logical assumptions:
1. It is the mass that causes dynamic imbalance (vibrations) in rotating objects. Since mountains are part of the Earth, we can assume they have similar densities, which cancel each other out.
2. Volumes or further weight of the mountains vary and will involve complex calculations. We will consider only heights (i.e., length dimensions) in our calculations, although this will make our calculations more biased toward the Earth/mountain, as Mountains are conical-shaped and have less mass at the top.

The above two assumptions will make our calculation safer, as detailed calculations will yield results that favour the argument that mountains provide more balanced rotation.

Understanding the Components

1. Defining the Objects:
- **Mountain on Earth:** Mountains vary significantly in size. For this comparison, let's consider Mount Everest, the tallest mountain above sea level, with a height of approximately 8,848 meters (29,029 feet).
- **Grain of Sand:** The size of a grain of sand can vary, but typically, it ranges from 0.05 mm to 2 mm in diameter. For this comparison, let's take an average size of about 1 mm.
- **Cricket Ball:** A standard cricket ball has a diameter of about 7.2 to 7.3 cm (or approximately 72 mm).
- **Baseball:** A standard baseball has a diameter of about 7.3 to 7.5 cm (similar to a cricket ball, roughly 73 mm).

Objective Analysis of God

2. Calculating the Ratios:
The comparison appears to be about the relative size of a mountain compared to the Earth versus a grain of sand compared to a cricket ball or baseball.

- **Mountain to Earth Ratio:**
  o Earth's diameter: ~12,742 km (or 12,742,000 meters).
  o Height of Mount Everest: ~8,848 meters.
  o Ratio = Mountain height / Earth diameter = 8,848 / 12,742,000 ≈ 0.000694 or 6.94×10^{-4}.

- **Grain of Sand to Ball Ratio:**
  o Diameter of a grain of sand: ~1 mm.
  o Diameter of cricket ball/baseball: ~73 mm.
  o Ratio = Grain diameter / Ball diameter = 1 / 73 ≈ 0.0137 or 1.37×10^{-2}.

Comparing the Ratios
Now, let's compare the two ratios:
- Mountain/Earth ratio: $\sim 6.94 \times 10^{-4}$
- Grain/Ball ratio: $\sim 1.37 \times 10^{-2}$

To see how many times larger one ratio is compared to the other:
$(1.37 \times 10^{-2}) / (6.94 \times 10^{-4}) \approx 19.74$
This means that the grain of sand on a cricket ball or baseball is roughly 20 times larger, relative to the ball, than Mount Everest is relative to the Earth.

Visualizing the Comparison
To put this into perspective:
- If Mount Everest's height compared to the Earth is represented by a specific small size, then the grain of sand on the ball is about 20 times that size relative to the ball.
- This suggests that a grain of sand on a cricket ball or baseball is significantly more prominent than Mount Everest is on Earth.

Alternative Interpretation: Height vs. Diameter
An alternative way to look at this is to consider that the height of a mountain is a linear measurement compared to the Earth's diameter. However, a grain of sand's size is also a linear measurement compared to the ball's diameter. Both ratios are linear, so the comparison holds in that regard.

But one might argue that a mountain's height is a one-dimensional protrusion from the Earth's surface, whereas a grain of sand sits on the surface of the ball. To make a more accurate comparison, perhaps we should consider the mountain's height relative to the Earth's radius (since the mountain protrudes from the surface, and the Earth's radius is more relevant for surface curvature).
- Earth's radius: ~6,371 km (6,371,000 meters).
- Ratio: $8,848 / 6,371,000 \approx 0.00139$ or 1.39×10^{-3}.

Now, compared to the grain/ball ratio:
$(1.37 \times 10^{-2}) / (1.39 \times 10^{-3}) \approx 9.86$

So, even when compared to the Earth's radius, the grain is about 10 times more prominent on the ball than Everest is on Earth.

Considering the Grain's Height vs. Ball's Diameter

Another perspective is that a grain of sand might not be perfectly spherical, and its "height" when placed on the ball could be slightly less than its diameter. If we assume the grain's height is about half its diameter (~0.5 mm), then:
- Grain height / Ball diameter = $0.5 / 73 \approx 0.00685$ or 6.85×10^{-3}. Compared to the Everest/Earth radius ratio:
  $(6.85 \times 10^{-3}) / (1.39 \times 10^{-3}) \approx 4.93$

Now, the grain's height is about 5 times more prominent on the ball than Everest is on Earth.

Real-world Analogies and Examples

To better understand, let's think of real-world examples or models:
- If we scaled down the Earth to the size of a cricket/baseball ball (~73 mm diameter), how tall would Mount Everest be?
  o Scale factor: Earth diameter / ball diameter = 12,742,000,000 mm / 73 mm ≈ 174,547,945.
  o Scaled Everest height: 8,848,000 mm / 174,547,945 ≈ 0.051 mm or 51 micrometers.

A grain of sand is about 1 mm, roughly 20 times larger than the scaled Everest height (since 1 mm / 0.051 mm ≈ 19.6). This confirms our earlier ratio calculation.

Implications of the Comparison

Given these calculations, it's clear that:
- A grain of sand on a cricket ball or baseball is significantly larger relative to the ball than Mount Everest is relative to the Earth.

Objective Analysis of God

- Therefore, if we're making a direct size comparison, the grain of sand is much more prominent in its respective sphere than the mountain on Earth.

Potential Missteps and Corrections
Initially, one might hastily assume that since both a mountain and a grain of sand are small compared to their respective spheres, the comparison is roughly equivalent. However, as the calculations show, the grain is much larger in relative terms.

Another potential source of confusion could arise from mixing different measurements—comparing a mountain's height (a linear measure from base to peak) to the Earth's diameter (a straight line through the Earth), versus comparing a grain's diameter to a ball's diameter. Ensuring that we're consistently comparing linear dimensions is crucial.

Alternative Comparisons
To further validate, let's consider another comparison:
- **Olympus Mons on Mars:**
  - Height: ~22 km (21.9 km).
  - Mars diameter: ~6,779 km.
  - Ratio: $21,900 / 6,779,000 \approx 0.00323$ or 3.23×10^{-3}.

Compared to grain/ball:
$(1.37 \times 10^{-2}) / (3.23 \times 10^{-3}) \approx 4.24$

Even the largest known volcano in the solar system, Olympus Mons, is only about 1/4 as prominent on Mars as a 1 mm grain is on a cricket ball.

Practical Visualization
Imagine holding a cricket ball with a grain of sand on it:
- The grain is easily visible to the naked eye, perhaps even feeling rough to the touch.
- If Mount Everest were scaled down proportionally on a model Earth the size of a cricket ball, it would be only about 0.05 mm tall—barely perceptible, like a very fine speck.

This illustrates how much smoother the Earth is at its scale compared to a cricket ball with a grain of sand.

Mathematical Confirmation
Let's express both ratios as percentages for clarity:

Section 5 – Islam
Questions from Muslims

- Everest/Earth: ~0.0694%
- Grain/Ball: ~1.37%

The grain is approximately 1.37 / 0.0694, ≈ or about 19.74 times more prominent.

Considering Surface Area
Another angle is to consider the surface area:
o Surface area of a sphere: $4\pi r^2$.
o Earth's surface area: ~510 million km².
o Everest's base covers an area of about 1,000 km² (approximate; actual base is irregular).
   o Ratio: $1,000 / 510,000,000 \approx 1.96 \times 10^{-6}$.
o Cricket ball surface area: $4\pi(36.5 \text{ mm})^2 \approx 16,740$ mm².
o Grain of sand area (assuming circular base with diameter 1 mm): $\pi(0.5)^2 \approx 0.785$ mm².
   o Ratio: $0.785 / 16,740 \approx 4.69 \times 10^{-5}$.

Comparing the two:
$(4.69 \times 10^{-5}) / (1.96 \times 10^{-6}) \approx 23.9$
From a surface coverage perspective, the grain covers about 24 times more of the ball's surface than Everest's base covers the Earth's surface.

Conclusion
After carefully analyzing the sizes and ratios involved, it's evident that:
- **A grain of sand on a cricket ball or baseball is significantly larger relative to the ball than Mount Everest is relative to the Earth.**

Specifically:
a) The height of Mount Everest is about 0.069% of the Earth's diameter.
b) A 1 mm grain of sand is about 1.37% of a cricket ball's diameter.

This means the grain is roughly **20 times more prominent** on the ball than Everest is on Earth.

Therefore, while the comparison seeks to draw an analogy between a minor feature on a large sphere, the scales don't align proportionally. The grain of sand is much more noticeable on its respective ball than the mountain is on our planet.

Objective Analysis of God

Conclusion

No, a mountain on Earth cannot be accurately compared to a grain of sand on a cricket ball or baseball in terms of relative size. A grain of sand is proportionally much larger compared to a cricket ball or baseball (about 1.37% of the ball's diameter) than Mount Everest is compared to the Earth (about 0.069% of Earth's diameter). The grain of sand is roughly 20 times more prominent on the ball than Mount Everest is on Earth. This means that the Earth's surface is much smoother at its scale than a cricket ball or baseball with a grain of sand on it.

Section 5 – Islam
Questions from Muslims

Question:
Benefits of Iron that Came from Space

M57

Analysis and background:
57:25: *"We sent our messengers with clear signs and Sent down with them the Book and the Balance so that people may uphold justice. **And We sent down iron, in which there is a strong force and benefits for people,** so that Allah may know who will help Him and His messengers unseen. Surely, Allah is Strong, Almighty."*

I have explained the importance of iron and its magnetic field as one of the reasons that we have life on Earth in later stages. Allah, stating Iron as "strong force / Great might / Military might," suggests that the Creator was not aware of iron's importance to life on Earth.

Without Iron, there would be no Earth (in its present form) and no life, so indicating Iron as beneficial to Humans shows that Allah is not all-knowing about other benefits of Iron—they were not known at that time.

The Arabic word **"anzala" (أَنْزَل) means "to send down," and it appears frequently in the Quran with both literal and metaphorical meanings. It comes from the root ن-ز-ل (n-z-l), which generally refers** to descent or something coming down.

(Please read more explanation on the next page before answering.) Additionally, logically, if iron were sent down to Earth, then Earth should exist, and iron should be more abundant at the surface; however, this is not the case, as explained in the following few pages.

Conclusion:
Again, the Quran states what the knowledge was about at that time, whereas the Creator should have known the actual benefits of iron and how it became part of the earth.

Please rate this Conclusion:

Objective Analysis of God

The Role of Iron (Quran 57:25)

There are multiple arguments against this verse, some facts:
- *Iron came to Earth when Earth was forming, not after Earth's formation*
- *That is the reason that the central portion of iron is in its core in molten form, which gives it its magnetic fields.*
- *The magnetic field is much more crucial and beneficial to life on Earth, as it deflects the sun's harmful radiation / UV rays, which can kill all living things in a few seconds on Earth and make it uninhabitable*

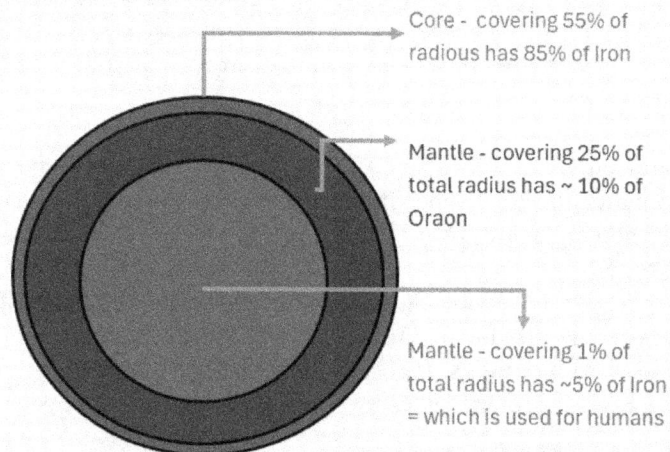

Core - covering 55% of radious has 85% of Iron

Mantle - covering 25% of total radius has ~ 10% of Oraon

Mantle - covering 1% of total radius has ~5% of Iron = which is used for humans

Why This Gradient?
- **Planetary Differentiation (4.5 BYA):** *Heavy iron sank to the core; lighter silicates rose outward.*
- **Core's Dominance:** *Earth's core holds ~90% of the planet's total iron, leaving the mantle/crust relatively Fe-poor.*

Why this word "sent down"/ Anzala:
- **Meteoric Iron:** *Long before smelting terrestrial iron, ancient civilizations used iron from meteorites. This "sky metal" was rare and prized. The earliest iron artifacts (e.g., beads in Egypt, circa 3200 BCE) were made from **meteoric iron**, not smelted ore. This "metal from the gods" was rare and used ceremonially.*
- *Egyptians (c. 3000 BCE): Called it "metal from heaven" and used it for ceremonial objects (e.g., beads in Gerzeh tombs).*
- *Mesopotamians: Referred to iron as "an-bar" (fire from heaven).*

- *Inuit and Native Americans: Used meteoritic iron for tools and weapons.*
- *Many cultures associated meteorites with divine or cosmic origins, though they lacked a scientific framework to explain their extraterrestrial source.*
- *So, when smelting started in ~1500 to 1200 BCE, in Anatolia/Turkey (followed by Africa, South Asia, China & Europe all over the world between 1500 and 500), iron ore was used, and the idea of "sky metal / Metal of God" transitioned into Iron coming from the sky*

Secondly, almost all iron came to Earth before it was even formed, which is why Iron is found in the Earth's core. It became part of the Earth when there was no Earth as such, and everything was coming together to form a shape, which we now know as the Earth and its surface.

Objective Analysis of God

Question:
The Sun and the Moon's Orbits

M58

Analysis and background:
21:33: *"It is He who created the night and the day, and the sun and the moon; each floating in its orbit/rounded course."*
Muslims claim that the Quran correctly states that the sun moves in an orbit.
Counterargument: The concept of the sun and moon having orbits was known long before the Quran, as evidenced in ancient Babylonian and Greek astronomy.

Ancient Civilizations (Pre-5th Century BCE)

Babylonians & Mesopotamians:
- Empirical Observations: Babylonians (c. 1800–300 BCE) tracked lunar and solar movements for calendars and astrology.
- Predictive Models: They used arithmetic (not geometric) models to predict eclipses and planetary positions but did not describe orbits as physical paths.
-

Vedic Texts (India): The ancient Indian text **"Āryabhaṭīya"** by **Āryabhaṭa**, written in **499 CE**, is a foundational treatise on astronomy and mathematics. It provides one of the earliest systematic explanations of planetary motion and celestial mechanics from the Indian tradition.
He was one of the first known thinkers to propose that the Earth rotates on its axis.
He explains that the apparent westward motion of stars is due to the Earth's eastward rotation, not because the sky is rotating. This was a significant deviation from the geocentric view held by most ancient cultures.
- Sanskrit (Aryabhatiya, Golapada 9~10): "Just as a person in a boat going forward sees the stationary objects as moving backward, so are the stationary stars seen by the people on Earth as moving exactly towards the west."
- Aryabhata described the elliptical orbits of celestial bodies, including the Moon and planets.
- He calculated the sidereal (true) and synodic (apparent) rotations of planets.
- He gave an accurate value for the Moon's revolution period

(27.3 days, close to modern calculations).

Greek Astronomy (5th Century BCE–2nd Century CE)
- Pythagoreans (5th–4th BCE): Proposed celestial bodies moved in perfect circles (a philosophical ideal).
- Eudoxus (4th BCE): Created a geocentric model with concentric spheres carrying the sun, moon, and planets.
- Aristotle (4th BCE): Formalized the geocentric model, asserting celestial bodies were embedded in rotating crystalline spheres.
- Ptolemy (2nd CE): Advanced the geocentric model with epicycles (small orbits within orbits) to explain retrograde motion.

Ancient Greek Models (Geocentrism)
- **Ptolemy (2nd century CE)**: Proposed a **geocentric model** where the sun, moon, and planets moved in **circular orbits (deferents) and smaller circles (epicycles)**. This system was mathematical and predictive, but not physically accurate.
- **Aristotle (4th century BCE)**: Believed celestial bodies were embedded in rotating crystalline spheres.

Pre-Islamic Arab Knowledge
- **Bedouin Astronomy**: Arabs observed stars and seasons for navigation and timekeeping, but lacked formal geometric models.
- **Poetic References**: The term فَلَك (falak) in pre-Islamic poetry sometimes referred to the celestial sphere or heavens, but not specifically to orbits as paths.

So, while ancient Greeks, Babylonians, and Indian civilizations recognized circular or cyclical patterns in celestial motion, circular motion was theorized in ancient times; however, orbits as we define them today were not understood until the Islamic era. **The Quran also does not explain the orbits, only mentioning circular motion. Whereas the motion of the sun and moon, looking from the outside, is different**

The Quran's 7th-century description of the sun and moon "swimming" in orbits (falak) reflected the observational knowledge

Objective Analysis of God

of its time.

Secondly, the word "Orbit" came into use later on. The actual word is فلك (falak), which refers to the **celestial orbits or paths** of the sun, moon, and other heavenly bodies. The circular motion of the Sun and the Moon was known before Islam:

Conclusion: The Quran states what was known about that time, whereas the Creator should have known that the motion of the moon and sun is distinctly different, as the moon moves in a non-circular spiral path.	Please rate this Conclusion:

Section 5 – Islam
Questions from Muslims

| **Question:** The Water Cycle – Quran might have completed the cycle – new information. | **M59** |

Analysis and background:
Muslims claim that the Quran describes the water cycle (evaporation, condensation, precipitation). Let's first analyze how it is stated in the Quran (bits and pieces), not in a complete cycle form:
1. Evaporation: Winds "fertilize" clouds (15:22, 35:9).
2. Cloud Formation: Winds stir and gather clouds (30:48, 24:43).
3. Rainfall: Water descends in measured amounts (23:18, 56:68-70).
4. Groundwater Storage: Rain seeps into the earth as springs (39:21).
5. Revival of Land: Rain brings dead land back to life (35:9, 50:9-11).

Here we will come back to the word "measured amount" in – 23:18 later on, before that, let's analyze the cycle and historical knowledge:
The **water cycle** (evaporation, cloud formation, precipitation, and groundwater renewal) was **partially observed and understood** by ancient civilizations before the advent of Islam. Still, their knowledge was often fragmented, mythological, or lacked scientific coherence. The Quran encompasses all aspects of the cycle but in a strangely uneven manner. We will provide benefits here, as this comprehensive knowledge, although it is not a complete full cycle (evaporation → clouds → rain → infiltration → revival of land), presents a cohesive system.

The **water cycle** (evaporation, cloud formation, precipitation, and groundwater renewal) was **partially observed and understood** by ancient civilizations before the advent of Islam. Still, their knowledge was often fragmented, mythological, or lacked scientific coherence.
- **Mesopotamia (c. 3000 BCE–500 BCE):**
  - Observed seasonal rains and river flooding (Tigris/Euphrates).
  - Linked rain to gods (e.g., Adad, the storm god).

Pg. 415
My-OAG.com

Objective Analysis of God

- - No systematic understanding of evaporation or groundwater.
- **Ancient Egypt (c. 3000 BCE–30 BCE):**
  - Noted the Nile's annual flooding and dependence on distant rains.
- **Greece (c. 600 BCE–200 CE):**
  - **Aristotle** theorized that water evaporates into the air and falls as rain (*Meteorologica*)
  - **Thales** claimed water was the primal element
- **India (Vedic Period, c. 1500–500 BCE):**
  - The **Rigveda** (7.101.1–2) describes clouds forming from ocean water and rain nourishing crops.
- **China (c. 1000 BCE–200 CE):**
  - Observed cloud formation and seasonal monsoons.

Here, I found no evidence of whole water known to any ancient civilization, so I will consider it new information (although it is in a fragmented form - spread out verses), making the water cycle like constructing a sentence from jumbled words.
However, I will still give credit to the Quran.

Conclusion: Suppose God knows about the cycle, and He should. In that case, He should have completed the loop and described it in a complete cycle, not in 7 different verses spread across 5 Surahs/chapters, just like the knowledge of pre-Islamic civilizations.	Please rate this Conclusion:

Section 5 – Islam
Questions from Muslims

Question:
The Barrier Between Fresh and Salt Water

M60

Analysis and background:
55:19-20: *"He released the two seas, meeting [side by side]; between them is a barrier [so] neither of them transgresses."* Muslims argue that the Quran describes the separation of fresh and salt water in estuaries.

The phenomenon of two bodies of water meeting but not immediately mixing—as described in Quran 55:19-20—has been observed in certain regions like the Strait of Gibraltar (where the Mediterranean Sea and Atlantic Ocean meet). Apparently, yes: These two bodies of water do not mix immediately, but at the point where they meet.

Greeks attributed oceanic phenomena to gods (e.g., Poseidon's trident stirring the seas).

There was no clear concept of a "barrier" (barzakh) preventing mixing; instead, myths described sea monsters or divine boundaries that served as barriers.

The Quran also does the same; credit this to Allah.

In actuality, Salty Mediterranean water flows outward beneath less dense Atlantic inflow, but turbulence from tidal currents and the strait's narrow geometry creates eddies. Over weeks to months, these forces blend the two water masses into the Atlantic.

Conclusion:
The Quran states what the knowledge was about at that time, whereas the Creator should have gone further and explained the reason rather than attributing it to Himself.

Please rate this Conclusion:

Objective Analysis of God

Question:
Expanding universe

M61

Analysis and background:
The only thing I find new in the Quran is the "expanding universe concept."
51:47 – *"We built the universe with great might, and We are certainly expanding it,"* present-day translation promoted by Muslims, taking it as proof of the Quran's divine origin

After some investigation, I realized the issue:
This is another example of fitting the Quran to science, as mentioned; Arabic is a language in which words can have multiple meanings and thus can be manipulated to fit the translator's requirements. Edwin Hubble discovered the expanding universe in approximately 1928; therefore, let us revisit translations written in those years or other authentic sources. One of the most authentic English translations is by Yousuf Ali, done around 1934, and the translation of 51:47 is quite different in that translation is ---

1. "With hands, we constructed the heaven. Verily., We can expand the vastness of space thereof" – **Ibn Khateer**
2. "We have built the firmament in the night. And we indeed have vast power" – **Yousuf Ali**
3. "We have built the heaven with Our might and We possess the Power for it" - **Maududi**
4. "And the heaven We constructed with strength, and indeed, We are [its] expander." – **Sahih International**
5. "We have built the heaven with might, and We it is Who make the vast extent (thereof)." **Marmaduke Pickthall**

لَمُوسِعُونَ – In older versions of translations of the Quran, it was not translated as "Expanding." This word becomes "expanding" only in new translations after Hubble discovered it in 1932.

Source/Translation	Year	Focus	Theological/Scientific Lens
Ibn Kathir (Tafsir)	1370	Divine power to create vastness	Classical theological focus
Yusuf Ali	1934	"Vastness of space"	Divine power and creation
Pickthall	1930	"Expanding it"	Direct action, literal
Sahih International	1997	"Expander" (active role)	Neutral, action-oriented
Muhammad Asad	1980	"Steadily expanding"	Explicitly aligns with cosmology
Muhsin Khan	1996	"Able to extend."	Emphasis on divine capability

The Arabic word وَإِنَّا لَمُوسِعُونَ has many meanings. Grammatically speaking, it is an agent noun constructed from the verb أوسع. This non-triconsonantal verb comes from the 3-consonant root (or 3CR) وسع.
So, the above Ayat can have any of the following interpretations:

Details of the above:
1. **Ibn Khateer**
   o "He is the One Who has expanded and extended it perfectly, making it vast and spacious."
   o Focuses on Allah's creative power and sovereignty
2. **Yusuf Ali**:
   "With power and skill did We construct the Firmament: for it is *We Who create the vastness of space.*"
   Interprets *mūsi'ūn* as creating vastness/capacity (focus on divine power).
3. **Pickthall**:
   "And the heaven we built with might and *are expanding it.*"
   Directly states ongoing expansion (similar to modern cosmology).
4. **Sahih International**:
   "And the heaven We constructed with strength, and indeed, *We are [its] expander.*"
   Emphasizes Allah's ongoing act of expanding the universe.
5. **Muhammad Asad**:
   "And it is We who have built the universe with [Our creative] power, and *verily, we are steadily expanding it.*"
   Explicitly links to the modern concept of cosmic expansion.
6. **Muhsin Khan**:
   "And We have built the heaven with might, and *We can extend the vastness of space.*"
   It focuses on Allah's ability to expand, which is not necessarily an ongoing process.

Once again, I find no truly objective rationale to justify the use of this particular word in the context of expansion, as previously discussed. It may simply be a coincidence that, with our current understanding of cosmology, the universe is expanding—a notion that happens to align with one possible interpretation of the phrase وَإِنَّا لَمُوسِعُونَ

Conclusion: Quran translation is still being revised to align it with discoveries, and translations/Tafaseers are making their best efforts to prove that it's the word of God, by manipulating and twisting facts.	Please rate this Conclusion:

Question: The Pain Receptors in Skin	**M62**

Section 5 – Islam
Questions from Muslims

Analysis and background:

4:56: "*Indeed, those who disbelieve in Our verses—We will drive them into a fire. Every time their skins are roasted through, We will replace them with other skins so they may taste the punishment. Indeed, Allah is ever Exalted in Might and Wise.*"

The verse is about punishment in the afterlife, not a scientific statement. Ancient cultures well understood the role of skin in sensing pain.

The argument given by Muslims is that the Quran correctly states that pain is felt in the skin. How can Allah know that only the skin can feel pain at that time? Only Allah, who created humans, knows it.

I submit that this is an obvious, known fact of that time, or since the first humans began to come to their senses.

The idea that pain receptors exist only in the skin is an outdated belief, likely to stem from early anatomical studies where external injuries were the most obvious source of pain. However, modern science has thoroughly debunked this myth. Below are key counterarguments proving that nociceptors (pain receptors) are found throughout the body, not just the skin.

1. Internal Organs Have Pain Receptors (Visceral Nociception)

Fact: The gut, heart, lungs, bladder, and other organs contain nociceptors that detect inflammation, stretching, and oxygen deprivation.

- A heart attack causes chest pain (angina) due to cardiac ischemia, even though the heart muscle itself has fewer receptors than the skin.
- Kidney stones trigger severe flank pain when they obstruct the urinary tract.
- Fracture of the bone also causes pain

If pain were only in the skin, internal diseases would not cause pain—yet they do, often severely.

2. Deep Tissue Pain (Muscles, Joints, Bones)

Fact: Muscles, tendons, and bones have nociceptors that respond to injury, pressure, or inflammation.

- Muscle cramps (from overuse or dehydration).

Objective Analysis of God

- Arthritis (joint pain due to cartilage damage).
- Bone fractures (direct nerve stimulation in the periosteum).

If pain were skin-only, broken bones or muscle tears would not hurt—but they do, often more intensely than superficial cuts.

3. Corneal Pain (Eye Surface)
Fact: The cornea is one of the most pain-sensitive tissues, despite not being skin."
- A tiny scratch (corneal abrasion) causes extreme discomfort.
- If pain were skin-exclusive, eye injuries wouldn't hurt—yet they do intensely.

So, in general, if pain were truly skin-only, medical conditions like appendicitis, heart attacks, and arthritis would be painless—but they're not. Modern medicine and neuroscience confirm that nociceptors are ubiquitous in the body, not just the skin.

The claim that "pain receptors are only in the skin" is a long-debunked myth.

Conclusion: This may be accepted as a symbolic or metaphorical statement, but it is not considered scientific proof of the Quran's divine knowledge.	Please rate this Conclusion:

Section 5 – Islam
Questions from Muslims

Question: Fingerprints | M63

Analysis and background:
Muslims claim that the following verse signifies that Allah knew about the uniqueness of fingerprints at that time

75:3-4 *"Does man think that We cannot assemble his bones? Nay, We are able to put together in perfect order the very tips of his fingers."*

My submission has two components:
Fingerprints were already known to be unique to individuals in ancient cultures. There is no evidence to suggest that this was a groundbreaking scientific insight.

- **Babylon & China (~2000 BCE – 300 CE)**
  Fingerprints were used as **marks of identity** on clay tablets (Babylon) and legal documents (China), but there's no evidence they understood uniqueness.
- **Chinese Qin Dynasty (221–206 BCE)** – Thumbprints were used as **seals**, but likely as a symbolic gesture rather than a means of identification.
- **Persia & Medieval Europe (~14th–17th Century)**
  Some contracts included fingerprints, but uniqueness was not formally recognized.

Now science has proven that not only are fingerprints unique, but there are multiple other parts which are unique to each individual, like Eyes (Iris Patterns), Ears (Otoacoustic Emissions), voice (vocal cord vibration), tongue print, lips print (Cheiloscopy), etc.

Linguistic and Semantic Aspects
It is another example of fitting Quranic words to scientific knowledge. To explain this, let us revisit the translation by Yusuf (first published in 1934) and the translation done by IFTA of Saudi Arabia.
They have mentioned the reference to fingertips is the use of an Arabic idiom, as explained in his tafseer 5812 – "An idiom for the most delicate parts of his body"

I have explained the use of idioms in the Quran, which has made the translation much more complex and misleading.

Objective Analysis of God

Key Arabic Terms:
بَنَانَهُ (banānahu): Traditionally translated as "his fingertips" (not "fingerprints"). Classical lexicons define banān as the "tips of fingers/toes," not the ridges or patterns (بصمات, basamāt) we call fingerprints.
نُسَوِّيَ (nusawwiya): Derived from سَوَّى (sawwā), meaning "to shape," "to proportion," or "to restore," but not explicitly "to recreate fingerprints."

Considering the above, the verse emphasizes God's ability to recreate the entire human body, including its minutest parts (like fingertips), not to highlight the uniqueness of fingerprint patterns. The focus is on resurrection, not forensic identification.
Early scholars (e.g., Ibn Kathir, Al-Tabari) interpreted the verse as affirming God's power to resurrect even the most minor body parts, not as a reference to fingerprint uniqueness.
Example: Ibn Kathir states, "*God will resurrect the decomposed fingertips to their original form, proving His ability to recreate humans.*"

Conclusion: Considering the above statements, it appears that this reference to fingertips is not specific to fingerprints, as the Creator Allah would likely be aware that many other parts of the body are also unique to individuals.	Please rate this Conclusion:

Section 5 – Islam
Questions from Muslims

Question: Earth Protective Layers	M64

Analysis and background:

21:32 - *"And we have made heaven heaven a roof, safe and well-guarded"*

Several ancient civilizations gained insights—either through observation, philosophy, or divine revelation—about the Earth's atmosphere acting as a protective layer. However, they described it in mythological or symbolic terms, much like the Quran. Therefore, if we reject them as proof, we must also reject similar statements in the Quran. Here's a concise breakdown:

1. Hindu / Vedic Texts (~1500–500 BCE)
- Rigveda (10.149.1) describes the sky as a protective shield: *"The atmosphere covers Earth like a blanket, guarding it from harm."*
- Surya Siddhanta (5th century CE, but based on older knowledge) refers to layers of air (*Vayu Mandala*) surrounding Earth, influencing climate and life.

2. Greek & Roman Philosophy (~500 BCE–200 CE)
- Anaximenes (6th century BCE) claimed air (*pneuma*) envelops Earth, sustaining life.
- Aristotle (4th century BCE) in *Meteorology* described the atmosphere as a "protective veil" that burns up meteors (observed as "falling stars").

3. Modern Science (Confirmed in the 19th–20th Century)
Earth's Atmosphere provides a covering from the following
- Ozone Layer (1913): Blocks UV rays.
- Atmospheric Layers (Troposphere to Exosphere): Absorb meteors, regulate temperature.
- Magnetic Field + Atmosphere: Shields against solar winds (Van Allen belts, 1958).

Many ancient civilizations, including those mentioned in the Quran, symbolically described the atmosphere's protective role.

Conclusion: Again, stating the knowledge of that time, while missing the key information that the Creator should have known.	Please rate this Conclusion:

Objective Analysis of God

| Question: Layers of darkness in the Ocean | M65 |

Analysis and background:
24:40: "Or [they are] like darknesses within an unfathomable sea which is covered by waves, upon which are waves, over which are clouds—darknesses, some of them upon others. When one puts out his hand [therein], he can hardly see it. And he to whom Allah has not granted light—for him there is no light."

There is no solid evidence that deep-sea diving existed in the BCE era, although ancient civilizations practiced shallow-water free diving for resources such as pearls and sponges. Greeks, Persians, and Indians used breath-holding and basic tools, with a range limited to around 30 meters.

Early Diving Activities (Pre-500 BCE)
- Free-Diving for Resources:
- Sponge and Pearl Diving: Ancient Greeks, Phoenicians, and Mesopotamians free-dived (breath-holding) to collect sponges, pearls, and red coral from shallow coastal waters (5–30 meters depth). The Greek Island of Kalymnos was famous for sponge diving as early as 3000 BCE.
- Pearl Diving: Evidence from the Persian Gulf, India, and Sri Lanka suggests pearl divers operated in shallow waters as early as 2000 BCE. Ancient Tamil texts (Sangam literature) describe pearl harvesting.
- Military and Salvage Diving: The Greek historian Herodotus (5th century BCE) describes Scyllias of Scione, a diver who sabotaged Persian ships during the Greco-Persian Wars by cutting anchor ropes underwater.
- Assyrian stone carvings (c. 900 BCE) depict soldiers using inflated animal skins as primitive breathing aids while crossing rivers.

Early explorers and researchers were aware of the ocean's layers and the concept of depth-related darkness, as documented in historical books from the past. This description is not unique or advanced in terms of scientific discovery.

Another argument is that the wording about layered darkness is not entirely aligned with the concept of continuous, gradual darkness in

the ocean.
Early knowledge of ocean darkness is also reflected in religious texts, and it is not unique to the Quran—Greek, Hindu, and biblical texts also mention deep-sea darkness in a similar symbolic manner.

- Greek & Roman Texts (e.g., Aristotle, Pliny, the Elder) mention the sea's depth and darkness.
- Hindu Scriptures (e.g., Vedas, Puranas) speak of cosmic darkness. Like
- Rigveda (10.129.3) – The Nasadiya Sukta (Hymn of Creation) – "There was darkness hidden in darkness in the beginning; all this was an indiscernible ocean of water"
- Atharvaveda (4.16.4) – Darkness in the Waters - "The back (depths) of the ocean is covered with darkness, and darkness is spread within darkness."
- Bhagavata Purana (2.5.23) – The Garbhodaka Ocean - "In that ocean (Garbhodaka), the thousand-headed serpent Ananta (Shesha) serves as the bed of Lord Vishnu, and the darkness is so dense that even the serpent's glowing jewels cannot dispel it."
- The Bible mentions deep waters - Psalm 88:6 - "You have put me in the depths of the pit, in the regions dark and deep."

Again, I will let you decide if these could be normal, known facts of the day, or some divine, completely original revelation.

Conclusion: The Quran states known knowledge of the time, whereas the Creator should have gone further and explained the reason, rather than providing superficial information.	Please rate this Conclusion:

Objective Analysis of God

| Question: The Earth's Spherical or Flat | M66 |

Analysis and background:
79:30: "And after that He spread the earth."
Old translations of this word "Dahaha" (دَحَاهَا), as spreading earth out as a flat carpet -:
Meaning of "Dahaha" (دَحَاهَا)
- **Ibn Kathir - Completed ~883 CE (270 AH)**: Explains it as **spreading out the Earth** like a bed or carpet (*firash*) for creatures to dwell.
- **Al-Tabari: Completed ~1350s CE** (Supports this, citing Prophet Muhammad's analogy of Earth being **"stretched like a carpet"** (Hadith in Musnad Ahmad).
- **Yiousuf Ali:1934** " And the earth moreover. Hadth He extended"
- **Maududi:** (1942-72) " And after that he spread the Earth"

Again, here we see the same approach of redefining words to align them with scientific facts. Here are some arguments:
- "Dahaha" (دَحَاهَا) comes from the root *daha* (د-ح-و), which can also imply:
- Spreading out (like an ostrich spreads out its nest, as some scholars explain).
- Making it rounded or egg-shaped (modern interpretations link this to Earth's geoid shape).

Later on, once the concept of a rounded earth became more popular, the word "Dahaha" changed its meaning to "curved earth."
This is a critical argument so that we will delve slightly deeper into the details.

The flat earth concept is mentioned in many places in the quran, like the following 10 examples:
1. 13:3 - Arabic word: مَدَّ (madda: He spread out)
   And He is the One Who spread out (madda) the earth and placed therein firm mountains and rivers, and from all the fruits He made two spouses; He covers the night with the day. Indeed, in there are signs for people who give thought.
2. 15:19 - Arabic word: مَدَدْنَاهَا (madadnāhā: We spread it)
   And the earth—We have spread it (madadnāhā) and cast therein

firm mountains and caused to grow therein [something] of every well-balanced thing.
3. 20:53 - Arabic word: مَهْدًا (mahdan: as a cradle/bed)
   [He who has made for you the earth a bed (mahdan) and inserted therein roadways for you and sent down from the sky water; and We have brought forth thereby various kinds of plants in pairs.
4. 43:10 - Arabic word: مَهْدًا (mahdan: a cradle/bed)
   [It is He] who made for you the earth as a cradle (mahdan) and made for you therein roads that you might be guided.
5. 50:7 - Arabic word: مَدَدْنَاهَا (madadnāhā: We spread it)
   And the earth—We have spread it (madadnāhā) and cast therein firm mountains and made grow therein [something] of every beautiful kind.
6. 51:48 - Arabic word: فَرَشْنَاهَا (farashnāhā: We spread it out/made it as a carpet)
   And the earth—We have spread it out (farashnāhā); how excellent are the Spreaders!
7. 55:10 - Arabic word: وَضَعَهَا (waḍa'ahā: He laid it down)
   And the earth He laid [out] (waḍa'ahā) for creatures.
8. 71:19 - Arabic word: بِسَاطًا (bisāṭan: an expanse/carpet)
   And Allah has made for you the earth an expanse (bisāṭan).
9. 78:6 Arabic word: مِهَادًا (mihādan: a cradle/bed)
   Have we not made the earth a cradle (mihādan)?
10. 91:6 - Arabic word: طَحَاهَا (ṭaḥāhā: He spread it)
    And by the earth and He who spread it (ṭaḥāhā).

Here you can see that the Quran is using several Arabic words to describe the earth's surface, including "bisāṭan" (carpet), "firāshan" (bed), "daḥāhā" (spread out or possibly "shaped like an egg"), and "sūṭihat" (flattened).

Out of all the words used to describe the flatness of the earth, mainly "Dahada", based on its root words, can also be interpreted as "made it egg-shaped,".

Historically, classical scholars and commentators interpreted these words as indicating a flat earth, in line with pre-modern cosmology—primarily as terms like "bisāṭan" and "sūṭihat" clearly denote something spread out flat, such as a carpet or a floor. However, over the centuries, as scientific understanding evolved and Muslim astronomers recognized the earth's sphericity,

Objective Analysis of God

interpretations shifted. Modern interpreters often highlight that root meanings for words like "daḥāhā" (from 79:30) could also refer to making something egg-shaped, drawing connections to the slightly oblate shape of the earth, especially referencing the ostrich egg.

Various translations include:
- Sahih International: "*And after that, He spread the earth.*"
- Yusuf Ali: "*And the earth, moreover, hath He extended (to a wide expanse).*"
- Ibn Kathir's tafsir explains it as making the earth flat for habitation after its creation.

The above example of the Arabic word "Dahaha" reinforces our previous argument about the complexity of the Arabic language and the ability of Muslim scholars to reinterpret the Quran. This raises questions about why the universe's creator chose Arabic, a language that has a single word for a flat, egg-like surface.

Conclusion: Same old story: Islamic scholars bending their backs to align Quranic verses with present-day facts. The creator of this earth would not use such words to explain the earth in so many places.	Please rate this Conclusion:

Pg. 430

Section 5 – Islam
Questions from Muslims

Question:	
The Role of Honey	**M67**

Analysis and background:
Claim: 16:69 - "There emerges from their bellies a drink, varying in colors, wherein is healing for people."

The knowledge of honey's healing properties dates back thousands of years, with evidence from ancient medicine, religious texts, and archaeological findings.

Here's a historical breakdown:
- Prehistoric & Ancient Civilizations (Before 2000 BCE) Stone Age (Prehistoric): Cave paintings (e.g., Spain's Cuevas de la Araña, circa 8000 BCE) depict honey harvesting, suggesting an early recognition of its value.
- Ancient Egypt (3000–500 BCE): The Ebers Papyrus (1550 BCE) lists honey in over 900 medicinal remedies for wounds, digestive issues, and embalming. Used as an antibacterial wound dressing (confirmed by modern science).
- Ayurveda & Traditional Indian Medicine (~1500 BCE) - Rigveda (1700–1100 BCE): Mentions honey (madhu) as a healing substance. Charaka Samhita (300 BCE–200 CE): Prescribes honey for eye diseases, cough, and detoxification.
- Ancient Greece & Rome (500 BCE–500 CE) Hippocrates (460–370 BCE): "Father of Medicine" used honey for pain relief, fever, and wound care. Aristotle (384–322 BCE) noted its use for eye infections and burns. Dioscorides (1st CE): Wrote in De Materia Medica that honey heals ulcers and soothes throat infections.

Conclusion:	Please rate this Conclusion:
The medicinal properties of honey have been known since ancient times. This is a general reference, not a novel scientific discovery.	

Objective Analysis of God

| Question: Female Bees | M68 |

Analysis and background:
16:68-69: "*And your Lord inspired to the bee, 'Take for yourself among the mountains, houses, and among the trees and [in] that which they construct. Then eat from all the fruits and follow the ways of your Lord laid down [for you]. There emerges from their bellies a drink, varying in colors, in which there is healing for people. Indeed, in that is a sign for a people who give thought.*"

Claim: Female bees are referenced here, as female bees perform these jobs, and the Quran informed us about it at a time when no one knew about it.

In Arabic, verbs reflect the gender of the nouns they describe, including non-human entities. This contrasts with English, which lacks gender-based verb conjugation for non-human subjects, often resulting in challenges when translating nuanced meanings. In this verse, the verbs used for the bee—"take" (اتَّخِذِي), "eat" (كُلِي), and "follow" (فَاسْلُكِي)—are all in the feminine form, suggesting that female bees perform the actions. This aligns with modern scientific knowledge, which indicates that only female worker bees collect nectar and produce honey. It is worth noting that Arabic grammar employs feminine forms for collective nouns, such as "al-nahl" (the bee), regardless of the biological sex of the entity being referred to. Similar to many other languages (e.g., Arabic, Hebrew, German, Urdu), nouns and verbs may follow grammatical conventions rather than biological realities. For instance, when referring to a general fox or fish in Urdu, the female gender is mainly used.

| **Conclusion:** The feminine verb form reflects standard usage rather than intentional scientific insight. | Please rate this Conclusion: |

Section 5 – Islam
Questions from Muslims

Question:
Moon's Reflected Light

M69

Analysis and background:
25:61: "Blessed is He who placed constellations in the sky and placed therein a lamp [sun] and a moon giving light."
Claim: Distinguishes the sun (source of light) vs. the moon (reflective).
Similar information is stated in 71:16

The understanding that moonlight is reflected sunlight developed gradually through observations and intellectual contributions across different cultures and eras. Here's a concise timeline of key milestones in various regions:

Ancient Greece:
- (5th century BCE): Anaxagoras of Clazomenae proposed that the Moon does not emit its light but instead reflects the Sun's light. He also correctly explained lunar eclipses as the Earth blocking sunlight from the Moon. His ideas were controversial and led to charges of impiety.
- Aristotle later supported this view, using the Moon's phases and the geometry of eclipses as evidence.

Vedic astronomy
- Jyotisha – Indian astronomy, especially texts like the Surya Siddhanta (possibly compiled between 1400 and 1200 BCE), describes the moon as receiving light from the sun. "The moon, being of the nature of water, receives light from the sun and reflects it." (Surya Siddhanta, Chapter 12).
- Then later in 400 CE – about 150 years before the Quran) Āryabhaṭīya – By Āryabhaṭa - Explicit Statement (Verse 4.36, Golapāda Section)"The Moon is always illuminated by the Sun, and thus it shines by reflected light."
- At the time when Quran was being revealed in 628 (Prophet Mohammed first claimed prophet hood at 610 CE and Quran was finalized in present form in about 655 CE)following was recorded in historical books - Āryabhaṭīya (499 CE) – By Āryabhaṭa I explicitly Stated (Verse 4.36, Golapāda Section) "The Moon is always illuminated by the Sun, and thus it shines by reflected light." About 27 years before the Quran was

Pg. 433

My-OAG.com

finalized.

Therefore, we can see that this information was outdated and approximately 5000 to 2000 years older than the Quran. There are multiple ways it could have reached a person in Mecca or while they were traveling. This reiterates that we lack information on the extent of discoveries made by ancient civilizations.

Conclusion: Again, Allah is narrating the same information available in the pre-Islamic era. My discussion earlier indicates that this was readily available to Prophet Mohhamed.	Please rate this Conclusion:

Section 5 – Islam
Questions from Muslims

Question:
Subterranean Water

M70

Analysis and background:
23:18: "… We store it [water] in the earth."
Claim: Groundwater reservoirs were revealed.
Storage of water is an ancient concept, and humans have been extracting water from the earth for approximately 10,000 years.

The oldest known ancient water wells discovered by *archaeologists* date back to the Neolithic period (New Stone Age), reflecting early human innovation in accessing groundwater. Here are the key examples:

1. Kissonerga-Mylouthkia Well (Cyprus) Age: ~10,000–9,000 years old (c. 8,000–7,000 BCE).
   Discovery: A circular, stone-lined well found in Cyprus, associated with some of the earliest farming communities in the Mediterranean.
2. Atlit Yam Well (Israel) Age: ~9,000–8,500 years old (c. 7,100–6,500 BCE).
   Discovery: A submerged Pre-Pottery Neolithic site off Israel's coast, featuring a stone-built well.
3. Kückhoven Well (Germany - Age: ~7,000 years old (c. 5,100 BCE).
   Numerous records show that Arabs used Wells to extract water from underground. People used wells for drinking, agriculture, and watering animals, particularly in trade hubs such as Mecca, Ta'if, and Yathrib (Medina). Many tribal wars occurred solely due to the ownership or use of the well.

This verse also mentions the measured quantity of rain. If it is measured quantities, why do we have frequent floods?

Conclusion:
It was common knowledge even among Arabs, and is not new information

Please rate this Conclusion:

Objective Analysis of God

| Question: Plant's pair | M71 |

Analysis and background:
20:53: "He who has made for you the earth a bed and the sky a canopy; and sends down rain... producing thereby pairs of plants."
Claim: The Quran revealed about Botanical sexual reproduction (male/female parts)

The Arabic phrase in question is "زُوجَيْن" (zawjayn), the dual form of "زَوْج" (zawj), which translates to "two of a pair" or "two kinds." However, older classical Quranic exegesis (tafsir) and translations widely interpret this term contextually to mean "many kinds of plants" or "various types of vegetation," emphasizing the diversity of creation rather than a strictly numerical "pair." Like Ibn Khateer –"Who has made earth for you like a bed, and has opened ways for you there in, and has sent down water (rain)from the Sky. And we have brought forth with its various kinds of vegetation."

In addition, the understanding of male and female reproductive structures in plants evolved through a combination of ancient practical knowledge and later scientific inquiry. Here's a structured overview:

Ancient Practices (Pre-Scientific Era):
Date Palm Cultivation (c. 700 BCE): Ancient Mesopotamians and Assyrians practiced hand-pollination of date palms, transferring pollen from male to female trees to ensure fruit production. While they recognized the practical need for this process, they likely did not conceptualize it in biological terms of "male" and "female." This is a given as plants' genders are not specified. Yes, it is established that pairs work together for reproduction, and only the roles of giving and receiving partners are defined as male and female, respectively.

While zawj can mean "pair" or "couple," in classical Arabic and Quranic usage, the plural azwāj (أزواج) often denotes "kinds," "species," or "varieties." The dual form (zawjayn) here likely serves a rhetorical purpose, highlighting multiplicity and diversity rather than a literal "two."
Even if we consider Quran words as Pairs (not male and female),

this was ancient knowledge, as mentioned above. The Quran also mentions pairs, not just male-female pairs.

Additionally, as discussed in the animal kingdom, where genders are not defined by birth, in the plant kingdom, it is more common for plants not to exhibit fixed genders. Plant kingdom distribution is as follows:
a. ~**85%** of plants are **hermaphroditic** (both sexes in one flower).
b. ~**5-10%** are **monoecious** (separate male/female flowers on the same plant).
c. ~**5-7%** are **dioecious** (strict male/female individuals)

Here is a further explanation of the above:
1. Dioecious Plants (True Male & Female Separation)
   - Definition: Species with distinct male and female individuals.
   - Examples:
   a) Papaya (Carica papaya) – Some trees bear only male flowers, others only female.
   b) Willow (Salix) – Separate male and female plants.
   c) Date Palm (Phoenix dactylifera) – Farmers must plant both male and female trees for fruit production.
   d) Science Confirms: Genetic studies have shown that sex chromosomes (such as XY in humans) control this separation.

2. Monoecious Plants (Both Sexes on One Plant)
   - Definition: A single plant has both male and female flowers.
   - Examples:
   a) Corn (Zea mays) – Tassels (male) and ears (female) on the same plant.
   b) Cucumber (Cucumis sativus) – Produces separate male and female flowers.
   c) Science Confirms: Hormones (like ethylene) regulate sex expression in such plants.

3. Hermaphroditic Plants (Perfect Flowers)
   - Definition: Flowers contain both male (stamens) and female (pistils) parts.
   - Examples:
     o Tomato (Solanum lycopersicum)

Objective Analysis of God

- - Rose (Rosa)
- Science Confirms: These plants can self-pollinate, but many still prefer cross-pollination.

The majority of plants – approximately 85%- do not have fixed or flexible sex pairs.

There are no "gender roles": Unlike animals, plants don't have behaviors tied to sex. Their reproductive structures are purely functional.
Fluid Sex Expression: Some plants (e.g., Cannabis) can change sex under environmental stress (like light exposure).
Evolutionary Strategy: Separating sexes (dioecy) reduces inbreeding, while hermaphroditism ensures reproduction even in isolation.

Conclusion: Surely, the creator of the universe, as well as plants, should know that not all plants are pairs; these words cannot be from the Creator.	Please rate this Conclusion:

Section 5 – Islam
Questions from Muslims

Question:
Photosynthesis

M72

Analysis and background:
36:80: "*He who produces for you fire from green trees, when behold you kindle therewith*"

Claim: Combustion requires stored solar energy (photosynthesis).

It is a very long stretch to convert the phrase "produces fire for you from green plant" and deduce that it refers to photosynthesis. Allah could have been more explicit, like "green plants make their food from sun rays."
Photosynthesis, the process of converting sunlight into chemical energy, involves energy storage, not combustion—burning wood releases stored energy through oxidation, a separate reaction. The reference to fire emerging from green trees cannot be directly linked to the process of photosynthesis.

Historically, the verse emphasizes Allah's power to create fire from an unsuitable source (moist, green wood) in a desert context where dry lumber was used.

I can say that Allah is informing us that humans can make fire from wood, which appears to be a more direct outcome of this sentence.

Conclusion:
This connection is entirely absurd, lacking any logical, scientific, or narrative basis.

Please rate this Conclusion:

Objective Analysis of God

Question: Frontal Lobe Deception	M73

Analysis and background:
96:15-16: "No! If he does not desist, we will seize him by the forelock—a lying, sinful forelock."

Claim: The prefrontal cortex governs decision-making and deceit.

Yes, there is an Arabic idiom that metaphorically associates the forehead with lying or deception: "يَكْذِبُ بِجَبْهَتِهِ" (Yakdhibu bijabhatih) -- "He lies with his forehead."

Explanation: This idiom implies that someone is lying so brazenly or shamelessly that their deception is "written on their forehead" (i.e., visibly apparent). The forehead symbolizes a person's face or demeanor, suggesting their dishonesty is unconcealed or audacious. It reflects cultural associations of the forehead (جَبْهَة/jabha) with pride, honor, or integrity.

Plus, scientifically, lying is not solely linked to the frontal lobe. While the prefrontal cortex (PFC)—particularly the dorsolateral and ventromedial regions—plays a central role in deception (e.g., planning lies, suppressing truth, and managing cognitive load), modern neuroscience highlights a broader neural network.
The **anterior cingulate cortex (ACC)** monitors conflicts between truth and lies, the **amygdala** processes emotional responses (e.g., guilt or fear), and the **parietal lobe** aids in attention and memory manipulation during deceit. Neuroimaging studies (fMRI) confirm that lying involves dynamic interactions across these regions, not isolated frontal lobe activity. Deception is a complex process that requires the coordination of executive, emotional, and social brain networks.

Conclusion: Another example, where an idiom was given a literal meaning as it fits new scientific knowledge	Please rate this Conclusion:

Section 5 – Islam
Questions from Muslims

| Question: Hygiene in Rituals | M74 |

Analysis and background:
5:6: "O believers! When you rise for prayer, wash your faces, hands up to the elbows, wipe your heads, and wash your feet..."

Cleaning oneself before praying was an ancient practice, even before the advent of Islam. Pre-Islamic Arabia (the Jahiliyya period) had rituals of purification associated with entering the Kaaba or participating in pilgrimage (Hajj) ceremonies. While these practices were not identical to the Islamic concept of wudu (ablution) or ghusl (full-body wash), they reflected a cultural and religious emphasis on ritual purity when approaching sacred spaces. Here are some key points:

Ritual Purity in Pre-Islamic Arabia: Before Islam, the Kaaba was already a revered sanctuary (Haram), and polytheistic tribes across Arabia performed pilgrimages to it. Ritual cleansing before entering the Kaaba or touching its sacred objects (like the Black Stone) was likely part of pre-Islamic practice:

Washing with Water: Some accounts suggest pilgrims washed themselves with water from the Zamzam well or other sources to purify themselves before approaching the Kaaba.

Avoiding "Impure" States: Entering the sanctuary while in a state of ritual impurity (e.g., after sexual intercourse, menstruation, or contact with the dead) may have been prohibited, similar to taboos in other ancient Near Eastern religions.

The Hums: Pre-Islamic Guardians of the Kaaba
The Hums (حمس) were a group of elite Meccans and allied tribes who, to distinguish themselves from others, enforced strict rules regarding the Kaaba and pilgrimage. They insisted that pilgrims wear specific garments (often

Objective Analysis of God

seamless, more like "Ihram") to enter the Kaaba's precincts, which may have been linked to notions of purity. As explained earlier, this is another example of old practices creeping into Islamic rituals.

Cleaning oneself was a common practice in ancient Egyptian and Mesopotamian civilizations, dating back to around 2400 BCE.

Conclusion: Islam did not introduce pre-prayer cleansing; it was already common among ancient civilizations and pre-Islamic Arabs.	Please rate this Conclusion:

Section 5 – Islam
Questions from Muslims

Question:
Fasting benefits

M75

Analysis and background:
2:183: "*O believers! Fasting is prescribed for you—as it was for those before you—so perhaps you will become mindful of Allah.*"
Claim: Intermittent fasting has health benefits (autophagy, metabolism).

Fasting as a practice—both for spiritual and health benefits—predates Islam and was practiced in ancient civilizations. Fasting as a spiritual practice existed in pre-Islamic Arabia, influenced by ascetic traditions and neighboring religions. Its health benefits were known to the Romans as early as 1550 BCE. It is also used to remove sins.

Civilization - The Ebers Papyrus (1550 BCE) references fasting as a remedy for specific ailments. Mesopotamia, Greece, and Roman - Hippocrates (460–370 BCE) prescribed fasting to treat diseases, stating, *"To eat when you are sick is to feed your illness. Hinduism and Buddhism - Ayurvedic texts associate fasting with balancing the bodily humors (doshas). Jews fast to atone for sins (Leviticus 16:29–31).*
Pre-Islamic Fasting Practices: Some pre-Islamic Arabs practiced fasting as part of personal spiritual or ascetic rituals. For instance, individuals might fast during meditative retreats (tahannuth) or times of reflection, though these were not standardized or communal obligations. Jewish and
Christian communities in Arabia observed fasting (e.g., Yom Kippur and Lent). The Quraysh tribe in Mecca adopted the practice of fasting on the Day of Ashura (the 10th of Muharram). Additionally, the Quran does not explicitly mention the physical health benefits of fasting. The focus of fasting in the Quran is spiritual/moral discipline.

Conclusion:
The health benefits of fasting were known before Islam and were practiced as a form of prayer and to atone for sins.

Please rate this Conclusion:

Objective Analysis of God

Question: Prohibition of Pork	M76

Analysis and background:
6:145: "*Say, 'I find nothing forbidden to eat except carrion, flowing blood, swine...'*"
Claim: Pork's health risks (parasites, cholesterol).

The Quran prohibits pork as an act of submission to Allah and a marker of spiritual purity (rijs). While health benefits are discussed in Islamic tradition, the Quran primarily focuses on theological obedience rather than scientific rationale.

Scientifically, lean pork and lean beef are nearly identical in nutrition and health impact when eaten in moderation. Neither is significantly healthier or riskier than the other, assuming they're unprocessed and adequately prepared. Both can fit into a balanced diet without significant differences in health risks.

Prohibiting pork in Abrahamic religions (Judaism and Islam) is rooted in ancient cultural, environmental, and practical considerations rather than arbitrary rules. While the Torah (Jewish law) and the Quran (Islamic law) frame prohibition as a divine command, historical and anthropological research suggests plausible reasons for this, which is more of a historical continuation of arbitrary beliefs adopted by religions.

Many pre-Judaic Semitic cultures (e.g., Canaanites, Phoenicians) avoided pigs. This taboo predates Abrahamic religions and may have later influenced Jewish and Islamic practices. Pigs were associated with settled agricultural societies (e.g., the Egyptians and Philistines) rather than nomadic pastoralists (such as the early Hebrews and Arabs).

Conclusion: There is no direct link between diseases and Pork; otherwise, most of the non-Muslim and Non-Jews would have died by now, considering their pork consumption.	Please rate this Conclusion:

Section 5 – Islam
Questions from Muslims

Question:
Everything in Pair-even Antimatter

M77

Analysis and background:
51:49: *"And of all things We created pairs, so perhaps you may be mindful."*
Claim: Particle-antiparticle pairs in quantum physics.

The concept of duality, where things are created in pairs, predates Islam and is found in many ancient civilizations and religious traditions. The concept of cosmic balance, encompassing the principles of male and female, or complementary forces, is a profoundly ancient and widespread idea.
- Taoism (Yin and Yang) - Everything in nature arises from the interaction of these dual energies.
- Zoroastrianism (Ahura Mazda vs. Angra Mainyu) - Central to its theology is the cosmic struggle between Ahura Mazda (good) and Angra Mainyu (evil)—a metaphysical duality.
- Ancient Egyptian belief (Geb and Nut, Isis, and Osiris) - They believed in the duality of nature: order vs. chaos, male vs. female, sky vs. earth (Nut and Geb)
- Greek philosophy (Plato's Forms and duality) - The concept of binary opposites was used to explain the structure of the cosmos
- Hinduism (e.g., Shiva–Shakti, duality in Samkhya)

Additionally, there are a few creatures that change their nature or gender, such as clownfish, Wrasses, Grouper, Parrotfish, and Slipper Limpets. Butterflies also exhibit characteristics of both genders due to genetic anomalies. Flatworms are hermaphroditic, meaning they can be both male and female simultaneously and can decide which gender they want to be, a decision that is not permanent.

Conclusion:
The notion of creation in pairs or dualities is deeply rooted in many pre-Islamic religions and philosophies.

Please rate this Conclusion:

Objective Analysis of God

| Question : Relativity of Time | M78 |

Analysis and background:
22:47: "A Day with your Lord is like 1,000 years of your counting."
70:4: "The angels and the Spirit ascend to Him in a day equivalent to 50,000 years."
Claim: The Quran refers to Time dilation in Einstein's relativity, which says time becomes immaterial when traveling at the speed of light.

These verses give an exciting situation from 2 aspects:

1. With the above given, if you apply it to Einstein's theory, that if we try to calculate "what will be the speed of God and angels", if they travel at the above ratio, that is, God has 1000 equal to 1 day on Earth. Result and calculation shown below, but before that, a few quick words - speed of God comes extremely close to the speed of light →
   - Time Dilation Ratio Required Speed
   - 1 day = 1,000 years ~99.9999999996% of speed of light
   - 1 day = 50,000 years   ~99.99999999999985% of speed of light
   - If we accept this calculation, then Angel's speed is more than the speed of Allah, indicating that Angels have more capability than the All-Potent Allah

2. And for the second, please see the calculation on the next page

Conclusion:
Even if we accept this concept, we must admit that Allah's capabilities are limited by the universal constant – the speed of light. Thus, He cannot be omnipotent.

Please rate this Conclusion:

Section 5 – Islam
Questions from Muslims

Calculation examples given below:

First, when I performed this calculation for 1000 years, I was astonished by the immediate results, which show that the Quran accurately represents the actual speed of light. However, upon further investigation, I realized that it was more of a coincidence than a deliberate effort.

According to **special relativity**, time slows down for objects moving at speeds close to the speed of light. This is called **time dilation**. The time experienced by a fast-moving observer (**proper time, t'**) compared to the time experienced by someone at rest (**t**) is given by:

$$t' = \frac{t}{\gamma}, \quad \text{where } \gamma = \frac{1}{\sqrt{1 - v^2/c^2}}$$

You want:

- $t = 1000$ years $= 365,000$ days
- $t' = 1$ day

Solving:

$$\frac{t}{t'} = \gamma = \frac{365,000}{1} = 365,000$$

Now solve for v:

$$\gamma = \frac{1}{\sqrt{1 - v^2/c^2}} = 365,000 \Rightarrow \sqrt{1 - v^2/c^2} = \frac{1}{365,000} \Rightarrow 1 - v^2/c^2 = \left(\frac{1}{365,000}\right)^2$$

$$v^2/c^2 = 1 - \left(\frac{1}{365,000}\right)^2 \Rightarrow v \approx c \cdot \left(1 - \frac{1}{2 \cdot (365,000)^2}\right)$$

That Allah was moving with almost the speed of light. That means you'd need to move at a speed:

Very, very close to the speed of light ($\approx 0.99999999999625 * c$)
That is about **299,792,458 m/s**

Whereas the speed of light is = 299,792,458 m/s

Objective Analysis of God

Earth Time Passed (days)	Lorentz Factor ($\gamma = t/t'$)	Required Speed (% of c)	Speed (m/s)
5 days	5	97.98%	293,228,745 m/s
10 days	10	99.50%	298,496,241 m/s
20 days	20	99.88%	299,416,224 m/s
50 days	50	99.98%	299,716,970 m/s
100 days	100	100.00%	299,782,245 m/s
1,000 days	1,000	100.00%	299,791,831 m/s
50,000 days	50,000	100.00%	299,792,457.99 m/s

Section 5 – Islam
Questions from Muslims

Question:
Black holes obliterate stars

M79

Analysis and background:
77:8: "When the stars are obliterated..."
Claim: Ayat is pointing to black holes, as black holes can obliterate stars, and stars collapse into black holes.

This is another example where translators and scholars utilize the complexity of the Arabic language to shape the sayings of the Quran in a way that makes Quranic verses appear to define fresh concepts verified by the latest science.

The word طُمِسَتْ can have multiple meanings, such as extinguished, obliterated, or dimmed. There is a clear difference in what was chosen by many originators' translators
- Ibn Khateer took: *"Then, when the stars lose their light"*
- Mouddudi took: *"When, then the start becomes dim"*
- Sahih International:- "*So when the stars are obliterated*"
- Yusuf Ali:-"*Then when the stars become dim;*"
- Pickthall:-"*When the stars are put out;*"
- Dr. Ghali (Muhammad Mahmoud Ghali): "*So, when the stars are obliterated,*"
- Mohsin Khan: -----"*So when the stars are extinguished;*"
Genetic Inheritance

Here, it is clear that the majority of translators have not taken the word, which will lead to translation as pointing to black holes.

Conclusion:
This verse does not point to the existence of black holes

Please rate this Conclusion:

Pg. 449
My-OAG.com

Objective Analysis of God

Question: The Pyramids of Egypt and Herman	M80

Analysis and background:
28:38 – *"And Pharaoh said, "O eminent ones, I have not known you to have a god other than me. Then ignite for me, O Haman, [a fire] upon the clay and make for me a tower that I may look at the God of Moses. And indeed, I do think he is among the liars."*

This verse portrays Pharaoh as arrogantly challenging the existence of Moses' God, instructing his minister Haman to construct a tower—presumably to ascend and confront the divine. However, this account raises several historical and archaeological concerns. There is no evidence in Egyptian records of a figure named Haman associated with Pharaoh or any major construction projects. The name "Haman" appears in the biblical book of Esther, where he is a Persian official under King Ahasuerus—not an Egyptian—and separated by centuries from the time of Moses.

The Great Pyramid of Giza and other monumental structures were built around 2600 BCE, during Egypt's Old Kingdom. Moses, however, is traditionally placed in the New Kingdom period, around 1300–1200 BCE—a gap of over a thousand years. This makes any connection between the Quranic tower and the pyramids chronologically implausible.

Additionally, there is no record of baked clay bricks being used in the construction of the pyramids. The pyramids were built primarily from limestone and granite, not fired bricks.

Islamic scholars generally interpret the tower not as a reference to the pyramids, but as a symbolic act of Pharaoh's arrogance—a metaphorical attempt to challenge divine authority. Still, the inclusion of Haman in this Egyptian context has led many critics to suggest a historical conflation, possibly merging elements from Biblical and Persian traditions into a single narrative.

Conclusion: This claim is fabricated, with no relation to actual verses in the Quran or historical facts; it merely attempts to match one unrelated event with another.	Please rate this Conclusion:

Section 5 – Islam
Questions from Muslims

M81

Question:
Sperms originating from where?

Analysis and background:
86:6-7:- *"He was created from a fluid, emerging from between the backbone and the ribs."*

Here, the verses are saying that "He (man) is created from a fluid, emerging from between the backbone (ṣulb) and the ribs (tarā'ib)." Now we know that the human sperm does not originate from any place close to the one mentioned in the Quran.

Greek and Hippocratic Embryology (c. 5th–4th century BCE): Greek physicians, including Hippocrates and later Galen (2nd century CE), significantly influenced medical theory well into the Islamic Golden Age. Their texts were translated into Syriac and later Arabic.
- Hippocrates wrote about semen originating from the whole body, particularly the brain and spinal marrow. He claimed that it "flows from the brain down the spinal column and through the bones," vaguely mirrors the Quranic language of something *"emerging from between the backbone and ribs."*
- Galen also described semen as originating from blood and having a connection to the spinal cord and nerves.

Early Greek medical ideas about the life fluid emerging from the spinal or upper body region may have influenced medical knowledge in Arabia.

This could have happened through cultural transmission, particularly in areas like Yemen, Hijaz, and Syria, where Arab Christians and Jews lived.

Conclusion:
The above proves that God did not know where the semen came from, but it also shows a possibility that the Quran's source of knowledge, as Prophet Mohammed said, was what the Greeks believed.

Please rate this Conclusion:

Objective Analysis of God

Question: People of the cave's year calculation	M82

Analysis and background:
18:25:- *"And they remained in their cave for three hundred years, and were exceeded by nine"*
18:26:- *"Allah knows how long they remained. To Him is [knowledge of] the unseen of the heavens and the earth. How clear of sight is He and keen of hearing! They have no protector besides Him, and He shares not His legislation with anyone."*
Claim: If you calculate the number of days of a solar year and then convert those days to a Lunar year, it comes to about 309 years. So, the Quran calculated Solar years in 1400.

Few aspects of this:
1. Here, it is strange that Allah is calculating years in Solar and days in the Lunar Calendar
2. Calculation comes close to 9, but it is 9 years and 4 months
   - There are 365 days in the solar Calendar
   - 354 x 300 = 109500
   - Converting into Lunar year which has 354 days = 109500/354 = 309.32 = 300+9 years and ~4 months
3. Also, check the next verse, where Allah says you cannot know and only Allah has the correct knowledge.

4. Plus, Solar-Lunar years were known knowledge at that time
   - The solar calendar—a calendar based on the Earth's revolution around the Sun—was developed by several ancient civilizations, thousands of years before Islam:
   - Ancient Egyptians (~3000 BCE): One of the first to create a solar calendar with 365 days based on the Sun and the Nile's seasonal cycles.
   - Babylonians and Greeks also tracked solar and lunar cycles, often combining them in lunisolar calendars
   - Julian Calendar (45 BCE): Introduced by Julius Caesar, the solar year was made more precise by introducing the leap year.
   - Gregorian Calendar (1582 CE): A reform of the Julian calendar, it is the modern solar calendar used globally today.

- Pre-Islamic Arabs were aware of the difference between the lunar year (354 days) and the solar year (365 days), and they had a practice to adjust for it.
- Intercalation (Nasi'):- They practiced a form of intercalation (called Nasi') to synchronize the lunar calendar with the solar year, so that seasonal events like Hajj would stay in the same season. This involved inserting an extra month every few years, similar to what lunisolar calendars do (such as the Hebrew calendar), and this was forbidden by verse 9:37: "Indeed, the postponing [of a sacred month] is an increase in disbelief..."

Given that these events occur outside the direct intervention of Allah, it's puzzling how some Muslim scholars assert that Quranic calculations align with various calendars. It often feels like a retrospective attempt to shape facts to fit a predetermined narrative.

Conclusion: Adding "plus 9" while converting Solar days into lunar days was common knowledge of that time.	Please rate this Conclusion:

Objective Analysis of God

Question: Matching numbers with words in the Quran	M83

Analysis and background:
On social media, you may have come across regular clips that explain how words mentioned in the Quran align with present-day knowledge, which was not available at the time of the Quran's revelation. This question is one that I will try to address in a single response.

First, please note that if you Google or use ChatGPT, they will provide the same information because their sources are the internet, and they are programmed to count the words in the Quran.

However, we have numerous websites and apps that perform the actual word counting and can provide you with the correct answer. The following are a few websites:

1. ParsQuran - http://www.parsquran.com/eng/
2. Quran Analysis Word Frequency tool – (easiest one) https://qurananalysis.com/analysis/index.php?lang=EN
3. Quran Word Counter by AL Quran Lab - https://www.alquranlab.com
4. Masjid Tucson Quran Word Count tools - https://www.masjidtucson.org/quran
5. Quranic Arabic Corpus - https://corpus.quran.com/

The list is very long – you can verify using any sources or doing actual counting, but please see some of the examples of how this is manipulated:

Conclusion: This false information has been disproved by many aspects, indicating that there is no miracle of numbers in the Quran.	Please rate this Conclusion:

Section 5 – Islam
Questions from Muslims

Question:
Cracks in Sky or Falling Sky

M84

Analysis and background:
At least at two places in the Quran, Allah has talked about his glory that the sky He has created does not have any cracks:
50:6 – *"Have they not looked at the sky above them—how We constructed it and adorned it, and how it has no rifts?"*
67:3 - *"He who created the seven heavens one above another; You see no disharmony in the creation of the Most Merciful. So return your vision to the sky, do you see any breaks?"*

The verses describe the sky as a flawless, solid structure with no cracks and refer to "seven heavens" seamlessly layered above one another. However, modern science reveals that the sky is not a solid dome, but instead Earth's atmosphere, which gradually transitions into space, and that there are not seven distinct heavens.
The ancient image of perfect, layered heavens does not align with our current understanding of the atmosphere or the universe, which contains no solid roof or neatly separated layers, as implied in these verses.

These verses reflect especially pre-modern, anthropocentric conceptions of the sky and cosmos as layered, solid, perfect structures. Modern science, reliant on empirical observation, demonstrates that the sky and space are neither constructed nor neatly layered, nor are they flawless in the idiomatic sense.

In at least two places, Allah has mentioned the falling Sky.
17:19 – *"... "Or you make the sky fall upon us in pieces, as you assert, or you bring Allah and the angels before [us] face to face..."*
34:9 - *"Have they not considered what is before them and what is behind them of the heaven and earth? If we choose to, we could cause the earth to swallow them or let fragments from the sky fall upon them. Indeed, that is a sign for every servant who turns [to Allah]."*
Verses 17:92 and 34:9 suggest a solid sky that could collapse or the earth swallowing people—reflecting ancient cosmology, not modern science. The sky isn't solid, and natural events like sinkholes or quakes aren't supernatural. Taken literally, these verses contain scientific inaccuracies.

Objective Analysis of God

Conclusion: These verses reflect a portrayal of the creator whose knowledge aligns with the prevailing beliefs of that era. Proving that these are words of the Creator	Please rate this Conclusion:

Section 5 – Islam
Questions from Muslims

Question:
Hanging Stars

M85

Analysis and background:
37:6 - *"Indeed, We have adorned the nearest heaven with an adornment of stars"*
41:12 - *"Then He completed them as seven heavens in two days and inspired in each heaven its command. And we adorned the nearest heaven with lamps as protection. That is the determination of the Exalted in Might, the Knowing."*

These verses describe the creation of the heavens, highlighting that the nearest heaven is adorned with lights often interpreted as stars or planets. From a scientific perspective, these verses contain inaccuracies. The depiction of a fixed, completed creation achieved in just "two days" contradicts the scientific understanding that the universe formed gradually over billions of years through dynamic processes.

Furthermore, the portrayal of the heavens as discrete, orderly layers with protective lights reflects an ancient geocentric cosmology. In contrast, modern astronomy reveals a vast, expanding universe without distinct celestial layers and no central point, such as Earth. The concept of stars or planets serving as "protection" also does not align with current astrophysics, where stars are massive nuclear bodies and planets orbit stars within galaxies, but do not function as protective shields.

Consequently, these verses align more with pre-modern theological views rather than with the empirical, evolving model of the cosmos that modern science provides.

Conclusion: God is narrating what a general human of that age saw, and not what these stars actually are; the creators of stars should have known better.	Please rate this Conclusion:

Objective Analysis of God

Question:	
Basic Ingredients of Humans / Life	**M86**

Analysis and background:
The Quran narrates multiple ways in which Allah created Humans or life. The following tables show the variation of the ingredients and how many times the same concept is repeated in the Quran:

Number	Starting ingriedenats	Verses
1	Semen	16:4, 75:37, 76:2, 80:19
2	Nothing	19:9, 19:67
3	Water	21:30. 24:45, 25:54
4	A clot of congealed blood	96:2
5	Base Material	79:39
6	Earth	20:55
7	Dust	3:59, 22:5, 31:11, 40:67
8	Mud	15:26, 15:28, 15:33
9	Clay (or its base)	6:2, 7:12, 17:61, 18:76, 21:7, 23:12
10	Sticky Clay	37:11
11	Ringing Clay	55:64
12	Sounding Clay	15:26, 15:28, 15:33

12 methods to create one Adam? Additionally, notice numbers 2, 8, and 12 are: Nothing, Mud, and Sounding clay. It appears that when narrating ingredients close to each other, Allah was consistent, yet He occasionally forgot what He had said before, which is more characteristic of human behavior.

Conclusion:	Please rate this Conclusion:
Allah has mentioned at least 12 different types of basic ingredients; either He cannot decide or, just like many humans, He forgot what He had said earlier.	

Section 5 – Islam
Questions from Muslims

Question:
Where is Allah – now (known history)

M87

Analysis and background:
8:17 – *"You did not kill them, but it was Allah who killed them. And you [Prophet], when you threw [dust], it was not you who threw, but Allah threw so that He might test the believers with a good test; indeed, Allah is Hearing, Knowing."*

This verse highlights logical issues, where actions by humans—like fighting in battle or throwing dust—are attributed directly to Allah, raising questions about agency, responsibility, and causality. The verse's language challenges the concepts of free will and individual accountability, suggesting that God is ultimately behind all human actions, which creates philosophical difficulties regarding justice and the rational evaluation of deeds.

When this idea is extended to historical claims of divine intervention—like the miraculous story of the birds (ababil) stopping the attack of elephants on the Kaaba (21:69, 11:50-83, 26:63, 2:65, 7:166, etc)more examples —it becomes apparent that such unmistakable, protective interventions are absent in recorded modern history.

Despite countless instances of horrible suffering and atrocities against innocents, especially children, we do not observe clear, direct divine intercessions of this kind today. This absence deepens the logical and moral questions around claims of selective or exceptional intervention and the broader issue of why, if such acts were possible or real, they are not witnessed in the face of ongoing extreme injustice and suffering.

Conclusion: In the stories stated in the Quran, Allah seems to be very active and regularly participating in oppressing evil and oppressors. Still, He cannot be seen anywhere after that, in known and validated history.	Please rate this Conclusion:

Objective Analysis of God

Question:
The Quran correcting itself

M88

Analysis and background:
New verses replaced some existing verses; these are referred to as

Abrogation (Naskh). Following is the list of such possible verses: Some other commonly cited examples:

It is a long list; the following are only a selection; some scholars, such as Ibn Salama, counted as many as 238 cases.

Abrogated Verse (Mansūkh)	Abrogator Verse (Nāsikh)	Subject (Summary)
2:115	2:144	The direction of prayer (Qibla) changed from Jerusalem to Mecca
2:180	4:7, 4:11	Inheritance rulings: bequest for parents/kin abrogated by fixed shares
2:183, 2:184	2:185	Fasting rules updated for Ramadan
2:217	9:36	Fighting in the sacred months (allowed after abrogation)
2:240	2:234	Mourning period for widows reduced from one year to 4 months and 10 days
3:102	64:16	Fear Allah as you can (instead of "as He should be feared")
4:15	24:2	Punishment for adultery: from confinement to flogging
4:33	8:75	Inheritance for those "your right hand was pledged to" abrogated by blood kin as heirs.
5:2	9:36	Violation of sacred months—allowed due to fighting orders
5:42	5:49	Discretion in judging between Jews—made mandatory to judge by divine law
5:106	65:2	Bequest witnesses—changed to divorce witness procedure
8:65	8:66	Battle ratios for fighting unbelievers have been reduced
9:41	9:91, 9:122, 24:61	Obligation to go to war clarified/exempted for some
24:3	24:32	Marriage restrictions for adulterers eased
24:58	24:59	Privacy rules for children/servants before adulthood
33:52	33:50	Prophet's marriage restrictions modified
58:12	58:13	Charity before a private consultation with the Prophet was cancelled
73:2	73:20	Night prayer obligation eased

And the list goes on, like some other commonly cited examples: 2:109: Forgiveness for People of the Book abrogated by 9:29 ("Fight those who do not believe...")

2:190, 2:191, 2:192, 2:256: Early restrictions on fighting/compulsion abrogated by 9:5 ("Verse of the Sword")

2:219, 4:43: Gradual prohibition of wine, entirely prohibited by 5:90

The most commonly referenced verse that is said to abrogate is 9:5 ("Verse of the Sword"), which some claim abrogates more than 100 peaceful or restrictive verses relating to fighting and coexistence. Other abrogations involve dietary laws, waiting periods, and social regulations.

The question arises here: why would an all-knowing Allah need to correct what He has said earlier? Some of these changes are minor, but since they come from Allah as His command, they should not even have the slightest difference.

Conclusion: These abrogations show that the commands are not coming from an all-knowing and all-perfect Allah.	Please rate this Conclusion:

Objective Analysis of God

Question: Burden in life and Suicides	M89

Analysis and background:

2:286: *"On no soul doth Allah Place a burden greater than it can bear...."*

However, the reality we see in the world today appears to contradict this statement in a very literal and painful way.

Globally, around 720,000 to 746,000 people die by suicide each year — that's about 2,000 suicides every single day, or roughly one every 43 seconds. If we take the verse at face value, these deaths suggest that many individuals were burdened beyond what they could bear. In other words, their suffering, pain, or life circumstances exceeded their capacity to endure, pushing them to end their own lives.

If every 43 seconds someone dies by suicide, it can be argued that this verse is effectively proven false dozens of times each minute — at least 45 times per half-hour — in the real world. The existence of such widespread and ongoing self-inflicted death strongly implies that some human beings face pressures, traumas, and mental states that surpass their ability to cope.

Seen in this light, rather than being a universal truth, Quran 2:286 might represent a moral or emotional comfort statement that does not withstand measurable human experience. The evidence from global suicide rates shows that some burdens are indeed too significant for some people to bear, making the verse's claim factually false if read literally.

Conclusion: This raises questions about Allah's knowledge of the burdens and stress an individual can bear. It seems that His claimed capabilities do not reflect His own limits.	Please rate this Conclusion:

Section 5 – Islam
Questions from Muslims

Question:
Stories in the Quran

M90

Analysis and background:
Pre-Islamic Stories in the Quran
Many stories and motifs found in the Quran have origins in the pre-Islamic world. There are about 50 stories of prophets and other figures, and in terms of verses, these stories comprise about 30% of the Quran's total verses.

All these stories, in one form or another, have been taken from either the Bible or were part of the cultures in the areas where Prophet Mohammed spent his days. In most of the stories, the narration has been changed slightly, but one can still find an obvious link, especially in the stories of prophets with names. Strangely, God could not come up with new stories and guidance to teach humans the morals, as the older version failed to make any impact. Additionally, one can read the stories to discover the teachings and moral values, although they may appear somewhat limited in scope. So, the Quran is the old product in "new packaging."

Other aspects include the length of these stories, which Mullah mentions contain teachings and morals.

Another aspect is the length of coverage given to these stories in the last message, as mentioned earlier, about 30% of the Quran consists only of Praises of God. Now we realize that about 32% has been assigned to stories that were already known to the people of the time (or present-day humans would have obtained those from earlier resources, such as the Bible). This is not an effective way to convey the final message to humans.

Conclusion:
Allah adds old stories and gives them so much importance, despite knowing they have had no impact on humans, which shows that Allah "has not learnt from his earlier mistakes."

Please rate this Conclusion:

My-OAG.com

Objective Analysis of God

Concluding Religion Topic:

Towards the end of my submissions on religions, I will provide my opinion and state what I have concluded after going through the same process.

> *My premise was to analyze YAHWEH, GOD, and ALLAH and determine, in my opinion, whether these concepts can be considered valid, primarily based on the texts and fundamental teachings of the respective religions. After performing this Objective Analysis, my number comes close to about 9.5 and I concluded that the so-called All-Knowing, All-Merciful, and Omnipotent Abrahamic God, as described in the Holy Books and Scriptures, probably does not exist. On the other hand, I also see a few very profound pieces of evidence in nature that are difficult to explain by theories like evolution, and these appear to be the result of an intelligent design. Religion takes these examples and jumps directly to their favourite God, without linking them to God.*

Between these two extremes, I consider that the facts are much closer to the concept of a natural God and further away from the Abrahamic religious God, which has evolved.

In the following pages, we will discuss the possible and probable chemical and biological processes. In the final remarks, we will address the possibilities regarding God.

Life on Earth began about 3.6 billion years ago, whereas our known history spans approximately 4,000 years, which is roughly 0.000111% of the total time. Many unknown things could have happened during this period, which we may discover later. So, I would say that only 3-4 major interjections can explain the whole development of Humans and remove the Abrahamic God.

Objective Analysis of God

The following lines aim to explain the entire process of world formation. This could have only 3-4 fill-in-the-blanks, which someone will fill in at the appropriate time.

Before closing this topic, I'd like to highlight one positive aspect of religion: its ability to create coherence and community, something we need as social beings. Like any group, its value depends on how it is managed and how it contributes to the well-being of its members and society as a whole. The same applies to religious groups—and you are the best judge within your local context.

Religion's social benefit: A Platform for Human Connection

Religion has been vital in human societies for centuries, serving as a spiritual guide and a robust social platform. One of its most significant benefits is its ability to unite people, fostering interaction, shared values, and a sense of belonging. In an increasingly fragmented world, religion offers a space where individuals can connect, collaborate, and discover a shared purpose.

Building Community and Belonging

Religious institutions—such as churches, mosques, temples, and synagogues—serve as gathering places where people from diverse backgrounds come together to share common beliefs and values. These spaces foster social interaction, enabling individuals to form meaningful relationships. Weekly services, festivals, and prayer groups create regular opportunities for people to engage, reducing loneliness and fostering a sense of community.

Encouraging Moral and Social Values

Religions often promote ethical principles such as compassion, honesty, and charity. These shared values create a framework for social harmony, encouraging cooperation and mutual respect. Many religious traditions emphasize the importance of helping the less fortunate, leading to organized charity work, food drives, and community support initiatives that benefit society.

Providing Emotional and Psychological Support

During difficult times, religious communities offer emotional comfort and practical assistance. Whether through counselling, prayer groups, or a network of supportive individuals, religion provides a safety net for those facing hardship. This communal support strengthens mental well-being and resilience.

Facilitating Cultural and Intergenerational Bonds

Religious traditions often include rituals, stories, and celebrations that have been passed down through generations. These practices preserve cultural heritage while allowing younger and older members to bond over shared experiences.

Conclusion

While religion is often discussed in terms of faith and spirituality, its role as a social platform is equally important. By fostering connections, promoting shared values, and offering support, religion helps build cohesive and compassionate communities. In a world where isolation is a growing concern, the social benefits of religion remain invaluable.

Section 6

Different Roads

Section- 6 – Different Roads

Atheism - Where evolution failed me

I will not discuss alternatives (Different Roads) to the destination in any detail. Considering the volume of this book, I will only touch the tip of the iceberg.

Before moving on, let's set some boundaries for the terms we generally use in similar discussions, as there is a spectrum of belief systems between Religious beliefs and atheism:

- **Theism**: Belief in the existence of at least one god.
- **Atheism**: Atheism is the lack of belief in gods or deities, ranging from simple disbelief to the conviction that no gods exist.
- **Naturalism:** holds that everything arises from natural causes and laws. Believing that life, consciousness, and the universe itself developed through natural processes without invoking miracles or divine intervention
- **Agnosticism**: Neither belief nor disbelief—holding that the existence of gods is unknown or unknowable.
- Scientific Materialism: A stricter form of naturalism that claims matter and energy are the fundamental reality.
- **Secularism:** A political/social stance about keeping religion separate from governance, not the same as atheism.
- **Theory of Evolution:** The theory of evolution, developed by Charles Darwin and others, is a scientific explanation for the diversity of life through natural selection and random variation. It does not directly address the existence of God—only how species develop and change over time

Relationship between the Theory of Evolution and Atheism:
- Evolution challenges literal interpretations of creation stories (e.g., in the Bible or Quran).
- Some atheists embrace evolution as it provides a naturalistic explanation for life, reducing the need to invoke a divine creator.

Objective Analysis of God

- Atheism and Theory of Evolution are two independent phenomena, but as Atheists find refuge in Theory and they consider it as proof of their concept, and Religious believers consider it something that is shaking the very foundation of religious general beliefs, both argue about it.
- This has often caused tension with religious groups, particularly those that hold to creationism or intelligent design.
- Thinkers like Richard Dawkins have argued that evolution makes atheism intellectually satisfying because it explains complexity without God.
- In recent years, as more and more undeniable evidence for the theory has emerged, many so-called broad-minded scholars have started embracing it partially nd are molding their religious beliefs around it.
- So now, not all religious people reject evolution. Many religious groups (including Catholicism, parts of Protestantism, and some Muslim scholars) accept theistic evolution, seeing evolution as the method through which God creates.
- In a strict sense, Aethism is "The lack of belief in gods or deities." It does not commit to how the universe or humans came to be. So, atheism does not require belief in evolution, the Big Bang, or any specific theory—it only rejects divine involvement.
-

I will try to simplify these and will restrict to what is totally against the Religious beliefs of the belief of All-Knowing, omnipotent, and omnipresent God, who is testing humans and will give individuals the path to go to Heaven or Hell.

For this discussion, I will consider Atheism, supported by the theory of evolution, as it provides an explanation and an alternative to the Abrahamic God.

I will also not go into the "known"– "unknowns" like:
1. The first creator–ultimate cause
2. Consciousness
3. Creation of the First Life form
4. Nature of reality
5. … etc,

I will only discuss what I consider the limitations of the Theory of Evolution, or the concepts that "all is happening by itself while adapting to the environment.".s

I will provide only a few examples from the known world that defy the logic of evolution, specifically the concept that the fittest survive or adapt well to their surroundings. I could not figure out why those behaviors or characteristics in animals exist, and how they can develop through general evolution. At present, these few examples point to an "intentionally designed" world.

> *Until now, we were mainly highlighting what does not make sense with the religious God and how the religious institute has (maybe) made a fool out of us. Now we will shift our gears and try to point out what is illogical on the other side (like the Evolution theory)*

Seven (7) Limitations of Evolution

Evolution by natural selection operates within fundamental constraints that limit its ability to achieve specific outcomes or explain all biological phenomena. Evolution excels at explaining adaptation but hits walls when addressing perfection, altruism, sudden complexity, and non-utilitarian traits. Its blind, incremental nature makes it powerful yet limited, shaping life's diversity without intent, foresight, or guarantees of survival. Recognizing these boundaries helps us appreciate where other forces (culture, intelligence, or even metaphysical explanations) might come into play.

Yet we see numerous examples of the following traits, which are limitations of the Evolution process.
Here are the key limitations of evolutionary processes:

1. Evolution is Reactive, Not Proactive

Evolution operates through natural selection, genetic mutations, and environmental pressures—it cannot anticipate future scenarios or plan for unforeseen events. Organisms adapt based on their immediate survival needs, rather than long-term strategies. For example, a species may evolve camouflage to evade current predators, but if a new predator or sudden climate shift emerges, existing traits may become obsolete. This reactive nature means extinction can occur when changes outpace adaptation. Unlike intentional design, evolution is a blind process shaped by randomness and necessity, leaving species vulnerable to unpredictable challenges. While it fosters remarkable diversity, its lack of foresight highlights the fragility of life in a dynamic world.

2. Evolution Lacks Contingency Planning

Evolution is a process driven by immediate survival pressures, not foresight. It cannot build "backup systems" or prepare for hypothetical "what-if" scenarios. Traits develop in response to existing environmental challenges—not future uncertainties. For example, a species may evolve thick fur for cold climates but lack an adaptive failsafe if temperatures rise abruptly. Unlike engineered systems with redundancy (like spare parts or backup circuits), biological traits emerge only when directly favored by selection. Random mutations occasionally provide unexpected advantages, but these are accidental, not preemptive. Consequently, evolution leaves species vulnerable to sudden changes, such as shifts in climate, the emergence of new predators, or the spread of diseases. Its strength lies in adaptability, but its limitation is its inability to anticipate or "plan," making life resilient yet perpetually at the mercy of unpredictable change..

3. The "Good Enough" Problem

Evolution does not produce perfect designs—it favors traits sufficient for survival and reproduction. This leads to functional but flawed structures, such as the human spine (prone to injuries due to our evolutionary shift to bipedalism) or the recurrent laryngeal nerve's inefficient route in giraffes. Unlike an engineer, evolution cannot "fix" suboptimal designs if they don't impede reproduction.

- Issue: Evolution cannot retroactively fix suboptimal traits.
    - Example: Humans evolved upright posture from quadrupedal ancestors, but the spine—originally adapted for horizontal movement—now struggles with vertical weight-bearing. This leads to chronic back pain, herniated discs, and susceptibility to injuries. Evolution favored immediate mobility benefits over long-term structural perfection.

4. The Mystery of Selfless Acts

Kin selection helps explain why animals often sacrifice themselves for their relatives, such as bees dying to protect the hive. But it doesn't fully explain why living beings sometimes go out of their way to help strangers or even members of other species. Consider human philanthropy or instances where animals adopt babies from a completely different species. Since these acts don't bring clear survival or reproductive advantages, they hint that culture, empathy, or other non-Darwinian forces may also play a role in shaping morality...

- Issue: Altruism toward non-relatives lacks clear Darwinian logic.
    - Example: Vampire bats regurgitate blood meals to feed unrelated, starving roost-mates—even when it costs them calories. Reciprocal altruism (helping those who may return favors) explains some behavior, but not why bats often help strangers without a guarantee of repayment.

5. Irreducible Complexity

Some biological structures (e.g., the eye, bacterial flagellum, blood clotting cascade) require multiple interdependent parts. Critics argue that these systems could not evolve through incremental steps, as intermediate stages might offer no survival advantage. While evolutionary biologists propose plausible pathways (e.g., co-option of existing parts), the question remains contentious.

- Issue: The Gradual evolution of complex structures is hard to explain.
    - Example: The vertebrate eye requires the cornea, lens, retina, and optic nerve to function. Critics argue that partial versions (e.g., a retina without a lens) would be useless. However, biologists point to intermediate forms in nature (e.g., light-sensitive patches in flatworms) as evidence of stepwise evolution.

6. Non-Adaptive Traits

Not all traits arise from survival needs. Human capacities, such as art, music, and abstract mathematics, provide no obvious reproductive edge. Did these emerge as byproducts of other adaptations (e.g., increased brain complexity), or do they hint at

other evolutionary drivers, such as sexual selection or cultural evolution?
- Issue: Some traits seem to defy survival logic.
    - Example: The peacock's ornate tail hampers escape from predators and requires energy to maintain. Its sole purpose is sexual selection—females prefer flashy mates, showing that evolution can prioritize reproduction over survival.
- Issue: Evolution cannot preemptively adapt to novel threats.
    - Example: Sea turtles mistake plastic bags for jellyfish (their prey). Their instincts, shaped over millennia, offer no defense against this human-made hazard. Evolution lacks a mechanism to "prepare" for such rapid environmental changes.

7. Universals' Moral

Many societies share innate moral instincts (e.g., fairness, disgust at injustice). While some argue these evolved for group cohesion, their universality and emotional depth suggest influences beyond mere survival logic, possibly pointing to a deeper cognitive or spiritual layer.

We have discussed the development of morals and society's survivors' "collective wisdom," which explains at least this aspect of evolution's limitations, so we will not delve further into this aspect of evolution.

Examples: Where nature defies the Evolution process

Now we will go into further general examples

1. **Baby Iguanas vs. Racer Snakes** - BBC documentary series "Planet Earth II" (2016), specifically Episode 1: "Islands." - Galápagos Islands (Fernandina Island)
   - Marine iguanas – Newly hatched babies must cross dangerous terrain to reach the shore. Galápagos racer snakes – Fast-moving predators that hunt by detecting movement. The documentary captures an incredible survival strategy. As baby iguanas sprint from their nests towards the ocean, they race to the rocky shore to escape snakes. However, when snakes get too close, the hatchlings instinctively freeze completely, as snakes primarily detect prey through motion. The snakes slither right past motionless iguanas, unable to see them. Once the snakes pass, the iguanas bolt again toward safety.
   - In an Evolutionary sense, how come newly hatched babies know the limitations of the snakes by birth, where there is no mechanism to develop this detailed knowledge into genes, while surviving the snakes over the ages?

2. **Salmon Reproduction seems "suicidal**
   Pacific salmon after spawning undergo rapid physiological breakdown (organ failure, skin rotting) and die. Evolution favors traits that maximize reproduction, yet salmon invest so heavily in a single reproductive event that it often results in their death.
   - Evolution is based on survival, and this behavior negates Evolution. One argument presented is that this "Semelparity" ensures that nutrients from their corpses are passed on to their offspring. Still, the strategy seems extreme when iteroparity (multiple breeding cycles) is observed in other fish. Additionally, it is unclear how this could have been genetically coded over numerous generations, a period that could have led to the extinction of the species.

Objective Analysis of God

3. **Male Praying Mantis Self-Sacrifice During Mating**
   Many mantis species (e.g., Mantis religiosa), while mating, females often decapitate and eat males during copulation, while males continue mating even after decapitation (nerves in the abdomen prolong sperm transfer).
   - How could a trait that eliminates the male's future reproduction persist? While some suggest that the nutritional boost to the female increases egg production, indirectly favoring the male's genes, can this behavior be coded into the genes logically

4. **Ant Colonies with "Useless" Workers**
   Some Pheidole ant colonies produce "super soldiers" with giant heads, which are rarely used in defense.
   - Considering evolution, energy-intensive traits (useless ants) should be discarded if they don't enhance survival, but it has not

5. **Suicidal Pollination Strategy of the Amazonian Giant Water Lily**
   One of nature's most dramatic examples of extreme coevolution. The Plant (the world's largest water lily, with pads over 3m wide) and an Insect Pollinator, a scarab beetle, pull this through. Plants lure the beetle by opening their huge, white flowers at dusk, releasing an intense, fruity fragrance that generates heat (thermogenesis) and attracts beetles. The flower's petals form a *temporary trap*, with downward-pointing hairs preventing escape. The plant keeps the beetle prisoner for ~24 hours, maintaining a warm microclimate (up to 10°C above ambient temperature). The beetle becomes covered in pollen while struggling inside the male-phase flower. After 24 hours, the flower changes to the female phase on the second night and releases the pollen-covered beetle. Exhausted and often injured from escape attempts, many beetles die shortly after.
   - The Evolutionary Paradox is why the beetle has not developed a genetic knowledge about its death and developed some mechanism, as it is a case of borderline parasitism—the beetle gains no nectar reward, and the physical toll often proves fatal.

Section- 6 – Different Roads
Examples: Where nature defies the Evolution process

6. **The Orchid's Deadly Deception: A Bee's One-Way Journey to Death**
My favorite - Featured in ***The Private Life of Plants*** **(BBC, 1995)**

In the steamy depths of the Amazon rainforest, an orchid lures its unsuspecting pollinator into a trap with no escape. This is the story of Catasetum, a cunning orchid that tricks male euglossine bees into a fatal mission that ends in their demise but ensures the orchid's survival. As dawn breaks, the male Catasetum orchid unfurls its waxy petals and releases an intoxicating fragrance, mimicking the scent female bees use to attract mates. Drawn in by this irresistible perfume, male euglossine bees—known as "perfume collectors"—descend upon the flower, eager to douse themselves in the alluring aroma. The moment the bee lands, the orchid strikes. In a burst of movement, it hurls its pollen sacs onto the bee's back with such force that the insect is often knocked sideways. Disoriented but still alive, the bee struggles to recover, now unwittingly carrying the orchid's genetic payload.

- Unlike typical flowers, male and female Catasetum orchids grow at different heights, (Male Flowers: Grow at 1–3 meters (3–10 feet) above ground, low enough for bees to easily spot and land on, while Female Flowers, tower much higher, nestled 5–10 meters (16–33 feet) up in the canopy, often obscured by leaves.) The pollen-laden bee flies upward - a behavior hardwired into euglossine bees, which associate height with better mating opportunities—going straight to the female orchid. The female flower's entrance is a tight, slippery chamber, designed to imprison the bee. As it thrashes in panic, the pollen is scraped off, fertilizing the orchid. Exhausted and battered, many bees never break free. They die inside the flower.
- Guaranteed Pollination: The orchid ensures cross-pollination by attracting bees to move from low (male) to high (female) flowers. If the female flowers grew at the same height, the bees might learn to avoid them. But hidden in the canopy and with a different appearance, the trap stays lethal.
- It is tough to imagine that this whole process of specialized flowers and bees' behavior and size could have evolved through evolution. To me, it is a very innovative and cruel design.

Objective Analysis of God

7. **Male Octopus Self-Sacrifice**
   Contradiction: Programmed death after mating
   - Example: Male octopuses enter a state of self-destruction after mating, stopping eating and slowly dying. While this ensures resources for offspring, it eliminates potential future reproduction opportunities, which seems counter to evolutionary fitness. The trait persists because it's genetically hardwired despite its apparent inefficiency.

8. **Infanticide in Langur Monkeys**
   Contradiction: Killing of one's own species' offspring
   - Example: Male langurs systematically kill infants when taking over a new troop. While this brings females back into estrus (benefiting the male's genes), it destroys existing genetic material - a paradox where short-term reproductive strategy conflicts with long-term group survival.

9. **Worker Bee Sterility**
   Contradiction: Voluntary reproductive sacrifice
   - Example: Worker honeybees are genetically capable of reproduction but remain sterile, devoting their lives to supporting the queen's offspring. While kin selection explains this through shared genes, the complete abandonment of personal reproduction contradicts individual evolutionary advantage.

10. **Same-Sex Behavior in Animals**
    Contradiction: Non-reproductive sexual behavior
    - Example: Over 1,500 species exhibit homosexual behavior (penguins forming same-sex pairs, male fruit flies courting other males). These energy-intensive behaviors don't contribute to direct reproduction, challenging the notion that all evolved behaviors must enhance fitness.

11. **Humans' backup "organs"**
    The human body has several built-in "backup systems" or redundancies—components or functions that can compensate when others fail or are damaged. Here are 5–6 examples where the body has a **distinct backup by design**:
    - **Kidneys – Paired Organs with Full Redundancy**

- A person can donate one kidney and live an everyday life with the remaining one.
- Backup mechanism: Each kidney contains about 1 million nephrons (filtering units). One kidney alone can perform the full function of removing waste, balancing fluids and electrolytes, and regulating blood pressure.
- Clinical evidence: Many kidney donors experience no long-term health issues, and patients with one functional kidney (e.g., due to injury or disease) often have no significant health limitations.

12. Lungs – Bilateral Organs with Partial Functional Redundancy
- After a pneumonectomy (surgical removal of one lung, e.g., due to cancer), the remaining lung expands and increases its oxygen exchange efficiency.
- Backup mechanism: The alveoli (air sacs) in the remaining lung may increase in number or size, and the breathing rate may increase slightly to maintain oxygenation.
- Real-world case: People who undergo a single-lung transplant or live with one lung can engage in moderate physical activity and lead relatively everyday lives.

13. Liver – Regenerative Redundancy
- In living donor liver transplants, a segment of the liver (as little as 30%) is transplanted into a recipient. Both donor and recipient livers regenerate to near full size.
- Backup mechanism: The liver's hepatocytes (liver cells) divide and grow back to compensate for lost mass, often within weeks.
- Real-world case: A healthy liver can recover from damage due to partial resection, drug toxicity, or viral infections like hepatitis, thanks to its regenerative capability.

14. Brain – Functional and Pathway Redundancy
- After a stroke in the left hemisphere (typically responsible for language), the right hemisphere can sometimes compensate, especially in children or with therapy.
- Backup mechanism: Cortical reorganization Occurs When Nearby or opposite hemisphere areas take over functions.

Objective Analysis of God

- Plasticity: Neural circuits rewire to restore lost functions like speech or motor control.
- Real-world case: In hemispherectomy (removal of one cerebral hemisphere, usually in children with severe epilepsy), many patients regain speech, mobility, and even reading skills over time.

15. Adrenal Glands – Paired Hormone-Producing Organs
- If one adrenal gland is surgically removed (e.g., due to a tumour), the remaining gland typically increases hormone production to maintain normal endocrine balance.
- Backup mechanism: The remaining gland compensates by upregulating cortisol, aldosterone, and adrenaline secretion.
- Clinical relevance: Patients post-adrenalectomy often maintain normal hormone levels without needing lifelong hormone replacement, unless both glands are removed.

16. Muscles and Motor Control – Distributed and Synergistic Systems
- In foot drop (inability to lift the front of the foot due to nerve injury), other muscles (like the hip flexors) can partially compensate for foot lifting.
- Backup mechanism: Synergistic muscles (e.g., hamstrings and glutes for hip movement) work together to share the load.
- Neural plasticity helps reroute motor commands via alternate motor neurons or muscle groups.
- Rehabilitation: After spinal cord injuries or strokes, patients often regain function using alternate muscle groups, aided by physical therapy.

17. Circulatory System – Vascular Redundancy (Collateral Circulation)
- In patients with gradual coronary artery blockage, tiny new blood vessels (collaterals) form to bypass the blocked area.
- Backup mechanism: Over time, these vessels enlarge and provide alternative ways for blood to reach the heart tissue.
- Clinical relevance: Due to robust collateral circulation, some patients survive major artery blockages with few symptoms.

Section- 6 – Different Roads
Examples: Where nature defies the Evolution process
And my favorite

18. Visible arteries at the back of your hand

Let's examine the dorsal hand (back of your hand), which features a network of arteries that ensures a continuous blood supply to the fingers even if one vessel is damaged. This redundancy is achieved through anastomoses (interconnected blood vessels) and a well-organized contingency system—like nature's built-in backup.

The visible arteries on your hand are part of a resilient vascular network. Through redundancy, dual supply, and interconnection, your hand ensures that critical areas, such as the fingers, remain perfused even if one path fails—an elegant, natural form of contingency planning.

Visible Arteries on the Back of the Hand: Overview
- Without going into medical terms, you can see and analyze that the artery system shown has multiple backups at different levels.

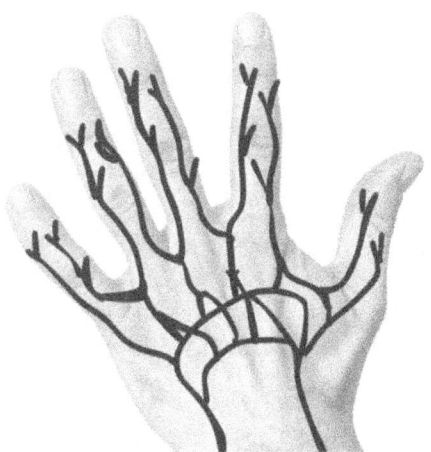

The whole human body is filled with examples of backups and contingency planning; here are a few more examples. Here are four other anatomical systems in the human body with built-in contingency and backup mechanisms, like the vascular system of the hand:

Objective Analysis of God

19. **Circle of Willis (Brain Blood Supply)**
    - Function: Ensures uninterrupted blood flow to the brain.
    - Structure: A circular network of arteries (anterior cerebral, posterior cerebral, internal carotid, etc.) at the base of the brain.
    - Contingency: If one artery is blocked (e.g., stroke), others can reroute blood to maintain cerebral perfusion.

20. **Coronary Artery Collateral Circulation (Heart)**
    - Function: Supplies oxygen-rich blood to the heart muscle.
    - Structure: Small arteries that interconnect major coronary vessels.
    - Contingency: In chronic blockages (e.g., atherosclerosis), these collateral vessels enlarge over time to bypass the obstruction, thereby reducing damage during heart attacks.

21. **Lymphatic Drainage Overlap (Immune/Circulatory)**
    - Function: Drains interstitial fluid and supports immune defense.
    - Structure: Lymph nodes and vessels with overlapping territories.
    - Contingency: If one lymph vessel is damaged (e.g., surgery or infection), nearby vessels can compensate to maintain drainage and immune surveillance.

22. **Kidney Functional Reserve (Renal System)**
    - Function: Filters blood, balances fluids/electrolytes.
    - Structure: Two kidneys, each with millions of nephrons.
    o Contingency: One healthy kidney can compensate if the other fails (up to 75% loss of total renal function) due to redundant nephron capacity.

Incredible Creatures That Defy Evolution:

Incredible Creatures That Defy Evolution is a documentary series featuring Dr. Jobe Martin, a medical doctor and former evolutionist who, after extensive study of various animal species, concluded that traditional evolutionary theories cannot adequately explain the complexity and specificity of biological design in these creatures. His professional background in medicine equipped him with the tools to critically analyze the anatomical and physiological features of living organisms.

Over more than twenty years, he collected evidence indicating that many creatures exhibit designs that must have been created "all at once," as any incomplete intermediate structure would render the organism non-viable—challenging the assumption that gradual, stepwise evolution could produce complex organs, behaviors, or systems without the presence of the entire integrated mechanism from the start.

The Bombardier Beetle: Master of Chemical Warfare
The bombardier beetle is notable for its highly sophisticated defense mechanism. When threatened, it ejects a chemical spray from the tip of its abdomen that detonates in a series of rapid, small explosions, producing a loud popping sound and releasing a noxious hot gas that deters predators.

- The spray results from the beetle mixing two separate chemical compounds—hydroquinones and hydrogen peroxide—in a reaction chamber inside its abdomen.
- The reaction is catalyzed in a precise, controlled manner so the beetle is not harmed by the heat and pressure generated.
- Additionally, the beetle has two tailpipes that can aim the spray in different directions to target predators accurately.

From a biological design perspective, this system comprises multiple specialized components, including chemical production organs, precise storage compartments to separate chemicals until use, catalytic enzyme systems, and targeting mechanisms. According to Dr. Martin, such a complex defense could not have evolved incrementally because any partially developed version would be ineffective or even deadly to the beetle itself.

The Giraffe's Cardiovascular System: Engineering Marvel

Giraffes face unique challenges to blood circulation due to their towering height and long necks, which can reach up to 18 feet tall and be as long as 6 feet.

- To pump blood to the brain, giraffes have a huge heart, approximately 2.5 feet long, capable of pumping at a very high pressure.
- They also possess specialized valves in their neck veins to prevent excessive blood pressure from damaging their brains when they lower their heads to drink water.
- Their arterial walls are thickened to withstand the high pressure necessary to circulate blood efficiently.

The integration of heart size, blood pressure regulation, valve systems, and vasculature highlights an intricate adaptation that works seamlessly. The design must be fully operational, lest the giraffe suffer a brain hemorrhage or fainting spells, implying that all parts must have appeared together, which challenges the gradualist evolutionary view.

Bird Navigation: The Mystery of Long-Distance Migration

Particular bird species, such as the Pacific Golden-Plover and Arctic Tern, undertake migrations spanning thousands of miles across featureless oceans and landscapes, relying on extraordinary navigation skills.

- These birds use celestial cues, magnetic fields, and possibly even patterned olfactory guides to maintain precise routes.
- They possess an internal magnetic compass involving specialized proteins like cryptochromes in their eyes, reportedly capable of sensing the geomagnetic field.
- The neurological and sensory integration required for such navigation is highly sophisticated.

This intricate navigation system cannot be the product of trial and error over long timescales, as it needs to be fully present and effective from the initial migrations for survival, challenging the notion that gradual refinement could have led to this outcome.

The Gecko's Feet: Climbing Experts

Geckos can effortlessly climb vertical surfaces, even smooth glass walls, thanks to the unique structure of their feet.

- Their feet contain millions of tiny, hair-like structures called setae, each of which splits into hundreds of even smaller projections called spatulae.
- These structures work through van der Waals forces—weak intermolecular forces that collectively provide significant adhesion.
- The foot anatomy is specially designed to allow geckos to both adhere strongly and detach easily as they walk.

The complexity and fine control implied by the gecko's foot microstructure and mechanics seem irreducible: partial development would hinder adhesion and mobility, making survival impossible.

Fireflies and Bioluminescence: Cold Light Creation

Fireflies, glowworms, and certain marine animals produce bioluminescence—light created by a chemical reaction without heat emission.

- The luciferin-luciferase reaction produces light with nearly 100% energy efficiency, a feat human-made lights cannot match.
- The control of light patterns for communication, especially in mating displays, requires refined neural and biochemical control.

The sophistication in both biochemical efficiency and behavior cannot sustain the development process over many generations of the animals.

The Woodpecker's Skull and Tongue

The woodpecker withstands repetitive high-impact pecking without brain damage:

- Its skull and neck muscles absorb shock and protect the brain from trauma.
- It has a specialized barbed tongue coated with a sticky saliva that can extend to extract insects from holes without sticking to itself.

Such adaptations suggest a multi-layered solution that involves anatomy, physiology, and behavior. These birds cannot continue to evolve these systems over hundreds and thousands of generations and survive, and continue their routine.

The concept of *irreducible complexity* — that specific biological systems require all their parts to be fully present and coordinated to function — has been countered by slow and gradual change, such as

Objective Analysis of God

the Giraffe's neck extending over many generations. As evolution progressed, it continued to adapt to the external environment. However, it still does not provide an answer to the last valve of Girrafe's system, which stores the blood so it can be used when Girrafe suddenly raises its head. Additionally, Partial systems or gradual incremental steps would produce non-functional intermediates, making survival impossible.

The Koala's Dietary Specialization
- Problem: Extreme specialization without backup options
    - Example: Koalas evolved to eat only eucalyptus leaves, which are toxic to most species. They developed specialized gut bacteria to detoxify them, leaving them vulnerable. When habitats shrink, they starve rather than adapt to new food sources. Their physiology cannot quickly develop alternatives when their food source becomes scarce.

Dodo Bird's Lack of Predator Defenses
- Problem: No preparation for new environmental threats
    - Example: Evolving on predator-free Mauritius, dodos lost the ability to fly and became fearless. When humans and invasive species arrived, they had no contingency behaviors, such as hiding or fleeing. Their evolutionary path gave them no proactive defenses against novel predators

---

These are only a few examples to illustrate that the Theory of Evolution, in its strict sense, does not hold in many aspects of nature and requires revision.

The idea of "Intelligent Design":

A hallmark of intelligent design is the incorporation of fail-safe, redundant, and contingency planning features that anticipate potential failures and ensure continued functionality. Biological systems exhibit this foresight, suggesting deliberate engineering rather than unguided evolutionary processes.

Intelligent Design (ID) suggests that some features of the universe and living things are too complex to have arisen by chance or natural processes alone, and instead point to an intelligent cause. Supporters often present it as a scientific alternative to the theory of evolution. Yet from the very beginning, ID has faced intense pushback—scientists question its methods and evidence, and in the U.S., it has even been challenged in court over whether it should be included in public-school classrooms.

A tornado makes an airplane.
  (There are multiple such analogies, but I am referring to only one)
  - Taking a cue from William Paley's "Watchmaker analogy" in his book Natural Theology (1802). It would be highly improbable for a tornado to assemble a flying plane randomly, and it's also unlikely that the universe and life came about by chance without some purposeful design.
  - In this analogy:
    o The tornado represents chaos or random chance.
    o The flying plane represents something highly complex and organized, like the universe or life.

The argument typically suggests that just as a tornado can't reasonably be expected to create a plane due to the improbability of the specific, intricate design that a plane requires, the complexity of the universe, life, or the existence of moral values can't reasonably be explained by pure random chance.

Intelligent design is often referred to as an attempt by religious groups to promote Creationism under the guise of science, promoted by the "Discovery Institute".

Objective Analysis of God

At its heart, intelligent design claims that certain features of living organisms—or even the universe itself—display patterns of complexity or 'specified complexity' that, based on human experience, suggest the action of an intelligent agent. Proponents point to examples such as the intricate molecular machinery within cells, the information-rich code of DNA, or so-called 'irreducibly complex' systems, where removing a single part would supposedly cause the system to fail. They argue that these structures cannot be fully explained by current evolutionary theory and therefore imply an intelligent cause. Modern ID advocates often frame these arguments in scientific-sounding terms, using concepts like information theory and probability, while avoiding explicit references to traditional religious figures.

Key figures in the ID movement include William Dembski, Michael Behe, and Stephen Meyer, and institutions like the Discovery Institute have played a central role in promoting it academically and publicly. Their work presents intelligent design as the 'best explanation' for specific natural patterns that they claim are unlikely to arise through undirected processes alone.

ID supporters generally focus on a few key arguments:
- **Specified complexity/information:** They claim that specific biological systems contain patterns of information—similar to human-created codes, like written language or computer programs—that point to an intelligent source. By this logic, the complex information in nature suggests design.
- **Irreducible complexity:** Some molecular structures, such as the bacterial flagellum, are described as "irreducibly complex," meaning that if any single part were removed, the system would fail. Advocates like Michael Behe argue that such systems could not have evolved gradually through natural selection.
- **Gaps and improbabilities:** ID supporters often point to areas where evolutionary explanations seem unlikely or incomplete, arguing that an intelligent cause is a reasonable explanation for these low-probability events.

ID camp suggests it as a scientific approach, claiming it relies on empirical observation and logical inference. Critics, however, contend that the movement cloaks religious ideas in scientific-sounding language rather than offering genuine testable science.

Science or not Science

Many scientific associations have described this concept as non-scientific. Intelligent design struggles as a scientific theory because it cannot be tested or falsified, offers little peer-reviewed research, and relies on supernatural explanations that fall outside standard scientific methods. Moreover, historical and legal evidence shows that ID is closely tied to earlier creationist movements, making it more a repackaged religious idea than a genuinely new scientific alternative.

US Court Decision

This concept took a significant hit due to a U.S. court decision.

In October 2004, the Dover Area School District in Pennsylvania implemented a policy requiring ninth-grade biology students to read a statement suggesting that evolution is "just a theory" and directing them to Of Pandas and People, a book promoting intelligent design. Concerned parents filed a lawsuit, arguing that the policy violated the Establishment Clause of the First Amendment by effectively promoting a religious viewpoint. The ACLU and allied groups represented the plaintiffs, while the National Center for Science Education (NCSE) provided expert scientific testimony.

Case (Sept–Nov 2005): Over several weeks, the U.S. District Court heard testimony from scientists, educators, and historians. Experts explained the nature of scientific inquiry and evolutionary theory, while historians traced the direct connections between creationism and the ID movement. Crucial evidence included early drafts of Of Pandas and People that had initially used the term "creationism" before later replacing it with "intelligent design," highlighting ID's roots in religious thought.

Decision (Dec 20, 2005): Judge John E. Jones III issued a detailed 139-page ruling, finding that the Dover policy violated the Establishment Clause. The court concluded that intelligent design is not science and "cannot uncouple itself from its creationist, and thus religious, antecedents." The ruling permanently prohibited the school board from compelling teachers to challenge evolution or teach ID as an alternative. The decision thoroughly examined both the historical context and the scientific merits of ID, as well as the motives of the school board.

Objective Analysis of God

While the ruling slowed or stopped attempts to teach ID as science in public schools, it did not erase the intellectual or political influence of ID proponents. ID continues to have an audience in some religious communities and among confident policymakers. There is a detailed NOVA documentary on this case on YouTube.

Judgment Day: Intelligent Design On Trial (creationism vs evolution)

Case of Intelligent Design case:

Critics of ID (scientists, philosophers, and atheists who reject design analogies as oversimplified) and also some of the points I have highlighted in "7 limitations..." argue that:

1. Analogies to human design (like watches, machines, or preplanned backups) don't accurately reflect how natural processes such as evolution, natural selection, and cosmology work.
2. Complexity does not require an intelligent designer but can emerge naturally over long timescales.

However, the existence of interdependent systems, self-repair mechanisms, proactively designed backups, and optimized redundancies in biology, which go beyond the "good enough" standard, is seen by some as evidence of purposeful design, since such features suggest anticipation and planning rather than step-by-step adaptation alone. Additionally, the evolutionary process requires vast amounts of time—often thousands to millions of years—for organisms to adapt to new environments and develop mechanisms to counter emerging challenges. This gradual pace means that many species cannot keep up with sudden or extreme environmental changes. In such cases, entire populations may decline or even go extinct before beneficial adaptations can take hold.

Is this the reason that 99% of all species that have ever lived have died?

Both sides failed

Neither religious creationism nor evolutionary theory can definitively refute others because they operate within fundamentally different frameworks. Religion relies on faith, revelation, and metaphysical explanations, while evolutionary science depends on empirical evidence, natural processes, and methodological naturalism. This divide makes mutual exclusivity impossible to prove.

For religious believers, life's complexity and design point to a Creator, but science cannot confirm or deny supernatural agency because it operates within observable, testable phenomena. Conversely, evolutionary theory explains biodiversity through the processes of natural selection and genetic mutation. Still, it cannot address existential questions, such as why life exists or whether purpose underlies questions that religion seeks to answer.

Additionally, both perspectives face unresolved gaps. Evolution struggles to explain the origin of consciousness, irreducible complexity in cellular machinery, and the fine-tuning of the universe's fundamental constants. Religion, meanwhile, cannot empirically demonstrate divine intervention in biological history without invoking untestable claims.

Ultimately, the debate persists because each system answers different questions—science explains how, while religion addresses why. Since neither can fully encompass the other's domain, the search for a definitive resolution remains elusive, leaving room for coexistence or continued disagreement.

Section 7

Possibilities

Section 7 - Possibilities

What might have happened?

Earth's process for evolving living cells

Before moving on, please consider two things:
1. The Earth and the universe have been developing over immense spans of time. Across these ages, natural processes such as star explosions created complex elements, while Earth's unique conditions allowed those elements to combine into increasingly complex compounds
2. Earth happens to occupy a position in the universe that provides conditions suitable for life as we know it. From a statistical perspective, such natural conditions are likely to occur on many other planets as well. This does not necessarily mean there are other planets with humans, but it does suggest that some form of alien life is likely to exist elsewhere.

> *Out of the billions of planets in the universe, each with its own unique conditions and compositions, it is possible that at least one Earth-like planet could bring together the right combination of factors to give rise to life. Such a life would not appear suddenly but would emerge through a long process shaped by favorable conditions over time.*

Now, as noted above, we turn to the process by which basic elements gave rise to complex living organisms. While many prominent scientists acknowledge that not all steps are yet fully explained, it is worth remembering that modern science is only a few centuries old. Given its rapid progress, it is reasonable to expect that these gaps will be filled in the future. In fact, many of the key steps are already well understood and have been successfully demonstrated in laboratories, as outlined below.

The transition from simple chemicals to living cells is an interesting journey, defined as "abiogenesis", which describes the gradual emergence of life from nonliving matter. Although some steps remain uncertain, scientists have outlined plausible sequences supported by experimental evidence and theoretical models. The following overview explores how simple chemicals could evolve

Objective Analysis of God

into living cells, with environmental conditions acting as a natural 'catalyst' to drive the process:

Starting from hydrogen in the universe:

The formation of complex elements from hydrogen in the universe is called nucleosynthesis. It occurs through several stages, primarily driven by nuclear fusion in stars and explosive events. Here's a brief overview:

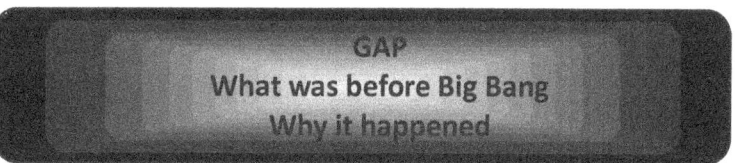

1. **Big Bang Nucleosynthesis**
   Timeframe: A few minutes after the Big Bang (~13.8 billion years ago).
   Process: The extreme heat and density of the early universe enabled hydrogen nuclei (protons) to fuse, forming helium (He), as well as trace amounts of lithium (Li) and beryllium (Be).
   Outcome: The universe is composed of approximately 75% hydrogen and 25% helium by mass.

2. **Stellar Nucleosynthesis**
   Location: Inside stars.
   Process: Hydrogen Fusion (Main Sequence Stars): In stars like the Sun, hydrogen nuclei fuse to form helium via the proton-proton chain or CNO cycle.
   Helium Fusion (Red Giants): When hydrogen is exhausted, helium fuses to form carbon (C) and oxygen (O).
   Advanced Fusion (Massive Stars): In heavier stars, fusion continues to produce elements like neon (Ne), magnesium (Mg), silicon (Si), and up to iron (Fe) in the core.
   Outcome: Stars act as "element factories," creating elements up to iron through fusion.

3. **Supernova Nucleosynthesis**
   Location: During supernova explosions of massive stars.

Section 7 - Possibilities
Earth's process for evolving living cells

Process: The immense energy and neutron flux in a supernova allow the formation of elements heavier than iron (e.g., gold, uranium) through the rapid neutron-capture process (r-process). Elements are scattered into space, enriching the interstellar medium.
Outcome: Supernovae produce and distribute most of the heavy elements in the universe.

4. Cosmic Ray Spallation
Location: Interstellar space.
Process: High-energy cosmic rays collide with heavier nuclei, breaking them apart and forming lighter elements like lithium, beryllium, and boron.
Outcome: This process accounts for certain light elements not forming significantly during the Big Bang or stellar nucleosynthesis.
Summary
   a) Hydrogen (the simplest element) formed shortly after the Big Bang.
   b) Stars fused hydrogen into helium and heavier elements up to iron.
   c) Supernovae created elements heavier than iron and dispersed them into space.
   d) Cosmic rays contributed to the formation of some light elements.

This nucleosynthesis process, which has occurred over billions of years, has produced all the complex elements in the universe, including those essential for life.

From Elements to elementary compounds – gases

The conversion of elements into gases, such as methane (CH_4) and other simple organic molecules, is a chemical process that occurs under specific conditions. These processes are crucial for understanding the origins of life and the chemistry of planets, moons, and interstellar space. Here's how elements like carbon (C) and hydrogen (H) are converted into gases like methane:

1. Formation of Methane (CH_4)
- Basic Reaction: Carbon (C) reacts with hydrogen (H) to form methane (CH_4).

$$C+2H_2 \rightarrow CH_4 C+2H_2 \rightarrow CH_4$$

Objective Analysis of God

- **Conditions Required:**
  Presence of Hydrogen: Hydrogen gas (H_2) must be available.
  Catalysts: Certain minerals or surfaces (e.g., nickel, iron) can act as catalysts to speed up the reaction.
    - **Energy Source:** Heat, pressure, or electrical discharges (e.g., lightning) can provide the energy needed for the reaction.
- **Natural Occurrence:**
    - Planetary Atmospheres: On planets like Earth (in its early atmosphere) or Saturn's moon Titan, methane forms through reactions between carbon and hydrogen under reducing (oxygen-poor) conditions.
    - Hydrothermal Vents: In deep-sea hydrothermal systems, methane is produced by chemical reactions between water, carbon dioxide (CO_2), and minerals like olivine (serpentinization process).

2. Formation of Other Gases

- **Ammonia (NH_3):**
  - Nitrogen (N_2) reacts with hydrogen (H_2) under high pressure and temperature, often with a catalyst like iron:
    $$N_2 + 3H_2 \rightarrow 2NH_3$$
  - This process is known as the Haber-Bosch process and is used industrially, but it also occurs naturally in specific environments.
- **Water Vapor (H_2O):**
  - Hydrogen (H_2) reacts with oxygen (O_2) to form water:
    $$2H_2 + O_2 \rightarrow 2H_2O$$
  - This reaction releases a lot of energy and is common in stellar environments or during planetary formation.
- **Carbon Dioxide (CO_2):**
  - Carbon (C) or carbon monoxide (CO) reacts with oxygen (O_2):
    $$C + O_2 \rightarrow CO_2$$
  - This occurs in combustion processes or the presence of oxidizing agents.

3. Role of Environmental Conditions

- **Reducing Atmosphere**: An oxygen-poor (reducing) environment is essential for the formation of methane and ammonia. Early Earth and other celestial bodies (e.g., Titan, Jupiter) have or had such atmospheres.

- **Energy Sources**: Heat, pressure, lightning, or UV radiation can drive these reactions.
- **Catalysts**: Minerals (e.g., nickel, iron) or surfaces (e.g., clay, rocks) can lower the activation energy required for these reactions.

4. Interstellar and Planetary Chemistry
- **Interstellar Medium**: In space, simple molecules like methane, ammonia, and water form on the surfaces of dust grains through reactions catalyzed by cosmic rays and UV radiation.
- **Planetary Moons**: On moons like Titan, methane is produced through geological processes and atmospheric photochemical reactions.

Summary
Elements like carbon, hydrogen, and nitrogen are converted into gases like methane, ammonia, and water through chemical reactions under specific conditions:
- **Reducing environments** (oxygen-poor).
- **Energy sources** (heat, lightning, UV radiation).
- **Catalysts** (minerals, surfaces).

These processes are fundamental to planetary chemistry, the origins of life, and the composition of atmospheres on Earth and other celestial bodies

From elementary gases to complex living compounds

So, now we have an abundance of heavy elements scattered in the universe, some of which also arrive on Earth in reasonable quantities.

1. Formation of Simple Organic Molecules
- **Primordial Earth Conditions**: Around 4 billion years ago, Earth's atmosphere was rich in gases such as methane (CH_4), ammonia (NH_3), water vapor (H_2O), and carbon dioxide (CO_2), but lacked free oxygen. Volcanic activity, lightning, and UV radiation provided energy.
- **Key Experiments**: The Miller-Urey experiment (1953) demonstrated that simple organic molecules (e.g., amino acids, nucleotides) could form spontaneously under

conditions simulating early Earth. These molecules are the building blocks of life.
- **Role of Environmental Conditions:** Energy sources (e.g., lightning, UV radiation) acted as catalysts to drive chemical reactions, while the absence of free oxygen prevented oxidation of these fragile molecules.

2. **Polymerization of Organic Molecules**
Formation of Complex Molecules: Simple organic molecules began to link together to form more complex polymers, such as proteins (formed from amino acids) and nucleic acids (formed from nucleotides).
    - **Role of Environmental Conditions:**
        - **Wet Dry Cycles:** Tidal pools or hydrothermal vents provided environments where wet-dry cycles could concentrate molecules and facilitate polymerization.
        - **Mineral Surfaces:** Clay minerals and hydrothermal vent structures may have acted as catalysts, providing surfaces for molecules to align and react.

3. **Emergence of Self-Replicating Molecules**
    - RNA World Hypothesis: RNA (ribonucleic acid) is thought to have played a crucial role in early life. RNA can store genetic information (similar to DNA) and catalyze chemical reactions (like proteins), making it a strong candidate for the first self-replicating molecule.
    - **Role of Environmental Conditions:**
        - Protective Microenvironments: Pores in rocks or lipid vesicles could have protected RNA molecules from degradation.
        - Chemical Gradients: Hydrothermal vents provided energy and chemical gradients that could drive the replication and evolution of RNA.

4. **Formation of Protocells**
- **Encapsulation of Molecules:**
    Lipid molecules spontaneously form bilayers and vesicles in water, creating compartments that can encapsulate self-replicating molecules, such as RNA.
- **Role of Environmental Conditions:**

- Lipid Availability: Early Earth had an abundance of fatty acids and other lipids, which could be used to form membranes.
- Energy Sources: Chemical gradients across these membranes could drive primitive metabolic processes.

5. **Development of Metabolism and Cellular Life**
   Metabolic Pathways: Protocells developed simple metabolic pathways, such as glycolysis or chemiosmosis, to harness energy from their environment.
- **Role of Environmental Conditions:**
   - Hydrothermal Vents: Alkaline hydrothermal vents provided a steady supply of energy and chemicals, acting as natural reactors for early metabolic processes.
   - Natural Selection: Protocells that could better harness energy and replicate efficiently outcompeted others, driving the evolution of more complex cells.

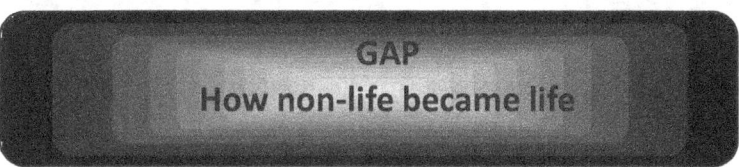

6. **Transition to True Cells**
   DNA Takes Over: DNA eventually replaced RNA as the primary genetic material due to its greater stability and capacity for storing information.
- **Role of Environmental Conditions:**
   - Oxygenation of the Atmosphere: The rise of photosynthetic bacteria (cyanobacteria) led to the accumulation of oxygen in the atmosphere, enabling more efficient energy production through aerobic respiration.
   - Evolution of Enzymes: Enzymes evolved to catalyze specific reactions, increasing the efficiency of cellular processes.

Summary of Environmental "Enzymes"
Environmental conditions on early Earth acted as catalysts (like enzymes) to drive the chemical evolution of life:
- Energy Sources: Lightning, UV radiation, and hydrothermal vents provided energy for chemical reactions.

Objective Analysis of God

- Concentration Mechanisms: Wet-dry cycles, mineral surfaces, and lipid vesicles concentrate and organize molecules.
- Protective Environments: Microenvironments, such as pores in rocks or lipid bilayers, protect fragile molecules from environmental damage.
- Chemical Gradients: Hydrothermal vents and other environments provided gradients that drove metabolic processes.

This step-by-step process, driven by chemistry and environmental conditions, ultimately led to the emergence of the first living cells, setting the stage for the evolution of all life on Earth.

Overall summary of the process

Here's a high-level summary of the evolutionary processes that explain the formation of complex elements from hydrogen, the conversion of elements into gases like methane, and the emergence of life from simple chemicals to living cells:

1. Cosmic Evolution: From Hydrogen to Complex Elements
   - Big Bang Nucleosynthesis: Hydrogen and helium formed in the first few minutes after the Big Bang.
   - Stellar Nucleosynthesis: Stars fuse hydrogen into helium and heavier elements (up to iron) through nuclear fusion.
   - Supernova Nucleosynthesis: Massive stars exploded in supernovae, creating elements heavier than iron and scattering them into space.
   - Cosmic Ray Spallation: Cosmic rays broke apart heavier nuclei, forming lighter elements like lithium and boron.
   - Outcome: The universe became enriched with complex elements essential for chemistry and life.

2. Chemical Evolution: From Elements to Simple Molecules

Section 7 - Possibilities
Earth's process for evolving living cells

- Formation of Gases: Under reducing (oxygen-poor) conditions, elements such as carbon, hydrogen, and nitrogen combine to form gases like methane (CH_4), ammonia (NH_3), and water (H_2O).
- Energy Sources: Heat, lightning, UV radiation, and mineral catalysts drove these reactions.
- Interstellar Chemistry: In space, simple molecules formed on dust grains and were delivered to planets via comets and meteorites.
- Outcome: Planetary atmospheres and surfaces were seeded with simple organic molecules.

3. Prebiotic Evolution: From Molecules to Life
    - Formation of Organic Molecules: Experiments, such as those conducted by Miller and Urey, demonstrated that amino acids and nucleotides could form under the early Earth's conditions.
    - Polymerization: Simple molecules linked to form polymers (e.g., proteins, RNA) in environments like tidal pools or hydrothermal vents.
    - RNA World Hypothesis: Self-replicating RNA molecules emerged as precursors to life, capable of storing genetic information and catalyzing reactions.
    - Protocells: Lipid membranes encapsulated self-replicating molecules, creating the first cell-like structures.
    - Metabolism and Cellular Life: Protocells developed metabolic pathways, ultimately leading to the emergence of true cells, which possess DNA, proteins, and enzymes.
    - Outcome: The first living cells emerged, setting the stage for biological evolution.

Key Drivers of Evolution
   a. Energy Sources: Stellar fusion, supernovae, lightning, UV radiation, and hydrothermal vents provided energy for chemical reactions.
   b. Environmental Conditions: Reducing atmospheres, wet-dry cycles, and mineral surfaces acted as catalysts.
   c. Natural Selection: Molecules and cells that replicated more efficiently outcompeted others, driving complexity.

Objective Analysis of God

Other contributing factors:

Earth is protected from harmful cosmic and solar radiation, as well as from impacts by asteroids and comets, by a combination of **internal properties** and **external factors**. These protective mechanisms have played a crucial role in making Earth habitable. Here's a breakdown of these factors:

1. Earth's Internal Properties
- Magnetic Field (Magnetosphere):
  - Generated by the motion of molten iron and nickel in Earth's outer core (geodynamo effect - **mechanism by which molten iron and nickel in Earth's outer core produce a magnetic field**).
  - **Protective Role**:
    - Deflects harmful **solar wind** and **cosmic rays**, preventing them from stripping away the atmosphere.
    - Shields the planet from high-energy charged particles that could damage life and disrupt electronics.
  - **Auroras**: The interaction of solar wind with the magnetosphere creates auroras near the poles.
- Atmosphere:
  - Composed of nitrogen (78%), oxygen (21%), and trace gases like ozone (O_3).
  - **Protective Role**:
    - **Ozone Layer**: Absorbs harmful ultraviolet (UV) radiation from the Sun, protecting life from DNA damage.
    - **Ablation**: Burns up smaller meteoroids before they reach the surface.
    - **Heat Distribution**: Regulates temperature to maintain a stable climate.
- Plate Tectonics:
  - The movement of Earth's lithospheric plates recycles carbon and regulates the planet's climate over long timescales.
  - **Protective Role**:
    - Helps maintain a stable atmosphere and climate, essential for life.

2. External Factors
- **Jupiter's Gravitational Influence**:
  - Jupiter, the largest planet in the solar system, acts as a "cosmic vacuum cleaner."
  - **Protective Role**:
    - Its strong gravity deflects or captures many comets and asteroids that might otherwise collide with Earth.
    - However, Jupiter can also perturb some objects into the inner solar system, so its role is complex.
- **The Moon**:
  - Earth's large moon stabilizes the planet's axial tilt.
  - **Protective Role**:
    - Prevents extreme climate fluctuations that could make the planet less habitable.
- **Asteroid Belt**:
  - Located between Mars and Jupiter, it acts as a buffer zone.
  - **Protective Role**:
    - Most asteroids are confined to this region, reducing the likelihood of impacts on Earth.

Protection from Radiation
- **Solar Wind and Cosmic Rays**:
  - Earth's magnetosphere deflects most charged particles from the Sun and deep space.
- **UV Radiation**:
  - The ozone layer in the stratosphere absorbs most of the Sun's harmful UV radiation.
- **Galactic Cosmic Rays**:
  - The atmosphere and magnetosphere together reduce the intensity of these high-energy particles.

4. Protection from Impact Events
- **Atmospheric Friction**:
  - Smaller meteoroids burn up due to friction with the atmosphere, appearing as shooting stars.
- **Planetary Defence**:
  - Larger impacts are rare, but Earth's size and gravity help it withstand and recover from such events.

Objective Analysis of God

- **Geological Activity**:
    - Plate tectonics and erosion erase evidence of past impacts, reducing their long-term effects.

5. Cosmic and Solar Shielding
- **Heliosphere**:
    - The Sun's magnetic field and solar wind create a bubble (heliosphere) that shields the solar system from some interstellar radiation.
- **Local Interstellar Cloud**:
    - The solar system passes through a space region with a lower density of interstellar material, reducing exposure to harmful particles.
- **Molten iron core of the Earth:**
    - At the beginning of the Earth's formation, a heavy volume of iron was in the Earth's molten core. This considerable quantity of Iron also gave Earth its magnetic field, which in turn provided a shield to protect Earth's atmosphere and its inhabitants from the sun's rays.

Summary of Protective Mechanisms
- **Earth's Magnetic Field**: Shields against solar wind and cosmic rays.
- **Atmosphere**: Blocks UV radiation and burns up small meteoroids.
- **Jupiter's Gravity**: Acts as a gravitational shield for Earth.
- **The Moon** Stabilizes Earth's climate.
- **Heliosphere**: Protects the solar system from interstellar radiation.

These factors work together to create a stable and protective environment, allowing life to thrive on Earth despite the harsh conditions of the cosmos.

Section 7 - Possibilities
Earth's process for evolving living cells

Overall Summary

1. Cosmic Evolution: Hydrogen → Helium → Complex Elements (stars, supernovae).
2. Chemical Evolution: Elements → Simple Molecules (methane, ammonia, water).
3. Prebiotic Evolution: Simple Molecules → Polymers → RNA → Protocells → Living Cells.

This interconnected process, spanning billions of years, explains how the universe evolved from simple hydrogen to the complex chemistry of life on Earth.

Future discoveries may complete the puzzle by providing missing pieces.

Section 8

Ending

Section 8 – Ending

Interpreting your numbers:

Please visit my-oag.com to download calculation sheet for your results

By now, you have completed "Your Objective Analysis of Your GOD" and put your numbers against each question, tabulating the outcome. Please note that it could be Gs +Cs or Gs+Ms or Gs+Cs+Ms, fully or partially; the following applies to all scenarios. Please take the average of your answers and match the following indicative explanation. This is your position and actual standing, as accurately and unbiasedly represented by the numbers you have chosen.

Result 9-10 - The Liberated Skeptic

After years of questioning and deep study, you've reached a painful but liberating conclusion: the religion you were raised in is built on deception. Your once-unshakable trust in scholars and teachers has shattered, replaced by the certainty that they misled you—whether out of ignorance, tradition, or control. The more you learned, the clearer it became that dogma contradicts reason, evidence, and even morality. Now, you openly reject the idea that religion holds any monopoly on truth. You've broken free from its psychological chains, and though the journey was lonely, you speak boldly about your disillusionment. To you, spirituality, if it exists, must be sought beyond rigid doctrines, critical thought, empathy, and the unflinching pursuit of reality.

Result 7-8 -The Thoughtful Seeker

You once unquestioningly followed the faith of your upbringing, but over time, deep-seated doubts began to take root. The more you studied your religion's doctrines, the more inconsistencies and unanswered questions you found—until you couldn't ignore them. This led you to explore other belief systems, comparing philosophies, ethics, and histories. While you've nearly abandoned the rituals of your original faith, stop short of declaring a complete break, whether out of residual attachment, family ties, or intellectual humility. You can articulate your skepticism clearly in debates,

Objective Analysis of God

challenging dogmas without outright rejection. You're unsure what you believe, but you know blind adherence is no longer an option.

Result 5-6 - The Socially Observant Skeptic
You occasionally participate in religious practices, more out of social expectation than personal devotion. You've read about other faiths, even questioned some of your traditions—why certain rituals exist, whether they hold more profound meaning, or are just relics of tradition. Yet, you keep observing them, half out of respect for your community, half because it's what you've always known. Your faith isn't blind, but it's not fiery either. You nod along during ceremonies, but your mind wanders to the contradictions, the cultural parallels, the unanswered "whys." You belong, but you wonder. You comply, but you doubt. And that's where you linger—between custom and curiosity.

Result 3-4 – Resilient followers
You are deeply rooted in your childhood faith, forming an unshakable core belief system. However, intellectual curiosity led you to explore other sects, perhaps only within your religion, or to study different faiths superficially. Despite this exposure, your foundational beliefs remain unwavering. You may appreciate aspects of other traditions or engage in comparative analysis, but your original convictions stay intact, sometimes even reinforced by the process. Your faith is not blind but resilient, having withstood scrutiny without yielding. You embody a balance between steadfast devotion and a willingness to acknowledge diversity; yet, ultimately, your spiritual anchor remains firmly rooted in the belief system you first adopted.

Result 1-2 - Blind followers
You are a devout believer who anchors life entirely in religious doctrine, accepting teachings given from birth as absolute truth without question. Your faith, shaped by tradition and authority, dictates morality, purpose, and worldview. You reject doubt, avoiding exploration beyond prescribed beliefs (not even to different sects of the religion), and you are convinced that your path is the only correct one. Rituals and scriptures reinforce your certainty, offering unwavering comfort and reassurance. For you, faith isn't just belief; it's an unshakable identity, leaving no room for curiosity or alternative perspectives. You always stand firm, convinced that your truth is the only truth.

Section 8 – Ending
Interpreting your numbers:

Please visit My-OAG.com

And download the Excel calculation program.

My conclusion

Based on my journey in this path, here is my conclusion of my thoughts as of today:

1. **In my opinion and understanding, the probability is extremely low that the religious God, as explained by Islam and Christianity, is the same as the Universe's God who has designed this universe**
   (as nothing is 100% confident in any world, based on our limited knowledge)
   a) When we compare the God who has the capability of designing, creating, and managing this universe, in terms of its length of time, its vastness, and its complexity at the cosmology or the atom/cell level
   b) When we see that the religious God makes very obvious and silly mistakes in His messages to Humans
   c) When we see that his method of teaching us how to live is full of gaps, could not develop a system or communicate a complete way of life, and has always passed it on to the likes of Priests, Pandits, and Mullas to interpret that and teach it further to other humans
   d) When we see that after so many attempts, He has not succeeded once, but keeps on making similar mistakes again and again– he could not effectively implement his desired way of life once or even for a minute in this world
   e) When he is confronted with a petty creature like Satan, compared to his stature
   f) When he shows that what is instructed is brutality against the Humans whom He is supposed to love
   g) When he completely fails to do justice by being biased or fails to develop a complete Just system
   h) When we see the cruel system that He has designed and maintains forever in the kingdom of non-human living beings
   i) When most of his messages were concentrated on a 5000 km² area, and less than 1% of the human time on earth.
   j) When we see that He only tried to communicate with less than 5% of the humans, and only when Humans did not have the knowledge to understand the Universe

Section 8 – Ending
My conclusion

- k) When we see that He has stopped communicating with Humans for most of the recorded history
- l) When we see that His so-called holy Text is full of errors and blunders
- m) When we fail to create any cohesion in creating this universe because of the Human test
- n) When have Humans stopped communicating with Humans? When did Humans start understanding the universe

❖ **Plus, also note who the Beneficiaries of this religious system are.**
  - ✓ Only **the elite rulers and religious institutions** are the beneficiaries of implementing religion.
  - ✓ The North American Church's overall budget is more than the combined revenue of the top five firms
  - ✓ All religious rituals involve money, reaching religious institutes directly or indirectly
  - ✓ A priest in church earns more than a manager in most corporations, and that is without tax and major living expenses
  - ✓ Almost all religious leaders have made themselves above the law and have been doing so against their preachings and also against the law of the land
  - ✓

So, in conclusion:
  - ✓ If there is a God, that god is not the one that has been communicated to us by the known religions, so the religious God does not exist
  - ✓ Religion has never been able to develop and enforce moral values; it is the collective wisdom of humans and their will to live together that has created morals – which religion has given you traffic laws
  - ✓ Ask a question why the omnipotent God needs your money, take the money out of the religion, and this whole religious system will fall to the ground
  - ✓ Even if you need more time to think, read, and understand the original holy text, do not just listen to preachers. They have their hidden agenda and manipulate the sacred text. Ask yourself why your God gave you His text instructions, and then do not accept reading them.

My submission will be limited to arguments:

Objective Analysis of God

We know nothing about this world or the universe. Our current knowledge, which accounts for approximately 99% of what we have acquired in the last 100 years, still has many unknowns. The more we know about this world, the more we realize we do not know. Therefore, we do not have clear answers to every argument about how highly complex creatures were developed, how life and consciousness originated, or how this universe began, etc.

Now, trying to answer about making complex things with a random process, I would like to submit the example of ice crystals formed: Now, moving on to the time of this universe, we only know / human history for about 4000 years.
Based on archaeological evidence, Homo sapiens have inhabited the Earth for approximately 200,000 years. If we follow Abraham's religion, the total history is only about 3500 years at most. But without any evidence
Moses received the Torah in approximately 1312 BCE, and the Vedas date back to around 1500 BCE; therefore, our religions are approximately 3500 years old.

So, all recent religions have only existed for about 0.0175% of human history. According to one scientific method, the Earth is said to be 13.8 billion years old. In contrast, the religion, which is believed to be the cause of creating this universe, according to its own narrative, accounts for only about 0.00000025% of the time.

> *All religions promote core values rooted in collective social survival, suggesting they originally emerged to support group cohesion and endurance. Over time, deities were introduced as symbolic anchors to strengthen group identity, offering promises of reward and threats of punishment both in this life and beyond, reinforcing loyalty through hope and fear.*

Section 8 – Ending
My conclusion

Scarboro Mission in Canada were kind enough to use the following poster, which Paul McKenna developed. In addition to promoting interfaith commonality, it also, I believe, depicts the basic common theme and origin of all religions, which are primarily rooted in human needs and requirements.
(https://www.scarboromissions.ca/golden-rule)

Closing the loop...

We started our journey from

"God or no God", → *"Which God is The God"*

After going through the above journey, I would say if there is a God or Creator of this universe, then that creator does not fit into the God who has tried to communicate to Humans using these three sacred texts (Torah, Bible, and Quran)

At the same time, considering the known history, if there is a God or creator of this universe (if one exists), then that entity is either merely watching humans or is unconcerned about them.

If God wants to test humans in this world, then the actual test would be to create humans with built-in traits and free will, given the ability to use those traits, and set them free in this world — without intervening and guiding during the examination. And then see where individual humans end up – without providing any guidance in the examination room – that is called CHEATING ☺

Section 8 – Ending
Closing the loop...

Please help me get the

answers or challenge me.

My-OAG.com

one@MyAOG.com

Stay Curious

Stay Inspired

My-OAG.com

Our other channels of

communication

YouTube → @My-OAG

Facebook → My OAG

X - Twitter → @MyOAGod

TikTok → @myoagod

Objective Analysis of God

Section 8 – Ending
Closing the loop...

Objective Analysis of God

www.ingramcontent.com/pod-product-compliance
Lightning Source LLC
Chambersburg PA
CBHW050326010526
44119CB00050B/696